The Armenian Massacres
in Ottoman Turkey

The Armenian Massacres
in Ottoman Turkey

A Disputed Genocide

Guenter Lewy

THE UNIVERSITY OF UTAH PRESS
Salt Lake City

10   09   08   07   06   5   4   3   2

 The Defiance House Man colophon is a registered trademark of the
University of Utah Press. It is based upon a four-foot-tall, Ancient Puebloan
pictograph (late PIII) near Glen Canyon, Utah.

LIBRARY OF CONGRESS CATALOGING-IN-PUBLICATION DATA

Lewy, Guenter, 1923-
 The Armenian massacres in Ottoman Turkey : a disputed genocide / Guenter
Lewy.
   p. cm.
 Includes bibliographical references and index.
 ISBN-13: 978-0-87480-849-0 (cloth : alk. paper)
 ISBN-10: 0-87480-849-9 (cloth : alk. paper)
 1. Armenian massacres, 1894-1896. 2. Armenian massacres, 1909. 3. Armenian
massacres, 1915-1923. 4. Armenians—Turkey—History. 5. Armenia—History—
1901- 6. Turkey—History—20th century. I. Title.
 DS195.5.L49 2005
 956.6'20154—DC22

                                                              2005023322

Acknowledgment is made to the following source for permission to use previously
published material from the article "The Case for the Armenian Genocide
Revisited," published in *The Middle East Quarterly,* Fall 2005.

Interior printed on recycled paper with 50% post-consumer content.

Contents

List of Maps   *viii*

Preface   *ix*

I. THE HISTORICAL SETTING

1. Armenians in the Ottoman Empire during the Nineteenth
    Century   3
2. The Armenian Revolutionary Movement   11
3. The Massacres of 1894–96   20
    Carnage in the Wake of an Attempted Reform   20
    Who Was Responsible for the Massacres?   26
4. The Young Turks Take Power   30
    Armenian Guerrilla Warfare   30
    An Uneasy Alliance   32
    The Armenian Reform Agreement of 1914   37

II. TWO RIVAL HISTORIOGRAPHIES

5. The Armenian Case (1): Genocidal Plans   43
    Turkish Nationalism, Turanism, and the Role of
      Ziya Gökalp   43
    The "Ten Commandments"   47
    The Secret CUP Meeting of February 1915 Described by
      Mevlanzade Rifat   51
    Genocidal Consequences   53
6. The Armenian Case (2): The Implementation of Genocide   63
    Aram Andonian's *The Memoirs of Naim Bey*   63
    The Turkish Courts-Martial of 1919–22   73
    The Role of the Teskilat-i Mahsusa (Special Organization)   82
    The Covert Nature of the Genocide   88
7. The Turkish Position   90
    The Armenian Rebellion   90
    The Revolt of Van   95
    Armenian Support for the Allied War Effort   100

The Punishment of Excesses 109

Armenian Atrocities: A Civil War within a Global War 115

The Release of the Malta Prisoners 122

III. HISTORICAL RECONSTRUCTION: WHAT WE KNOW
AND WHAT WE DO NOT KNOW

8. The Sources 131

Turkish Archives 131

The Political Archive of the German Foreign Ministry 133

Other German Eyewitnesses 135

The British Blue Book "The Treatment of Armenians
in the Ottoman Empire" 137

American Archives 139

Missionary Reports 142

Armenian Survivor Testimony 144

9. The Deportation Decision 150

Antecedents 150

The Deportation Decree 151

The Reasons for the Deportation Order 155

The German Role 159

10. The Course of the Deportations 162

Erzurum 162

Harput 168

Trebizond 178

Cilicia: Mersina, Adana, Marash 183

The Baghdad Railway Route 187

Aleppo 191

Urfa 198

Constantinople and Smyrna 203

The End of the Deportations 205

11. Resettlement 209

Ras-ul-Ain 209

"The Route of Horrors" 212

Der-el-Zor 215

The *Vilayet* of Damascus 218

12. Who Were the Perpetrators of the Massacres?   221
    The Role of the Kurds   221
    The Wartime Gendarmerie   224
    Circassians, *Chettes,* and "Similar Scum"   226
    The Fate of the Labor Battalions   228
    The Power of Local Officials   231
13. The Number of Victims   233
    The Size of the Prewar Armenian Population   234
    The Number of Survivors   236
    An Estimate of the Losses   240

IV. THE STATE OF THE CONTROVERSY
14. Conclusion: The Question of Premeditation   245
    A Spectrum of Views   245
    Critique   250
    An Alternative Explanation   252
Epilogue: The Politicization of History   258
    The Campaign for Recognition of the Genocide   258
    Pressure Tactics   262
    The Future of Turkish-Armenian Relations   269

Abbreviations and Glossary   273
Notes   275
Works Cited   333
Index   359

Maps

1. Anatolia at the time of the First World War   5
2. Resettlement in the Syrian Desert   211
3. Boundaries of Armenia as claimed at the Paris
   Peace Conference (1919)   238

Preface

The literature on what Armenians call the first genocide of the twentieth century and what most Turks refer to as an instance of intercommunal warfare and a wartime relocation is voluminous. Yet despite the great outpouring of writing, an acrimonious debate over what actually happened almost one hundred years ago continues unabated. The highly charged historical dispute burdens relations between Turkey and Armenia and increases tensions in a volatile region. It also crops up periodically in other parts of the world when members of the Armenian diaspora push for recognition of the Armenian genocide by their respective parliaments and the Turkish government threatens retaliation.

The key issue in this quarrel, it should be stressed at the outset, is not the extent of Armenian suffering, but rather the question of specific intent: that is, whether the Young Turk regime during the First World War intentionally organized the massacres that took place. Both sides agree that large numbers of Christians perished and that the deportation of the Armenian community was accompanied by many excesses. Several hundred thousand men, women, and children were forced from their homes with hardly any notice; and during a harrowing trek over mountains and through deserts uncounted multitudes died of starvation and disease or were murdered. To the victims it makes no difference whether they met their death as the result of a carefully planned scheme of annihilation, as the consequence of a panicky reaction to a misjudged threat, or for any other reason. It does make a difference for the accuracy of the historical record, not to mention the future of Turkish-Armenian relations.

The situation today is highly polarized and is characterized by two distinct and rigidly adhered to historiographies. The Armenian version maintains that the Armenians were the innocent victims of an unprovoked act of genocide by the Ottoman government. Large numbers of Western scholars have embraced this position. The Turkish version, put forth by the Turkish government and a few historians, argues that the mass deportation of the Armenians was a necessary response to a full-scale Armenian rebellion, carried out with the support of Russia and Britain, and that the large number of deaths—the "so-called massacres"—occurred as a result of famine and disease or as a consequence of a civil war within a global war. Both sides make their case by simplifying a complex historical reality and by ignoring crucial evidence that would yield a more nuanced picture. Professional historians in both camps copy uncritically from previous works when a reinvestigation of the sources is called for. Both parties use heavy-handed tactics to advance their cause and silence a full debate of the issues. The Turkish government has applied diplomatic pressure and threats; the Armenians have accused all those who do not call the massacres a case of genocide of seeking to appease the Turkish government. In 1994 the well-known Middle East scholar Bernard Lewis was taken to court in France and charged by the plaintiff with causing "grievous prejudice to truthful memory" because he denied the accusation of genocide.

This book subjects the rich historical evidence available to the test of consistency and (as much as the state of knowledge allows) attempts to sort out the validity of the rival arguments. Unlike most of those who have written on the subject of the Armenian massacres and who are partisans of one side or the other, I have no special ax to grind. My purpose is not to put forth yet another one-sided account of the deportations and mass-killings; still less am I in a position to propose a conclusive resolution of the controversies that have raged for so long. Important Turkish documents have disappeared, so that even a person who knows Turkish and can read it in its old script most likely would not be able to write a definitive history of these occurrences. My aim has been to deal with this emotion-laden subject without political preconceptions and to carry out a critical analysis of the two historiographies. Time and again, it will be seen, authors on both sides have engaged in highly questionable tactics of persuasion that include willful mistranslations, citing important documents out of context, or simply ignoring the historical setting altogether. After this uninviting task of "cleaning out the stables" (the results of which probably will please neither side), I attempt a historical reconstruction of the events in question—to show what can be known as established fact, what must be considered unknown as of today, and what will probably have to remain unknowable. My hope is that such an undertaking will clarify and advance our understanding of these fateful occurrences and perhaps also help build bridges between the two rival camps.

The Turkish government has issued collections of pertinent documents in translation, but the material from Western sources outweighs the available Turkish records (translated and untranslated), if not in quantity then in importance. The reports of American, German, and

Austrian consular officials who were on the spot in Anatolia and Meso-potamia have been preserved, and many of them have written memoirs that draw on their personal observations. American, German, and Swiss missionaries who witnessed the tragic events have written detailed accounts. We have a large memoir literature composed by Armenian survivors and their descendants. Also of interest are the published recollections by members of the large German military mission who held important positions of command in the Turkish army. The availability of these highly informative sources in Western languages means that even scholars like me who do not read Turkish can do meaningful work on this subject. Indeed, a requirement that only persons fluent in the Turkish language be considered competent to write on this topic would disqualify most Armenians, who also do not know Turkish.

I had the opportunity to immerse myself in the rich holdings of the archive of the German Foreign Ministry in Berlin, the Public Record Office in London, and the National Archives in Washington. All of these sources yielded some findings that I believe are new. More importantly, many of the documents cited by Turkish and Armenian authors and their respective supporters, when looked at in their original version and proper context, yielded a picture often sharply at variance with the conclusions drawn from them by the contending protagonists. Both Turkish and Armenian authors, it turns out, have used these materials in a highly selective manner, quoting only those points that fitted into their scheme of interpretation and ignoring what Max Weber called "inconvenient facts." Both the Turkish and the Armenian sides, in the words of the Turkish historian Selim Deringil, "have plundered history"; and, as if the reality of what happened was not terrible enough, they have produced horror stories favorable to their respective positions.

While working on this book, I sometimes had the feeling that I was a detective working on an unsolved crime. Clues to the perpetrators of gruesome massacres lay hidden in dusty old books and journals. I experienced the surprise and amazement of finding still another footnote that did not substantiate what the author in question claimed for it. It was fascinating to find corroboration for hunches in unexpected places, which made it possible to firm up conclusions. I hope that my readers too, while following the unfolding argument of this work, will share some of the satisfaction I experienced in finally coming up with an interpretation of these calamitous events that is supported by the preponderance of the evidence and is plausible. I may not have solved the crime in all of its complicated aspects, but I hope to have thrown some significant new light on it.

In the interest of a treatment in depth, I have limited the scope of this study to the events of 1915–16, which by all accounts took the greatest toll of lives and lie at the core of the controversy between Turks and Armenians. I make only brief references to the fighting between Turks and Russian Armenian units in 1917–18 and to what Armenian historians call the "Kemalist aggression against Armenia" in the wake of the Treaty of Sèvres of August 10, 1920. These topics raise important but different questions that deserve treatment in their own right. I also quite intentionally have not discussed each and every allegation, no matter how far-fetched, made by Turkish and Armenian authors in their long-standing war of words. To do so would have required a tome of many hundreds of pages. Moreover, it would have resulted in a work of gossip rather than history that no serious person would have been interested in and willing to read.

Finally, I have endeavored to avoid becoming entangled in problems of definition and nomenclature. For example, the question of what constitutes genocide—whether according to the Genocide Convention approved by the General Assembly of the United Nations on December 9, 1948, or in terms of other rival definitions—is often far from simple; and the attempt to decide whether the Armenian massacres in Ottoman Turkey fit all, some, or none of these definitions strikes me as of limited utility. I have therefore concentrated on what appears to me to be the far more important task of clarifying what happened, how it happened, and why it happened. The issue of the appropriate label to be attached to these occurrences is relevant for the ongoing polemics between Turks and Armenians. It is of secondary importance at best for historical inquiry, because the use of legal nomenclature does not add any material facts important for the history of these events.

As those familiar with the field of Middle Eastern studies know, English transliterations of Turkish and Armenian words have produced great variations in the spelling of places and personal names. As much as possible I have resorted to the most common styles; I have not changed the spelling in quotations, though I have omitted most diacritical marks. The difference between the Ottoman or Julian calendar and the European or Gregorian calendar (twelve days in the nineteenth century and thirteen days in the twentieth century) presented another problem. In most cases I have used the dates given in the sources utilized. The few instances where the interpretation of an event depends on the precise date have been noted in the text.

I would like to express my thanks to the archivists and librarians, here and abroad, who have aided me in my research, as well as to those who have translated some important Turkish materials for me. I also acknowledge with gratitude a grant from the German Academic Exchange Service (DAAD). As it is customary to note, none of these institutions and individuals are responsible for the opinions and conclusions reached in this work, which remain my personal responsibility.

Part I

THE HISTORICAL SETTING

Chapter 1

Armenians in the Ottoman Empire during the Nineteenth Century

Armenian history reaches back more than two thousand years. In AD 301 the Armenians were the first people to adopt Christianity as their official religion; the Holy Apostolic and Orthodox Church of Armenia (also known as the Gregorian Church) has played an important role in the survival of a people who for much of their history have lived under the rule of foreigners. The last independent Armenian state, the Kingdom of Cilicia, fell in 1375, and by the early part of the sixteenth century most Armenians had come under the control of the Ottoman Empire. Under the *millet* system instituted by Sultan Mohammed II (1451–81) the Armenians enjoyed religious, cultural, and social autonomy. Their ready acceptance of subservient political status under Ottoman rule lasted well into the nineteenth century and earned the Armenians the title "the loyal community."

Over time large numbers of Armenians settled in Constantinople and in other towns, where they prospered as merchants, bankers, artisans, and interpreters for the government. The majority, however, continued to live as peasants in the empire's eastern provinces (*vilayets*), known as Great Armenia, as well as in several western districts near the Mediterranean called Cilicia or Little Armenia. We have no accurate statistics for the population of the Ottoman Empire during this period, but there is general agreement that by the latter part of the nineteenth century the Armenians constituted a minority even in the six provinces usually referred to as the heartland of Armenia (Erzurum, Bitlis, Van, Harput, Diarbekir, and Sivas). Emigration and conversions in the wake of massacres, the redrawing of boundaries, and an influx of Muslims expelled or fleeing from the Balkans and the Caucasus (especially Laz and Circassians) had helped decrease the number of Armenians in their historic home. Their minority status fatally undermined their claim for an independent or at least autonomous Armenia within the empire—aims that had begun to gather support as a result of the influx of new liberal ideas from the West and the increased burdens weighing upon the Christian peasants of Anatolia.

Until the beginning of the nineteenth century Armenians had not suffered from any systematic oppression. They were second-class citizens who had to pay special taxes and wear a distinctive hat, they were not allowed to bear or possess arms, their testimony was often rejected in the courts, and they were barred from the highest administrative or military posts. The terms *gavur* or *kafir* (meaning unbeliever or infidel) used for Christians had definite pejorative overtones and summed up the Muslim outlook.[1] Still, as Ronald Suny has noted, despite all discriminations and abuses, for several centuries the Armenians had derived considerable benefit from the limited autonomy made possible by the *millet* system. "The church remained at the head of the nation; Armenians with commercial and industrial skills were able to climb to the very pinnacle of the Ottoman economic order; and a variety of educational, charitable, and social institutions were permitted to flourish." Living in relative peace with their Muslim neighbors, the Armenians had enjoyed a time of "benign symbiosis."[2]

In the eastern provinces the Armenians lived on a mountainous plateau that they shared with Kurdish tribes. During the second half of the nineteenth century relations with the Kurdish population deteriorated. Large numbers of Armenian peasants existed in a kind of feudal servitude under the rule of Kurdish chieftains. The settled Armenians provided winter quarters to the nomadic Kurds and paid them part of their crop in return for protection. As long as the Ottoman state was strong and prosperous this arrangement worked reasonably well. When the empire began to crumble and its government became increasingly corrupt, however, the situation of the Armenian peasants became difficult—they could not afford to pay ever more oppressive taxes to the Ottoman tax collectors as well as tribute to their Kurdish overlords. When they reneged on their payments to the Kurds, the tribes—never very benevolent—engaged in savage attacks upon the largely defenseless Armenian villagers that led to deaths, the abduction of girls and women, and the seizure of cattle. Ottoman officials, notoriously venal, were unwilling or unable to provide redress. The reforms introduced in 1839 and 1856 under Sultan Abdul Mejid I, which sought to establish elements of the rule of law and religious liberty and are known in Turkish history as the Tanzimat, did little to change the dismal situation of the common people and of the Armenian minority. In a

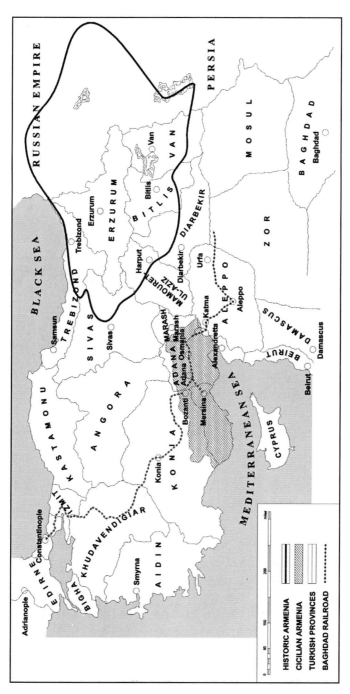

ANATOLIA AT THE TIME OF THE FIRST WORLD WAR

period of twenty years before 1870 Armenian patriarchs, as heads of the Armenian community, submitted to the Ottoman government more than 500 memoranda in which they detailed the extortions, forcible conversions, robberies, and abductions common in the provinces.[3]

The constitution of 1876 proclaimed the equal treatment of all nationalities, but Sultan Abdul Hamid II suspended it in 1878 and began a period of autocratic rule that was to last thirty years. The situation of the Armenians soon went from bad to worse, accelerating the growth of Armenian national consciousness and the spread of revolutionary ideas. Armenian nationalistic feelings had begun in the diaspora and in the larger towns, from which they gradually permeated the eastern provinces. Protestant missionaries and their schools played an important role in this process of radicalization. Both the government and the Armenian church tried to discourage the influx of these foreigners and their Western ideas, but the number of missionaries, most of them American and German, kept growing. By 1895, according to one count, there were 176 American missionaries, assisted by 878 native assistants, at work in Anatolia. They had established 125 churches with 12,787 members and 423 schools with 20,496 students.[4] Even though the missionaries denied that they instilled Armenian nationalistic, let alone revolutionary, sentiments, the Ottoman government saw it differently. As Charles Eliot, a well-informed British diplomat with extensive experience in Turkey, put it:

> The good position of the Armenians in Turkey had largely depended on the fact that they were thoroughly Oriental and devoid of that tincture of European culture common among Greeks and Slavs. But now this character was being destroyed: European education and European books were being introduced among them.... The Turks thought that there was clearly an intention to break up what remained of the Ottoman Empire and found an Armenian kingdom.... "Onward, Christian soldiers, marching as to war," in English is a harmless hymn, suggestive of nothing worse than a mildly ritualistic procession; but I confess that the same words literally rendered into Turkish do sound like an appeal to Christians to rise up against their Mohammedan masters, and I cannot be surprised that the Ottoman authorities found the hymn seditious and forbade it to be sung.[5]

The reports sent home by the missionaries made the outside world aware of the unhappy life of their downtrodden fellow-Christians in Anatolia. The missionaries were hardly impartial observers, but the

The suspension of the Constitution. Rights provided in the Constitution caused an increase in Armenian national identity

injustices and indignities suffered by the Christian population were indeed quite real. The Ottoman authorities, for their part, as Suny has written, "interpreted any manifestation of cultural revival or resistance, however individual or local, as an act of national rebellion.... Turkish officials and intellectuals began to look upon Armenians as unruly, subversive, alien elements who consorted with foreign powers."[6] The Ottoman government began to protest the growing European interest in the fate of the Armenians, regarding it as interference in Ottoman affairs. They suspected, not without justification, that the European powers were using the Armenian problem as a convenient pretext for further weakening of the Ottoman Empire. It was felt that Russia, in particular, which had seized some of the Armenian lands following the Russo-Turkish war of 1828–29, was encouraging the Armenian agitation in order to annex the remaining Armenian provinces in eastern Anatolia.

Matters came to a head in the wake of the Bulgarian revolt against Ottoman rule in 1876. Reports reaching the West about the ferocious manner in which the rebellion had been suppressed helped solidify the image of the "terrible Turk." Russian public opinion clamored for help to the Southern Slavs, and in April 1877 Russia declared war upon Turkey. The commander of the Russian army invading eastern Anatolia was a Russian Armenian, Mikayel Loris-Melikov (his original name was Melikian). The Russian troops included many Russian Armenians; Armenians from Ottoman Anatolia were said to have acted as guides. The spread of pro-Russian sentiments among the Armenians of Anatolia, who hoped that Russia would liberate them from the Turkish yoke, was well known. All this alarmed the Ottoman government and raised doubts about the reliability of the Armenians. The transition from "the most loyal *millet*" to a people suspected to be in league with foreign enemies was complete. Consequently, when the Russian troops withdrew, Kurds and Circassians pillaged Armenian villages in the border region, and thousands of Armenians took refuge in the Russian Caucasus. The massacres of 1894–96 are unintelligible without taking note of this decisive change in the Turko-Armenian relationship.

After some initial setbacks, the war of 1877–78 ended with a complete victory for Russia. In January 1878 Russian troops approached Constantinople; on the Caucasian front they took Erzurum. At the urging of the Armenian patriarch, the Treaty of San Stefano, signed on March 2, 1878, included a provision aimed at protecting the Armenians. According to article 16, the Sublime Porte (the Ottoman government) agreed "to carry out, without further delay, the ameliorations and reforms demanded by local requirements in the provinces inhabited by the Armenians, and to guarantee their security against the Kurds and Circassians."[7] Russian troops were to remain in the Armenian provinces until satisfactory reforms had been implemented.

The harsh provisions of the Treaty of San Stefano stripped the Ottoman state of substantial territories in the Balkans and yielded Russia the Armenian districts of Ardahan, Kars, and Bayazid as well as the important Black Sea port of Batum. These gains aroused the fears of the British that Turkey would become a client state of Russia, thus upsetting the balance of power in the eastern Mediterranean.[8] Hence Russia, under pressure from the European powers, had to agree to the Treaty of Berlin several months later (July 13, 1878), which greatly reduced Russian gains. The creation of a Bulgarian vassal state subservient to Russia was shelved; the Armenian district of Bayazid was returned to Turkey and Batum converted into a free port; the independence of Serbia, Montenegro, and Rumania was reaffirmed; and Bosnia-Herzegovina was to be occupied and administered by Austria-Hungary. The new treaty also required Russia to withdraw its troops from Ottoman territory and placed the responsibility for enforcing the Armenian reform provisions of the Treaty of San Stefano (article 61 of the new treaty) upon the entire Concert of Europe. As George Douglas Campbell, Duke of Argyll, a former cabinet minister, later observed correctly: "What was everybody's business was nobody's business."[9] In the separate Cyprus Convention of June 4, 1878, which allowed Britain to occupy the island of Cyprus, the Porte made an additional promise to introduce reforms into Armenia; but all these commitments remained mere words.

The overall result was to increase antagonism between Turks and Armenians. The agreements raised the expectations of the Armenians, while they provided no effective security for them. The sultan was angry over the continuing interference of the European powers in Turkey's internal affairs. He became more fearful of the Armenians, whose lands constituted a crucial segment of the reduced empire, and hence was more inclined to use violence. The Armenians had become pawns in the European struggle for power and dominance.

The contribution of the Treaty of Berlin and the Cyprus Convention to the Armenian tragedy was noted by Lord James Bryce, a great friend of the Armenians. Writing in 1896, after a wave of Armenian massacres, he remarked:

If there had been no Treaty of Berlin and no Anglo-Turkish Convention, the Armenians would doubtless have continued to be oppressed, as they had been oppressed for centuries. But they would have been spared the storm of fire, famine, and slaughter which descended upon them in 1895.... Before the Treaty of Berlin the Sultan had no special enmity to the Armenians, nor had the Armenian nation any political aspirations. It was the stipulations then made for their protection that first marked them out for suspicion and hatred, and that first roused in them hope of deliverance whose expression increased the hatred of their rulers. The Anglo-Turkish Convention taught them to look to England, and England's interference embittered the Turks.[10]

The European powers did nothing to enforce the treaty provisions designed to help the Armenians. Having an uneasy conscience, they repeatedly remonstrated with the sultan. Yet these remonstrations only further irritated Abdul Hamid and stiffened his back. He would rather die, he told the German ambassador in November 1894, than yield to unjust pressure and grant the Armenians political autonomy.[11]

In 1891, fearful of Russia's continuing interest in the eastern Anatolian region and of Armenian revolutionaries on both sides of the Russian border, the sultan decreed the formation of Kurdish volunteer cavalry units. Modeled after the Russian Cossacks, the Hamidiye regiments, named after the sultan, were to strengthen the defense of the border provinces. They also had the purpose of bringing the Kurds under some control and using the Hamidiye as a counterweight to the Turkish notables of the towns, who often challenged the sultan's writ.[12] By 1895 the Hamidiye consisted of fifty-seven regiments and probably close to fifty thousand men.[13] Their marauding also affected the settled Muslims, but the Armenian peasants were the hardest hit. For them the new Kurdish armed bands meant more depredations and further pillaging of their villages. The fox, it appeared, had been put in charge of the henhouse. During the disturbances of 1894–96 the Hamidiye participated in punitive expeditions against the Armenian population.

Archbishop Mugrdich Khrimian, who had been one of the spokesmen of the Armenians at the Congress of Berlin in 1878, preached a sermon in the Armenian cathedral of Constantinople upon his return. He had gone to Berlin with a petition for reforms, a piece of paper, he told the large crowd, while the other small nations—Bulgarians, Serbians, and Montenegrins—had come with iron spoons. When the European powers placed on the table of the conference a "Dish of Liberty," the others were able to scoop into the delicious dish and take out a portion for themselves. The Armenians, however, had in their hands only the fragile paper on which their petition was written. Hence when their turn came to dip into the dish of liberty, their paper spoon crumbled, and they were left without any share of the meal. Archbishop Khrimian's famous sermon was a not so subtle appeal for the use of arms—"iron spoons."[14] During the following decades a growing number of Armenians were to act upon this call for armed struggle.

Chapter 2

The Armenian Revolutionary Movement

Disappointed by the failure of the European powers to enforce the protective provisions of the Treaty of Berlin and encouraged by the successes of other oppressed nationalities in the Ottoman Empire, especially the Greeks and Bulgarians, young Armenian intellectuals began to organize for armed struggle. The revolutionary movement began in the European diaspora and spread from there into Anatolia. Another important base was the Russian Caucasus, where the large Armenian population embraced the idea of national liberation with growing fervor. The poet Kamar-Katiba called upon the Turkish Armenians across the border to defend themselves and not to rely upon Europe, which was too far, or upon God, who was too high.[1]

During the early 1880s several secret societies sprang up in eastern Anatolia. Its leaders exploited the abuses of Abdul Hamid's autocratic regime and insisted that the national aspirations of the Armenian people could not be realized without the use of force. A group called the Defenders of the Fatherland was arrested in the city of Erzurum in 1883, and forty of its members were condemned to prison terms of five to fifteen years. At the same time, another secret organization, the Patriotic Society, operated in Van. After its detection by the government, this group changed its political aims and became a moderate-liberal organization that took the name Armenakan (after the newspaper *Armenia* published in Marseilles). This party existed well into the twentieth century, but its influence remained limited.[2]

In 1887 a group of Armenian students in Geneva, Switzerland, organized the Hunchakian Revolutionary Party (after the journal *Hunchak,* meaning "Bell"). The Hunchaks, as they became known, were influenced by Russian Marxist revolutionary thought. The immediate objective was the resurrection of historic Armenia, which was to include the Armenians in Turkey, Russia, and Persia; the ultimate goal was a socialist government. Armenian independence was to be achieved by oral and written propaganda as well as by the armed struggle of guerrilla fighters. Showing the impact of the Russian Narodnaya Volya revolutionaries, committed to direct action, the Hunchaks embraced political terror as a means of eliminating opponents, spies, and informers. Article 6 of the program of the Hunchak party stated: "The time for the general revolution [in Armenia] will be when a foreign power attacks Turkey externally. The party shall revolt internally."[3] In due time this program of course became known to the Turkish government, and during World War I the Young Turks used the clause to justify the deportation of the Armenians.

In June 1890 Russian Armenian students convened a meeting in Tiflis, in the Russian Caucasus, to discuss the unification of all revolutionary forces in a new organization. After long and stormy sessions a new party was founded that took the name Armenian Revolutionary Federation (Dashnaktsuthiun, meaning "Federation," or Dashnaks for short). The Hunchaks at first joined but soon withdrew and continued their separate existence. In 1896 the Hunchak party divided into two hostile factions, and this split reduced its effectiveness. The main revolutionary player in the Armenian community became the Dashnak party.

The platform of the Dashnaks was adopted at their first general convention, held in Tiflis in 1892. The central plank read: "It is the aim of the Armenian Revolutionary Federation to bring about by rebellion the political and economic emancipation of Turkish Armenia." The majority of the delegates were socialists, but many of them felt that the inclusion of the demand for socialism would harm the national cause. Socialism, writes Anaide Ter Minassian, "was to remain as it were the bad conscience of the Dashnak party."[4] The platform spoke of a popular democratic government to be elected in free elections, freedom of speech and assembly, distribution of land to those who were landless, compulsory education, and other social reforms. In order to achieve these aims "by means of the revolution," revolutionary bands were "to arm the people," wage "an incessant fight against the [Turkish] Government," and "wreck and loot government institutions." They were "to use the weapon of the terror on corrupt government officers, spies, traitors, grafters, and all sorts of oppressors."[5]

On the whole, then, as Louise Nalbandian has noted, "there was no radical difference between the Dashnak *Program* of 1892 and the aims and activities of the Hunchaks."[6] Both organizations were committed to armed struggle to achieve their goals and accepted the use of terror (i.e., recourse to assassinations). To be sure, the Hunchaks explicitly demanded an independent Armenia, while the Dashnaks embraced the vaguer notion of a "free Armenia." In the eyes of the Ottoman government this was not a very important distinction, however, and both ideas were considered anathema. Even when the Fourth General Convention of the Dashnaks held in 1907 revised the party's platform and adopted the goal of Armenian autonomy within a federative system, the general attitude in the country—including that of many Young Turks, before and after their assumption of power in 1908—remained one of sharp distrust. The demand for an autonomous Armenia was seen as simply the opening wedge for complete separation and the breakup of the empire.

Operating from bases in the Russian Caucasus and Persia and taking advantage of eastern Anatolia's mountainous terrain, Armenian guerrilla bands attacked Turkish army units, gendarmerie posts, and Kurdish villages involved in brigandage. There were charges of massacres of Muslim villagers. British consuls regularly mention the killing of Turkish officials. In late November 1892 an Armenian villager tried to assassinate the *vali* (governor) of Van. Upon interrogation, the British vice-consul reported, the villager stated that his brother and several others, including the village priest, had led him to believe that "the Armenian national cause would thereby be advanced."[7]

The recruitment of fighters from among the Armenian peasantry was not easy, and the revolutionaries therefore carried out an active campaign of propaganda against what they considered the slavish mentality of the Armenian masses. They stressed the valor and heroism of the men known as *fedayee*s, a word derived from the Arabic, meaning dedicated patriots prepared to lay down their lives for the cause. The exploits of the guerrillas against superior Ottoman forces assumed legendary proportions, and this hero worship continues to the present day. For example, in a book richly illustrated with pictures of ferocious-looking fighters, proudly displaying their weapons, an American author describes his compatriots in Ottoman Turkey in language that recalls the legend of Robin Hood. Armenian guerrilla companies, he writes,

> roamed the hillside and the plains defending the hard-pressed peasants, redressing wrongs, executing revolutionary justice and inflicting punishment on the tormentors of their people.... It might truthfully be said that the Fedayee was the finest and noblest creation of the Armenian revolution. Dedicated to the cause of his people, fearless in battle,

chivalrous toward women, generous to his foes and yet terrible in his vengeance, the Armenian Fedayee renounced the comforts and pleasures of life, gave up his family and loved ones, endured the privation and suffering of a wanderer's life, and became a living Madagh [sacrificial offering] for the liberation of his people.[8]

In contrast, the picture of the Turk painted in Armenian revolutionary propaganda was one of utter depravity and fiendish cruelty. Hundreds of books, pamphlets, and articles, making the most of Turkish oppression, were disseminated in Europe (especially in England) and in the United States. At least some of these reports, as Nalbandian has pointed out, exaggerated Turkish atrocities.[9] No doubt, the British diplomat Eliot noted, "Turkish prisons present most of the horrors which can be caused by brutality and neglect .... No doubt, too, such rough punishments as the bastinado are freely employed." Yet many of the "hellish" and "unutterable" forms of torture of which the Turks were freely accused were "largely the invention of morbid and somewhat prurient brains. Medical testimony makes it certain that no human being could survive the tortures which some Armenians are said to have suffered without dying."[10]

Despite great efforts to build up mass support, the Armenian revolutionaries often enjoyed no more than a modicum of sympathy among the largely apolitical peasants and the more prosperous urban Armenians, who were fearful of losing their privileged position. There is general agreement, writes Vahakn N. Dadrian, that "the revolutionaries were not only opposed by the bulk of the Armenian population and of its ecclesiastical leadership, but in fact comprised a very small segment of that population."[11] Hence they were often driven to resort to terror against their own people. British consular reports mention several attempts to assassinate Armenian patriarchs and many instances of Armenians killed for failure to contribute to the costs of the revolutionary struggle or accused of being traitors or spies. A report from Marsovan, dated May 27, 1893, noted that the "terrorism they [the revolutionaries] exercised over their more tranquil compatriots was increasing, and some murders which had recently occurred of supposed informers or lukewarm supporters had deepened the fears of the peaceable."[12] The son of a leading member of the Armenakan party describes in a memoir how "the Dashnak Central Committee in Van resorted to the use of terrorists to put my father away."[13]

Dashnak literature contained long lists of persons liquidated by execution. "Early issues of the Dashnak *Droshag* [Standard]," writes a historian of the Dashnaks, "frequently carry notices of those against whom the death penalty has been served or about those who had met the penalty."[14] This way of enforcing revolutionary justice was considered fully justified, for, as another more recent defender of this practice put it, "The revolutionary avenger was the Archangel Gabriel whom to oppose was unthinkable. He was sinless and impeccable, the executor of the will on high. He was invisible and invulnerable. His hands were always clean." After all, he added, the revolutionary terror affected only "those baneful elements which jeopardized the safety of the people and the progress of the emancipatory cause."[15]

Well-informed observers on the scene were convinced that despite increased revolutionary activity and frequently voiced bombastic threats the Ottoman regime was in no danger. The number of Armenian militants was small, and they were fighting among each other. The great majority of the Armenians, wrote the American missionary Edwin M. Bliss, strongly opposed any seditious activity, and the idea of a general uprising was considered madness. Yet ill feeling between Christians and Muslims, he noted, was on the increase: "and there were not a few cases during 1893 and in the early part of 1894, when Turkish officials had all they could do to restrain the hostile manifestations of the Moslem communities."[16] The authorities in Constantinople, fed alarmist reports from provincial officials, became edgy. The sultan, in particular, was said to be in a state of increasing paranoia and panic. Interpreting any minor raid or skirmish as a full-scale rebellion, he ordered severe measures of repression that drew widespread condemnation in Europe. In the summer of 1892 the new Liberal government in England, headed by William Gladstone, sent sharp notes of protest to the Porte that further inflamed the situation. In the eyes of many patriotic Turks the Armenians were, now more than ever, disloyal subjects in league with the European powers that sought to dismantle the Ottoman Empire.

In their attempts to suppress the revolutionary agitation the Ottoman authorities in the eastern provinces made little effort to differentiate between the guilty and the innocent. Following the appearance of revolutionary placards in Marsovan in January 1893, the police arrested over seven hundred Armenians. In other towns, too, large-scale arrests and imprisonments on the most frivolous charges were common. The British ambassador reported to London on March 28, 1894: "The inability of the officials to distinguish between harmless criticism and active sedition; their system of making indiscriminate arrests in the hope of finding somewhat [*sic*] that will justify the arrest; the resort not infrequently to torture in order to obtain testimony; the use made by unprincipled officials of existing excitement in order to ruin personal enemies or to extort money by means of baseless charges . . . threaten to make rebels more quickly than the police can catch them."[17] The Armenians, noted another British diplomat, "would be a perfectly contented, hardworking, and profitable part of the subjects of the Sultan, provided that they were protected against the Kurds; given a fair share in the administration of those districts where they form a large proportion of the inhabitants; and, what would follow as a natural consequence, treated, civilly and personally, on an equal footing with their Mahommedan neighbours."[18]

In the summer of 1894 the rugged Armenian villagers of Sassun, under the prodding of Armenian revolutionaries, refused to pay the customary tribute to Kurdish chiefs. Unable to subdue their former underlings, the Kurds appealed for help to the Ottoman government, which sent regular army units. After prolonged and sharp fighting and having been promised amnesty if they laid down their arms, the Armenians surrendered. Yet large numbers of villagers, without distinction of age or sex, were massacred. Christian missionaries and European consuls voiced their revulsion, and the sultan was forced to agree to a commission of inquiry with British, French, and Russian participation as well as to a number of reform measures.[19]

first massacres caused by a refusal to pay tribute to Kurds

The Turks insisted that Armenian armed bands had provoked the affair, had committed atrocities against the inhabitants of Muslim villages in their way, and thus had forced the government to send in troops to establish order.[20] Some authors have argued that this and other incidents were part of a strategy on the part of Armenian revolutionaries, especially the Hunchaks, to provoke the Turks to commit excesses that would draw the attention of the Christian world and bring about European intervention. Perhaps the best known spokesman for what has become known as the "provocation thesis" is the historian William L. Langer. The revolutionaries, he contends, organized incidents to "bring about inhuman reprisals, and to provoke the intervention of the powers." Yet the Europeans never followed through long enough to achieve lasting reforms. The net result was that "thousands of innocent Armenians lost their lives, and there was no real gain to be shown."[21]

More recently Justin McCarthy and Carolyn McCarthy have put forth the same argument:

Provocation thesis opposed to Ottoman responsibility

Only the intent to spark massacre in retaliation can explain the seeming madness of Armenian attacks on members of Kurdish tribes. Such attacks were a constant feature of small-scale rebel actions. Individual members of powerful Kurdish tribes were assassinated, undoubtedly in expectation of reprisals that would touch the heart of Europe. For example, the 1894 troubles in Sassun were preceded by Armenian attacks on the Bekhran and Zadian tribes, which resulted in armed battles between the Armenian revolutionaries and Kurdish tribesmen.[22]

Most supporters of the Armenian cause have rejected the provocation thesis. According to Richard Hovannisian, "those who have made it have failed to provide proof."[23] Suny has argued that Langer and "those who have followed him seriously distort the aims and motives of the revolutionaries." The provocation thesis, he suggests, "is based on a misreading of the sources, a disregard for the causes of the Armenian resistance, and inadequate consideration of the reasons for the Turkish perceptions of the Armenian threat."[24] In the eyes of Robert Melson, the provocation thesis "neglects the independent predispositions toward violence, the perceptions, and the actions of the perpetrators." It fails "to inquire into the intentions of the sultan, his view of the Armenians, or the context of Armenian-Ottoman relations which might have exaggerated the Armenian threat."[25] In a foreword to a book by Melson on the Armenian genocide, Leo Kuper maintains that the provocation thesis makes the Armenians "the agents of their own destruction, [and] offers a parallel to the Nazi ideology of Jews engaged in international conspiracy against the Third Reich."[26]

These reactions, I believe, are needlessly defensive. To take note of the tactical designs of the Armenian revolutionaries does not mean to ignore or excuse the malevolent intentions and deeds of the Turkish authorities. Given the weakness of the Armenian side, the need for great power intervention (especially on the part of Britain and Russia) was always an essential part of Armenian thinking. The provocative intentions of at least *some* of the Armenian revolutionaries to bring about such an intervention are well documented and are mentioned by many contemporary observers of the events in question. For example, an "eloquent defender of the revolution" explained to Cyrus Hamlin, the founder of Robert College in Constantinople, how Hunchak bands would use European sympathy for Armenian suffering to bring about European intervention. They would "watch their opportunity to kill Turks and Kurds, set fire to their villages, and then make their escape into the mountains. The enraged Moslems will then rise, and fall upon the defenceless Armenians and slaughter them with such barbarity that Russia will enter in the name of humanity and Christian civilization and take possession." When the horrified missionary denounced this scheme as immoral, he was told: "It appears so to you, no doubt; but we Armenians have determined to be free. Europe listened to the Bulgarian horrors and made Bulgaria free. She will listen to our cry when it goes up in shrieks and blood of millions of women and children.... We are desperate. We shall do it."[27] The program of the Hunchaks, Louise Nalbandian notes, required that the people were to be "incited against their enemies and were to 'profit' from the retaliatory actions of these same enemies."[28]

In a message sent on May 6, 1893, to ambassador Clare Ford, British consul Robert W. Graves in Erzurum reported on the interrogation of an Armenian prisoner that he was allowed to attend. The self-declared revolutionary, "showing the boldest front possible," told his questioners that he was a socialist by conviction and was prepared to use any means to attain his ends. "He was paid for this work by funds from abroad, and the attention of the movement was, he declared, to cause such disturbances in the country as should attract attention to the oppressed condition of his fellow-countrymen and compel the interference of foreign powers."[29]

In his memoirs published in 1933 Graves elaborated upon the intentions of the revolutionaries:

> They counted upon the proneness to panic of the Sultan, and the stupidity, misplaced zeal or deliberate malevolence of the local authorities to order and carry out unnecessarily punitive measures, which would degenerate into massacre as soon as the fanaticism and blood-lust of the ignorant Turk and Kurd populations had been sufficiently aroused. Then would come the moment for an appeal to the signatory Powers of the Treaty of Berlin to intervene and impose upon the Sultan such administrative reforms as would make life at least endurable for his Armenian subjects. They were quite cynical when remonstrated with on the wickedness of deliberately provoking the massacre of their unfortunate fellow-countrymen, with all its attendant horrors, without any assurance that the lot of the survivors would be any happier, saying calmly that the sacrifice was a necessary one and the victims would be "Martyrs to the National Cause."[30]

Other contemporaries report similar statements; it is clear that the actions of the revolutionists did not just consist of self-defense, as most pro-Armenian authors are prone to argue. The American author George Hepworth, a highly regarded observer and friend of the Armenians, noted that "the revolutionists are doing what they can to make fresh outrages possible. That is their avowed purpose. They reason that if they can induce the Turks to kill more of the Armenians, themselves excepted, Europe will be forced to intervene."[31] The veteran British correspondent Edwin Pears noted that Russia had turned against the Armenian revolutionists in the Caucasus, fearful that they would succeed in undermining the tsar's autocratic rule, and that under these circumstances an Armenian revolt against the Ottomans had no chance of success. "Some of the extremists declared that while they recognised that hundreds of innocent persons suffered from each of these attempts, they could provoke a big massacre which would bring in foreign intervention."[32] More recently the British writer Christopher Walker has acknowledged that such a plan "was endorsed by some of the revolutionaries" but goes on to argue that this "was not the cold, vicious calculation that it has some times been represented to be ....In reality, the extreme measures to which they sought to provoke the Porte were only a speeded-up version of what was happening all the time to Armenians. There was little to choose between a thousand dying in a week and a thousand dying in a year."[33]

To prevent misunderstandings it is well to state again that the existence of plans on the part of at least some Armenian revolutionaries to provoke massacres neither excuses the actions of the Turks who acted upon these provocations with vicious attacks upon innocent people nor amounts to blaming the victim. Given the avowed aims of all of the revolutionists to achieve a "free Armenia," a harsh and hostile reaction on the part of the Ottoman authorities would undoubtedly have been forthcoming even in the absence of the provocative acts. Whether the number of victims would have been as high as it turned out to be will have to remain a matter of speculation. That the attacks greatly increased tension between Muslims and Christians is a matter of record. The observation of Consul Graves in Erzurum, made about two years before the horrible massacres of 1895–96, turned out to be sadly prophetic. A "spirit of hostility and race hatred," he noted on July 1, 1893, "has been aroused among the hitherto friendly Turkish population which may some day, if further provoked, find vent in reprisals and atrocities."[34] Unfortunately, that is exactly what happened.

Chapter 3

The Massacres of 1894–96

By 1894 tensions between Armenians and Turks in eastern Anatolia had reached a dangerous point. Armenian revolutionaries were active in all of the provinces, while Turkish authorities were displaying increased severity. There were mass arrests and new reports of the use of torture in the prisons. The Kurds felt encouraged in their new role as the irregular soldiers of the sultan; former consul Graves called them "licensed oppressors of their Christian neighbors in the Eastern provinces."[1] Events in the district of Sassun in the *vilayet* of Bitlis, mentioned briefly in the previous chapter, set off a round of massacres all over Anatolia that were to echo around the world.

CARNAGE IN THE WAKE OF AN ATTEMPTED REFORM

The report of the Turkish commission of inquiry set up after the bloodshed in the summer of 1894 in the Talori region of the district of Sassun blamed the entire episode on Armenian provocation. Hunchak organizers were said to have incited an uprising on the part of the villagers that required the dispatch of regular troops. Heavy fighting lasted over twenty-three days before the disturbance was put down. Muslim villages were said to have been burned by the Armenian bandits, and their inhabitants slaughtered. No more than 265 Armenians had been killed.[2] European consuls, however, denied that there had been an uprising. The villagers had refused to pay double taxation and had taken up arms to defend themselves against attacking Kurds. Turkish troops and Hamidiye regiments had massacred those who had surrendered and many others, including women and children. The total number of Armenian dead was reported to have reached several thousand.[3] Missionary accounts speak of women being "outraged to death" and describe atrocities such as Armenian villagers being burnt alive in their houses and "children [being] placed in a row, one behind another, and a bullet fired down the line, apparently to see how many could be dispatched with one bullet. Infants and small children were piled one on the other and their heads struck off."[4]

After considerable delay, in July 1895 the three European delegates attached to the Turkish commission of inquiry issued their own report, in which they complained about the difficulties put in their way by Ottoman authorities when they had tried to interview Armenian survivors. The delegates conceded that there had been isolated acts of brigandage by an Armenian band and resistance to the troops, but they denied the charge of an open revolt. The three delegates failed to agree on the number of Armenians killed (their views ranged from nine hundred to four thousand), but they were unanimous in reporting widespread massacres.[5] More recently Dadrian has acknowledged that "the Hunchakists... exacerbated the situation by their intervention in the conflict when two of their leaders, through agitation, tried to organize an armed insurrection." But this agitation, by all accounts, had only limited success and certainly does not justify the massacres of villagers that appear to have taken place.[6]

The events of Sassun, as one writer puts it, "opened the floodgates to a torrent of Turcophobia in Europe and the United States."[7] Just as after the Bulgarian atrocities of 1876, there was an outcry of protest, and the press of Britain and America demanded action. The ambassadors of Britain, France, and Russia now began to pressure the sultan to accept political reforms for the six eastern provinces of Anatolia. According to the plan, there was to be an amnesty for Armenian political prisoners, one-third of all administrators were to be Armenians, the gendarmerie was to be mixed, and the Kurdish Hamidiye regiments were to operate only in conjunction with regular army units. The appointment of governors was to be subject to confirmation by the European powers, a control commission was to be established, and a high commissioner was to implement the plan. Many of the Armenians as well as Britain had hoped for more far-reaching reforms, but Russia was adamantly opposed to any scheme that might eventually lead to full Armenian independence or to the use of military pressure to gain acceptance of the plan.[8]

Sensing the lack of unanimity on the part of the Europeans, the sultan raised objections to many of the reform provisions. Diplomatic exchanges continued all through the summer of 1895 while tensions between Christians and Muslims increased steadily. The Armenian revolutionaries were reported to threaten an insurrection; Muslim conservatives organized to prevent the implementation of the reforms, which they regarded as another example of European imperialism that would eventually lead to Armenian independence and the destruction of the Ottoman Empire. One group of Muslims in Bitlis, the British consul in Erzurum reported on July 10, had vowed "to shed blood in case the Sultan accepts the scheme of reforms." The Turkish ambassador to Great Britain told the foreign secretary on August 11 that "knowledge of the encouragement given in England to the Armenians taken in connection with the outrages committed by them, might excite the Mussulman population to acts of retaliation, which would lead to a very serious state of affairs."[9]

On September 30, 1895, the Hunchaks organized a demonstration in Constantinople that was to support the reform proposals of the European powers. A petition was to be presented to the grand vizier, but many of the approximately four thousand demonstrators were armed with pistols and knives. Several hundred yards from the government offices police and troops blocked the procession, shots were fired, and in the resulting skirmish sixty Armenians and fifteen gendarmes were killed and many more wounded. An outbreak of mob action all over the city ensued, in which Armenians were hunted down and hundreds brutally killed. It is not clear who fired the first shots, but European diplomats believed that the authorities had a hand in the violent repression that followed the demonstration. The German ambassador reported to his government on October 4 that the police had equipped the mob with thick cudgels.[10] Some two thousand Armenians took refuge in various churches of the city. When they were eventually allowed to leave, more than ten percent were found to have arms.[11] Both sides, it appears, had prepared for a violent collision.

A few days later an attempt in Trebizond (today's Trabzon) on the life of Bahri Pasha, a former governor of Van, led to another round of killings. The attackers apparently were members of a revolutionary committee; and the attack, coming in the wake of the events in Constantinople, led to furious retaliation. On October 8 large numbers of rowdies attacked the houses and shops of Armenians; police and soldiers participated in the looting and killing. The work of butchery went on for five hours; estimates of the number of killed in Trebizond and the nearby villages were as high as eleven hundred.[12] Turkish officials told the American George Hepworth that "the Armenians had brought the calamity on themselves by their ambition for autonomy"; but while Hepworth acknowledged that that there had been "great provocation," he also noted the "inexpressly cruel" mode of retaliation of the Turks that punished the innocent as well as the guilty.[13]

With renewed pressure from the European ambassadors, under whose eyes the killings in Constantinople had taken place, the sultan on October 17 finally agreed to issue a decree that embodied most of the reform proposals.[14] He refused to release the actual text, however, arguing that publication would inflame his Muslim subjects. The effect was an explosion of violence all across Anatolia. Rumors had it that the sultan had agreed to Armenian autonomy, and Muslim conservative elements retaliated by organizing widespread massacres. "The provocations of the revolutionaries (real or imagined), paled beside the reprisals of Turks and Kurds," writes one student of the subject.[15]

One of the first of many such outbursts of large-scale killings took place in Bitlis, a stronghold of Muslim fanaticism. On Friday, October 25, while Muslims were attending services in the mosque, a shot was fired. Assuming that it came from an Armenian, Muslims, many of them armed, poured out of the mosque and attacked every Armenian in sight. According to information obtained by the British vice-consul in Mush, between five hundred and eight hundred Armenians were killed that day and their shops pillaged. "The Kurds," he reported on October 29, "are profiting by the situation and commit outrages in every direction."[16] Armenian villages were being attacked and their men murdered. The authorities were unable or unwilling to control the mobs. A similar report was received from Van, where the Kurds had pillaged villages and killed the men.[17]

Erzurum exploded on October 30. Tension had been building up steadily during the month of September, with Armenian revolutionaries becoming more active and Muslims accusing the Armenians of wanting to create an independent state. Marauding bands of Kurds and Laz were attacking Armenian villages. "The feeling of enmity between the Turk and the Armenian had been fermenting for a long while," wrote Hepworth, "and it only needed a proper occasion to give itself vent."[18] That occasion was the news that the sultan had agreed to far-reaching reforms. According to Consul Graves, the massacre apparently had been carefully planned, "for before it began hundreds of Turkish women flocked into town carrying sacks in which to remove the loot of the Armenian quarter. The killing of Armenian men in the streets was started by a bugle-call and ended four or five hours later with another, and the plundering of Armenian shops and houses was carried out systematically, the lives of women and children being spared." [19] Foreign observers noted that soldiers had actively participated in the looting and killing. The number of Armenians killed was said to have been several hundred, all of them men.[20] Similar massacres took place in other Anatolian towns and villages. In each of these incidents, notes a balanced scholar, "the local government stepped aside and let them run their course until they could safely step back in and restrain the Muslims. No attempts were made to introduce troops into the area, which could have garrisoned the cities and suppressed the Kurds, until the winter, when most of the activity had subsided anyway." [21]

In two instances Armenian revolutionaries decided to strike first. In the mountain town of Zeitun, located about 170 miles north of Aleppo and inhabited by strong-willed Armenians with a long history of militancy, Hunchak organizers had passed the word that the British and French fleets would come to the aid of an uprising. In late October the Zeitunis overwhelmed the local garrison and for several weeks successfully defended their stronghold against a large Turkish force that soon arrived on the scene and laid siege to the town. The rebellion finally ended with an amnesty, arranged with the help of European consuls.[22] In Van, a center of Armenian nationalist feeling, revolutionaries barricaded themselves in the Armenian quarter. Here, too, a siege was resolved through the mediation of foreign consuls.[23]

During the winter of 1895–96 Armenian widows and orphans who had survived the wave of killing suffered from want of food and shelter, and large numbers died of cold, hunger, and exposure. Meanwhile, the British ambassador reported on December 19, "accounts from the Asiatic provinces show that the ravages of the Kurds remain unchecked. The perpetrators of the massacres remain unpunished, while innocent Armenians are committed to prison on frivolous charges." [24] With the reform proposals effectively stalled, the leadership of the Dashnaks decided upon a dramatic act that would bring the Armenian problem back on the European agenda. In the early afternoon of August 26, 1896, a group of revolutionaries, armed with firearms and dynamite, seized the Imperial Ottoman Bank in Constantinople and threatened to blow up the bank if their demands for the introduction of reforms in Armenia were not granted. The demands included the appointment of a European high commissioner for the Armenian provinces and a general amnesty for Armenians convicted on political charges. Bombs were also thrown in several other parts of the city.[25]

It appears that both the Turkish police and the Armenian community knew of the audacious plan before it took place. Many well-to-do Armenian families had left the city on the morning of the attack. The authorities may have thought that the seizure of the bank would discredit the bomb-throwers in the eyes of Europe and that they could teach the Armenians a lesson by organizing a brutal retaliation. At six o'clock the same evening, bands of Muslims, chiefly lower-class Kurds and Laz armed with iron bars and wooden clubs, appeared in the streets and began to kill all the Armenians they could find. It was clear to observers on the scene that this was not a spontaneous reaction on the part of the Turkish population but a carefully prepared mob. "It is fairly certain," concludes Langer, "that the government had learned of the revolutionaries' plans some days before they were put into execution, and that these Turkish bands had been organized and armed. The clubs were mostly of one design and the men who wielded them were rarely residents of the neighborhood in which they operated."[26] Few soldiers participated in the orgy of killing, but neither did they try to stop it. The mob was in control of the city until the evening of the next day. It is estimated that five thousand to six thousand Armenians lost their lives, most of them poor porters. Again, as in the earlier massacres in Anatolia, very few women or children were killed—another indication that this was not a blind outburst of popular fury but a planned massacre with carefully chosen victims.[27]

If the revolutionaries had hoped finally to bring about a decisive intervention of the European powers, they were again disappointed. Through the mediation of the first dragoman (interpreter) of the Russian embassy the survivors of the attack on the Ottoman Bank were able to obtain nothing more than a promise of safe passage to France, and by midnight of August 26 they had quietly left the bank. The European diplomats submitted notes of protest; the European press published lurid accounts of the killings, illustrated with gruesome pictures; and in the capitals of the continent there were numerous meetings demanding help for the persecuted Christians—but that was all. Once again the Armenian revolutionaries had brought about nothing but more suffering for their unfortunate and innocent compatriots.

On October 1 the sultan appointed a commission of inquiry into the disturbances in Constantinople, which included three European officers. The Prussian general Kamphövener Pasha resigned ten days later because he was unwilling to participate in an inquiry, which, he believed, was designed to whitewash the police.[28] Meanwhile the news from Constantinople sent new tremors through the provinces. Consul Graves in Erzurum described the atmosphere of panic that ensued:

> At Erzerum the events of Constantinople had a disastrous effect, the surviving Armenians being more terrified than ever, while Moslem fanaticism was stirred to its depths by exaggerated accounts of Armenian seditious activity, to which colour was given by the foolish and criminal attempt on the Ottoman Bank. Incendiary placards appeared on the walls, calling for vengeance on the enemies of the religion and the state, and a further migration of Armenians from the frontier districts into Russian territory took place, while the work of our relief agents became more and more difficult and dangerous.[29]

The events of 1895–96 took a heavy toll in human lives. Estimates of Armenian deaths range between twenty thousand (a figure given by a Turkish diplomat and historian in 1985) and three hundred thousand (the number of victims claimed by two members of the Armenian Academy of Sciences in Erevan in 1965).[30] Figures produced closer to the time of the events in question reveal a somewhat smaller disparity. The Ottomans gave the figure of 13,432.[31] Hepworth speaks of fifty thousand dead.[32] On December 11, 1895, the German ambassador reported an estimate of sixty thousand to eighty thousand killed.[33] In the absence of reliable inquiries there is of course no possibility of reconciling these conflicting figures; as Jeremy Salt puts it, "the sensible reader may well arrive at the conclusion that more Armenians died than the Ottomans were prepared to admit but fewer than Armenian propagandists would like the world to believe."[34] Whatever figure is accepted, there can be little doubt that the events of 1895–96 created misery on a vast scale. Thousands of houses and shops were plundered and destroyed, many Armenians were forced to convert or made to flee for their life, and in the aftermath of the massacres hunger and disease added to the human toll. The loss of life, one should add, would have been even higher if (as several sources indicate) many Armenians had not been protected by their Muslim neighbors.[35]

WHO WAS RESPONSIBLE FOR THE MASSACRES?

Given the similarity with which the disturbances played themselves out in the various locations it is tempting to consider the killings the result of a centrally planned plot, the personal responsibility of the sultan. The massacres, noted Eliot, "were executed with military precision. Each lasted only a short time, generally twenty-four or forty-eight hours, and often began and ended with the sound of the trumpet. The authorities did not interfere, and in some cases encouraged the mob. The victims were only Gregorian Armenians; other Christians, and even Catholic Armenians, remaining as a rule untouched."[36] The American missionary Bliss reported that special care was taken everywhere to avoid injury to the subjects of foreign nations and to kill men only.[37] Small wonder, therefore, that the European press everywhere placed the blame for the massacres on Abdul Hamid, an autocratic ruler known for giving minute attention to the internal affairs of his empire. Prime Minister Gladstone called him the "Grand Assassin" and "the unspeakable Turk."[38] The "Red Sultan," wrote ambassador Henry Morgenthau in 1918, had wanted to get rid of the Armenians and had to desist from complete annihilation only because of the protests of England, France, and Russia.[39] A more recent author speaks of "a conscious plot to wipe out a race of people…and that is what leads us to label it as genocide."[40] Dadrian refers to a "continuum of a genocidal policy" that links the actions of Abdul Hamid and those of the Young Turks in 1915.[41] Still another writer calls the massacres "a dress rehearsal for the 'final solution' of 1915."[42]

And yet the evidence for the personal responsibility of Abdul Hamid is weak, and the accounts of observers on the scene make other explanations more plausible. Eliot did not think that "orders were issued for a deliberate and organized slaughter of Armenians." He believed that the sultan, misled by local officials, genuinely feared an uprising by the Armenian revolutionaries and therefore commanded severe measures. "Probably the orders issued to the local Ottoman authorities warned them to be on guard against any revolutionary movement of the Armenians, and, should there be any reason to apprehend one, to take the offensive without delay."[43] The Turks, according to Hepworth, really feared an insurrection. Unreasonable as this fear may have been, they "really thought that the whole country was infested with rebels, and that unless the most heroic measures were taken, the government would be overthrown." In many cases, Hepworth relates, local officials invented revolutionary plots. Told by the sultan to put these down with all severity, they organized massacres, reported these as the successful suppression of a rebellion, and collected their medals.[44]

The German ambassador reported to Berlin on October 26, 1895, that he did not think that the central government had ordered the recent outrages. It was more likely, he believed, that provincial authorities were

responsible for the killings. The sultan, he added on November 13, had
given orders to crush the Armenian rebels, and that had unleashed the
bloody revenge against the hated Armenians.[45] The crucial role played
by local officials is demonstrated by the instances where no massacres
took place due to the intervention of such officials. The acting British
consul in Angora noted on October 26, 1895: "The Vali [governor] has
made strenuous and hitherto successful efforts to prevent disturbances
of any kind." On November 24, 1895, British consul Henry D. Barnham in Aleppo praised Lt. Gen. Edhem Pasha, the local commander,
who, despite high tension and small incidents, had been able to prevent
a riot.[46] Similar interventions occurred in other places.

Many contemporaries who witnessed the massacres also stressed
the responsibility of the Armenian revolutionaries, whose inflamma-
tory propaganda had created an atmosphere of fear, and the empty
promises of support by the European powers that had helped bring
about the violent reaction of the Turks. The pamphlets of the revolutionaries, noted the American journalist Sidney Whitman, had called
for an uprising to throw off the Turkish yoke. The Turks had taken
these threats seriously, and this had led to the horrors and "the suffering of the innocent for the guilty."[47] The revolutionaries, led by men
safely ensconced in the capitals of Europe, had issued irresponsible
threats of violence, wrote the British official Ardern Hulme-Beaman.
They had pursued "their infamous and futile programme of attempting
to force the hand of Europe by outrages on innocent people, Christians
like themselves." The responsibility for the ruthless massacres therefore "rests divided between the cowardly Committees abroad and the
braggart and ineffectual intervention of Europe."[48] England, in particular, argued Hepworth, had promised protection for the persecuted
Christians, "but her protection is a sham and a shame. She can talk elo-
quently about oppression, and she can play the simple and easy game
of bluff; but when deeds are to be done she retires from the field."[49]
European intervention was constant enough to produce fury among the
Turks but was never forceful and effective enough to provide meaningful protection for the Armenians who relied upon the promises of
assistance.

Whoever the instigators of the massacres were, where did they find
the hatchet men to do the actual killing? At a time when the Ottoman
Empire was losing choice provinces in Europe, Asia, and Africa, the
idea of granting the Armenians equal political rights drew widespread
opposition. Muslims felt that their supremacy was at stake and that the

Armenians, aided by the Europeans, would gain the upper hand unless forcefully suppressed and taught a lesson. Muslim refugees from the Balkans spread horror stories of how their homes and properties had been taken from them by the Christians and how Muslims had been butchered. After the Russo-Turkish war of 1877–78 more than a half million Bulgarian Muslims alone had become permanent refugees in Anatolia and were known for their strong anti-Christian hatred. Some of these refugees are known to have been heavily implicated in the massacre of their neighbors. "The great mass have joined heart and soul in murder, pillage and outrage," wrote Bliss. "This motive has undoubtedly been mixed. Political fear, religious fanaticism, lust for booty, have all entered in varying proportions in different places."[50]

There was also much envy of the relative prosperity of the hard-working Armenians. A large part of the general dislike of the Armenians, noted Hepworth, probably originated "in their remarkable aptitude and their exceptional talent." Even though a large majority of the Armenian population eked out a difficult living as downtrodden peasants in the countryside, many Armenians in the towns were doctors, pharmacists, or successful traders. "The Turk had not the ability to compete with him, and was a constant loser, much to his disappointment and indignation." The feeling of enmity had been growing steadily and only needed a proper occasion to explode in violence.[51] The result was an orgy of violence that shocked the civilized world.

Chapter 4

The Young Turks Take Power

After the massacres of 1895–96 Abdul Hamid's rule lasted another twelve years. Until the Young Turks' successful seizure of power in 1908, Armenian revolutionaries kept up their attacks and even came close to assassinating the hated autocrat. They also tried again to achieve the intervention of the European powers. None of this brought the Armenians closer to their goal of liberation from Turkish rule. Indeed, there are indications that these activities stiffened the back of the Turks and eventually led to a new rupture between Armenians and Turks with even more disastrous consequences than during the reign of Abdul Hamid.

ARMENIAN GUERRILLA WARFARE

In late July of 1897, one year after the ill-fated raid upon the Ottoman Bank in Constantinople, a force of 250 Dashnaks left their base on the Persian border and attacked the encampment of the Mazrik Kurdish tribe in the plain of Khanasor near the city of Van. The attack is said to have been a revenge for the tribe having wiped out an Armenian village.[1] Benefiting from the element of surprise, the Armenians scored a major victory described by Armenian writers in various ways: "a major part of the tribe was killed," "part of the menfolk were massacred outright," or "the entire tribe was annihilated."[2] According to Langer, the Armenians "killed or barbarously mutilated men, women and children."[3] The Khanasor raid was widely reported by the European press, but its major effect was on the Armenians. They experienced a sense of encouragement, and hope grew that they would able to attain their political freedom by themselves rather than having to rely on impotent European promises.[4]

Clashes between Armenian revolutionaries and Turks and Kurds continued in various parts of eastern Anatolia. A survivor recalls that hundreds of young men brought in arms and ammunition from Persia and Russia to be sold to Armenian peasants and city folks alike.[5] Innumerable epic encounters ensued, writes a historian of the Dashnaks: "It was an era of both glory and of heroic self-sacrifice."[6]

Twenty years after the first bloody fighting in the region of Sassun, a new battle broke out there in the spring of 1904. The Dashnaks had been distributing weapons and organizing fighting units for some time; according to a chronicler of the struggle, this was done "with a view to a general uprising in the future."[7] Led by some of their best-known commanders, such as Andranik (Ozanian) and Murad of Sebastia, the Armenians managed to fight off an attacking force of fifteen thousand Turkish troops for three weeks but finally had to withdraw into the mountains. Several attempts by Armenian fighters in the Russian Caucasus to provide relief failed when they were intercepted and killed by Russian border troops. During the summer of 1905, according to two English missionaries, some three hundred Dashnak fighters conducted guerrilla operations on a fairly large scale in the district of Mush and to the west of Lake Van that cost five thousand lives.[8]

The larger purpose of these and similar engagements fought by Armenian revolutionaries during these years was not always clear. Some Armenian writers, admirers of the Dashnaks, speak of "immortals" who fought "the Armenian battle of liberation."[9] They describe legendary heroes larger than life who managed to survive against heavy odds, sometimes through all kinds of miraculous escapes. The revolutionaries are referred to as avengers, who do not hesitate to risk their own lives or to kill those regarded as oppressors. One such *fedayee,* Kevork Chavoush, is called "the man with the dagger who was always ready to punish those who molested the defenseless people." After the defeat of the rebellion of Sassun in 1904 four of his men went after a particularly cruel Kurdish chief, "raided the Agha's mansion, dispatched the whole family of four," and got away.[10] Another author calls such acts "terroristic retaliation" carried out as "self-defense."[11] The arming of the population is sometimes described as preparation for an uprising; at other times it is called self-defense against marauding Kurds and other aggressors. During the period in question the propaganda of the revolutionaries accented the goal of national liberation, to be achieved through armed struggle, while information meant for foreign consumption stressed the defensive aims of the violence. It is tempting to conclude that the obfuscation was deliberate, and the Turkish authorities facing the attacks of the Armenian revolutionaries may be forgiven if they were not always able to determine exactly what they were dealing with.

Whatever ambiguity may have been attached to the fighting in Anatolia, the attempt of the Dashnaks to assassinate the sultan was a manifestly offensive act. On Friday, July 21, 1905, as Abdul Hamid was saying his prayers in a Constantinople mosque, the revolutionaries managed to plant dynamite in his carriage. Only the fact that the sultan had delayed his departure from the mosque by a few minutes saved his life. The carriage exploded before he had reached it, killing twenty-six members of his retinue and wounding fifty-eight.[12] Had the assassination succeeded, the repercussions for the Armenians might have been another large-scale massacre.

AN UNEASY ALLIANCE

The first congress of the Ottoman opposition convened in Paris in February 1902. Among the chief players were the Ottoman liberals, the Committee of Union and Progress (CUP) or Ittihad ve Terakki, known as the Young Turks, and an Armenian delegation in which the Dashnaks played an important role. All agreed that the present sultan had to be replaced, but the CUP was split over the issues of Armenian autonomy and foreign intervention. The largest faction, led by Prince Mehmed Sabaheddin, was willing to grant the national minorities of the empire a great measure of autonomy and to accept the help of the European powers in implementing the necessary reforms. A group around Ahmed Riza, however, denounced such intervention as an act of imperialism and opposed any form of regional self-rule. The final pronouncement of the congress demanded the reestablishment of the constitution that had been suspended in 1878 and called upon the European powers to carry out the treaty obligations that they had assumed. This pleased the Armenians, who had insisted upon the "immediate execution of article 61 of the treaty of Berlin" and other reform provisions. But the resolution also deepened the rift between the two CUP factions.[13]

During the following years the nationalist wing of the CUP with its anti-imperialist agenda grew in influence, and tension increased between the Young Turks and the Armenians. After the victory over Abdul Hamid in 1908, however, the old disagreements were relegated to the background. In the face of reports that England and Russia planned to partition Turkey, a group of officers in Macedonia joined the CUP. Other garrisons followed suit, and the Young Turks took power in a bloodless coup. On July 24, 1908, Abdul Hamid was forced to restore the constitution that he had suspended in 1878, and Turks and Armenians together celebrated the principles of liberty and equality that they had achieved in their joint struggle. There were scenes of public reconciliation; Young Turk leaders such as Mehmed Talaat, Ismail Enver, and Ahmed Djemal visited churches, and prayers were said for the future of the new order of national harmony. The Dashnaks announced that while they would maintain their revolutionary organization they would abandon the armed struggle and would operate in the open as a political body.[14]

The new friendly relations between the Dashnaks and the CUP survived even a new massacre of Armenians in Adana and other parts of Cilicia that took place in the wake of a conservative countercoup in April 1909. For some time, it appears, the leader of the Armenian community of Adana, Archbishop Musheg, had urged his people to acquire arms, had voiced chauvinistic ideas, and had engaged in what was perceived as contemptuous behavior toward the Muslims. The Armenians of Cilicia, Pears was told by several observers on the scene, "had asserted their liberty and equality with Moslems in terms which were unnecessarily offensive."[15] Muslim religious figures, in turn, had come out against the newly proclaimed idea of equality for all religions and had incited the mobs against the Armenians. The first wave of massacres took place on April 14, a few hours after the reactionary group had taken power in Constantinople. Troops sent to restore order participated in the plundering and killing. After European warships had entered the port of Mersina and on the day the Young Turks retook Constantinople a second wave of massacres followed. Altogether the violent explosion resulted in an estimated death toll of close to twenty thousand, most of them Armenians.[16]

Some Armenian writers have blamed the massacres on agents sent from Constantinople by Abdul Hamid and the rebelling reactionaries.[17] Others have accused the Young Turks.[18] Adana, writes Dadrian, "served as a test case from which the party was able to profit by improving its organizational network and putting that network into operation during the subsequent Armenian genocide."[19] There is little evidence to support any of these interpretations, and the true causes of the disturbances may never be known. The massacres were limited to Cilicia, which would tend to suggest that local factors loomed large. A well-informed contemporary British author, H. Charles Woods, stressed the "smouldering embers of Mohammedan jealousy against the Armenians of this district," who, largely untouched by the massacres of the 1890s, had increased both in numbers and in wealth. The events of 1909, he writes, "were probably remotely caused by the talk of equality which roused the Moslems to a state of fury, by the extreme orators of both religions, by the somewhat foolish actions of a very small section of the Armenian community, and by the feebleness and negligence of the governmental officials in the localities in which massacres actually occurred."[20] Another foreign observer on the scene attributes most of the killings in the villages around Adana to Kurds, who resented the role of the Armenians as moneylenders and usurers.[21]

The CUP, reinstalled in power, moved quickly to repair the damage. Money was appropriated for the relief of the victims; on May 1 the chamber of deputies voted almost unanimously to set up a court-martial to try those guilty of the massacres. Eventually fifty Turks were condemned to death for murder and incitement to riot; twenty of these were actually executed—the first time that Muslims had been hanged for murdering Christians. Five Armenians were also among those condemned to death. At least three of them were probably innocent. The hotheaded Archbishop Musheg escaped.[22]

After the defeat of the reactionary countercoup, Abdul Hamid, suspected of complicity in the plot, was forced to abdicate in favor of his brother, Mohammed V. The Armenians now became the most ardent defenders of the new regime. At their fifth congress (held in the fall of 1909) the Dashnaks affirmed their policy of cooperation with the Young Turks, and they decided to discontinue their underground activities.[23] Still, the collection of arms continued, ostensibly for self-defense. The ox has its horns, the cat has its claws, and the dog has his fangs, the veteran guerrilla leader Murad is supposed to have told a group of villagers in the Sivas area. "Can it be that you do not have as much understanding about your needs as they have?"[24]

Some contemporary authors have blamed the Dashnaks for inadequately preparing the Armenian population for the treachery of the CUP and the disastrous events of 1915.[25] During the years prior to World War I the Young Turks supposedly gave ample indication of their increasingly chauvinistic outlook, and their embrace of pan-Turkish ideas should have warned the Armenian minority of the dangers that lay ahead. Other writers have pointed out that "the leaders of the CUP were not ideologues but men of action. They were ideologically eclectic and their common denominator was a shared set of attitudes rather than a common ideological programme."[26] As their liberal strategies failed to prevent the continuing decline of the empire, Suny observes, "the Young Turk leaders gradually shifted away from their original Ottomanist views of a multinational empire based on guarantees of civil and minority rights to a more Turkish nationalist ideology that emphasized the dominant role of Turks."[27] Still, Suny adds, the leadership of the CUP never agreed on a clear ideological orientation, and their political thinking represented an uneasy mixture of Ottomanism and Pan-Islamism. The notion of Turanism—the idealization of the imaginary homeland of all Turks in central Asia and potentially an expansionist ideology—was espoused by the sociologist and prominent educator Ziya Gökalp, but he and his followers constituted a fringe movement in Young Turk politics. Moreover, even for Gökalp Turanism never represented a program of action. Still less did it envision the genocide of the Armenian minority, as has been charged by some writers.[28]

More serious in their eventual impact on Turkish-Armenian relations than ideological developments within the CUP was the series of devastating foreign policy defeats experienced by the Ottoman government during the years 1908–13. These defeats, it must be remembered, came on top of a steady loss of Ottoman territory ever since the failed siege of Vienna in 1683. From this point on the Ottoman Empire entered its period of decline, losing parts of Persia in 1736, the Crimea in 1784, Greece in 1832, and Egypt in 1840. In the early twentieth century the dissolution of the empire gathered momentum. On October 5, 1908, Bulgaria declared its independence, and within hours Austria-Hungary announced the annexation of Bosnia-Herzegovina. At the same time, Greek leaders on the island of Crete proclaimed their merger with Greece. On September 29, 1911, Italy invaded the Ottoman province of Tripoli (today's Libya). The Balkan wars of 1912–13 added to these setbacks. After the Ottoman government had been forced to sign the Treaty of Bucharest on August 10, 1913, the empire had lost 32.7 percent of its territory and 20 percent of its population. Put differently, by 1913 the Ottomans had forfeited 83 percent of their European territories. Not surprisingly, all this had a profoundly demoralizing effect on the Young Turk leadership and increased nationalistic sentiments. They developed a siege mentality and strong resentment of the Christian states that had brought about these humiliating defeats.[29]

Tension between Turks and Armenians increased, especially in the wake of the Balkan wars. Turkish Armenians were said to have served loyally in the ranks of the Ottoman military, but the Turkish government did not fail to take note of the fact that one of the most famous Armenian commanders, Andranik, had relocated to Bulgaria, where he organized a group of volunteers to fight alongside the Bulgarians against Turkey. The Armenians of the Caucasus also agitated for Russian intervention against the Ottomans.[30] Still more baneful was the influx of almost half a million Muslim refugees who had been forced to flee from their homes in the lost European provinces of the empire. Once again, as after the exodus following the Russian-Turkish war of 1877–78, there were tales of massacres; many of the refugees had died during their flight. The survivors were filled with hatred for all Christians, whom they blamed for their misfortune.[31]

During the parliamentary election of 1912 the Dashnaks and the CUP still agreed on a common platform, but by early 1913 relations had become strained.[32] In the eastern provinces of Anatolia Kurdish depredations were on the rise. Formally the Dashnaks were still committed to a program of reform and autonomy within the empire, but increasingly many Armenians tended to look to Russia as their only effective protector.[33] A Hunchak congress held in Constanza (Rumania) in September 1913 decided to move from legal to illegal activity, which included a plot to assassinate Talaat, the minister of the interior. In January 1913 he had been one of a group of nationalistic CUP leaders who had overthrown the cabinet and effectively enthroned themselves as dictators. The attempt to assassinate Talaat was not carried out,[34] but it reflected the new more radical mood among many Armenian revolutionaries. Meanwhile Dashnak leaders, the heads of the Armenian church, and Armenians in the diaspora, seeking to take advantage of the militarily defeated Turkey, renewed their efforts to bring about a solution of the "Armenian question" through the intervention of the European powers. For the CUP leadership this appeal for outside help was proof of the unpatriotic and provocative attitude of the Armenians. "Nowhere in the world," Talaat is supposed to have told the Armenian patriarch, Archbishop Mikayel Zaven, some two years later, "can you find a people which seeks the intervention of foreigners in the affairs of government by running from one capital to another."[35]

THE ARMENIAN REFORM AGREEMENT OF 1914

Afraid that an uprising by the Turkish Armenians in eastern Anatolia might spread to their own territory, the Russians took the lead in proposing a far-reaching program of reform. "Transcaucasia, with its varied and not over-peaceful population," Russian foreign minister Serge Sazonov recalled in his memoirs, "was dangerous ground for any kind of disturbance, and the local administration feared nothing more than to see the Turkish border provinces become the theatre for an armed rebellion."[36] The Russian proposal was drafted by André N. Mandelstam, the first dragoman of the Russian embassy and a noted international lawyer. It included the appointment of an Ottoman Christian or European governor for a new single Armenian province that was to be established in the six eastern *vilayets*; the creation of an administrative council, a provincial assembly, and gendarmerie units composed of both Muslims and Christians; the dissolution of the Kurdish Hamidiye regiments; and the institution of similar reforms in other provinces inhabited by Armenians, especially Cilicia. In accordance with the provisions of the Treaty of Berlin, the six European powers were to guarantee the implementation of all clauses of the agreement.[37]

During the summer of 1913 the ambassadors of Russia, Great Britain, France, Germany, Austria-Hungary, and Italy in Constantinople and a commission appointed by them deliberated about the Russian plan. The Ottoman government, excluded from these negotiations and seriously concerned about the loss of the eastern provinces, sought to prevent the adoption of the European initiative by proposing its own reform for the entire empire, but this maneuver failed.[38] The Russian draft was supported by France and England but was opposed by Germany and Austria-Hungary, which sought to curry favor with Turkey and enlarge their influence in the Near East.

While these negotiations dragged on, the situation in eastern Anatolia became steadily worse. Rumors spread that the proposed reforms would curtail the movement of the nomadic Kurdish tribes and that the Muslim Kurds would fall under the control of a Christian state.[39] "The Ambassadors of the Great Powers," Sazonov writes, "received daily reports from their Consuls on the spot, informing them of the ceaseless oppression and violence of Turks and Kurds."[40] Finally a compromise agreement was worked out that involved several concessions to the Turkish point of view championed by Germany. The six eastern *vilayets* were to be grouped into two provinces, each under a European inspector. There was no mention of the words "Armenia" or "Armenians," and the program of reform did not include Armenian populations living outside the two inspectorates, as in Cilicia. The European powers, acting through their ambassadors, were given the right to supervise the execution of the reforms, but the obligation to guarantee their success was eliminated. On February 8, 1914, Russia (on behalf of the Europeans) and Turkey signed the revised accord.[41]

The Russian chargé d'affaires in Constantinople, M. Goulkévich, hailed the reform: "The Armenians must now feel that the first step has been taken towards releasing them from the Turkish yoke."[42] Richard Hovannisian notes that the reform did not fulfill all Armenian expectations but adds that "it did represent the most viable reform proposed since the internationalization of the Armenian Question in 1878."[43] Many Armenians at the time, however, took a more cautious view. The Geneva organ of the Dashnaks warned that "before placing our trust in diplomatic reforms, the Nation must subject itself to basic renovations; it must extirpate the curse of cowardly passiveness; it must be inspired by the healthy and redeeming principle of self-assistance; it must arm and be prepared!"[44]

The skeptical attitude toward the reform agreement expressed by the Dashnaks in Geneva turned out to be the more realistic view. The Ottoman government had signed the accord under duress, threatened by Russian armed intervention, but it had no intention of implementing it. Not until April did the sultan approve the choice of the two inspectors, the Dutch civil servant L. C. Westenenk and the Norwegian officer Hoff, who arrived in Constantinople a few weeks later to receive their instructions. There were more delays as the parties haggled over the authority of the inspectors. By the early summer of 1914 Hoff had actually reached Van and Westenenk was about to leave for Erzurum, but on June 28 the assassination of the Austrian Archduke Francis Ferdinand at Sarajevo provided the spark that set off World War I. On July 29 Germany declared war on Russia, and on August 8 Turkey ordered general mobilization. Soon thereafter the two inspectors were dismissed. In December 1914, after Turkey had entered the war on the side of Germany, the reform agreement was annulled.[45]

And there is more to be said. Not only was the Armenian reform of 1914 never implemented, but there is reason to think that it contributed to the disastrous events of 1915. Like the autocrat Abdul Hamid earlier, the Young Turk leadership also deeply resented the intervention of the European powers on behalf of the Armenians. The Russian role, in particular, created strong fears. The rights granted the Armenians in the aborted reform agreement, writes Feroz Ahmad, "seemed like a prelude to a Russian protectorate over eastern Anatolia, with eventual Armenian independence."[46] Hence when many Armenians manifested open sympathy in 1915 for the Russian invaders of the eastern provinces, the Young Turks became convinced that only a radical measure such as the wholesale displacement of the Armenian population would provide a permanent solution to the recurring treasonous conduct of the Armenian minority. The Armenians had regarded the reform agreement as a kind of down-payment on the eventual complete liberation from Turkish rule. They did not realize that the Turks would do anything in their power, no matter how ruthless, in order to prevent the loss of what they regarded as the heartland of Turkish Anatolia. The strong desire to be free from the shackles imposed by the Armenian reform agreement may have been one of the reasons that led the Young Turks to sign the secret military alliance with Germany on August 2, 1914, and eventually to enter the war on the side of Germany several months later.[47]

Part II

Two Rival Historiographies

Chapter 5

The Armenian Case (1): Genocidal Plans

To this day, the prevailing view of the Armenians is that the deportation of hundreds of thousands of their compatriots in 1915 represented a state-organized plan of annihilation. The Ottoman government, dominated by the Committee of Union and Progress (CUP), it is argued, used the cover of war in order to fulfill its long-term ideological goals. "The method adopted to transform a plural Ottoman society into a homogeneous Turkish society," writes Richard Hovannisian, "was genocide." More than half of the Armenian population perished, "and the rest were forcibly driven from their ancestral homeland."[1] Most defenders of the Armenian position also adhere to the view that plans for the extermination of the Armenian nation had been worked out well before the outbreak of war in 1914 and thus help to prove the element of premeditation. By the time of the Saloniki congress in November 1910, Dadrian has maintained, the central objective of the CUP had become "the forcible homogenizing of Turkey."[2] Finally, authors invoke the large number of Armenian deaths—genocidal consequences—as proof that the massacres that took place must have been part of an overall plan to destroy the Armenian people.[3]

TURKISH NATIONALISM, TURANISM, AND THE ROLE OF ZIYA GÖKALP

As noted in the last chapter, some elements of the CUP leadership had been concerned from an early date about the spirit of nationalism growing among the non-Muslim minorities of the empire and gradually had come to embrace a chauvinistic ideology that stressed the dominant role of the Turks—their language, culture, and religion. However, there is only hearsay evidence that this shift included plans for the forcible elimination of the Armenians.

From the beginning of his analysis, Terry inclused that evidence the CUP was planning the real annihilation of the Armenians is only hearsay + nothing true

43

On August 6, 1910, several weeks before the opening of the Salon-iki congress, Talaat is supposed to have delivered a secret speech at a CUP strategy meeting in which he rejected the constitutional equality of Muslims and infidels and advocated the use of the army to homog-enize the empire. This plan allegedly included the elimination of vari-ous troublesome nationalities and was ratified at a secret session of the Saloniki congress. The "projected extermination of the Armenians," writes Dadrian, "was but one phase of a comprehensive plan in which other nationalities, considered to be alien, discordant, and unsettling, were to be targeted."[4]

The sources reporting on these secret proceedings all rely on second-hand information, and none speak specifically of a planned destruc-tion of the Armenian community. The British vice-consul at Monastir, Arthur B. Geary, is said to have been one of several foreign diplo-mats who obtained the text of Talaat's secret speech; but, according to his report rendered on August 28, the relevant part of the speech mentioned nothing worse than the needed "task of Ottomanizing the Empire."[5] Others claiming knowledge of the secret decisions include Galib Bey, the former director of post and telegraph in Erzurum and a participant at the congress. According to Dadrian, Galib "confided to his close friend Dikran Surabian, a Catholic Armenian and official interpreter at the French Consulate in Erzurum, that these plans 'make one's hair stand on end' (*faire dresser les cheveux sur la tête*)." As the main source for this information Dadrian cites the memoirs of Jean Naslian, the bishop of Trebizond.[6] However, even pro-Armenian authors such as James H. Tashjian and Yves Ternon acknowledge that Bishop Naslian's work has numerous errors.[7] Moreover, the chain of transmission for the damaging information is rather lengthy—Galib confiding to Surabian, who presumably told Bishop Naslian. Dadrian is aware of the "limita-tions and problems" of such sources,[8] and most readers probably will regard this as an understatement.

Ternon, referring to the allegation that the Saloniki congress accepted the idea of the Armenian genocide, writes: "This assumption is not based on any solid proof."[9] The British historian Andrew Mango uses even stronger language: "I know of no evidence to support the assertion that in several secret conferences of the 'Committee of Union and Progress,' held in Salonica from 1910 onward, the elimination of all Armenians was adopted as a central object of Young Turk policy."[10]

The allegation that the noted sociologist and educator Ziya Gökalp (1878–1924) and his espousal of Turanism played an important role in the planning for the extermination of the Armenians has even less factual support, and yet it is often repeated. "What Wagner was to Hitler," writes the historian James Reid, "Gökalp was to Enver Pasha." Gökalp's theory and its pragmatic application are said to have meant "the eradication of all non-Turkish societies in the shrinking Ottoman Empire."[11] According to Stephan H. Astourian, Gökalp embraced a "mystical vision of blood and race" that turned out to be "devastating for the Armenians and many other non-Turks."[12] Peter Balakian calls Gökalp "a virulent racist...foreshadowing the leading Nazi propagandists Alfred Rosenberg and Joseph Goebbels."[13] Haigazn Kazarian maintains that Gökalp's teachings "set the philosophical base for the eradication of the Armenians," and he includes Gökalp among the 160 Turks he considers most responsible for the massacres.[14]

Such a reading of Gökalp's ideas appears to be strained, not to say outright wrong. Gökalp became a member of the CUP's central committee in 1909 and, with justification, has been called "the spiritual father of Turkish nationalism" and "the philosopher of the Atatürk Revolution."[15] He sought to exalt the Turkish nation and to encourage pride in Turkish culture. In the last stanza of his poem "Turan," published around 1911, Gökalp declared that the fatherland of the Turks was not Turkey but "a vast and eternal land: Turan." The idea of Turan, an ancient Iranian name for the area lying northeast of Persia, was for him a symbol of the cultural unity of all Turkish people. "Turan," Gökalp wrote in his book *The Principles of Turkism,* "is the great fatherland of all Turks, which was a reality in the past and may be so again in the future." He believed that the cultural unity of all Turks, once achieved, could serve as the basis for an eventual political unity. The Turkish nation was to be based on "a sharing of education and culture," not on a racial or ethnic group. The Ottomans, by contrast, had traveled "the road of imperialism, which was so detrimental to Turkish culture and life."[16]

Practically all interpreters of Gökalp's thought stress that his notion of Turan or Turanism did not involve any expansionist plans. Gökalp's nationalism, writes Taha Parla, "rests unequivocally on language and culture." Gökalp was "a man of vast humanitarian concerns." Turkish nationalism meant for him "a cultural ideal," "the basis of social solidarity" as taught by Emile Durkheim. His nationalism "was a non-racist, non-expansionist, pluralistic nationalism."[17] Gökalp, argues Gotthard Jäschke, interpreted Turanism in an unpolitical manner. Fantasies of a large empire "ran counter to his entire inner nature."[18] Niyazi Berkes stresses that Gökalp never advocated "anti-Western jingoism" or "racism" and that in his later years he even ceased to mention the word "Turan."[19] It is true that at the beginning of World War I Gökalp, caught up in the general outpouring of patriotism, wrote a poem in which he predicted that the "land of the enemy shall be devastated, Turkey shall be enlarged and become Turan." As late as April 1918 Gökalp expressed the hope that the Turks in Russia would produce a leader who would undertake the task of liberating Turan. However, even Uriel Heyd, who refers to these utterances, acknowledges that Gökalp soon abandoned these calls for a political union of all Turks and emphasized that "the first task was to unite all the Turkish people on the cultural side."[20]

In any event, one should add that there is a big difference between longing for a revival of Turkish national greatness and encouraging the violent elimination of all ethnic minorities. Dadrian has called Gökalp an advocate of ethnic cleansing, one of the "party chieftains in this exterminatory enterprise,"[21] but he provides no substantiation for this accusation other than quoting an ominous-sounding sentence from Uriel Heyd's intellectual biography of Gökalp: "A considerable part of his suggestions were accepted by the Party and carried out by its Government during the First World War."[22] The same sentence is quoted by Robert Melson, who also seeks to blame Gökalp for supporting genocide.[23] But both Dadrian and Melson distort the position of Heyd, who in the sentences preceding the quoted passage makes it quite clear that the suggestions in question were made in the autumn of 1917, well after the Armenian deportations, and concerned religious education, pious foundations, and family law. "As a member of the Central Council of the Union and Progress party," Heyd writes, "Gökalp dealt with social, legal and cultural problems. He investigated the history of the Turkish guilds, the development of the dervish orders and the question of minorities, especially of the Armenians."[24] Gökalp was a respected advisor on cultural and educational issues, but he never became one of the CUP's policy makers on political matters.[25]

After the defeat of Turkey and the armistice of 1918, Gökalp was arrested and brought before a military court set up by the new Turkish government to try the Young Turk leadership. Unlike many of his colleagues, Gökalp, apparently believing that he had not done anything wrong, refused to flee the country and stayed on lecturing at Constantinople University. When he was questioned at the trial about his concept of Turanism he denied that he had espoused it in order to provoke harm to any of Turkey's minorities. These trials and the significance to be attached to their findings are examined in detail in the next chapter.

THE "TEN COMMANDMENTS"

In early 1919 a British official in Constantinople obtained several Turkish documents, the most important of which, he explained in a memo that accompanied the documents to the Foreign Office in London, "is believed to be the original draft instructions issued by the Committee of Union and Progress relative to their plan for massacring Armenians. It is known as the Ten Commandments of the Committee of Union and Progress." The documents had been offered to him in return for a large sum of money by a member of the Turkish Department of Security, but he had finally acquired them without payment by promising the Turkish official who had stolen or rescued the documents protection "if in the future he gets into trouble." The "Ten Commandments" were an unsigned and rough draft, but the handwriting was said to be that of Essad Bey, who at the time the document was drafted (December 1914 or January 1915) was one of the confidential secretaries keeping secret archives in the Ministry of the Interior. According to the informant, present at the meeting when this draft was drawn up were several high-ranking CUP officials, including Talaat Pasha, Dr. Behaeddin Sakir, and Dr. Nazim as well as Colonel Sefi, the subdirector of the political section of the Ministry of War. The instructions were to be sent to the *vali*s in the different provinces "with instructions to read these orders to them and then return the originals which were to be destroyed."26

According to Dadrian, the "Ten Commandments" were the product of a series of secret meetings held by top CUP leaders during the early part of World War I. The draft, he argues, was the result of the decision to commit genocide and was meant as an operative plan. "Both the decision and the blueprint reflect the fact that the crime committed against the Armenians was premeditated and the intent was the wholesale extermination of the victims."27 Christopher Walker also relies on this document,28 which, if considered authentic and taken at face value, indeed provides a powerful indictment of the CUP leadership. The text, in the British verbatim (and rather crude) translation, reads as follows:

DOCUMENTS RELATING TO COMITE UNION AND
PROGRESS ORGANIZATION IN THE ARMENIAN MASSACRES:
THE 10 COMMANDMENTS OF THE COMITE UNION AND PROGRES

(1) Profiting by Art: 3 and 4 of Comité Union and Progres, close all
Armenian Societies, and arrest all who worked against Government at
any time among them and send them into the provinces such as Bagdad or Mosul, and wipe them out either on the road or there.

(2) Collect arms.

(3) Excite Moslem opinion by suitable and special means, in places as
Van, Erzeroum, Adana, where as a point of fact the Armenians have
already won the hatred of the Moslems, provoke organized massacres as
the Russians did at Baku.

(4) Leave all executive [sic] to the people in provinces such as Erzeroum,
Van, Mamuret ul Aziz, and Bitlis, and use Military disciplinary forces
(i.e. Gendarmerie) ostensibly to stop massacres, while on the contrary
in places as Adana, Sivas, Broussa, Ismidt and Smyrna actively help the
Moslems with military force.

(5) Apply measures to exterminate all males under 50, priests and
teachers, leave girls and children to be Islamized.

(6) Carry away the families of all who succeed in escaping and apply
measures to cut them off from all connection with their native place.

(7) On the ground that Armenian officials may be spies, expel them
and drive them out absolutely from every Government department or
post.

(8) Kill off in an appropriate manner all Armenians in the Army—to
be left to the military to do.

(9) All actions to begin everywhere simultaneously, and thus leave no
time for preparation of defensive measures.

(10) Pay attention to the strictly confidential nature of these instructions, which may not go beyond two or three persons.[29]

It appears that British officials in Constantinople in early 1919
regarded the "Ten Commandments" as genuine and hoped that they
would help bring to justice those responsible for the Armenian massacres. Yet (as we will see in more detail in chapter 7) when the law offi-

cers of the Crown a year later were seeking to build a legal case against the Turkish officials whom the British had arrested and taken to Malta, they made no use of the "Ten Commandments" and complained that no proper evidence was available that would satisfy a British court of law.[30] By that time the British authorities in Constantinople also had begun to realize that not every alleged secret document floating around was genuine. A good number of foreign secret service organizations are operating in the Turkish capital, a British officer reported in February 1920, "and all are naturally anxious to obtain original documents or photographs of the same. This state of affairs affords a very large market for salable goods of this description, and has resulted in the regular production of forgeries for the purposes of sale."[31] The press, too, was filled with sensational revelations of all kinds. The Armenian newspaper *Verchinlour* publicized the text of the "Ten Commandments" on March 23, 1919.

The article in *Verchinlour* containing the "Ten Commandments," albeit in a different translation, was forwarded to Washington by American high commissioner Lewis Heck on March 26, 1919. Heck commented: "It is not known whether this document is authentic, but it can at least be stated that the instructions therein contained are of a nature which were followed during the deportations."[32] Dadrian invokes the same argument: "Evidence that the procedure described in the Ten Commandments and the other documents was followed during the genocide would support Essad's [in whose handwriting the document is alleged to be] veracity." He goes on to refer to testimony accepted by one of the Turkish courts-martial of officials accused of participation in Armenian massacres held in March 1919 by the new Turkish government. This tribunal makes no mention of the "Ten Commandments" but does make reference to the testimony of an officer who reported that he received secret orders regarding the massacres relayed to the provinces. "In other words," Dadrian concludes, "Essad's document on the transmission of an official order by the Ottoman War Minister [the third of the documents acquired by the British in early 1919] is verified by the testimony of a military commander who received the order. The demonstrated authenticity of the one document provided by Essad points to the authenticity of the others."[33]

There are several problems with this way of reasoning. At the time when Commissioner Heck expressed his view of the nature of the instructions followed during the deportations, little reliable evidence regarding these instructions was as yet available; and Heck undoubtedly was relying on sources that cannot be considered truly probative. The same difficulty arises in connection with the court-martial testimony invoked by Dadrian. Of the proceedings of the trial in Yozgat (see chapter 6), where the testimony in question was supposedly given, only the verdict has been preserved;[34] Dadrian's account of this testimony therefore has to rely on an article in a Constantinople newspaper, *Renaissance*. The original text of the testimony is not available. This, I submit, is hardly the kind of evidence that can be used to demonstrate the authenticity of a document.

The British official who forwarded the "Ten Commandments" to London at the time had suggested that Essad be arrested "to prove to the hilt the authenticity of the draft 'Ten Commandments' document."[35] Once they had him in custody they presumably could have compared his handwriting with that of the document he was supposed to have compiled in his capacity as secretary in the secret archives of the Ministry of the Interior. This was never done, however, as Gwynne Dyer has shown in careful analysis of the "Ten Commandments." Indeed there was no need to arrest Essad: as other Foreign Office files show, Essad was employed as an agent by the British High Commission in Constantinople at least until September 1919. The intelligence operative controlling him described him as "a low class intermediary" involved in the courier system functioning between the capital and the CUP exiles abroad. The fact that the British made no inquiries of him about the "Ten Commandments" suggests that they soon had come to doubt the authenticity of this document.[36] As mentioned earlier, it was never noted or used by the law officers collecting evidence against the Young Turks.

Dadrian has attempted to establish the authenticity of the "Ten Commandments" by pointing to the similarity between the provisions of this blueprint and the actual course of the deportations. His version of these events is certainly not to be considered the last word on the subject. However, even if his description of the deportations was to be accepted as fully accurate, the similarity between the provisions of the "Ten Commandments" and the deportations would not necessarily rule out forgery. Dyer has summed up the overall impression that one obtains from reading the "Ten Commandments": they "resemble the result of an attempt after the fact to reconstruct what might have been said, had the actual events of April 1915–mid 1916 all been foreordained in a single comprehensive official document months before their initiation."[37]

The Secret CUP Meeting of February 1915
Described by Mevlanzade Rifat —

Still another secret meeting that is said to substantiate the element of premeditation and the guilt of the CUP leadership for the massacres is described in memoirs written by a purported member of the central committee of the CUP, Mevlanzade Rifat. The book in question, *Türkiye inkilabinin ic yübü* (The Inner Aspects of the Turkish Revolution), was published in Aleppo in 1929. According to several Armenian authors, Mevlanzade Rifat participated in this meeting, held in February 1915, in which "the savage plan to destroy the Armenian people was first formulated."[38]

The meeting is said to have been chaired by Talaat and attended by several other high-ranking CUP leaders. The main report, Rifat relates, was given by Dr. Nazim, who proposed the total destruction of the Armenian minority:

> If we are going to be satisfied with the kind of local massacres that occurred in Adana and other places in 1909 ... if this purge is not going to be universal and final, instead of good, it will inevitably result in harm. It is imperative that the Armenian people be completely exterminated; that not even one single Armenian be left on our soil; that the name, Armenian, be obliterated. We were now at war; there is no more auspicious occasion than this; the intervention of the great powers and the protests of the newspapers will not even be considered; and even if they are, the matter will have become an accomplished fact, and thus closed forever. The procedure this time will be one of total annihilation—it is necessary that not even one single Armenian survive this annihilation.[39]

After some of the other central committee members had expressed their views, Rifat goes on, a resolution embodying Dr. Nazim's proposal to exterminate the Armenians to the very last man was adopted unanimously:

> The Ittihad ve Terrake Party recommended that a special organization be set up for carrying out this decision, made up of criminals and murderers under the direction of the "three-man executive committee," composed of Dr. Nazim, Dr. Behaettin Shakir, and the Minister of Education, Shoukrie.[40]

Following this vote, Dr. Sakir is said to have spelled out the plan of execution. The police officers accompanying the convoys of deportees from the various cities would hand the Armenians over to the special force of convicts released from the prisons, who would be waiting "at various suitable points on the road designated by us." These assassins would put to death every last Armenian, throw them into pits prepared in advance, and appropriate the money, jewelry, and other personal belongings found on the murdered Armenians.[41]

Among the relatively few authors who have bought into the story told by Mevzanlade Rifat is Hovannisian.[42] In 1973 Walker invoked this source in support of his argument that the killing of the Armenians was premeditated and represented a carefully planned plot, but by 1997 he had changed his mind and conceded that Rifat's account of the secret CUP meeting "appears to be a fraud and cannot be accepted as sound evidence, at least until a comprehensive bibliographical inquiry is published on the origin of the book and the authenticity or otherwise of its content."[43] Florence Mazian (in a book supporting the genocide thesis published in 1990) refers to the work of Rifat, whom she calls "a former member of the *Ittihad* Central Committee."[44] For reasons that will become obvious in a moment, the Kurdish historian Kamal Madhar Ahmad also cites the memoirs of the "leading Unionist" Rifat as proof of the Turkish government's plans to exterminate the Armenians.[45]

The generally skeptical reception of Mevzanlade Rifat's account has been due primarily to the painstaking research into the background of the alleged Young Turk leader by Gwynne Dyer published in 1973, which has since been backed up by other scholars.[46] Rifat, it turns out, was a Kurd who never belonged to the CUP. Still less was he a member of its central committee and in a position to have access to secret plans for the annihilation of the Armenians. To the contrary, from the time of the 1908 revolution on Rifat led a party in bitter opposition to the Young Turks; in 1909, when he was implicated in the reactionary coup against the CUP, a court-martial sentenced him to ten years' banishment from Constantinople. After the armistice of 1918 Rifat was back in the Turkish capital, where he participated in Kurdish efforts to obtain independence for Kurdistan; but following the assumption of power by the Kemalists he went into political exile again.

Despite the prominent Kurdish role in the wartime massacre of the Armenians, Kurds and Armenians had begun to cooperate at the Paris peace conference and continued their efforts to build a common front against the Kemalist regime in the following years.[47] During this time Rifat acted as liaison between Kurds and Armenians; his book, published in 1929, must be seen in this context. It represented an attempt to absolve the Kurds of responsibility for the wartime massacres by putting all the guilt for the killings on the CUP leaders and on the ex-convicts mobilized by them. "Presumably," writes Michael M. Gunter, "such 'revelations' would facilitate an Armenian-Kurdish alliance."[48] Dyer concludes that the book could ease Armenian-Kurdish cooperation by "transferring all blame to evil Ittihadist Turks who had prearranged and guided the entire operation from Istanbul."[49]

Dadrian acknowledges that Rifat was a Kurd and an "avowed Ittihadist opponent" but nevertheless cites him as a source of information for "one of the super-secret meetings of Ittihad, during which the decision for the Armenian genocide was being debated."[50] Dadrian fails to explain how an "avowed Ittihadist opponent" could obtain information about decisions taken at one of the "super-secret meetings" of the CUP.

To the best of my knowledge, Suny is the only scholar on the Armenian side who has openly and publicly expressed his skepticism of the kind of evidence that Dadrian and other like-minded authors have put forth in support of the premeditation thesis. While stating his belief that the massacres represented an act of genocide, Suny has denied that this crime resulted "from long-term planning by militant nationalists." When criticized by Dadrian for his more "balanced" approach, Suny reaffirmed that he remained "unconvinced that there was premeditation and prewar initiation of plans for genocide as Dadrian has often argued."[51]

GENOCIDAL CONSEQUENCES

Many authors of Armenian origin point to the large number of their people who perished during the course of the deportations of 1915–16 as proof that the large death toll must have been part of a premeditated plan of annihilation. Attained results, argues Dadrian, can give us an indication of the objectives of the Young Turk regime—an exterminatory intent is best revealed in an exterminatory outcome. It is possible to ascertain the aims of the CUP by posing the question: "Were the Ottoman Armenians in fact largely exterminated or not?"[52]

This approach, of course, raises a difficulty of logic, for objective results are not the same as subjective intent. Finding a man with a smoking gun standing next to a corpse tells us nothing about the motive for the killing—it may have been murder or a case of self-defense. Indeed, we cannot even be sure that this man is the killer. Similarly, the fact that large numbers of Armenians died or were killed during the course of the deportations can give us no reliable knowledge of who is to be held responsible for these losses of life. The high death toll certainly does not prove in and of itself the guilt of the Young Turk regime; nor can we infer from it that the deaths were part of a genocidal plan to destroy the Turkish Armenian community. Large numbers of Turkish civilians died as a result of severe shortages of food and epidemics; large numbers of Turkish soldiers, especially the wounded in battle, perished for lack of adequate medical care and as a result of neglect and incompetence on the part of their own officers; and large numbers of British prisoners of war lost their lives as a consequence of inattention and the kind of gross mismanagement rampant in the Ottoman regime (see the discussion below). Yet these results surely do not prove that the Ottoman government—ultimately responsible for all of these conditions—sought and intentionally caused the death of its own civilian population, of its own soldiers, and of its prisoners of war. The Turkish wartime government may deserve to be severely rebuked for its corruption and bungling misrule as well as for indifference to the suffering of its population during World War I. The Young Turk regime may be subject to special moral censure or condemnation on account of its treatment of its Christian minorities. Yet all this does not prove that this regime intended to annihilate the Armenian community. A large death toll, no matter how reprehensible, is not proof of a premeditated plan of extermination.

Most authors supporting the Armenian cause completely ignore the severe shortages of food that eventually were to afflict most classes of the Turkish population and led to widespread famines. The mobilization of large numbers of peasants in 1914 as well as the reckless requisitioning of their horses, oxen, and carriages had made it impossible to bring in the harvest, eventually left many fields untilled, and was one of the reasons for the growing food shortage. The American consul in Smyrna, George Horton, reported on November 14, 1914, that there was much misery to be seen and that "people are actually beginning to starve."[53] The domestic situation in the spring of 1915, American ambassador Henry Morgenthau noted, "was deplorable: all over Turkey thousands of the populace were daily dying of starvation."[54] In the late spring and summer of 1915 Palestine, Lebanon, and Syria were devastated by a plague of locusts that destroyed everything in its wake and led to famine conditions. On October 18, 1915, Enver told Morgenthau that the possibility of shortages of flour existed even in Constantinople and that "therefore it is not certain if they can furnish bread to the Armenians all through the winter."[55]

By the fall of 1916, the provincial governor told a German physician, sixty thousand had died of hunger in the Lebanon alone; entire villages had become desolate and abandoned.[56] According to the Austrian military attaché, the death toll in the Lebanon during the winter of 1915–16 was a hundred and fifty thousand.[57] Syria and Lebanon had always imported large amounts of food from Egypt. When allied warships blockaded the coast, all trade with the outside came to a halt and the consequences for the food supply were severe.

On March 23, 1916, the American chargé d'affaires in Constantinople cabled the secretary of state on behalf of the Red Cross:

> Great suffering throughout the country, particularly at Constantinople and suburbs along the shores of Marmora, at Adriano, Broussa and Smyrna. In these regions five hundred thousand, not comprising Armenian refugees, need help for bread. Hundreds dying of starvation. No relief in sight. Sugar and petroleum oil at famine prices. Typhus is spreading, high mortality.[58]

The food situation soon became even more severe. From 1916 until the end of the war in 1918, an Armenian pastor has written, the city of Urfa was plagued with famine, and many of the local poor died of starvation. "Starving Armenians and Turks were begging side by side in front of the same market and together were gathering grass from the fields."[59]

The shortages of food were made worse by the hoarding of speculators, who sold goods at exorbitant prices, and the widespread corruption. Some food supplies bought for the army never reached the fighting units. The troops, reported a German officer in November 1916, received a maximum of one-third of the rations they were supposed to get, and undernourishment was at a dangerous level.[60] The Turkish soldiers concentrated in Palestine, another observer noted, "had not enough bread to maintain their strength. They received almost no meat, no butter, no sugar, no vegetables, no fruits."[61] Whatever supplies were available in the rear had trouble reaching the troops in the front lines as a result of severe transportation problems. The few existing one-track railroads were overburdened. At times locomotives could not be used because of severe shortages of coal and wood. A crucial tunnel on the line toward Syria (the famous Baghdad railway) was finished only in September 1918. Because of these transportation difficulties the feeding of soldiers "varied enormously, depending on whether they were close to, or far away from, grain producing areas."[62] A German officer reported in February 1917 that soldiers had started to eat grass because the bread ration was completely insufficient.[63]

The worst situation prevailed during the winter of 1917–18. The German ambassador, Count Johann von Bernstorff, informed Berlin on March 30, 1918: "There is actually a famine, which is only veiled by the fact that no one troubles whether the poor die."[64] The head of the German Turkish military mission and inspector-general of the Turkish army, Otto Liman von Sanders, reported to the German ambassador on June 20, 1918, that by April of that year seventeen thousand men of the Turkish Sixth Army in Iraq had died of hunger and its consequences.[65]

Descriptions of the horrible life in the camps to which the Armenians had been sent leave the impression that it was only the deported Armenians who suffered from starvation. Yet, in fact, similar conditions at times prevailed even for soldiers in the Turkish army. European travelers and missionaries who witnessed the misery in the camps in the Syrian desert reported that the Armenians at best received a small quantity of bread at irregular intervals and gradually were reduced to eating grass roots and even dead animals. A German engineer, who had visited the Armenian encampments along the Euphrates River, on September 10, 1916, reported to Jesse Jackson (the American consul in Aleppo) that in Abou Herrera he had seen women "searching in the dung of horses barley seeds not yet digested to feed on." The unfortunates were gradually dying of hunger.[66] All this bears a striking similarity to what a German officer wrote on conditions in an artillery unit of the Turkish Fourteenth Infantry Division during the winter of 1915–16: "The men received, if they were lucky, a handful of barley. They began to gnaw at the carcasses of dead animals and scraped meager seeds from the dung of horses that originated from still better times. Gradually they fell victim to hunger-typhus and pined away....None of them survived the month of January."[67]

This comparison, I should stress, is not meant to belittle the misery of the deported Armenians or to ignore the mass killings that we know to have taken place. Neither do I suggest that the situation of all Turkish soldiers was as bad as that of the deportees. However, at a time when even soldiers in the Turkish army were dying of starvation, it is hardly surprising that little if any food was made available to the deported Armenians, who were seen as in league with Turkey's enemies.

Given the gradually worsening severe food shortages, the lot of the deported Armenians soon went from bad to worse. Walter Rössler, the German consul in Aleppo, on February 14, 1917, expressed the view that despite great efforts to provide relief for the deportees in Rakka (Mesopotamia), carried out with American money and distributed with the permission of the Turkish authorities, most of them would surely perish. "For hunger now exists not only among the Armenians but also among the population of Rakka, so that the distribution of food to the deportees by the government has stopped almost completely." Typhus had broken out, and twenty were dying daily.[68]

A Turkish historian has argued that the Armenians actually were better off than the Muslim population: "The Turkish citizens were starving while the Armenians were fed by American relief workers with money raised as a result of anti-Turkish propaganda."[69] This appraisal is unsupported by any evidence and is undoubtedly false. The relief effort never had enough money or supplies to prevent the death of thousands of Armenians by starvation and disease. It is clear that the lot of the Armenians was made infinitely worse by their relocation. Still, it is important to see these events in their proper context. The corruption and incompetence of the Ottoman government, aggravated by a natural catastrophe, led to severe food shortages and sporadic famine that afflicted the Muslim civilian population as well as the Turkish army. In this situation, the high death toll among the Armenian deportees resulting from lack of food and disease in and of itself does not prove that the Ottoman government aimed at the annihilation of the Armenian community.

The mistreatment of the simple Turkish soldier by his officers and the neglect of the wounded are another part of the historical setting missing from Armenian accounts of the events of 1915–16. These conditions led to the avoidable death of many thousands of Turkish soldiers, and they help explain why the Armenian deportees for the most part lacked any kind of medical care. If the Turkish authorities were unable or unwilling to provide adequate clothing, decent hygienic conditions, and appropriate medical attention for their Muslim soldiers, why would one expect them to be concerned about the fate of the Armenian deportees, whom they regarded as a fifth column?

The lack of regard for the welfare of their soldiers on the part of the Ottoman authorities was the main reason for the incredibly high number of deserters, which is estimated as one and a half million.[70] The mistreatment of the ordinary soldier was the subject of many comments by contemporaries. "Provisions and clothing had been confiscated to supply the army," wrote an American missionary in Van, yet "the soldiers profited very little by this. They were poorly fed and poorly clothed when fed or clothed at all."[71] The Danish missionary Maria Jacobsen noted in her diary on February 7, 1915: "The officers are filling their pockets, while the soldiers die of starvation, lack of hygiene, and illness."[72] Many of the soldiers had neither boots nor socks, and they were dressed in rags. "The treatment received by these men by their officers," wrote another American missionary and president of Euphrates College, Henry Riggs, "offered spectacles every day that made the blood boil." Cruelty on the drill ground was common. "It was not at all unusual to see an officer step up to a soldier standing in the line, and for some offense equally unintelligible to the bystander and to the soldier, slap him in the face, or, if the offense was more serious, knock him down, or, as I have seen once or twice, kick him in the stomach."[73]

The treatment of sick soldiers was especially appalling and was characterized "by a callous brutality that is unbelievable," Riggs wrote:

> One day I saw a squad of sick soldiers being taken to the hospital. For want of an ambulance they were trying to walk, and as I approached, I saw that one poor fellow had dropped down in the road. The spruce young officer who was escorting them ordered him to get up, and when he failed to do so, struck him several times with a horsewhip. As I drew near, I could hear the torrent of curses and abuses with which the horsewhip was being explained, but it was of no use. The man evidently could not get up. So, finally, the officer kicked the man over into the ditch beside the road.[74]

A similar episode is described by an Armenian in Aleppo during the typhus epidemic of 1916, who "saw a Turkish soldier lying sick with typhus in acute fever and coma." A passing young Turkish officer simply kicked the dying man aside in order to clear his way.[75]

During the fighting in eastern Anatolia, which had no railways and often not even regular roads, soldiers wounded in combat and trying to reach a hospital were lucky when they were able to catch a ride on the horse-drawn carriages or ox-carts on which Muslim refugees were making their way westward. Many had to walk on foot and never reached any hospital. The American consul in Harput, Leslie Davis, described the situation in the winter of 1915–16:

> All that winter sick and wounded Turkish soldiers came from the front to Mamouret-ul-Aziz. Notwithstanding what we know about the way the Turks treated the Armenians, it seemed incredible that their own soldiers fared little better. They were sent away from Erzerum and other distant places in midwinter, without food and with little clothing. They were told to go to the hospitals in Mamouret-ul-Aziz, which were the nearest to them. As no means of transportation was provided, they were obliged to make the journey of several weeks on foot, begging or stealing something to eat in the villages through which they passes [sic] and occasionally stealing a donkey on which to ride. I often met them as they were approaching the town. All but the hardiest ones, of course, had died on the way....Those who did arrive were often so exhausted that nothing could be done for them.[76]

Those fortunate enough to reach the hospitals were not necessarily on the road to recovery, for conditions in most of these hospitals were horrendous. Because of the lack of beds, patients shared beds or simply lay next to each other on the floor, some on mattresses, others on blankets. Many hospitals had neither running water nor electricity; there was a shortage of medications, syringes, medical instruments, and clean linen. Hygienic conditions were catastrophic. There were not enough doctors and nurses, and pharmacists and orderlies had to substitute for regular medical personnel. The training of the doctors was not up to date. The American missionary Clarence Ussher described how on a visit to the military hospital in Van he

> could hardly find room to step between the men as they lay on the floor. They were covered with vermin, for facilities for keeping clean were very insufficient....The windows were kept closed because of the cold and patients and orderlies smoked almost constantly to counteract the stench. The army doctors refused to enter the wards. They would stand at the doors and inquire of the orderlies how many men had died and what were the diseases of the others.[77]

According to Maria Jacobsen, the situation was no better in Harput. "The Turkish doctors did literally nothing for the sick because, firstly, they have little knowledge, and secondly, a human being counts as nothing with them. If he lives, he lives. If he dies, he dies."[78] The efforts of German doctors gradually brought about some improvement in this situation, but a high mortality rate continued to take its toll. A German nurse recalled that in the hospital in which she worked in the fall of 1917 forty to fifty percent of the patients admitted died of exhaustion and undernourishment before it was possible to treat them.[79] Hygienic conditions, too, continued to be a serious problem. A German inspector visited the military hospitals only after prior notice. "In this way I could be sure that at least on the occasion of my visit the hospitals were cleaned thoroughly."[80]

In view of these conditions it is not surprising that typhus, cholera, dysentery, and other infectious diseases spread rapidly among the troops. Two Red Cross surgeons reported on March 3, 1915, from Erzinjan that an epidemic of typhus, made worse by the lack of sanitary arrangements and sufficient medical help, was decimating the ranks of the military "in a manner unthinkable under German conditions."[81] A German doctor estimated that the death toll from typhus among Turkish soldiers at times reached fifty percent, while among German military personnel it was about ten percent.[82] According to Consul Davis in Harput, as many as seventy-five to eighty soldiers died of typhus there on some days during the winter of 1914–15.[83] Maria Jacobsen noted in her diary on May 24, 1916, that cholera had broken out in Malatia, and one hundred soldiers were dying every day. "The army there will soon be wiped out without a war."[84]

Facilitated by the disastrous sanitary conditions prevailing in the convoys and in the camps to which they were sent, typhus was rampant among the Armenian deportees. The Swiss missionary Jakob Künzler called the disease the "great consoler," because the afflicted person soon lost consciousness and, without medical care, experienced a relatively quick death.[85] From the deportees the disease spread to the Muslim population. Lice carried in clothing brought typhus to villages and towns along the routes of deportation. Typhus was also spread by the thousands of Turkish refugees who fled the Russian offensives of 1915 and 1916.[86] An American intelligence agent estimated in July 1915 that three hundred thousand had died from typhus in eastern Anatolia.[87] In Aleppo more than thirty-five thousand were reported to have died from the disease between August 1916 and August 1917.[88]

Even though Ottoman casualty figures are incomplete, it is clear that Turkish military losses from disease by far exceeded those resulting from combat. According to a new history of the Ottoman army by Edward Erickson, the Turkish armed forces experienced 243,598 combat deaths, while 466,759 soldiers died of disease. Another 68,378 succumbed to their wounds.[89] Nearly seven times as many Turkish soldiers died of illnesses as died of wounds experienced in combat.[90] No other army in World War I appears to have had such a disastrous ratio of losses from disease and wounds versus the number lost in combat. Furthermore, it is estimated that at least one and a half million Muslim civilians died as a result of the war, most of them probably from disease and malnutrition or starvation.[91]

The terrible death toll among Turkish Muslims quite obviously does not excuse the horrible fate of the Armenians, but neither can it be ignored. Many of the Turkish deaths, as we have seen, could have been prevented by better sanitary conditions and medical care. A government as callous about the suffering of its own population as was the Young Turk regime could hardly be expected to be very concerned about the terrible human misery that would result from deporting its Armenian population, rightly or wrongly suspected of treason. The Ottoman government decided to dislocate an entire community—men, women, and children—and send them on a trek of hundreds of miles. The Armenians from eastern Anatolia had to pass through the most inhospitable terrain, a voyage that would have exacted a heavy cost in lives even during the best of times. As it turned out, thousands died of starvation or disease, while large numbers of others were massacred. Still, we can account for this tragedy without the hypothesis of a CUP genocidal plan. As discussed later in this book, other explanations of this human catastrophe are supported by far better evidence and are far more convincing.

Finally, the treatment meted out to Turkish prisoners of war is another illustration of how a great number of deaths can occur without a plan of extermination. The largest number of prisoners to fall into Turkish hands resulted from the successful siege of Kut-al-Amara in Mesopotamia, which ended with the surrender of the starving Anglo-Indian garrison on April 29, 1916. The captives were composed of about three thousand British troops and ten thousand Indian soldiers. Eleven hundred of the worst hospital cases were repatriated, but the remaining twelve thousand or so were sent into captivity. Of these over four thousand ultimately perished (i.e., roughly one-third).[92] By contrast, only 4 percent of British and American troops captured in World War II died in German captivity.

Many of the captives of Kut-al-Amara never reached a prison camp. Though starved and weak from the long siege, they were marched across the hot Mesopotamian desert. There was little food or water. Hundreds died each week from exhaustion and dysentery. A British government report described the situation: "The way in which an operation of this kind may be mismanaged in Turkey is almost incredible, familiar as the details become by repetition. It is a fact that these men were sent off without food for the journey, and that no provision was made for them at any point on the road."[93] Those who survived the death-march were put to work on the construction of the Baghdad railway; but they were too weak to do any real work, and the dying continued. Eventually those still alive were sent to a prisoner-of-war camp.

Survivors later testified that there had been some brutality by the guards, but there also were cases where Turkish soldiers shared their meager ration with the captives.[94] The guards, a British officer recalled, were not cruel or even hostile. For the most part, the prisoners died as a result of sheer neglect, incompetence, and mismanagement.[95] Of the British rank and file who went into captivity, 70 percent lost their life; yet all this occurred without any plan to murder the prisoners. The treatment of the British prisoners-of-war does not disprove the proposition that the Young Turks sought to destroy the Armenian community, but it is another example of how in a setting of Ottoman misrule an extremely high death toll could take place without a premeditated scheme of annihilation.

Chapter 6

The Armenian Case (2): The Implementation of Genocide

Authors supporting the Armenian cause maintain that there exists abundant documentary evidence to prove that in 1915 the CUP and the Turkish government implemented plans for the total destruction of the Armenian community. The materials used to substantiate this charge include telegrams allegedly sent out by minister of the interior Talaat Pasha, ordering the extermination of the Armenians, and similar documents presented to the courts-martial of Young Turk officials held in 1919–20 by the Turkish government. The Special Organization, a covert special forces unit, is said to have been the primary instrument in the implementation of the plan of extermination.

ARAM ANDONIAN'S *The Memoirs of Naim Bey*

Aram Andonian was an Armenian, employed as a military censor at the time of mobilization in 1914, who was arrested and deported from Constantinople in April 1915. After a series of escapes and rearrests he reached Aleppo, where he managed to obtain a permit for a temporary residence. After the liberation of the city by British troops in October 1918, Andonian collected the testimonies of Armenian men, women, and children who had survived the deportations. As he relates the story, he also made contact at that time with a Turkish official by the name of Naim Bey, who had been the chief secretary of the deportations committee of Aleppo. Naim Bey handed over to Andonian his memoirs, which contained a large number of official documents, telegrams, and decrees that, he stated, had passed through his hands during his term of office. Andonian translated these memoirs into Armenian; and, after some delay, they were published in Armenian, French, and English editions. The Armenian version, which appeared in Boston in 1921 under the title *Medz Vodjiru* (The Great Crime), is the most complete.

The French and English editions, published in Paris and London in 1920, reveal substantial differences from the Armenian edition as well as from each other. Much of the material that is presented as the words of the Turkish official in the English edition is narrated by Andonian himself in the French edition, making it difficult to decide whether the text was written by Naim Bey or by Andonian. Many passages in the French edition (168 pages long) are omitted in the English version, which consists of a mere 84 pages.[1]

The French edition, *Documents officiels concernant les massacres arméniens,* contains fifty documents, including thirty-one alleged telegrams from Talaat Pasha. The English edition, *The Memoirs of Naim Bey: Turkish Official Documents Relating to the Deportations and Massacres of Armenians,* contains the text of forty-eight documents, thirty of which are said to be Talaat Pasha telegrams. These documents, especially the telegrams of the wartime minister of the interior, undoubtedly are the most damning and incriminating evidence put forth by the Armenians. If accepted as authentic, they provide proof that Talaat Pasha gave explicit orders to kill all Turkish Armenians—men, women, and children.

Several of the documents directly implicate the Committee of Union and Progress in the plan of extermination. A dispatch from the governing body of the CUP, dated March 25, 1915, states: "It is the duty of all of us to effect on the broadest lines the realisation of the noble project of wiping out the existence of the Armenians who have for centuries been constituting a barrier to the Empire's progress in civilisation." A telegram of Talaat Pasha dated September 16, 1915, notes that the CUP has "decided to destroy completely all the Armenians living in Turkey. Those who oppose this order and decision cannot remain on the official staff of the Empire. An end must be put to their [the Armenians'] existence, however criminal the measure taken may be, and no regard must be paid to either age or sex nor to conscientious scruples." The same odd tone of self-accusation and acknowledgment of criminality is sounded in another directive from the CUP of February 18, 1915:

> The Jemiet [CUP] has decided to save the fatherland from the ambitions of this cursed race, and to take on its own patriotic shoulders the stain which will blacken Ottoman history.
>
> The Jemiet, unable to forget all old scores and past bitterness, full of hope for the future, has decided to annihilate all Armenians living in

Turkey, without leaving a single one alive, and it has given the Government a wide scope with regard to this.[2]

The utter ruthlessness of Talaat Pasha is a recurring theme in the documents. An undated telegram by the interior minister to the authorities in Aleppo gives the order to "collect the children of the Armenians" and to "take them away on the pretext that they are to be looked after by the Deportations Committee, as not to arouse suspicion. Destroy them and report." On September 21, 1915, Talaat informs the government of Aleppo: "There is no need for an orphanage. It is not the time to give way to sentiment and feed the orphans, prolonging their lives. Send them away to the desert and inform us." In another undated telegram Talaat notes that by "continuing the deportation of the orphans to their destinations during the intense cold, we are ensuring their eternal rest."[3]

The demonization of Talaat Pasha in Andonian's work, it should be noted in passing, represents an important change from the way in which many Armenians regarded Talaat's character before the events of 1915. For example, on December 20, 1913, British embassy official Louis Mallet reported to London that the Armenians had confidence in Talaat Bey "but fear that they may not always have to deal with a Minister of the Interior as well disposed as the present occupant of that post."[4] Similarly, after the German missionary Liparit had visited Turkey in December 1914, he stated that Talaat was a man "who over the last six years has acquired the reputation of a sincere adherent of Turkish-Armenian friendship."[5] Some others who later came into close contact with Talaat continued to adhere to this favorable appraisal. William Peet, the American head of the international Armenian relief effort in Constantinople, recalls that Talaat Pasha always "gave prompt attention to my requests, frequently greeting me as I called upon him in his office with the introductory remark: 'We are partners, what can I do for you today?'"[6] Count Bernstorff, from September 1917 until October 1918 the German ambassador to Turkey, acknowledges Talaat's failure to prevent the crimes against the Armenians but adds that he has come to respect him and calls him a man of "absolute integrity."[7] Perhaps the Turkish statesman at some point indeed turned into the vicious fiend that Armenian writers have accused him of being ever since the deportations and massacres. Or could it be that the Armenians after 1915 simply got it all wrong?

Practically all Armenian authors writing on the subject of the massacres have accepted the documents reproduced in the memoirs of Naim Bey as genuine and consider them the centerpiece of their case against the Turks. The Andonian documents, writes Stephan Astourian in a typical appraisal, "establish without the shadow of a doubt the intent and involvement of the highest Ottoman authorities" in the massacres.[8] Among recent supporters of the Armenian cause who have relied upon the Naim-Andonian documents are David Lang and Robert Melson.[9] Yves Ternon has defended the authenticity of the work but has suggested that it is preferable not to use it in view of the great difficulty of proving its genuineness.[10]

As proof of the authenticity of the documents appearing in the memoirs publicized by Andonian, several writers refer to the 1921 trial of Soghomon Tehlirian, who was charged with the assassination of Talaat Pasha in Berlin on March 15, 1921. At that trial, it is alleged, five of the Talaat Pasha telegrams were authenticated and accepted by the court as evidence.[11] However, the stenographic record of the trial, published in 1921, yields a rather different picture. Andonian had come to Berlin and had made five telegrams, supposed to be originals, available to Tehlirian's lawyers. Yet when defense counsel Adolf von Gordon sought to introduce these five telegrams as evidence, the prosecutor objected on the ground that the question of Talaat's guilt could not be resolved by the court. To do so, he submitted, required a historical inquiry, "for which quite different material than what is here available would be needed." The prosecutor argued, furthermore, that the question of whether Talaat was indeed responsible for the Armenian massacres was irrelevant. It was enough to take note of the fact that the accused Tehlirian had been convinced of Talaat's guilt. "This fully clarified his motive." Defense counsel von Gordon thereupon withdrew his motion to introduce the five telegrams into evidence.[12]

Not only were the Talaat telegrams not admitted into evidence, but they were never authenticated either. Tehlirian's lawyers, before using the documents, sought to make sure that they were genuine. With the help of Dr. Johannes Lepsius, a longtime supporter of the Armenian cause, they therefore contacted Dr. Walter Rössler, who had been German consul in Aleppo from 1910 to 1918 and who had witnessed the tragic events of 1915. In a letter dated April 25, 1921, Rössler gave his assessment of Andonian's book and of the documents contained therein. While the author appeared to be carried away by his passions and lacked the ability to be objective, Rössler wrote, "the content of the book gives an impression of authenticity. The published documents coincide with the course of events and share a similarity with reality." Nonetheless, it was difficult to establish the genuineness of the telegrams said to be sent from Constantinople, "because these telegrams contain only the handwriting of the telegraph officials and the individuals responsible for their decoding." Rössler concluded that he could not see how the authenticity of the telegrams could be proven.[13]

Some of the documents in the Naim-Andonian book are also reproduced as facsimiles. None of the originals of these documents were ever made available for inspection by outside observers, however, which adds to the difficulty of establishing the genuineness of the documents. According to Andonian, in the summer of 1920 some of the originals were sent to Constantinople at the request of the Armenian patriarch there, to be used at the forthcoming trial of a Turkish official, Abdulahad Nuri Bey. This man is described by Andonian as the Aleppo representative of the general deportations committee and as Naim Bey's boss. As it turned out, this trial never took place, because Abdulahad Nuri escaped from custody. In a letter dated July 26, 1937, Andonian states that he never learned what happened to these originals.[14]

Nothing is known of the subsequent fate of the five original documents (mentioned earlier) that were taken by Andonian to Berlin in 1921 in order to be used at the Tehlirian trial. Other originals are said to have been deposited at the Bibliothèque Nubar in Paris, the main library of the Armenian General Benevolent Union, where Andonian served as curator until his death in 1951. According to Dadrian, however, "Nubar library no longer has these documents, believed to have been transferred to Soviet Armenia in the 1960s."[15] As of today, all of the originals of the documents reproduced in the Naim-Andonian book have disappeared.

Sinasi Orel and Süreyya Yuca, two Turkish authors who have undertaken a detailed examination of the authenticity of the documents in the Andonian volume, suggest that the Armenians may have "purposely destroyed the 'originals,' in order to avoid the chance that one day the spuriousness of the 'documents' would be revealed."[16] Orel and Yuca argue that the documents in question are "crude forgeries," and they justify this conclusion by pointing to numerous discrepancies between authentic Turkish documents and those reproduced in the Naim-Andonian book. Some examples:

1. The signature of Mustafa Abdülhalik Bey, the governor of Aleppo, which appears on nine of the documents, does not jibe with actual specimens of the governor's signature.

2. Andonian either was unaware of or carelessly neglected to account for the differences between the Ottoman and European calendar. These errors destroy the system of reference numbers and dates that he used for his documents.

3. An examination of the dates and reference numbers that are found in the ministry of the interior's registers of outgoing ciphered telegrams reveals that the reference numbers on Andonian's documents bear no relationship to the actual reference numbers used on ciphered telegrams sent from Constantinople to Aleppo in the period in question.

4. All but two of the documents are written on plain paper with none of the usual signs found on the official paper used by the Ottoman government during World War I.

5. The documents contain mistakes in grammar and language that only a non-Turkish writer would make.[17]

Orel and Yuca have searched for the name of Naim Bey in various official registers but have not found any reference to such a person. In this situation, they conclude, "it seems impossible to make a definite judgment on the question of whether or not Naim Bey was an actual person." If not a fictitious person created by Andonian, he clearly must have been a very low-ranking official, who "could not have been in a position to have access to documents of a secret and sensitive nature."[18] If Naim Bey was in fact an actual person, he is described in a highly contradictory way by Andonian. In the French edition of the book Naim Bey is portrayed as an honest and kind individual, who provided the documents to Andonian because his guilty conscience prompted him to expiate for this misdeeds as an official of the deportations committee. "Although his financial situation was not good, Naim Bey declined any offer of money."[19] However, in the letter composed in 1937 (referred to earlier) Andonian gives a totally different account:

> There were matters which I could neither disclose in my book, nor to Tehlirian's lawyers in order not to blacken Naim Bey's character which was in reality not that good....He was addicted to alcohol and to gambling, and in reality it was these shortcomings which dragged him into treachery. The truth of the matter is that everything which he provided

us in the way of documents, we bought from him in return for money.... In my book I gave an entirely different portrayal of Naim Bey, because to have unveiled the truth about him would have served no purpose. Naim Bey was a totally dissolute creature.[20]

It would appear, suggest Orel and Yuca, that Andonian in his book published in 1920 lied about the character of Naim Bey, for "he did not want to risk anything which would threaten the credibility of the 'memoirs' and 'documents' provided by Naim Bey. Andonian knew, of course, that no one could be expected to believe the 'memoirs' of an alcoholic, gambler or dissolute character."[21] It also would not have been opportune to admit that the material was bought, especially from a depraved character like Naim Bey, who would be suspected of having manufactured the documents to obtain money for his destructive and expensive habits.

Andonian links his work on the memoirs of Naim Bey to his endeavor to preserve the memory of the horrible suffering of the Armenian community. However, Orel and Yuca point out that the publication of the book was in fact "part of a larger organized undertaking....The book's appearance coincides with the extensive attempts on the part of various Armenian circles to persuade the Entente Powers to establish an independent Armenian state in Eastern and South-Eastern Anatolia, in the wake of the Ottoman Empire's defeat in the First World War."[22] The documents contained in the book, depicting the Young Turk leadership and indeed the entire Turkish people as utterly ruthless and evil villains, were to influence public opinion in America and Western Europe and provide ammunition for Armenian lobbying at the Paris Peace Conference. This is why the Armenian National Union, formed under the leadership of the veteran Armenian statesman Boghos Nubar Pasha, bought the documents. Andonian confirms this interpretation in a letter to Tehlirian's lawyers dated June 10, 1921: "I was entrusted with the duty of bringing these documents to Europe in the name of the Armenian National Union in Aleppo, and to submit them to the delegation of the Armenian National Union at the Peace Conference."[23]

At the time when Andonian was taking the documents to Europe, the British were searching archives all over the world for evidence that could be used against the Ottoman officials they had arrested, taken to Malta, and planned to try for the massacre of the Armenians (see chapter 7). Among the materials that came into their hands in Constantinople were the Naim memoirs. Several telegrams from the

Naim-Andonian book were included in a dispatch sent to London in March 1921.[24] They also appear in the dossiers of the Malta detainees. Yet the British government never made use of these telegrams. As in the case of the "Ten Commandments" discussed in chapter 5, the law officers of the Crown apparently regarded the Naim-Andonian book as another of the many forgeries that were flooding Constantinople at the time.

While Andonian willingly undertook the mission given him by the Armenian National Union, he apparently was not entirely happy with the way in which the Armenians who brought out the English and French editions of the book treated his text. In his letter of July 26, 1937, he concedes that Consul Rössler's criticism of the book as lacking in objectivity was warranted. However, he goes on to say that Rössler "forgets that my book was not a historical one, but rather aiming at propaganda. Naturally, my book could not have been spared the errors characteristic of publications of this nature….I would also like to point out that the Armenian Bureau in London, and the National Armenian Delegation in Paris, behaved somewhat cavalierly with my manuscript, for the needs of the cause they were defending."[25]

It is possible that the repeated instances in the documents where Turkish leaders confess their guilt on account of the drastic measures that they are forced to take against the Armenians are the result of changes made by Andonian's British and French editors. The dispatches and telegrams, note Orel and Yuca,

> are full of expressions which simply are out of character with what Ando-
> nian would have us believe was the typical behaviour of the leaders of the
> Committee of Union and Progress. Is it conceivable that the leaders of
> Union and Progress, who it is claimed made a "premeditated," "cold-
> hearted" decision to "massacre the Armenians," would have referred to
> their decision in this respect as the "shame which will besmirch Ottoman
> history," or state that they had been "obliged to take, unfortunately,
> bloody measures in this respect"?…The aim of the individual who con-
> cocted these forged "letters" was nothing less than the desire to have the
> Turks themselves acknowledge (in advance of the events themselves) the
> "guilt of the Turks," to confirm as it were the Armenian claims against
> the Turks. In short, to have the Turks say what the Armenians them-
> selves wanted to say.[26]

The admission made by Andonian (in order to protect his own reputation) that the book was written for propaganda purposes and was then further embellished by zealous editors seriously undermines the value of the work. When all is said and done, we are left wondering what credence to give to any of the documents, knowing that they were purchased and publicized as part of a propaganda effort.

In 1986 Dadrian published an article in which he sought to answer the strong criticism of the Naim-Andonian book by Orel and Yuca. Andonian, wrote Dadrian, assembled the book "in the turmoil and chaos of the armistice"; it was a "penchant for propaganda that prompted Andonian to rush the documents to London with a view to influencing public opinion and Allied diplomats who were to elaborate the terms of peace with defeated Turkey. A valuable opportunity was thus lost for submitting the documents to Ottoman authorities for possible authentication." Dadrian acknowledged that "all three versions—Armenian, French, and English—suffer from a series of typographical and editorial errors, including inaccuracies of dates....The result is incongruities in the interrelationships of the various pieces as well as in the chronology of the events depicted." Nevertheless Dadrian decided that the flaws in the documents were mere "technicalities" and that "it may be concluded with a high degree of certainty that the two letters and the 50 decoded ciphers that constitute the Naim-Andonian material are true documents."[27]

Dadrian arrived at this conclusion by dismissing the points raised by Orel and Yuca as inconsequential and asserting that "their own volume... is teeming with identical errors"—"errors of dates, date conversion, and typography." It is difficult to provide "a strictly legal authentication of the material," Dadrian conceded; there are other ways of arriving at the truth, however, such as the "method of *content verification.* The principal actors covered by the Naim-Andonian material are repeatedly depicted [in other sources] in the same roles of arch-perpetrators and with reference to the same atrocities in identical or similar circumstances pinpointed in that material." According to Dadrian, the findings of the Turkish military tribunals convened in 1919–20 in particular confirm the veracity of the Naim-Andonian documents. "These findings were based on authenticated official documents, sworn testimony, and depositions provided by a plethora of high-ranking officials, civilian and military, who independently verified the direct complicity of the men prominently figuring in the Naim-Andonian documents." Other corroboration comes from reports of German and Austrian diplomats.[28]

But what if these other sources are not as reliable and conclusive as Dadrian suggested? In the case of the Turkish military tribunals of 1919–20, the "official documents, sworn testimony, and depositions" relied upon by Dadrian do not actually exist; they are known to us simply from reports of the legal proceedings—official and unofficial. The originals of these documents and depositions are lost. The findings of the Nuremberg tribunals that judged the Nazi war criminals after World War II have become an invaluable historical source because they were based on thousands of original Nazi documents that everyone can consult in the archives of the Federal Republic of Germany. By contrast, not a single original Turkish government document used by the Turkish tribunals has been preserved. The reports of German and Austrian diplomats contain plenty of valuable information on the deportations and killings, but little solid evidence on who is to be held responsible for the massacres that took place. In other words, Dadrian's attempt to authenticate the Naim-Andonian documents through the method of content verification stands or falls with the reliability of the sources he has invoked for this purpose. As the reader will learn later in this chapter, these sources do not provide conclusive evidence regarding the responsibility for the massacres, and the attempt to use them to prove the genuineness of the Naim-Andonian material must therefore be regarded as a failure. "Dadrian and his supporters," writes a critic, "are trying to prove what is a *good* case in regards to the general theme of massacres with *bad* evidence about a premeditated genocide."[29]

All Turkish authors regard the Naim-Andonian documents as forgeries. But even a number of non-Turkish writers have raised questions about the Naim-Andonian materials. Generally pro-Armenian, Christopher Walker had abandoned his earlier acceptance of the Talaat telegrams by 1997 and noted that "doubt must remain until and unless the documents or similar ones themselves resurface and are published in a critical edition."[30] Hilmar Kaiser, who supports the charge of genocide, refers to several extant Turkish documents from the Ottoman ministry of the interior that "confirm to some degree the contents of two other telegrams ascribed to Talaat in Andonian's book." Orel and Yuca did not use these sources, and therefore "their thesis is to be put into question and further research on the 'Naim-Andonian' documents is necessary."[31] The Austrian historian Wolfdieter Bihl has called the Naim-Andonian material "controversial" and notes that Artem Ohandjanian, the Armenian author of several well-researched books on the massacres, does not rely on them.[32] (It should be noted here that Dadrian himself, in two books on the Armenian genocide published in 1995 and 1999 respectively, similarly does not refer to the Naim-Andonian documents and does not even list Andonian's work in the bibliographies of these books.)[33]

Other Middle East specialists have been more forthright. In a review article published in 1989, Michael Gunter called the works of Mevlanzade Rifat and Andonian "notorious forgeries."[34] The Dutch historian Erik Zürcher argued that the Andonian materials "have been shown to be forgeries."[35] The British historian Andrew Mango speaks of "telegrams dubiously attributed to the Ottoman wartime Minister of the Interior, Talât Pasha."[36] The controversy over the authenticity of the Naim-Andonian documents, it is clear, will only be resolved through the discovery and publication of relevant Ottoman documents, and this may never come to pass. Until then, I would argue, Orel and Yuca's painstaking analysis of these documents has raised enough questions about their genuineness as to make any use of them in a serious scholarly work unacceptable.

THE TURKISH COURTS-MARTIAL OF 1919–22

Following the defeat of Turkey in World War I and the signing of the armistice of Mudros on October 30, 1918, the new Turkish government formed on November 11 accused the Young Turk regime of serious crimes. These accusations led to the convening of special courts-martial to try the leadership of the Committee on Union and Progress and selected officials of the former government. Several contemporary Armenian writers cite the findings of these proceedings as crucial support for the charge of genocide. Vartkes Yeghiayan argues that they "are primary evidence of Turkish confessions and condemnations which corroborate and authenticate the Armenian witness' accounts of the genocide."[37] Dadrian, as we have seen above, invoked the trials to confirm the genuineness of the Naim-Andonian documents.

After losing the war, the Young Turk government was badly discredited, and harsh criticism of the CUP became the chief theme in the Turkish press.[38] Public clamor for the punishment of the Young Turk leadership gathered strength after the escape from Constantinople of seven top CUP leaders, including Talaat Pasha, on board a German destroyer during the night of November 1. British high commissioner Arthur G. Calthorpe informed London on November 29 that planning was underway to try Enver, Talaat, and their associates by court-martial. There is hardly an organ of the press, he added, "which is not vehemently attacking these men either for the incalculable harm they have brought to the country or for their share in the massacres of the various Christian races."[39] A committee of the Turkish parliament and a commission convened in the ministry of the interior undertook the gathering of evidence and procured a large number of relevant documents that were later used by the courts-martial.[40]

By all accounts, the most important reason for the establishment of the military tribunals was massive pressure by the victorious Allies, who insisted on retribution for the Armenian massacres. As early as May 24, 1915, the Allied governments had warned the Sublime Porte that they would "hold personally responsible [for] these crimes all members of the Ottoman government and those of their agents who are implicated in such massacres."[41] When the Turkish cabinet made the formal decision on December 14 to set up the courts-martial, writes Taner Akcam, author of the most detailed study of the trials, "the political pressure of the British played a decisive role."[42] Dadrian also speaks of the Allies' eagerness for punitive justice.[43] It is most certain, Dadrian writes in another article, that the convening of the courts-martial "was dictated by political expediency. On the one hand, it was hoped that it would be possible to inculpate the Ittihadist Party leadership as primarily, if not exclusively, responsible for the Armenian massacres, thereby exculpating the rest of the Turkish nation. On the other, many representatives of the victorious Allies nurtured a strong belief that the punishment of the perpetrators might induce the victors to be lenient at the Peace Conference."[44]

The wartime plans of the Allies had provided for the dismemberment of the Ottoman Empire. According to the so-called Constantinople agreement of March 18, 1915, Russia was to annex Constantinople and parts of eastern Thrace as well as an adjoining area in Asiatic Turkey. The Sykes-Picot agreement of May 16, 1915, negotiated between Mark Sykes and Georges Picot for Britain and France and ratified by the Russians, divided large areas of Asiatic Turkey among France, Russia, and Britain.[45] Understandably, the Turks were greatly concerned about these plans, and they decided early on that only full cooperation with the Allies would help minimize the loss of territory. They also unleashed an elaborate publicity campaign to convince the world that the Young Turks alone were to blame for the crimes that had been committed. According to an American intelligence report of December 10, 1918, the Turks had created a commission of propaganda "in order to persuade civilized people that the Turk is worthy of their sympathy, throwing all the responsibility for the massacres on the Young Turk Government."[46]

The National Congress, an umbrella group of more than fifty political and cultural organizations, issued several pamphlets addressed to the West, sounding a theme that was to be echoed by some of the courts-martial. The National Congress argued that the deportations of the Armenians had become necessary because of the treasonous activities of the Armenian revolutionary organizations and the "numerous outrages against the Musulman population" but that the massacres that had taken place were inexcusable. It accused the CUP of having carried out an "infernal policy of extermination and robbery" but maintained that the Turkish people should not be held responsible "for a criminal aberration against which its conscience protested from the outset." Muslims as well as Armenians had suffered greatly from the reign of the Young Turks. "All classes, all nationalities were the victims of its tyranny."[47] Grand Vizier Damad Ferid, appearing before the Paris peace conference, argued likewise that the responsibility for Turkey's entry into the war on the side of Germany and for the crimes committed against the Christians lay strictly with the CUP.[48]

Large-scale arrests of leading Ittihadists began in January 1919. A list of suspects had been compiled by the Greek-Armenian section of the British high commissioner, which drew on the assistance of the Armenian patriarchate; others arrested were nationalists opposed to the armistice or political enemies of the Liberal Union party now in power, which sought to settle old accounts. The charges included subversion of the Turkish constitution as well as massacres of Greeks and Armenians and wartime profiteering. The main trial judged key cabinet ministers and high CUP functionaries. Several other courts took up crimes in provincial cities where massacres had taken place. Due to inadequate documentation, the total number of courts is not known. Taner Akcam arrives at a count of twenty-eight, but there may have been more.[49] An attempt of the Turkish government in February 1919 to have representatives of four neutral governments (Denmark, Spain, Sweden, and Holland) participate in the investigation of the massacres was foiled by British and French opposition.[50] All of the proceedings took place in Constantinople.

The first of the tribunals, focused on Yozgat (province of Ankara), began on February 5, 1919, and lasted until April 7. It charged several Turkish officials with mass murder and plunder of Armenian deportees.

Of 1,800 Armenians who had been living in the town of Yozgat before the war, only 88 were still alive in 1919. The court heard testimony by survivors who told of killings, robbery, and rape and accepted as evidence documents that contained orders to kill the Armenians. For example, a letter by one of the defendants, commander of the gendarmerie for the districts of Chorum and Yozgat, contained a telegram to one of this subordinates, telling him that "the Armenians are to be eradicated."[51] On April 8 the court-martial found two of the defendants guilty; the case of the third defendant was detached to another trial.

The main trial got underway in Constantinople on April 28. Twelve of the defendants (among them important members of the CUP's central committee and several ministers) were present in the dock; but seven key figures who had fled (including Talaat, Enver, and Djemal) had to be tried in absentia. "Embedded in the Indictment," writes Dadrian, "are forty-two authenticated documents substantiating the charges therein, many bearing dates, identification of senders of the cipher telegrams and letters, and names of recipients."[52] Among these documents is the written deposition of Gen. Mehmet Vehib Pasha, commander of the Turkish Third Army, who testified that "the murder and extermination of the Armenians and the plunder and robbery of their property is the result of decisions made by the central committee of Ittihad ve Terakki [CUP]."[53] In another document quoted in the indictment, a high-ranking deportation official, Abdulahad Nuri, admits having been told by Talaat that "the purpose of the deportation was destruction."[54] The court-martial ended with a verdict handed down on July 22. Several of the defendants were found guilty of having subverted the constitutional form of government by force and of being responsible for massacres in various part of the country. Talaat, Enver, Djemal, and Nazim were sentenced to death (in absentia). Others were given lengthy prison sentences.[55]

The verdict of yet another trial (of the representatives of the CUP in various cities) implicated a unit called Teskilat-i Mahsusa (Special Organization) in the massacres.[56] The actions of the Special Organization were also discussed at length during the main trial, and the court is said to have compiled a special file called "The Residual Special Organization Papers." According to Dadrian, the proceedings of the main court-martial and other trials are replete with references to the crimes of "massacre and destruction" of the Armenians on the part of the Special Organization.[57] (The Special Organization is discussed in more detail later in this chapter.)

Despite widespread hatred of the discredited Young Turk regime, the trials of the CUP leaders received only limited support from the Turkish population. The funeral of Mehmed Kemal, former governor of Boghazliyan who had been hanged on April 10, led to a large demonstration, organized by CUP elements. It is probable, reported the British high commissioner to London, that many here "regard executions as necessary concessions to Entente rather than as punishment justly meted out to criminals."[58] Speaking of the continuing arrests of former government officials, the American high commissioner Lewis Heck reported to Washington on April 4, 1919, that "it is popularly believed that many of them are made from motives of personal vengeance or at the instigation of the Entente authorities, especially the British."[59]

Many Armenians, too, voiced their skepticism. Aram Andonian called the trial of the CUP leadership "a political ruse [rather] than a work of justice. The present Government in Turkey simply wanted to throw dust in the eyes of Europe."[60] Opposition to the trials increased dramatically following the Greek occupation of Smyrna (today's Izmir) on May 15, which caused a strong outburst of patriotic and nationalistic feeling. "This provocative move," writes James Willis, "raised fears that the Allies favored territorial annexations by the ancient enemy of Turkey."[61] Under the leadership of Mustapha Kemal, a highly decorated Turkish officer, a nationalist movement now emerged that eventually was to overthrow the government of the sultan in Constantinople. From the beginning, the Kemalists criticized the sultan for his abject surrender to the Allies, and they increasingly expressed the fear that the trials were part of a plan to partition the Ottoman Empire. The atrocities committed by the Greek forces upon landing in Smyrna remained largely unpunished while the Allies pressured the Turks to persecute the Young Turk leaders, which made the Allies appear to be hypocritical and adhering to a double standard.[62]

Between May 20 and 23 Constantinople saw several large demonstrations against the Allied occupation. To appease the nationalists the Ottoman government freed forty-one prisoners. The British had long been concerned about the lax discipline at the prisons and the large number of escapees. They now feared the release of all of the prisoners. Hence on May 28 British forces seized sixty-seven of the detainees, including some already on trial, and transferred them to Malta. As the Kemalist movement gathered strength, the work of the courts-martial slowed down more and more. On March 16, 1920, the Allies occupied

Constantinople, but the signing of the Treaty of Sèvres by the Ottoman government on August 10 further weakened the Turkish courts-
martial. The treaty envisaged an international tribunal that would
judge those suspected of serious war crimes and thus undermined the
relevance and importance of the Turkish courts. The last Ottoman government uncovered several mistakes in the proceedings of the military
tribunals. The trials formally ended on March 28, 1922. An amnesty a
year later freed those still in custody.[63]

Dadrian considers the military tribunals of 1919–20 "a milestone
in Turkish legal history." The courts, he concedes, suffered from insta-
bility in structure and personnel. There was much turnover among presiding judges and prosecutors. The proceedings failed dismally "in the
area of retributive justice." Despite the enormity of the crime, there were
only fifteen death sentences, only three of which were actually carried
out. Still, Dadrian argues, the trials "demonstrated beyond reasonable
doubt that the Ittihad, which had become a monolithic governmental
party, intended to destroy the Armenian population of the empire and
for that purpose had organized and implemented its scheme of genocide."[64] Hovannisian concludes similarly that, although justice was not
done, "the relevant documents stand as reminders of the culpability of
the Young Turk regime."[65] According to Melson, "the courts-martial
demonstrate that Turkish authorities once did exist with the integrity
not to deny but to face up to the truth of the Armenian Genocide."[66]

Armenian writers and their supporters have praised the contribution of the military tribunals to the discovery of historical truth,
despite serious problems concerning our knowledge of these proceedings and the reliability of their findings. It is of course not surprising
that the proceedings in 1919–20 lacked many basic requirements of
due process. Few authors familiar with Ottoman jurisprudence have
had many positive things to say about the Turkish court system, especially the military courts. Dadrian notes that military tribunals in 1915
"hanged countless Armenians on the flimsiest charges," and he cites
with approval a German memo that referred to these tribunals as "kan-
garoo courts."[67] In January 1916 the German ambassador, Paul von
Wolff-Metternich, demanded the supervision of Turkish courts by German officials, "since one cannot have confidence in Turkish jurisprudence."[68] In July 1915 and again early in 1916 a Turkish military court
condemned to death a total of seventy-eight leading citizens of Syria.
"Many, probably a large majority," writes one student of the subject,
"were innocent of anything which would justify such a sentence."[69]

To be sure, the military tribunals of 1919–20 passed few death sentences, but this was not the result of improved legal procedures. "It is interesting to see," commented British high commissioner Richard Webb on July 7, 1919 (on the just-concluded trial of Talaat and other Young Turk leaders), "how skillfully the Turkish penal code has been manipulated to cover the acts attributed to the accused, and the manner in which the sentences have been apportioned among the absent and the present as to effect a minimum of real bloodshed."[70] In other words, while there were fewer death sentences than during the war years, political interference continued to afflict these court proceedings just as before. If Armenian writers like the trials of 1919–20, one is inclined to conclude, it is less because the leopard changed its spots but rather because they are happy about the findings of these courts with regard to the responsibility of the Young Turk leadership for the Armenian massacres.

The legal procedures of Ottoman military courts, including those operating in 1919–20, suffered from serious shortcomings when compared to Western standards of due process of law. Nineteenth-century American courts-martial, for example, granted the accused or their counsels the right to question and cross-examine witnesses concerning the alleged offense.[71] This right is embodied in Articles 32 of the Uniform Code of Military Justice, enacted by Congress in 1950, which provides that the accused be able "to cross-examine witnesses" and to obtain evidence in their own behalf.[72] Even the much-criticized rules of procedure for the military tribunals proposed by the administration of George W. Bush in 2002 to try terrorists grant the accused the right to present evidence in their defense and to cross-examine witnesses.[73] By contrast, the Ottoman penal code did not acknowledge the right of cross-examination, and the role of the judge was far more important than in the Anglo-American tradition. He weighed the probative value of all evidence submitted during the preparatory phase and during the trial, and he questioned the accused.[74] At the trials held in 1919–20 the presiding officer, when questioning the defendants, often acted more like a prosecutor than like an impartial judge.

In line with Ottoman rules of procedure, defense counsels at the courts-martial held in 1919–20 were barred from access to the pretrial investigatory files and from accompanying their clients to the interrogations conducted prior to the trials.[75] On May 6, 1919, at the third session of the main trial, defense counsel challenged the court's repeated references to the indictment as proven fact, but the court rejected the objection.[76] Throughout the trials, no witnesses were heard; the verdict of the courts rested entirely on documents and testimony mentioned or read during the trial proceedings but never subjected to cross-examination. Commenting on the Yozgat trial that had just started, American high commissioner Heck noted with disapproval on February 7, 1919, that the defendants would be tried by "anonymous court material."[77] "After the establishment of the Turkish republic," writes a Turkish legal officer, "the military justice system developed during the Ottoman Empire was generally considered to be unconstitutional, and an entirely new *Turkish Military Criminal Code and Military Criminal Procedure* were prepared and accepted by the Turkish Great National Assembly in 1930."[78]

Probably the most serious problem affecting the probative value of the 1919–20 military court proceedings is the loss of all the documentation of these trials. This means that we have none of the original documents, sworn testimony, and depositions on which the courts based their findings and verdicts. We know of some of this material from reports of the legal proceedings that are preserved in selected supplements of the official gazette of the Ottoman government, *Takvim-i Vekayi,* or from press reports; but, of course, such reproductions can hardly be considered a valid substitute for the original documentation. In many cases we do not know whether the official gazette or the newspapers covering the trials reprinted all or only some of the text of the documents reproduced. Neither can we be sure of the accuracy of the transcription. According to Dadrian, "before being introduced as accusatory exhibits, each and every official document was authenticated by the competent staff personnel of the Interior Ministry who thereafter affixed on the top part of the document: 'it conforms to the original.'"[79] However, in the absence of the original documents and without the ability of defense counsel to challenge the authenticity of this material, we have to take the word of the officials in question—and that is indeed a tall order. It is doubtful that the Nuremberg trials would ever have attained their tremendous significance in documenting the crimes of the Nazi regime if we had to rely on a few copies of such documents in the trial record or in the press covering the trials instead of the verdicts being supported by thousands of original German documents preserved in our archives.

In the absence of the complete original documents, we have to be content with selected quotations. For example, General Vehib Pasha in his written deposition is supposed to have described Dr. Behaeddin Sakir, one of the top CUP leaders, as the man who "procured and engaged in the command zone of the Third Army the butchers of human beings....He organized gallow birds as well as gendarmes and policemen with blood on their hand and blood in their eyes."[80] Parts of this deposition were included in the indictment of the main trial and in the verdict of the Harput trial,[81] but without the full text we lose the context of the quoted remarks. The entire text of the deposition is supposed to have been read into the record of the Trebizond trial on March 29, 1919, but the proceedings of this trial are not preserved in any source; only the verdict is reprinted in the official gazette.

Other highly incriminating testimony is said to have been given at the Yozgat trial, but here again only the verdict was published in the official gazette. Dadrian, who quotes this testimony, has to rely on accounts of these proceedings in Turkish newspapers, all of which were operating under the dual prior censorship of the Turkish government and the Allied high commissioners.[82] Moreover, much of this testimony must be considered hearsay at best. For example, former Turkish official Cemal is supposed to have testified that Ankara's CUP delegate Necati had told him that the time had come to begin "the extermination of local Armenians."[83] Similar hearsay evidence is contained in the indictment of the main trial. The Turkish official Ihsan Bey had heard Abdulahad Nuri Bey, the Aleppo representative of the deportations committee, say: "I have taken up contact with Talaat Bey and have personally received the orders of extermination."[84] In the absence of corroboration from other reliable sources, it seems difficult to consider this testimony evidence in any meaningful sense of the term.

Contemporary Turkish authors dismiss the proceedings of the military tribunals of 1919–20 as tools of the Allies.[85] The victorious Allies at the time, however, anxious for retributive justice, considered the conduct of the trials to be dilatory and half-hearted. The trials, British high commissioner Calthorpe wrote to London on August 1, 1919, were "proving to be a farce and injurious to our own prestige and to that of the Turkish government."[86] In the view of commissioner John de Robeck, the trials were such a dead failure that their "findings cannot be held of any account at all."[87] Hence when the British considered conducting their own trials of alleged Turkish war criminals held at Malta they declined to use any of the inculpatory evidence developed by the Turkish tribunals (see chapter 7).

According to Dadrian, "several aspects of the court-martial proceedings merit attention for the quality of their judiciousness, despite the consideration of the fact that these trials were urged on by the victorious Allies, under whose shadow they took place." Among the features that deserve praise Dadrian notes that the trials were held in public, that the defendants had able defense counsel, and that the verdicts pronounced by the tribunals were based almost entirely on authenticated official documents.[88] As explained earlier, however, the authenticity of documents admitted into evidence cannot be established by assertion on the part of the prosecuting authority. Moreover, none of the testimony, written depositions, and documents put forth by the prosecution were subjected to cross-examination by the defense, which makes it impossible to consider these materials conclusive proof. Some of these materials are reproduced in the indictments, but an indictment is not tantamount to proven guilt. The serious violations of due process as well as the loss of all of the original documentation leave the findings of the military tribunals of 1919–20 unsupported by credible evidence.

THE ROLE OF THE TESKILAT-I MAHSUSA (SPECIAL ORGANIZATION)

Several of the courts-martial held in 1919–20 made references to the destructive role of the Special Organization, and Dadrian accepts this appraisal. "The stated responsibilities of the Special Organization," he writes, "included intelligence, counter espionage, and the prevention of sabotage." As it turned out, however, the members of this unit eventually became the primary instrument used by the CUP to carry out its plan to exterminate the Armenians. "Their mission was to deploy in remote areas of Turkey's interior and to ambush and destroy convoys of Armenian deportees."[89] The Special Organization's "principal duty was the execution of the Armenian genocide."[90]

According to Philip Stoddard, author of the only scholarly full-scale study of the subject, the Special Organization (SO) developed between 1903 and 1907; from 1913 on it used the name "Special Organization." Under the overall direction of Enver Pasha (minister of war since January 1914) and led by many talented officers, the SO functioned like a Special Forces outfit. Stoddard calls it "a significant Unionist vehicle for dealing with both Arab separatism and Western imperialism," which at its peak enrolled about thirty thousand men. During World War I it was used for special military operations in the Caucasus, Egypt, and Mesopotamia. For example, in 1915 units of the SO seized key oases along the Ottoman line of advance against the Suez Canal. The SO was also used to suppress "subversion" and "possible collaboration" with the external enemy. However, according to Stoddard, this activity targeted primarily indigenous nationalist activities in Syria and Lebanon. He maintains that the SO played no role in the Armenian deportations.[91]

Several recent authors have discussed some aspects of the secretive organization, but due to the loss of most documentation our knowledge of the operations of the SO remains spotty at best. Jacob Landau stresses the pan-Turkic and pan-Islamic activities of the SO, which led to the dispatch of agents even before the outbreak of World War I. During the war SO operatives were sent to Transcaucasia, Mesopotamia, Afghanistan, and India.[92] Dogu Ergil speaks of an organization "composed of the most dynamic officers of the army," who, in cooperation with local organizations, sought to foment nationalist revolutions in Mesopotamia, Turkestan, Egypt, Libya, and Tunis.[93] Donald McKale refers to the SO as originally being Enver Pasha's "private secret service," which later, under the leadership of Sulayman Askeri Bey, functioned "as a wartime intelligence and guerilla organization."[94] According to Erik Zürcher, the SO was "in effect a secret service directly responsible to Enver and paid out of secret War Ministry funds." It was sometimes quite successful in its counterespionage, as for instance in Syria. But, he concludes, "its 'offensive' operations were an almost total failure."[95]

The indictment of the main trial maintained that the SO, after having participated in the war, carried out "criminal operations and activities" against the Armenians. For this purpose the CUP is said to have arranged for the release of convicts who participated in the murder of the deportees.[96] Dadrian's argument is based on this indictment:

> In other words, following the abortive guerilla operations against Russian forces in the Transcaucasus, the Ittihadist leaders redeployed the brigand units for use on the home front internally, namely against the Armenians. Through a comprehensive sweep of the major cities, towns and villages, containing large clusters of Armenian populations, the Special Organization units, with their commanding officers more or less intact, set to work to carry out Ittihad's blueprint of annihilation.[97]

Turkish as well as German civilian and military sources, Dadrian maintains, confirm this information, including the employment of convicts in the killer units of the SO. Yet when checking the references that he provides for this assertion it becomes clear that these sources do not always say what Dadrian alleges. It is generally known and undisputed that the Ottoman government during World War I released convicts in order to increase its manpower pool for military service.[98] Yet there is no credible evidence other than the assertion of the indictment of the main trial for the allegation that the SO, with large numbers of convicts enrolled in its ranks, took the lead role in the massacres.

Dadrian quotes German documents in support of the alleged link between the SO and the Armenian massacres. One of these documents is a report on the Armenian deportations by a German officer, Colonel Stange. In this document, dated August 23, 1915, Stange reports that Armenian villagers, deported from the area north of Erzurum, "were murdered, with the acquiescence and even the assistance of the military escort, by so-called Tschettes (volunteers), Aschirets [tribesmen] and similar scum."[99] Dadrian, in quoting from this document, leaves out the phrase "with the acquiescence."[100] More importantly, the term "Special Organization" does not appear in the Stange report. It is in Dadrian's gloss that Stange "confirmed the swift transfer of the brigands employed in guerilla war to mass murder duties";[101] and it is Dadrian, not Stange, who equates the "scum" involved in this massacre with released convicts and enrolls them into the ranks of the SO.

Dadrian uses the same technique when quoting from a report by the German consul in Aleppo, Walter Rössler. This German official supposedly "described the Special Organization massacre details as 'convicts, released from the prisons, and put in military uniform.'"[102] But again it is Dadrian and not Rössler who blames the killing not just on released convicts but on the SO. The question of who murdered the Armenian deportees and who, if anyone, made them do their ghastly deeds is difficult to resolve conclusively (see chapter 12). Dadrian finds an easy solution to this problem by manipulating the statements of contemporary observers.

And there is more. In an apparent attempt to increase the credibility of Stange and to link this German officer to the SO, Dadrian describes him as "the highest-ranking German guerilla commander operating in the Turko-Russian border."[103] In another place Dadrian calls him "'Special Organization' Commander, 8th Infantry Regiment, and in charge of a Turkish *Teshkilati Mahsusa* Detachment, of regimental strength, operating on the Russian border area."[104] Yet there is no credible evidence to support this assertion about Stange's service as an SO commander; and in view of the well-known tension between the Turkish and German secret services it is a highly unlikely assignment.[105] At the beginning of the war SO units did indeed operate, without much success, in the border area, and some of them are said to have included released convicts.106 However, according to German Foreign Ministry files and other sources, during the winter offensive of 1914–15 Stange commanded a unit of regular Turkish troops, the Eighth Infantry Regiment of the Third Turkish Division. Although this unit, known as the Stange Detachment, was reinforced by two thousand to three thousand irregulars, these irregulars were not released Turkish convicts but Georgian Muslims (Laz and Acar) who had volunteered to fight the Russians.107 Even if Stange's appointment as commander of a regular army unit is regarded as camouflage and the detachment was in fact part of the SO, there is no evidence anywhere that this or any other SO detachment was diverted to duty involving the Armenian deportations. The Stange Detachment, according to another German officer, also included Armenians, who are said to have fought well.108 The supreme irony of this situation is rather striking: here is an alleged unit of the SO, the organization that Dadrian calls the primary instrument in the implementation of the Armenian genocide, that included Armenians!

Dadrian takes similar liberties with a Turkish source that deals with the leading SO official, Esref Kuscubasi. At the outbreak of World War I Esref was director of SO operations in Arabia, the Sinai, and North Africa. After his capture on a mission to Yemen on January 13, 1917, he was sent to Malta, where he was held until 1920. Esref was interrogated by the British, but he denied any involvement with the Armenian massacres. He died in 1964 at the age of 91.109 According to Dadrian, Esref admitted in an interview with the Turkish author Cemal Kutay that he "had assumed duties [in operations that revolved around] the covert aspects of [the Armenian deportations]." He also defended the former grand vizier, Said Halim, against charges of "complicity in crimes associated with the Armenian deportations. As a man deeply involved in this matter I firmly reject this false accusation."110 The text in which these sentences appear, as Dadrian acknowledges, is taken from pages 18, 36, and 78 of a book by Kutay on the SO in World War I,111 and indeed it is only through shrewd juxtapositions of words and insertions (which he puts in square brackets) that Dadrian ends up with the desired result—the well-known SO operative Esref Kuscubasi now acknowledges his responsibility for the crimes against the Armenians.112

Two other examples of the way in which Dadrian uses interpolations and rephrasing to make his points should be mentioned. When discussing the release of convicts, Yusuf Kemal Bey (undersecretary in the Ministry of Justice) is quoted as telling the Ottoman senate in 1916 that "these people are not being sent directly to the theaters of war as soldiers but are being used for special services e.g., in the ranks of the Special Organization." In Dadrian's assessment this testimony is said to mean that the convicts "are being used for special services [killing operations] in the ranks of the Special Organization" (the words in square brackets are inserted by Dadrian).[113] Also addressing the issue of the released convicts, Behic Bey (the deputy director of the Department of the Army in the Ministry of War) is quoted as testifying during the same debate that "the majority of these criminals was not made part of the military troops but was placed under the command of the Special Organization in which outfit their involvement proved profitable." When Dadrian summarizes this testimony, "the majority of these criminals" becomes "virtually all of the felons," and placement "under the command of the Special Organization" is said to mean "deployment in the interior provinces of Turkey for an extra-military mission, meaning the liquidation of the Armenian element, as subsequently documented by the Turkish Military Tribunal."[114] Again, it is Dadrian's gloss and not the original text quoted that includes the incriminating words.

In order to establish a connection between the SO and the Armenian massacres, Dadrian quotes repeatedly from the indictment of the main court-martial of 1919; but neither the proceedings of this trial nor the verdict support the allegation. Under questioning by the presiding judge of the main trial, several defendants confirmed the use of the SO for covert operations behind enemy lines on the Russian front, described the use of released convicts, and explained the way in which the SO had cooperated with the army and had been paid out of a secret fund of the Ministry of War. They also testified that individual CUP functionaries had served in the SO and had helped to recruit volunteers, describing this participation as a patriotic duty. The defendants denied any connection between the SO and the central committee of the CUP, however, as well as any role of the SO in the Armenian deportations and massacres.[115]

When the presiding judge kept on insisting that the SO had participated in the massacres, defendant Riza Bey finally expressed his "conjecture" that locally recruited reinforcements for the gendarmerie, which did not have enough manpower to carry out the deportations, could also be called "special organization." However, he insisted that these forces and the units of the SO were "completely different things."[116] All of the defendants rejected the idea, repeatedly put forth by the presiding judge, that the SO had two parts, one functioning under the direction of the Ministry of War and the other under the central committee of the CUP. I know of no credible evidence that proves their testimony to have been false.

Until the main court-martial of 1919, nobody had linked the SO to the Armenian deportations. The reports and writings of foreign consular officials, missionaries, and German officers who served in Turkey are a rich source of information about the deportations and massacres, but the SO is never mentioned. It would appear that the SO was selected by the prosecutors in 1919 as an easy target. Engaged in covert activities, the SO had regularly destroyed its papers. Moreover, practically all of whatever documentation may have been available at the end of the war had disappeared after the collapse of the Young Turk regime. Little was known about the organizational structure of the SO. All this made it tempting to use the SO as a scapegoat and attribute to it all kinds of nefarious activities.

The Turkish journalist Ahmed Emin Yalman revived the story about the involvement of the SO in the Armenian massacres in a book published in the United States in 1930. The SO, he wrote, "was in some cases directly instrumental in bringing about attacks and massacres."[117] Yalman cited no sources or evidence to back up this statement. In 1971 Kazarian published an English translation of the indictment of the main trial that contained references to the SO, and in a 1976 article he called the SO the instrument that carried out the killing of the Armenians.[118] Walker, in an exchange with Dyer in 1973, relied upon Yalman and two other secondary sources when he attributed the "Ittihadist planned extermination of the Armenians" to the "bands of Teskilat-i Mahsusa (Special Organization)."[119] Dyer, at the time a senior lecturer at the Royal Military Academy at Sandhurst and one of the few persons to have done research in the Ottoman military archives, responded that in his understanding the SO had been employed "mainly in furthering the Holy War among the Muslim peoples on and beyond the Ottoman borders. It was certainly not primarily involved in the Armenian events of 1915–1916." With regard to such an involvement, Dyer noted that he had seen "little evidence apart from gossip like that quoted by Mr. Walker."[120]

This is where matters stood until Dadrian began to write about the courts-martial of 1919–20 in the late 1980s and to publicize the accusations against the SO made by these tribunals. Dadrian fully accepted the charges made by the military tribunals and considered the SO to have played a central role in the program of genocide. Several authors apparently were persuaded by his argument. The SO, wrote Hovannisian in 1992, had the responsibility to oversee the deportations and "used as agents of death and destruction" hardened criminals released from the prisons as well as predatory tribes.[121] Zürcher, who in 1984 had discussed the SO without any reference to the Armenian deportation, in 1997 referred to "indications" that an inner circle within the CUP leadership, under the direction of Talaat Pasha, had pursued a policy of extermination and had used the relocation as a cloak for this policy. "A number of provincial party chiefs assisted in this extermination, which was organized through the *Teskilat-i Mahsusa* under the direction of its political director (and CUP central committee member) Bahaeddin Sakir."[122] Akcam, for the most part relying on the proceedings of the courts-martial as well as on the work of Dadrian, similarly concludes that after its failures on the Russian front the SO was used to organize and carry out the extermination of the Armenians.[123] Repeating the charge without any new supporting evidence, Donald Bloxham maintains that the irregular units of the SO were "the principal murderers of the Armenian deportees."[124]

The allegations of the involvement of the SO in the Armenian massacres are based upon testimony and documents introduced by the prosecution at the military tribunals of 1919–20 as well as on what Dyer has correctly characterized as "gossip." Given the limited credibility of this material, the role of the SO in the travail of the Armenians, too, must be considered not proven. The archive of the Turkish General Staff is said to contain ciphered telegrams to the SO,[125] but so far they have not been seen by any Western scholar. It is possible that authentic documentation concerning the SO may yet be discovered in Turkish or other archives that will throw additional light upon the activities of this secretive organization. Until then the allegations will remain just that—allegations unsupported by real evidence.

THE COVERT NATURE OF THE GENOCIDE

Dadrian has argued that the deportation order as well as the rules implementing the deportations were part of a scheme of deception and duplicity, for "subsequently these orders were superseded by secret orders decreeing the destruction of the convoys through massacre."

Both Talaat and Enver are said to have used for this purpose telegraphic apparatuses that they had installed in their homes.[126] According to Dadrian, Resit Akif Pasha, a veteran Ottoman politician and president of the council of state in the first postwar Turkish government in the fall of 1918, confirmed this nefarious practice in a speech before the senate on November 21, 1918. Dadrian refers to this speech as a "document [that] has extraordinary value. In this sense, it is perhaps the most damning piece of legal evidence, confirming the reality of the most critical feature of the Armenian Genocide: its covert and highly secret design, especially the resort to a two-track system of transmission of orders."[127]

In the speech in question Resit Akif Pasha stated that while occupying his last post in the cabinet he had become "cognizant of some secrets." The official order for the deportation of the Armenians had been followed by "an ominous circular order," sent by the central committee of the CUP to the provinces, "urging the expediting of the execution of the accursed mission of the brigands (*çete*). Thereupon, the brigands proceeded to act and the atrocious massacres were the result."[128] Unfortunately the existence of this circular order depends upon Resit Akif Pasha's word, which must be considered suspect. His speech was part of the elaborate propaganda campaign waged by the postwar Turkish governments that sought to heap all blame for the Armenian massacres upon the CUP leadership and thus forestall the dismemberment of the Ottoman Empire. This political purpose becomes clear in the remarks immediately following his mention of the secret circular order. Resit Akif here castigates the central committee of the CUP as a "vile and tyrannical body" that was more influential than the official government. This committee "*alone* is the cause of the immense catastrophes befalling this innocent state and nation, [and] emerges as the *singular* cause of this slaughter" (my emphasis).[129] Resit Akif never produced the circular order implicating the CUP leaders in the massacre of the Armenian convoys. The mere allegation that such an order was issued can hardly be considered "legal evidence," as Dadrian has claimed.

Chapter 7

The Turkish Position

The Turkish government denies that the Young Turk regime during World War I ordered the annihilation of the Armenian community and therefore was guilty of genocide. Until very recently, all Turkish historians took the same position. Their writings were heavily influenced by nationalism and, with few exceptions, were notable for extreme partisanship and a lack of critical self-reflection.[1] The relocation of the Armenians, it is argued in this literature, was an emergency measure made necessary by the treasonable activities of the Armenian revolutionaries who organized a full-scale rebellion behind the Turkish lines. Unable to tell who was and who was not in league with the enemy, the Ottoman government had no choice but to remove the entire Armenian community to a new location in the interior of the country. This removal was a relocation and not a deportation, they insist, since the destinations in Syria and Mesopotamia were part of the Ottoman Empire. During this relocation, most Turkish authors concede, unfortunate excesses took place, and many Armenians lost their life. However, the government did its best to prevent these killings and punished those who could be found responsible for them. There were no large-scale massacres; moreover, many Muslims, too, died as a result of what in effect was a civil war within a global war.[2]

THE ARMENIAN REBELLION

Turkey's entry into World War I on the side of Germany put the Armenian community in a difficult position. The Armenians were especially unhappy over the prospect of having to fight the Russians, whom they had come to regard as their protector. The fact that the Russian army of the Caucasus included large numbers of Russian Armenians added to the predicament. Still, the Armenian patriarch and even the Dashnaks went out of their way to affirm their loyalty to the Ottoman state, and most Armenians of military age at first responded to the call for military service.[3]

The Ottoman regime was not impressed by these declarations of support, and for good reason. As most Armenian authors concede, the sympathy of the great majority of their compatriots was in fact with the Allies. "Although most Armenians maintained a correct attitude vis-à-vis the Ottoman government," writes Hovannisian, "it can be asserted with some substantiation that the manifestations of loyalty were insincere, for the sympathy of most Armenians throughout the world was with the Entente, not with the Central Powers."[4] In view of the Ottoman legacy of massacres and despite "overt demonstrations of support for the Turkish war effort," acknowledges Dadrian, "it is fair to state that most (though not all) Armenians privately hoped for Turkish defeat and the end of Turkish domination."[5] Individual Armenians differed on the degree to which they wanted to involve themselves actively in the struggle against Turkey, but the general sentiment was clearly pro-Entente. A cartoon that appeared in the Turkish satirical paper *Karagöz* illustrated this attitude and also indicated that the Turks were well aware of the defeatist posture of the Armenians. The cartoon depicted two Turks discussing the war:

> "Where do you get your war news from?" asked Turk number one. "I do not need war news," replied Turk number two; "I can follow the course of the war by the expression on the faces of the Armenians I meet. When they are happy I know that the Allies are winning, when depressed I know the Germans had a victory."[6]

In September 1914, about a month after the general mobilization, the Ottoman government instructed provincial authorities to keep the activities of the Armenian organizations under surveillance and to seize any illegal arms.[7] This order led to widespread searches for weapons; several governors reported that they had discovered large stocks of arms and explosives, most of them of Russian origin. The Armenians claimed that these weapons had been prepared for self-defense only, but the Turks were unconvinced by this argument. By that time large numbers of Armenian conscripts had begun to desert, and some Armenian revolutionaries had started to engage in acts of sabotage. The Turkish army had just suffered a serious defeat at the Caucasus front; Armenian assistance to the enemy, it was charged, had played a crucial role in this debacle. There were reports of telegraph lines being cut and of armed clashes with bands of Armenian deserters. In some instances, villagers were said to have provided shelter for the Armenian bands; in other cases, they had refused.[8]

On February 25, 1915, the operations division of the Turkish General Staff sent a directive to all army units entitled "Increased Security Precautions." The order took note of the activities of Armenian brigands and deserters. "Although these incidents are not serious at the moment, they indicate that preparations for rebellion are being made by our enemies within our country." The General Staff gave commanders authority to declare martial law and directed that Armenians be removed from all military service.[9] Several days later, on February 28, Interior Minister Talaat informed the governors of the order from the General Staff and advised them to take "all necessary preventive measures in those matters affecting the civilian administration."[10]

By April 1915, Turkish authors and supporters of the Turkish cause argue, Armenian guerrilla activities had picked up momentum. Roads and communication lines were being cut. On April 22 the governor of Sivas informed the Ministry of the Interior that according to information supplied by arrested suspects the Armenians had thirty thousand armed men in the region: fifteen thousand had joined the Russian army and the other fifteen thousand would threaten the forces from the rear if the Turkish army suffered defeat.[11] Ambassador Morgenthau reported to Washington on May 25 that nobody put the Armenian guerillas "at less than ten thousand and twenty-five thousand is probably closer to the truth."[12] Armenian insurgents had seized parts of the city of Van, and there were also skirmishes in Cilicia. The Ottomans, writes Justin McCarthy, "were forced to withdraw whole divisions from the front to combat the rebels."[13] While the Turkish war effort was thus being weakened, Russian troops were advancing into eastern Anatolia, and a powerful British attack at the Dardanelles threatened Constantinople itself. In this situation of great stress, the Young Turk regime had become convinced that a general Armenian uprising was underway, a rebellion that endangered the very existence of the Ottoman state. The Armenian insurrection, writes the Turkish historian Yusuf Hikmet Bayur, was a fact, and it caught the Turkish government in a dangerously volatile situation.[14] The well-armed Armenian partisan forces operating in Anatolia, insists another Turkish historian, Selim Deringil, "were more than 'self-defense' units."[15]

Turkish authors have cited article 6 of the Hunchak program, adopted in the late 1880s, as proof that the Armenians in 1914–15 aimed at a general uprising. That article stated that the "most opportune time to institute the general rebellion for carrying out the immediate objective was when Turkey was engaged in war."[16] In 1919 the

National Congress of Turkey (an umbrella organization founded to discredit the Young Turks) publicized a proclamation of the Hunchaks allegedly issued after the outbreak of World War I, which called for a rebellion that would "drown ottoman tyranny in blood." The Hunchaks, it said, "will participate with the sword of insurrection in this gigantic fight for the existence of nations." The publication went on to describe how the Armenians, acting upon this call for rebellion, had attacked military convoys, cut off the retreat of Turkish troops, and also committed "numerous outrages against the Musulman population."[17] The Dashnaks also had drawn up a plan in January 1915 for a general uprising (according to a recently published history), but this plan was never implemented.[18] Another Dashnak publication praises the famous Murad of Sebastia for his uncompromising revolutionary role in 1914. Convinced that the Russian army and Armenian volunteers would soon enter Turkish Armenia, Murad "sent word everywhere for Armenians not to offer soldier conscripts to the Turkish army, to avoid military service, and to...fight, resist, and to die with honor." Unfortunately, the account continues, "Murad failed to persuade the Armenians of Sebastia to rise in rebellion."[19] According to these sources, then, the Hunchaks issued a call for rebellion, though it is not clear how many Armenians followed this order. The Dashnaks prepared plans for a general uprising but never carried them out.

Some European diplomats and other observers on the scene questioned whether the country in 1915 indeed faced a general Armenian uprising, and the issue continues to be the subject of controversy. On May 15, 1915, the Austrian consul in Trebizond relayed to his government Turkish reports of a widespread Armenian rebellion, though he added the caveat that these reports could be "exaggerations common in this country."[20] Max Erwin von Scheubner-Richter, who was German vice-consul in Erzurum from February 17 to August 6, 1915, in a report to Berlin acknowledged that Armenian revolutionaries had engaged in seditious activities, but he denied that there had been "a general and planned Armenian rebellion."[21] The same position was taken by the first dragoman of the Russian embassy, André Mandelstam.[22] On the other hand, German Vice-Consul Kuckhoff in Samsun considered it "a fact that a large Armenian conspiracy was excellently organized in all of Anatolia and was in constant contact with foreign powers. In all towns the conspirators were well supplied with weapons, ammunition and bombs."[23] Similarly, the high-ranking German officer Felix Guse (who as chief of staff of the Turkish Third Army was a witness to the events of 1915 in eastern Anatolia) insisted that the activities of the Armenian revolutionaries represented a "prepared undertaking" rather than simply a reaction to stepped-up persecution. "The seriousness and scope of the Armenian insurrection," he noted, "have not been sufficiently recognized and appreciated."[24]

Pro-Armenian authors have denied that the fighting in 1915 represented a general uprising. Dadrian acknowledges that "a number of Armenians, individually or in consort with the enemy, engaged in espionage and sabotage, mainly on the eastern border."[25] However, he denies the assertion of Guse and others that this was the result of a "prepared undertaking" or full-scale rebellion. Guse, Dadrian asserts, "was largely, if not exclusively, dependent upon the information fed to him by his Turkish subordinates as well as his Turkish superior, the Commander-in-Chief of the Caucasus, or the IIIrd Army. He had absolutely no alternative or supplementary source to check, modify, verify, or dismiss a flow of information with seemingly actual military implications but in reality with enormous political ramifications."[26] This assessment has some validity; yet after thus devaluing Guse as a reliable witness, Dadrian cited Guse in two writings published several years later as saying that "there was no proof that the Armenians had any plan or intention to mount a general uprising."[27] Dadrian's use of Guse's views raises several problems. First, if Guse's testimony is not to be trusted when he says that there was a "prepared uprising" because he had no independent sources of information, he should also not be considered a reliable source when he allegedly says that there was no planned uprising. Second, and more seriously, Guse nowhere states that there was no planned insurrection. Dadrian cites as his source Guse's 1925 article (quoted earlier), but Guse there maintains the opposite of what Dadrian makes him say—he affirms that there was indeed a large rebellion. Dadrian does not put Guse's words into quotation marks, but by falsely attributing an opinion to a source, even when not citing it verbatim, he once again commits a serious violation of scholarly ethics.

When all is said and done, we are left without firm knowledge as to whether the various guerrilla forces known to have operated in Anatolia were part of a general insurrection; the open-and-shut case claimed by Turkish authors is not substantiated. It is difficult to decide, observes Erickson in his history of the Ottoman army, when, where, and why the rebellions broke out—whether provoked by intolerable conditions imposed upon the Armenians or as part of a more encompassing

Turks say the armenians were in open rebellion against the Ottomans and actually fighting for the Russians.

scheme.[28] As it so often does, the assessment of Dyer appears to be the most sensible. Turkish allegations of wholesale disloyalty, treason, and revolt by the Ottoman Armenians, Dyer concludes, "are wholly true as far as Armenian sentiment went, only partly true in terms of overt acts, and totally insufficient as a justification for what was done [to the Armenians]."[29]

THE REVOLT OF VAN

One of the most important factors in the decision to deport the Armenian community was the uprising at Van. This important city, close to the Russian border and in the heartland of historic Armenia, for a long time had been a center of Armenian nationalist agitation, had developed a strong revolutionary tradition, and was considered a stronghold of the Dashnaks. As the Russians were advancing into eastern Anatolia in the spring of 1915—so goes the Turkish argument—the Armenians of Van began a revolt aimed at aiding the Russian offensive.

Relations between Armenians and Muslims in the Van area had been deteriorating for some time. Tension had been rising, especially between Armenian villagers and Kurds; depredations by Kurdish brigands led to stepped-up arming of the Armenian population. On July 9, 1913, the British vice-consul in Van reported that the "general lawlessness [is] worse than has existed at any time during the past three years."[30] Mobilization and the outbreak of war only aggravated the situation. The local Dashnak organization decided to oppose the conscription of young Armenians.[31] The government removed some of the gendarmerie for service at the front and created a militia, made up of Kurds and released convicts, to maintain local security. There are numerous reports that these forces used the excuse of requisitions in order to rob and pillage.[32] Following orders received from Constantinople, Armenian houses were burnt down as punishment for desertion.

By October 1914 Turkish military commanders reported increased Armenian desertions. The Russians were said to be distributing arms to Armenian bands. A dispatch dated November 29, 1914, stated: "From the confessions of two arrested spies it is understood that rebellion is expected in Van and in the province at any time now."[33] According to Turkish authors and their supporters, this insurrection, using Russian weapons, actually broke out in March 1915. Telegraph lines were cut, gendarmerie posts were attacked, and Muslim villagers were slaughtered. "The rebellion quickly took on the character of an inter-communal war. Armed Armenian bands attacked Kurdish villages. Kurdish tribesmen then retaliated by attacking Armenian villages. Wholesale massacres followed on both sides."[34] Armenian writers assert that it was the Turkish militia that—pretending to search for arms—repeatedly opened fire on unarmed Armenians and plundered and burned down entire hamlets. "Unable to stomach barbaric injustices, the village[r]s resisted and a fight ensued. The overwhelmed and terri-fied population escaped to nearby villages and eventually to Van."[35]

On April 20 (according to the European calendar) the Armenians of Van, under the leadership of the Dashnak leader Aram Manoukian, went on the offensive. The Turkish governor reported on April 24 that four thousand Armenian fighters had opened fire on the police sta-tions, had burned down Muslim houses, and had barricaded them-selves in the Armenian quarter. About fifteen thousand Armenian refugees from the countryside eventually joined the besieged rebels, creating overcrowding and near-starvation. Still, the Armenians were able to hold out for several weeks. The Turks used large cannons and made several attempts to storm the Armenian positions, but they were thrown back with heavy losses. The fighting was fierce. "Nobody gave quarter nor asked for it," wrote the South American soldier of fortune Rafael de Nogales, who served with the Turkish forces. "The Chris-tian or the Moor who fell into the enemy's hands was a dead man."[36] By the beginning of the fourth week of the siege the Armenians' sup-ply of ammunition had become very low, and they had suffered a large number of killed and wounded. The insurgents were eventually saved by the advancing Russian army. On May 17 the Turkish garrison had to retreat in the face of superior enemy forces; on May 20 Russian-Armenian units, followed a little later by Russian troops, entered Van.

The jubilant Armenians offered the commanding Russian gen-eral the keys to the city. In return, the Russian military authorities appointed Aram Manoukian, the head of the Armenian defense com-mittee, governor of the region. "Armenian political consciousness was stimulated," writes Hovannisian, "for the promised reward, an autono-mous Armenia under Russian protection, was within sight."[37] For the Turks, however, the fact that the rebellion of Van had succeeded with the help of the invading Russians was final proof that the Armenians were in league with Turkey's enemies; they were traitors against whom any retribution would be fully justified. Turkish hostility toward the Armenians was further increased as a result of the well-documented deeds of vengeance committed by the victorious insurgents. After the flight of the Turkish garrison, all important buildings in the city of Van were set on fire. Revenge for centuries of slavery under Turkish rule exploded in "a night of orgy, of saturnalia," wrote an eyewitness.[38] "It is impossible to even faintly depict the grandeur of the flaming night," Onnig Mukhitarian, the secretary of the Armenian defense council, recorded in his diary. "It would require the brush of a genius to put on canvas the crimson hue of the clouds created by the burning of Turkish military and administrative buildings, the dense smoke curling up from a dozen or more lairs of their unparalleled tyranny." The "burning and looting," he continued, went on for several days. "No authority could have curbed the uncontrollable vengefulness that had seized the Armenians of Van."[39]

According to Mukhitarian, none of the many Turkish prisoners taken were killed; but American and German missionaries on the spot tell a different story. After the departure of the Turks, writes the American missionary Clarence Ussher, the Armenians searched the city. "The men they put to death; the women and children they spared." Despite their protest, Dr. Ussher writes, this went on for two to three days. "They burned and murdered; the spirit of loot took possession of them, driving out every other thought."[40] The American mission compound, which earlier had sheltered five thousand Armenian refugees, now took in one thousand Turkish women and children. "These thousand fugitives," wrote Mrs. Ussher in a letter, "would all have been killed had we not opened our doors to them."[41] Another German missionary noted years later that the three days of Armenian revenge that she had witnessed in Van were difficult to forget. "The memory of these entirely helpless Turkish women, defeated and at the mercy of the victor, belongs to the saddest recollections from that time."[42]

The departing Turks had murdered their Armenian prisoners, including the wounded, and the Armenians now took their revenge. According to a Turkish Red Book published in 1916, the Armenians burned alive twenty-four sick Turkish soldiers who had been left behind at the military hospital.[43] This charge is not implausible. An Armenian boy, recalled Dr. Ussher, entered the Turkish military hospital and killed several patients who had been left behind.[44] Another eyewitness writes that some of the Armenians went to look for their wounded in the Turkish hospital, "and when they did not find them they were so infuriated that they killed some of the Turkish wounded and burned the building."[45] A Swiss missionary concluded with considerable

Armenians in Van were preparing for an uprising and w/ the advance of the Russians they were victorious for a while and sought revenge for what was done to them by inflicting the same atrocities on the muslims of the area.

understatement that the victorious Armenians of Van "did not act according to the provisions of the Geneva Convention and still less according to the words of Jesus Christ."[46]

The Turkish side, too, has made charges of atrocities. The grand vizier Said Halim told the American ambassador Henry Morgenthau in 1915 that the Armenian rebels had killed a hundred and twenty thousand Turks at Van.[47] A recent publication of the Assembly of Turkish American Associations alleges that after the Armenian takeover large numbers of Muslim inhabitants of the villages surrounding Van were murdered. "In one incident, Muslims from villages to the North of Van were herded into the village of Zeve, where all but a few of the approximately 3,000 Muslim villagers were killed. Similar incidents took place throughout the region."[48] Another publication by the same organization includes interviews with survivors of the Van region, who tell how the "Armenians skinned the men, castrated them, and raped and impaled the women." Women and girls threw themselves into rivers to escape their tormentors.[49] Many thousands of Armenians who feared punishment for the atrocities they had committed, writes a Turkish historian, fled with the retreating Russian troops into the Caucasus.[50]

Armenian writers, in contrast, speak of their people fleeing for their lives and being forced to leave all of their property.[51] They also make charges of massacres. According to Dadrian, after the Turks retook Van in August 1915 "some 55,000 Armenians in the outlying villages of Van were mercilessly hunted down and killed."[52] The figure of 55,000 murdered Armenians comes from Dr. Ussher, who reported that the Russians collected and cremated this number of dead Armenians in the province.[53] Accusations that wells ended up full of bodies and accounts of the suicide of violated women who drowned themselves in rivers appear in the writings of both sides. None of these allegations of atrocities are supported by hard evidence, but given the strong hatred that had developed between Armenians and Muslims by the spring of 1915 and in view of the known ferocity of the fighting, some of these charges may well be true.

Turkish authors maintain to this day that the rebellion at Van was designed and timed to facilitate the advance of the Russians. Whether intended for this purpose or not, the insurrection certainly had this effect. It forced the Turks to withdraw troops from their operations in the Caucasus region and Persia and move them to Van to suppress the rebellion.[54] Two German diplomats and officers on the scene, one of them friendly toward the Armenian cause, agreed that the insurrection was a premeditated undertaking. According to Scheubner-Richter, the German vice-consul in Erzurum, the Armenians at Van had been collecting arms for some time—at first only for defense against a possible massacre, "but later probably also for an armed uprising." Only in Van, he noted, did the Armenians prepare a revolution or insurrection; in other places it was a matter of self-defense.[55] The German staff officer Felix Guse, too, speaks of a "prepared undertaking."[56]

The Armenian position is that the insurrection, as Dadrian puts it, was aimed at preventing "the Turks from deporting and destroying the Armenian population of the city and its environs."[57] Two weeks earlier deportations had started in Cilicia. The new governor, Cevdet Pasha, was an avowed enemy of the Armenians and had started massacres in the villages of the province. The precipitating event is supposed to have been the murder of four Dashnak leaders, two of whom were members of parliament.[58]

Three American missionaries in Van—Clarence and Elizabeth Ussher and Grace Knapp—support the Armenian version of events. "Although the Vali calls it a rebellion," wrote Mrs. Ussher in her diary on the day the fighting started, "it is really an effort to protect the lives and homes of the Armenians."[59] Grace Knapp wrote that the governor had "planned a general massacre of his Armenian subjects."[60] The Russian foreign minister, Serge Sazonov, in a cable to his ambassador in London on May 15, 1915, expressed the view that the uprising undoubtedly had been the result of a bloodbath wreaked by the Turks.[61] The Englishman C. F. Dixon-Johnson, however, writing in 1916, saw "good and sufficient reasons for believing that the Armenians themselves commenced the troubles by rising in rebellion." The defeat of the Turkish army in the Caucasus and the absence of the greater part of the local garrisons and gendarmerie provided a propitious moment for the plans of the revolutionaries.[62] More recently Dyer has thought it "probable that Cevdet Pasha must bear most of the blame," though he added that he was "by no means entirely certain that some Armenians in Van did not have plans for a rising."[63] The organizers of the uprising for obvious reasons did not reveal their true intentions to anyone outside their own circle, so it is likely that the real causes of the insurrection will remain in dispute.

ARMENIAN SUPPORT FOR THE ALLIED WAR EFFORT

In August of 1914 (some sources give an earlier date), the Dashnaks held their eighth congress at Erzurum. There exists no documentary record of the proceedings of this gathering, which appears to have been secret, and Armenians and Turks report different conclusions. With war about to break out, representatives of the Young Turks are supposed to have made the following proposition to the Dashnaks:

> If the Armenians—the Turkish as well as the Russian Armenians— would give active cooperation to the Turkish armies, the Turkish government under a German guarantee would promise to create after the war an autonomous Armenia (made up of Russian Armenia and the three Turkish vilayets of Erzurum, Van and Bitlis) under the suzerainty of the Ottoman Empire.[64]

The Dashnaks, Hovannisian writes, agreed to support the government in a war with Russia but turned down the offer to foment rebellion among the Russian Armenians.[65] According to a Turkish source, it was a representative of the Dashnaks who approached the governor of Erzurum with this demand: "Should the Ottoman Government declare war on Russia and attack Caucasia, the Ottoman Government must make a concrete promise on the establishment of Armenia in order to propagate the arrangement for cooperation of the Armenians there with Turkey."[66]

The commander-in-chief of the Ottoman army reported that the Dashnaks at the Erzurum congress had adopted the following plans:

1. To preserve loyalty in tranquillity pending the declaration of war, but to carry on with the preparations for arming with weapons being brought from Russia and others to be obtained locally.
2. If war is declared Armenian soldiers in the Ottoman Army will join the Russian army with their arms.
3. If the Ottoman Army advances to remain calm.
4. Should the Ottoman army then retreat or come to a standstill position, to form armed guerilla bands and begin programmed operations behind army lines.[67]

A critic of the Dashnaks asserts that the Turkish Dashnaks did not keep their promises of loyalty to the Turkish cause and thus created a very dangerous situation for the Turkish Armenians. The "fate of two millions of their co-nationals in Turkey might not have proved so disastrous, if more prudence had been used by the Dashnag leaders during the war."[68] According to Yalman, the Turkish government "warned the Armenian leaders in Constantinople that the whole Armenian community would be held responsible, in case Armenian revolutionary organizations took any hostile action."[69] It is known that Minister of War Enver sent a personal note to the Armenian patriarch, in which he asked him to restrain the militants and their expressions of support for the Allies.[70] According to Ambassador Morgenthau, Enver told him repeatedly of warnings conveyed to the Armenian patriarch that "if the Armenians made any attack on the Turks or rendered any assistance to the Russians while the war was pending, he will be compelled to use extreme measures against them."[71]

After the outbreak of war between Turkey and Russia, Tsar Nicholas II personally visited the Caucasus front and conferred with Armenian leaders. Catholicos Gevorg V, the supreme head of the Armenian church, praised the Russian monarch and expressed regret that no political changes had been achieved despite the benevolence shown to the Armenians by Russia. "The salvation of the Turkish Armenians is possible only by delivering them from Turkish domination and by creating an autonomous Armenia under the powerful protectorate of great Russia." The tsar replied: "Tell your flock, Holy Father, that a most brilliant future awaits the Armenians." Hovannisian, who reports this exchange, comments: "Though soothing and comforting to the political mind of the Armenians, such statements disturbed the few who feared that the declarations would only deepen the suspicion of the Ittihad government toward its Armenian subjects."[72]

Soon after the Erzurum congress the Russian branch of the Dashnaks began to organize volunteers to fight the Turks on the Caucasus front. Most of the volunteers were Russian subjects, exempt from military service; but some of them came from as far as America and Western Europe, and Turkish Armenians, too, began to cross the border to join these units. An Armenian source put the total number of these volunteers at fifteen thousand.[73] According to one of his biographers, the famous Armenian military commander Andranik had arrived in the Caucasus on August 2 and in a meeting with General Mishlayevsky, commander of Russian forces in the Caucasus, pointed out "the routes through which the Russian army should advance on Turkey."[74] In addition to the volunteer detachments, led by veteran Armenian revolutionary figures such as Andranik, Dro (Igdir Drasdamat Kanayan), and Garo, about a hundred and fifty thousand Armenians served in the regular Russian armies.

The Russian government is supposed to have furnished a large sum of money for the provision of arms and training for Turkish Armenians,[75] though the exact number of Turkish Armenians who joined the Russian forces is not known. Turkish sources speak of fifteen thousand to fifty thousand.[76] Pro-Armenian authors cite smaller numbers. Souren Aprahamian states that General Andranik "commanded seven to eight thousand Turkish Armenian volunteers."[77] Among the several thousand Armenian volunteers, writes Dadrian, were only "a few hundred former Ottoman subjects."[78] In the eyes of the Turks the distinction was unimportant. As they saw it, the Armenian people the world over had thrown in their lot with the Allied cause and were arrayed against them in a fateful struggle.

One of the first Turkish Armenians to offer his services to the Russians was Garegin Pasdermadjian, the Dashnak revolutionary who had participated in the seizure of the Ottoman bank in 1896, later had become the Armenian deputy for Erzurum in the Turkish parliament, and was known by the revolutionary name of Armen Garo. He did so, recalled Pasdermadjian in his memoirs, despite warnings from some of his comrades that his service with the Russians "could have negative effects for the Armenians in Turkey."[79] Many Turkish Dashnaks are said to have expressed serious fears of a large-scale massacre.[80]

Armenian volunteer units contributed to the success of the Russian winter offensive. Turkish troops attacking on the Caucasus front at first had been very successful, but they were ill-prepared for the harsh winter in the high mountains and soon had to retreat amidst heavy losses. Of the original ninety thousand men in Enver's Third Army, only twelve thousand came back alive. The others were killed, captured, died of hunger and disease, or froze to death.[81] By January 4, 1915, Enver had to admit defeat, and he is supposed to have blamed the disastrous outcome on the treacherous activities of the Armenians.[82] The major factor in the Turkish rout, of course, was the lack of preparedness for a winter campaign. Still, the Armenian volunteer units, organized in six legions of battalion size each and reaching a total of eight thousand to ten thousand men, were of significant benefit to the Russians. Familiar with the rugged mountainous terrain, they acted primarily as scouts, guides, and advance guards. At the battle of Sarikamis, which marked the final defeat of Enver's offensive, their dedicated and courageous service drew the praise of Russian military commanders and even of the tsar.[83]

The Armenian volunteer detachments coming from Russian territory, the Turks charge, were joined by Armenian deserters from the Ottoman army, who destroyed bridges, raided convoys, and did everything possible to facilitate the Russian advance.[84] A historian close to the Dashnaks appears to confirm this charge when he speaks of guerrilla fighters in the Caucasian campaign who distributed arms to the peasants and thus saved many lives. Eventually, he writes, "the mountains swarmed with Armenian irregulars."[85] A French military historian, too, links the Ottoman Armenian volunteers to the partisans who attacked isolated Turkish units.[86] Pasdermadjian noted with pride that the Armenian resistance movement in the summer of 1915 tied down five Turkish divisions and tens of thousands of Kurds, who therefore were not able to fight the Russians on the Caucasus front.[87] Not surprisingly, the Turks eventually came to consider the Armenians a fifth column and decided to take decisive measures to put an end to these treasonable actions. Ambassador Morgenthau reported to Washington on July 10, 1915, that "because Armenian volunteers, many of them Russian subjects, have joined Russian Army in the Caucasus and because some have been implicated in armed revolutionary movements and others have been helpful to Russians in their invasion of Van district, terrible vengeance is being taken."[88] The Turkish position is that the issue was not revenge but national survival in a situation of extreme danger.

Threats of an Armenian insurrection were also a worrisome problem for the Turks in Cilicia. The first outbreak of violence took place in Zeitun, an Armenian town in the mountains northwest of Marash that had kept its independence well into the nineteenth century and was the center of a strong Hunchak organization. During the Turkish mobilization none of the inhabitants of Zeitun accepted enlistment in the army, and by the end of 1914 clashes between Armenian bands and gendarmes had taken place. On February 23, 1915, the French ambassador in Moscow reported that representatives of an Armenian revolutionary group in Zeitun had arrived in the Caucasus. Almost fifteen thousand men, the emissaries declared, were ready to attack Turkish lines of communication, but they lacked guns and ammunition. The commander of the Russian Caucasus army wanted to know whether British and French warships could bring them arms via the port of Alexandretta.[89] The British rejected this idea as impracticable because of the difficulty of transporting arms and ammunition into the interior. They suggested that if the Russians thought that the Armenian insurgents were of military value to them they should supply them through Black Sea ports under their control.[90]

In early April of 1915 Djemal Pasha, the commander of the Turkish Fourth Army, reported that "bandits staged an armed attack against a gendarmerie detachment carrying ammunition to Zeytun."[91] Assaults upon the local army barracks and the arrival of Turkish reinforcements followed. Eventually the Armenians retreated to a monastery on the outskirts of town and from there into the mountains. Armenian sources essentially confirm these accounts. Young Armenians, after attacking an army convoy carrying arms, had succeeded in killing five hundred soldiers who had pursued them. Eventually the rebels, facing twenty thousand Turkish troops, took refuge in the mountains.[92] An Armenian woman from Zeitun told the American journalist George Schreiner that armed Armenians, hearing that the British and French had taken Constantinople, had attacked the barracks of the Turkish battalion stationed in the town. After holding their own for two days they finally had to flee into the mountains.[93] Following the end of the fighting, the more than twenty thousand Armenian inhabitants were forced to leave the town. According to an Armenian pastor living in the region, Armenian guerrillas continued to operate in the mountains "for the whole four years of the war and caused the Turkish army much trouble."[94]

A still more serious threat to the Turkish military position in Cilicia came from outside the country. In December 1912 Catholicos Gevorg V had appointed the prominent Egyptian Armenian Boghos Nubar to head the Armenian National Delegation, which functioned as liaison with the Western Allies. After the outbreak of war, Boghos Nubar began to raise funds for Armenian volunteers in the Caucasus campaign. He also offered the help of the Turkish Armenians for a landing in Cilicia. Late in 1914 British and French warships bombarded the harbor of Alexandretta and other coastal points. Following these attacks, and especially after the Allied offensive at the Dardanelles had bogged down in the spring of 1915, the Armenians had hopes that the Allies would open a second front by landing troops at Alexandretta or Mersina. Such a force, it was believed, could cut the Baghdad railway (running only forty-five miles away from the coastline) and thus paralyze the Turkish forces in Mesopotamia and Palestine, whose supplies depended upon this railroad. Boghos Nubar assured Sir John Maxwell, the British commander in Egypt, that his compatriots in Cilicia would greet the British soldiers as liberators and would offer them "perfect and total support." All they needed was guns.[95] A similar assessment was made by the German consul in Adana. He had not come across any evidence of an Armenian conspiracy, he reported on March 13, 1915; but if the English or French carried out a successful landing, "they will be received with enthusiasm by all Christians."[96] About a month later the Turkish authorities accused several Armenians in the town of Dört Yöl (about twenty miles from Alexandretta) of having passed valuable information to Allied warships, and some were executed.[97]

Offers of military help soon also poured in from other parts of the Armenian diaspora. In early March of 1915 the Dashnak organization in Sofia proposed to land twenty thousand Armenian volunteers in Cilicia. Some ten thousand were to come from the Balkans, and another ten thousand from the United States. The volunteers knew the countryside and could count on the support of the local population.[98] The Armenian National Defense Committee of America in Boston informed the British foreign secretary on March 23, 1915, that after dispatching volunteers to the Caucasus it was now making "preparations for the purpose of sending volunteers to Cilicia, where a large section of the Armenian population will unfurl the banner of insurrection against Turkish rule, a circumstance which would greatly help to disperse and to prevent the onward march of the Turks against Egypt." The Defense Committee proposed to equip and arm the volunteers. The British and French government, it was hoped, would supply them with ammunition and artillery.[99] On July 24, 1915, the Armenian National Defense Committee in Cairo once again offered to Sir John Maxwell to undertake a landing on the shores of Cilicia.

> Allow us to state that the military campaign in question would require a force of 10,000 to 12,000 fighters to occupy Alexandretta, Mersin, and Adana (together with the defiles) and ensure the collaboration of 10,000 Armenian volunteers and the total Armenian population of the region. Because under those probable circumstances, it would be possible to rely on the 25,000 Armenian insurgents in Cilicia and on the more to come from nearby provinces. This formidable force of close to 50,000 would even be able to advance well beyond the borders of Cilicia and thus become an asset for the Allies. It would be just the reiteration of an oft repeated truth, when we state that in Turkey only the Armenians of Armenia and Cilicia are the inhabitants with obvious insurrectional tendencies against Turkish rule.[100]

The British took a dim view of these proposals. The Army Council had little confidence in the military ability of the Armenian volunteers or of the local insurgents. There was concern about the difficulty of transporting, training, and equipping the volunteers; it was enough of a challenge, they noted, to find a sufficient number of rifles for the British forces.[101] Moreover, and probably most importantly, in February 1915 a decision had been made to use all available military assets for the attack against the Dardanelles.[102] Summing up British policy on the subject, Sir Harold Nicolson noted in a minute of November 15, 1915, that "geographical, strategic and other reasons would render it impossible for the Allied troops to render such assistance to Armenian insurgents as would save them from extermination the moment the movement was discovered."[103] The evidence thus clearly contradicts Turkish assertions that the Allies incited the Armenians to rebel or ordered them to rise up.[104]

Boghos Nubar for some time had been concerned that the existence of Armenian volunteer units would provide the Turks with an excuse to commit atrocities, and he eventually concluded that in order to prevent Turkish retaliation Armenians should join the Allied forces rather than form a separate unit.[105] Other Armenians, however, kept pressing for a landing in Cilicia, hoping against hope that such an operation would hamper, if not halt, the deportations that were underway in all of Anatolia by the summer of 1915. "The mass deportations," wrote the Armenian National Defense Committee in Cairo to Sir John Maxwell on July 20, "will cause the annihilation of the Armenian population of the region if effective protection is not extended to them soon."[106] When the British showed themselves unwilling to reconsider their rejection of an Armenian volunteer force, the Armenians shifted their pressure to the French. On September 2 a French warship had rescued more than four thousand Armenians who had taken refuge on the mountain of Musa Dagh on the Mediterranean coast and had fought off Turkish troops for fifty-three days. Unwilling to sit idle in an Egyptian refugee camp, the leaders of this group approached the French and requested the formation of an Armenian unit that would fight alongside the French against the Turks.

The French government had its eyes on gaining a foothold in Syria and Cilicia, but pressed by the Germans they had been able to send no more than a small detachment of colonial troops to the Turkish front. Hence the Armenian offer of assistance had its appeal. During the fall of 1915 prolonged negotiations took place between the British and French about the formation and training of such a force; and on February 2, 1916, the French signed an agreement with the Armenian National Defense Committee in Egypt that provided for the creation of a unit of "irregular troops." Four hundred men from the refugees of Musa Dagh were to form the nucleus of this formation, but other Armenian volunteers could also join. The unit was to be employed "only in the districts of Cilicia and Lesser Armenia with which the Armenians are as natives familiar: and that at the earliest opportunity that may seem advisable from a military point of view." The Armenians had to agree that "the Allied Governments are free of any moral responsibility for reprisals or acts of violence on the part of the Turks that may be regarded as reprisals for the employment of these volunteers."[107] The British were asked to agree to the use of Cyprus for the training of the Armenian volunteer force, and this consent was finally given in September of 1916. Boghos Nubar also decided to go along, though he urged discretion.[108]

The French were well aware that the Armenians were hoping to use the military contribution of the volunteers to strengthen their claims for an independent Armenian state. Hence the French hedged when Boghos Nubar sought assurances that after the Allied victory the "national aspirations" of the Armenian people would be satisfied.[109] The same sentiment of caution may explain why, when the French Ministry of War formally established the new formation on November 15, 1916, it was given the name Légion d'Orient rather than Armenian Legion and why the volunteer unit had to wait nearly two years before it saw action. The French also opened the new unit to Syrians and Arabs, thus further diluting its special Armenian character.

Not surprisingly, Armenian recruiters were the most active; and by 1918 some four thousand Armenians from all over the world had arrived in Cyprus for military training. In July of that year the Légion d'Orient, composed of three battalions of Armenians and one company of Syrians, was finally sent to Palestine, where it participated in the victorious offensive of Gen. Edmund Allenby in Palestine and Syria. After the signing of the armistice of Mudros on October 30, 1918, the French sent the three Armenian battalions (now called the Armenian Legion and possessing its own flag) to occupy Cilicia. There the Armenian Legion quickly began to engage in acts of revenge against the Turkish population. Turkish authors speak of atrocities such as "raping the women, killing innocent women and children, and putting fire to the mosques after having filled them with local Muslims," but even outside observers concede that the Armenian troops committed numerous crimes.[110] Eventually the legion was disbanded, though many of its members stayed in Cilicia.

The extent to which the Turks knew of the Allied discussions and plans for an Armenian landing and insurrection in Cilicia is not clear. Coordinated for the most part by Boghos Nubar, appeals for enlistment and financial assistance to send volunteers to the Caucasus had appeared in European and American newspapers, though the recruitment for the Légion d'Orient was carried out more discreetly. In early May 1916 a Turkish court-martial in Constantinople, after having tried Boghos Nubar in absentia, sentenced the Armenian statesman to death for having collaborated with the French, English, and Russians and having raised funds for Armenian volunteers in the Caucasus.[111] The Turks also caught agents that the British had landed on the coastline of Cilicia and thus may have learned some details about the Allied plans.[112] Whatever the degree of Turkish knowledge, the Armenians' eagerness to fight alongside the Allies and their promise of an insurrection by local revolutionaries certainly speak for themselves. The fact that the Armenian volunteers actually joined the fighting against the Turks in Palestine and Syria only near the end of the war in the summer of 1918 is irrelevant in this context: as we have seen, the delay was not due to any Armenian restraint.

After the war had ended and at the Paris peace conference in 1919 the Armenians talked with pride about the important contribution they had made to the Allied victory. In a letter written on October 29, 1918, to French foreign minister Stephen Pichon, Boghos Nubar asserted that the Armenians in fact had been belligerents since they had fought alongside the Allies on all fronts. Between six hundred and eight hundred volunteers had served on the western front with the French Foreign Legion, and only forty were still alive; three battalions had taken the field in the Middle East and had been cited by General Allenby for their courage; and a hundred and fifty thousand had fought in the Russian army and had held the front in the Caucasus after the Russians had dropped out of the war in 1917.[113] The Armenians therefore deserved their independence and their own country. "We have fought for it. We have poured out our blood for it without stint. Our people have played a gallant part in the armies that have won the victory." Armenia, Boghos Nubar told the peace conference on March 8, 1919, had been devastated by the Turks "in retaliation for our unflagging devotion to the cause of the Allies."[114]

This rhetoric undoubtedly was designed to win the support of the peace conference for an independent Armenia, and in this respect the Armenians were not unduly modest. Encouraged by the promises of liberation from the Turkish yoke made by British prime ministers Herbert Henry Asquith and David Lloyd George, they claimed not only the six eastern provinces of Anatolia but also Cilicia in order to have a port on the Mediterranean. In none of these provinces did the Armenians constitute a majority of the population, and these extravagant demands therefore required powerful supporting arguments. Still, the essential facts put forth by the Armenian delegation were correct. The Armenians had supported the Allies in a variety of ways; and if more of them did not actually get to do battle against the hated Turkish foe it was not for want of trying. Authorized by their highest authorities, the commitment of the Armenians to the Allied cause had been strong, and they had expressed it in word and deed both during and after the war. In July 1915 Boghos Nubar had assured the British high command in Egypt that a landing in Cilicia would have the support of "the total Armenian population of the region," and from all we know this was not an idle boast. In eastern Anatolia, too, as we have seen, Armenian assistance to the Russians had been extensive. None of this can serve to justify what the Turks did to the Armenians, but it provides the indispensable historical context for the tragedy that ensued. Given this context, the Armenians can hardly claim that they suffered for no reason at all. Ignoring warnings from many quarters, large numbers of them had fought the Turks openly or played the role of a fifth column; not surprisingly, with their backs against the wall, the Ottomans reacted resolutely, if not viciously.

THE PUNISHMENT OF EXCESSES

Turkish authors have admitted that the deportations were accompanied by regrettable excesses, which deprived the deportees of their property and led to the killing of defenseless men, women, and children. Some of these killings are said to have been the result of the strong hatred between Muslims and Armenians; in other instances local officials condoned the murders. However, they insist, the Ottoman government did what it could to halt these excesses. "The government arrested those who were responsible for this, as far as it was able to determine the culprits and sent them to the martial law court. Quite a few of them were executed."[115]

Talaat Pasha himself acknowledged the occurrence of crimes against the deportees. In his posthumous memoirs the wartime Ottoman minister of the interior spoke of abuses and atrocities:

> I admit that the deportation was not carried out lawfully everywhere. In some places unlawful acts were committed. The already existing hatred among Armenians and Mohammedans, intensified by the barbarous activities of the former, had created many tragic consequences. Some of the officials abused their authority, and in many places people took the preventive measures into their own hands and innocent people were molested. I confess it. I confess, also, that the duty of the Government was to prevent these abuses and atrocities, or at least to hunt down and punish their perpetrators severely.[116]

The documentary record confirms that Talaat Pasha was aware of these excesses at the time that they occurred. In a message to Diarbekir province sent on June 29, 1915, Talaat Pasha expressed his concern about the massacres of Armenians that had occurred in the province (though his main interest in this dispatch appears to have been the protection of non-Armenian Christians):

> It has been reported to us that the Armenians of the province of Diyarbekir, along with other Christians, are being massacred, and that some 700 Armenians and other Christians, were recently slaughtered in Mardin like sheep after having been removed from the city through nightly operations. The number of people thus far slain through such massacres is estimated to be 2,000. It is feared that unless these acts are stopped definitely and swiftly the Muslim population of the region too may proceed to massacre the general Christian population. The political and disciplinary measures...adopted against the Armenians are absolutely not to be extended to other Christians as such acts are likely to create a very bad impression upon public opinion. You are ordered to put an immediate end to these acts lest they threaten the lives of the other Christians indiscriminately....Keep us informed of the true state of the matter.[117]

As Ambassador Morgenthau reported to Washington on May 2, 1915, Talaat had told him that "instructions had been sent by the Porte to provincial authorities to protect all innocent people from molestation and that any official who disobeyed these orders would be punished."[118] On August 28 Talaat repeated this warning: "In cases where the emigrants will be the object of an attack whether in the camps or during their journey, stop the assailants immediately and refer the case to the court martial with particulars." Those who accepted bribes or abused women were to be dismissed, court-martialed, and severely punished.[119] A similar order addressed to the governors of the provinces, issued on August 29, stressed that the aim of the Armenian relocations was the prevention of activities against the government; the "decision is not intended to destroy innocent people." The order provided for the prosecution of all those "who attack the convoys, and those who engage in robberies, and who commit rape, succumbing to bestial feelings." The provinces and districts were to be held responsible for any such incidents.[120] On September 2 the German ambassador, Prince Ernst Wilhelm Hohenlohe-Waldenburg, who had been given copies of these orders, reported to Berlin that Talaat had told him of his intention to proceed to the provinces as soon as the military situation allowed it, "in order to supervise the conscientious implementation of these orders."[121] On December 18, after his return from Anatolia, Talaat told ambassador Paul von Wolff-Metternich that he had taken comprehensive measures to ensure that offenses against the property and life of the Armenians would be punished severely. More than twenty persons found guilty of such offenses had been executed.[122]

The same acknowledgment of excesses can be found in a Turkish white paper of February 1916 that was distributed by the Ottoman government to the foreign legations in Constantinople on March 1. Entitled "The Truth about the Armenian Revolutionary Movement and the Measures Taken by the Government," it asserted that in order to assure the tranquillity and security of the country it had been necessary to transfer the Armenians to secure locations. "During the application of this measure, the Armenians were sometimes victims of regrettable abuses and violence," made "inevitable because of the profound indignation of the Moslem population against the Armenians who tried by revolution and treason to place in danger the existence of the very country of which they were citizens." In one case, several gendarmes guarding a convoy had even been "killed by the furious population." However, the government had taken all possible steps to protect the lives and property of the Armenians.[123]

On May 5, 1916, Talaat Pasha told a special correspondent of the *Berliner Tageblatt* in an interview that he knew that Armenian deportees had been massacred. "Unhappily bad officials, into whose hands the execution of these orders [deportation] had been committed, went into unreasonable excesses in doing their duty." These tragic events, he added, "have caused me more than one sleepless night."[124] In a report to the annual meeting of the CUP in late September of that year, Talaat is reported to have admitted the same excesses and mentioned the formation of commissions of inspection.[125] And in a speech at the last congress of the CUP on November 1, 1918, he again acknowledged "incidents," though he argued that these had been exaggerated by the Armenian and Greek press. "Many officials used force and violence more than was necessary. In many areas some innocent people unjustly fell victim. I admit this."[126]

The sincerity with which Talaat Pasha expressed these regrets and the forthrightness with which he responded to the excesses committed against the Armenians have been questioned—at the time as well as later. On September 3, 1915, the Austrian ambassador, who had been told of Talaat's order forbidding attacks on convoys, expressed his suspicion that this could represent an attempt to mislead foreign ambassadors. It remained to be seen whether this decree, if it was really issued, would be implemented.[127] The German consul in Adana, too, spoke of a "bold deception," since the decrees of late August were soon superseded by a second order that annulled the earlier provisions.[128] More recently, Taner Akcam has spoken of Talaat Pasha's two-track system in which publicly issued orders were later canceled by special emissaries or telegrams.[129] The evidence to substantiate such a system is slim. Ambassador Hohenlohe thought that Talaat's orders had failed to achieve their effect because of the arbitrary rule of the provincial authorities.[130] Or perhaps it was just the usual Turkish habit to assume that something would happen after an order had been nicely put down on paper.

As regards Djemal Pasha, commander of the Turkish Fourth Army in Syria and Palestine and another top CUP leader, there is reliable evidence that he took steps to prevent violence against the Armenians and actually punished transgressors. The German consul in Aleppo, Walter Rössler, reported on April 1, 1915, that a decree issued by Djemal Pasha on March 29 had forbidden private individuals to interfere with governmental affairs. Every Muslim who attacked an Armenian would face a court-martial.[131] Later that year Djemal Pasha proved that he meant to enforce this order. Two Turkish officers, Cerkez Ahmed and Galatali Halil, were implicated in atrocities against Armenian deportees in the *vilayet* of Diarbekir and were held responsible for the murder of two Armenian members of parliament (Krikor Zohrab and Seringulian Vartkes). At the request of Djemal they were arrested the moment they came into territory under his jurisdiction, tried by a court-martial in Damascus, and sentenced to be hanged.[132]

There are other examples of Djemal Pasha's efforts to punish those responsible for atrocities against the Armenians. After the transit camp at Islahia (north of Aleppo) had been the scene of repeated attacks by Kurds and women and children had been killed, Djemal ordered severe measures against the culprits; several Kurds who were caught were hanged.[133] On February 15, 1916, the Austrian consul in Damascus, Karl Ranzi, reported that due to the intervention of Djemal Pasha an officer of the gendarmerie was executed for serious offenses against the honor and property of Armenian refugees there.[134] Even Dadrian, who does not generally praise CUP leaders, concedes that Djemal Pasha was one of the few leading Ittihadists who "refused to embrace the secret genocidal agenda of the party's top leadership and whenever they could tried to resist and discourage the attendant massacres."[135] The other person credited by Dadrian with such a role is the commander of the Turkish Third Army, General Vehib Pasha, who in February 1916 is said to have court-martialed and hanged the commander of a gendarmerie unit and his accomplice responsible for the massacre of two thousand Armenians in a labor battalion.[136]

Turkish authors stress that the Ottoman government from an early date took note of the robbing and killing of Armenians being relocated and in the fall of 1915 therefore sent out commissions of inquiry to investigate these abuses. A special investigative council in the Ministry of War examined irregularities and performed this task until early 1918. According to the white paper of 1916, the government "promulgated a special law to safeguard property belonging to deported Armenians and it charged the application of this law to a commission composed of experienced and capable functionaries. It likewise sent inspection committees which made on-the-spot investigations and referred to court martials those whose guilt had been established."[137] The Turkish historian Kamuran Gürün, relying on an archival source, writes that 1,397 individuals were tried by military courts for offenses against Armenians and that some received the death penalty.[138]

The Turkish journalist Ahmed Emin Yalman (in a book published in 1930) questioned the effect of the investigations. "Some minor offenders were really punished; but those favoring the deportations being very influential in the Government, the whole thing amounted more to a demonstration rather than a sincere attempt to fix complete responsibility."[139] Dadrian, relying on copies of the reports of the commissions of inquiry preserved in the archives of the Armenian patriarchate in Jerusalem, asserts that the mandate of the commissions was limited to the misappropriation of property and that the matter of the massacres was not part of their investigative task. He quotes from several reports that indeed refer to plunder and fraud, though in one instance a report also speaks of the punishment of attacks against Armenians.[140] Edward Nathan, the American consul in Mersina, on November 6, 1915, mentions the arrival of an imperial commissioner "to investigate the abuses of local officials regarding the taking of the personal property of the deported Armenians."[141] The place in question saw no mass killings, so the fact that this investigation dealt only with the theft of Armenian property does not necessarily disprove the occurrence of investigations for killings in other places.

Talaat Pasha himself lends support to the argument that the investigations and consequent punishment were limited in scope. In his posthumous memoirs he writes that in "many places, where the property and goods of the deported people were looted, and the Armenians molested, we did arrest those who were responsible and punished them according to the law." However, he adds, although many of the guilty were punished, "most of them were untouched." This group of offenders included that large group of Turks who insisted that the Armenians be punished for the massacre of innocent Muslims and their help to the "Armenian bandits."

> The Turkish elements here referred to were short-sighted, fanatic, and yet sincere in their belief. The public encouraged them, and they had the general approval behind them. They were numerous and strong. Their open and immediate punishment would have aroused great discontent among the people, who favored their acts. An endeavor to arrest and punish all these promoters would have created anarchy in Anatolia at a time when we greatly needed unity....We did all we could, but we preferred to postpone the solution of our internal difficulties until after the defeat of our external enemies.[142]

Talaat's acknowledgment that most of the guilty remained unpunished does not distinguish between types of offenses. We do not learn from it whether the massacre of Armenians was punished less frequently than the unlawful appropriation of Armenian property. The documentary record has many references to the dismissal and punishment of officials who enriched themselves by seizing Armenian property, including governors.[143] However, practically all the punishments for killings that we know of took place in provinces under the jurisdiction of Djemal Pasha, whose record in this respect is unique, as we have seen. Turkish claims that the Ottoman government generally did what it could to investigate and prosecute crimes against the relocated Armenians thus appear to be less than convincing. The manner in which these prosecutions were implemented, as Talaat Pasha himself admitted, let most of the guilty escape and probably reached only a small number of those responsible for massacres.

ARMENIAN ATROCITIES: A CIVIL WAR WITHIN A GLOBAL WAR

The Turkish government and many Turkish historians argue that "the events of 1915 can best be described as a civil war within a global war."[144] In this civil war the number of Muslim deaths is said to have been far higher than the number of Armenian deaths. A Turkish-American publication issued in 1997 says that more than a million Muslims "lost their lives in intercommunal fighting."[145] According to the memoirs of Djemal Pasha published in 1922, one and a half million Turks and Kurds died as a result of Armenian atrocities.[146] The Turkish historian Mim Kemal Öke states that this figure is confirmed by statistical information gathered from documents discovered since Djemal Pasha made this estimate; in addition to massacres, however, he includes among the causes of death "migrations, diseases, war, famine and climatic conditions," most of which, of course, cannot be blamed on the Armenians.[147]

We do know that eastern Anatolia in 1915–16 was the scene of heavy combat and that Armenian volunteer and guerrilla units took an active part in these battles. Due to the changing fortunes of war and the seesawing front lines, the area was conquered and reconquered several times; hence the local population suffered greatly. No reliable information is available on the total number of civilian casualties that occurred during this period or on the role of Armenian atrocities in accounting for these losses. That the fighting was ferocious and little quarter was given by either side is mentioned in many sources. European missionaries in Van, as we have seen earlier, observed the brutalities committed by all parties to the conflict. Many allegations of atrocities are probably fabrications, and others involve gross exaggerations, but many are probably true. This is the larger context in which Turkish charges that the Armenians instigated a civil war and committed numerous atrocities must be evaluated.

Both Turks and Armenians have accused each other of horrible crimes while at the same time denying or minimizing the misdeeds committed by their own forces. In only a few instances have Armenian writers acknowledged the killing of Turkish civilians. In a memoir privately published in 1954, Haig Shiroyan recalled the sad fate of his hometown, Bitlis: "The Turks had killed and exiled all Armenians, looted their homes, burned down their houses. The Russian victorious armies, reinforced with Armenian volunteers, had slaughtered every Turk they could find, destroyed every house they entered. The once beautiful Bitlis city, under the retreating feet of defeated soldiers and incoming conquering armies, was left in fire and ruins."[148] Pastor Abraham Hartunian relates how Armenians in the village of Fundejak near the city of Marash, who faced deportation in late July 1915, "determined to rebel. Having disposed of about sixty Turks living in the village they were ready to fight for their lives."[149] The American relief worker Stanley Kerr, drawing on another Armenian source, confirms this massacre.[150] The pastor's choice of the word "dispose" to describe the killing of Turkish villagers is typical of Armenian writing, in which, as Dyer has correctly observed, "Muslim massacres of Christians are a heinous and inexcusable outrage; Christian massacres of Muslims are, well, understandable and forgivable."[151] Turkish writers, too, have said little about crimes committed by their compatriots, which has not prevented Western authors from dwelling on Turkish misdeeds while saying little about atrocities committed by Armenians. Turkish crimes, observed Arnold Toynbee in 1922, "are undoubtedly exaggerated in the popular Western denunciations, and the similar crimes committed by Near Eastern Christians in parallel situations are almost always passed over in silence."[152]

The Turkish side has published the testimony of Muslim villagers from the areas of Van, Bitlis, and Mush who are said to have survived Armenian massacres. Here is an example of the kind of experiences described in this book:

> I am from the Göllü village. The Armenians revolted when the army in Van retreated toward Erzurum. Our mothers and fathers were all slain by Armenians. My father, a gendarme, was among those killed. The villagers in Mollkasim, Amik, Sihayne, Göllü, Hidir, Kurtsatan, and Köprüköy were also murdered. Part of our village hid in Zeve and were later killed, but we were able to escape. Armenians tortured and inflicted all types of cruelties on the people they kidnapped. They cut up preg-

nant women and removed the unborn children with bayonets. They raided and burned all of the Muslim villages, murdering men, women, young and old.[153]

Similar accounts can be found in published documents from Turkish archives. A district governor reported on March 4, 1915, that local Armenians, in concert with Armenian volunteers in the Russian army, had murdered forty-two men and thirteen women in the village of Merhehu. They had raped, cut off breasts, burned a baby in an oven, and so forth.[154] Numerous reports tell of the destruction of mosques and other public buildings. According to the Turkish historian Salahi Sonyel, "the Dashnaktsutiun as a party bears a major portion responsibility, for it was often the leading force in perpetrating these massacres."[155] Nogales (a high-ranking South American officer in the Turkish army) states that when the Dashnak leader Pasdermadjian went over to the Russians he took with him "almost all the Armenian troops of the Third Army," only to return with them soon after, "burning hamlets and mercilessly putting to the knife all of the peaceful Musulman villagers that fell into their hands."[156] The Turkish journalist Yalman writes that within eighteen days almost the entire population of a hundred and forty thousand Muslims on the plain of Elashkird-Bayizid had been massacred by Armenian volunteer soldiers helped by local Armenians.[157] According to Felix Guse, both Russian and Turkish Armenians participated in these atrocities.[158]

Some allegations of massacres were made during and immediately after World War I.[159] The Austrian ambassador on August 19, 1915, wrote of "large-scale massacres of Turks" by Armenians that had taken place but added that it was not clear whether Turks or Armenians had started such killings.[160] At the main court-martial of the CUP leadership, the deputy prosecutor Resad Bey, seeking to justify the deportation of the Armenian community, charged that Armenian revolutionary bands in the provinces of Van, Bitlis, and Erzurum had massacred without mercy many thousands of women, children, and old people.[161] The Turkish senator Ahmed Riza, whom Dadrian praises as concerned about Armenian suffering and as a man who "valiantly challenged the Ittihadist power-wielders,"[162] in a memorandum dated March 17, 1919, called for an international inquiry into the crimes committed against the Muslim population by Armenian bands *before* the deportation of the Armenian community.[163]

Stronger evidence exists for the occurrence of Armenian atrocities during the last two years of the war. These crimes took place after the Armenian deportations and massacres of 1915–16 and therefore can be considered acts of revenge. Nevertheless, the large numbers and great cruelty of these killings prove that the Armenian side was fully capable of committing horrible deeds, and this finding lends some credibility to Turkish charges of earlier Armenian atrocities.

In January 1916 the Russians, led by advance guards of Armenian volunteers, took Diarbekir. "The Moslems who did not succeed in escaping," recalled the American missionary Grace Knapp, "were put to death."[164] According to Vatche Ghazarian, in July 1916 an Armenian volunteer unit "attacked seven Turkish villages, destroyed them, and killed the Turkish population. This attack had a two-fold purpose—to avenge hundreds of thousands of massacred Armenians, and to provide future security."[165] The special correspondent of the *Manchester Guardian*, M. Philips Price, in November 1916 spent several weeks with Russian-Armenian volunteers in the Lake Van area, during which time he observed the killing of several Kurdish villagers. This happened, he noted, because the Armenian volunteers saw "absolutely no difference between combatants and non-combatants."[166] One of the reasons for the eventual disbandment of the Armenian volunteer units is said to have been the charge that they were killing noncombatants in the occupied territories.[167]

A British political officer, Major E. W. C. Noel, reported on March 12, 1919, that after "three months touring through the area occupied and devastated by the Russian Army and the Christian Army of revenge accompanying them during the spring and summer of 1916, I have no hesitation in saying that the Turks would be able to make out as good a case against their enemies as that presented against the Turks." According to the unanimous testimony of local inhabitants and eyewitnesses, Noel wrote, the Russians, acting on the instigation and advice of the Nestorians and Armenians who were with them, had "murdered and butchered indiscriminately any Moslem of the civilian population who fell into their hands." There was "widespread wholesale evidence of outrages committed by Christians on Moslems." The destruction was enormous, and "anything more thorough and complete would be difficult to imagine."[168]

After the Russian revolution of March 1917 Russian soldiers deserted in large numbers. Most of the front lines from then on were held by Armenian units of the Russian army, who were joined by volunteers from the Turkish Armenian population.[169] The Turkish army was able to stage a successful offensive, and during the Armenian retreat numerous new atrocities were committed. When Turkish forces entered the city of Erzinjan in February 1918, they found a destroyed city and hundreds of bodies in wells and shallow graves. An Armenian author writes that the Armenian fighters who were forced to withdraw from the city, intent upon vengeance, fell upon the Turkish homes and "committed extraordinary acts."[170] A Turkish report speaks of people being forced into buildings that then were set on fire.[171] Erzurum fell soon thereafter; and there, too, large numbers of Muslim dead, including women and children, were discovered. A Turkish source speaks of 2,127 male bodies that were buried during the first days after the fall of the city.[172] The pro-Armenian French author Yves Ternon acknowledges that, following the Russian abandonment of the Caucasus front, Armenians massacred the civilian population of Turkish villages and committed "unspeakable crimes."[173]

Several foreign observers who toured the region some time later confirmed the Armenian atrocities. A report by two American officers, Emory N. Niles and Arthur E. Sutherland (who visited eastern Anatolia in the summer of 1919 in order to ascertain the need for relief aid), noted that in the region from Bitlis to Trebizond

> the Armenians committed upon the Turks all the crimes and outrages which were committed in other regions by Turks upon Armenians. At first we were most incredulous of the stories told us, but the unanimity of the testimony of all witnesses, the apparent eagerness with which they told of wrongs done to them, their evident hatred of Armenians, and, strongest of all, the material evidence on the ground itself, have convinced us of the general truth of the facts, first that Armenians massacred Musulmans on a large scale with many refinements of cruelty, and second that the Armenians are responsible for most of the destruction done to towns and villages.[174]

An American military mission to Armenia, led by Maj. Gen. James G. Harbord, reported in 1920 that the "retaliatory cruelties [of the Armenians] unquestionably rivaled the Turks in their inhumanity."[175] Muslims and Christians, wrote the British military attaché in Constantinople in a book published in 1925, "showed themselves equally villainous in their bestialities. Whichever side got on top massacred the other."[176] Taken together with what we know about events in the city of Van and the conduct of the Armenian Legion in Cilicia, these reports make it likely that at least some of the Turkish charges are true.

The two large waves of Muslim refugees generated by the Russian advances into eastern Anatolia in the winter of 1914–15 and the summer of 1916 are another indication of the prevalence of Armenian atrocities. An Ottoman commission on refugees reported that more than eight hundred and fifty thousand Muslims had to flee their homes in order to escape the fury of the conqueror. These were the officially registered refugees, and the total number may have been more than a million.[177] Armenian units were especially feared and apparently were a major factor in the flight of the Muslim population. The great suffering of these refugees has often been ignored by Western authors. That so many thousands of people were desperate enough to be willing to face a future of deprivation and death lends support to the Turkish argument that these Muslim villagers abandoned their homes because they feared being mistreated and massacred by Armenian bands. German staff officer Guse writes that those who failed to flee were frequently abused and killed by the Russians and Armenians.[178]

Many of the refugees had to travel large distances on foot, and the mortality from starvation and disease was high. A Turkish report on the resettlement of refugees from the war zone claims that by the end of October 1916 as many as 702,900 refugees had been "resettled, fed, and given medical care as well as clothes."[179] The report conceded that road conditions and the lack of transportation vehicles had hampered care for the refugees, but this was a great understatement. The large exodus caught the government unprepared, and the help that was eventually organized for the most part came too late. Only a few provinces provided real care; in most places the refugees were simply abandoned to their fate.[180] This crisis was a repeat performance of the failure of resettlement of refugees from Tripoli and the Balkans in 1914.

According to observers on the scene, the fate of the refugees was nothing short of catastrophic. The Austrian consul in Samsun reported on April 7, 1917, that the lot of the refugees was going from bad to worse. The distribution of bread had ceased weeks ago; and cases of death by starvation, especially among women and children, were becoming ever more frequent.[181] The American missionary Henry Riggs in Harput described the miserable condition of the refugees, who had been put into the houses still left standing after the deported Armenians had abandoned them:

Crowding was beyond all reason, and yet it was impossible to find place for all without crowding them into small quarters. In some of the houses which were designed for a single family, there were as many as fifty or sixty people, and at night the floor was literally covered with prostrate people trying to get a little sleep. Lying on the floor close together with only covering enough of one blanket for half a dozen people, and often not even that, it is not to be wondered at that disease became terribly prevalent. Hunger and privation had weakened the people, and herded together as they were, epidemic swept through them and carried off many.[182]

Other missionaries report similar conditions. Grace Knapp in Bitlis observed that "hundreds of the fleeing Moslem civilians died from illness and exposure."[183] Ernst Christoffel in Malatia took note of the efforts of the Turkish authorities to feed the refugees but concluded that there was not enough food and that "thousands perished on the way."[184] The German consul in Sivas, Carl Werth, returning from a journey to Erzurum and Erzinjan, reported that most of the refugees, fleeing from the Armenians who robbed and massacred them, died on the roads of hunger and cold.[185] The McCarthys estimate that "more than half of those who survived the first battles and massacres must have become refugees. Judged on the basis of the general wartime mortality of the Ottoman eastern provinces, more than half of the internal refugees in eastern Anatolia must have died."[186]

Armenian authors have ignored or denied the allegations of atrocities. They have also taken strong exception to the Turkish argument that the conflict in Anatolia was a civil war in which the Muslim population suffered a larger number of deaths than the relocated Armenians. As a result of the conscription of all able-bodied males, argues Dadrian, the Armenians were "an impotent, defenseless minority" who were completely unable "to engage in armed conflict with the omnipotent and dominant Turks and the other Muslims ruling over them."[187] Dadrian also challenges the McCarthys' numbers, which are said to be based on a faulty method of computation.[188] Vigen Guroian maintains that the relative number of victims is irrelevant and has no bearing on the charge of genocide.[189]

Dadrian's suggestion that the Armenians were "an impotent, defenseless minority" unable to engage in armed conflict is both true and false. It is true that the Armenians were never strong enough to prevent the deportations, which in most instances were carried out without encountering any organized opposition. However, as we have seen earlier, the Turkish Armenians were able to field large numbers of fighters from their own ranks; and on the Caucasus front they had the support of thousands of Russian Armenians, both regular troops and volunteer detachments. These well-armed Armenian units were strong enough to keep large numbers of Turkish troops tied down. Fighting here was fierce and protracted, and many innocent Muslims died.

On a more basic level, Dadrian is correct in pointing out that Muslim and Armenian losses of life were incurred in different situations. "By juxtaposing two disparate orders of events he [McCarthy] creates the impression that by and large these losses are integral components of a unitary event, namely war, whether civil or international."[190] Some of the Armenians who perished during those years died as a result of battling their Turkish enemy in intercommunal fighting. But many others lost their lives as a result of the deportations and the massacres that accompanied this forcible dislocation of the Armenian community. The Turkish argument that the losses of both sides should be subsumed under the label "civil war" undoubtedly has the purpose of deflecting attention from this basic fact. The large number of confirmed Armenian atrocities is irrelevant in this connection and does not make the "civil war" argument any more convincing. Dissenting from the prevailing national consensus, the Turkish historian Selim Deringil has insisted that "colossal crimes were committed against the Armenian people in eastern Anatolia and elsewhere" and that "no historian with a conscience can possibly accept the 'civil war' line, which is a travesty of history."[191] I agree with this view.

THE RELEASE OF THE MALTA PRISONERS

Fearing the release of all Turkish war crimes suspects, on May 28, 1919, the British seized sixty-seven of the detainees and moved them to the islands of Mudros and Malta (see chapter 6); eventually all the prisoners were held on Malta. Other Turkish political figures were arrested following the full military occupation of Constantinople on March 16, 1920, and further arrests continued during the rest of the year. Yet British plans to try these prisoners for various crimes, including the massacre of the Armenians, never materialized; and all of the detainees eventually were released. The fact that the British never prosecuted the prisoners for the Armenian massacres is cited by Turkish authors as another proof that these massacres never took place or, at least, that the Ottoman regime should not be blamed for them. The release of the Malta prisoners, write Orel and Yuca, ended the "fable" of Turkish responsibility for Armenian massacres.[192]

By August 1920 the number of prisoners held on Malta had risen to 118, but the legal machinery for their prosecution was moving very slowly. The Commission of Responsibilities and Sanctions of the Paris peace conference had proposed that a trial of Turkish war criminals be held by an international or Allied tribunal. The charges were to include the mistreatment of British prisoners of war as well as the deportations and massacres of the Armenians. However, the Allies soon began to disagree on the importance of establishing such a court. The French and Italians hoped to secure a foothold in Anatolia and therefore did not want to antagonize the increasingly powerful Kemalists, who were strongly opposed to having Turkish nationals prosecuted by a foreign court for war crimes. The British meanwhile were anxious to obtain the release of thirty British officers, soldiers, and nationals taken hostage by the nationalists on March 16, 1920, and they therefore eventually were forced to consider an exchange of the Turkish prisoners for their own men. Differences of opinion also emerged between the law officers of the crown, the War Office, and the Foreign Office about the scope and urgency of the prosecutions.[193]

One of the factors slowing up the prosecution of the Turkish captives was the difficulty of obtaining relevant evidence with regard to the Armenian massacres. The section of the British high commissioner's office entrusted with the collection of evidence most of the time consisted of only one officer, Andrew Ryan, who had no authority to search for evidence and who could merely pass on information that came into his office. Article 228 of the Treaty of Sèvres, signed by the Turkish government on August 19, 1920, required that government to "to furnish all documents and information of every kind" in order to ensure the prosecution of offenders. Article 230 called for the surrender of persons "responsible for the massacres" committed on the territory of the Turkish empire.[194] The sultan's government was steadily losing ground to the nationalists who refused to recognize the validity of the treaty, however, and it therefore quickly became a dead letter. Hence the British, for the most part, were limited to information from the Armenian patriarchate and items of such dubious value as Andonian's *Memoirs of Naim Bey.* Other sources were the Constantinople newspapers and the published proceedings of the Turkish military tribunals.[195] An undated minute on the "Work of the Armenian-Greek Section" in the office of the British high commissioner noted that "almost all our information is derived from the 'Bureau d'information armenienne' [of the Armenian patriarchate] or from Armenians from the provinces who themselves come to the High Commission with their complaints."[196]

In a minute dated November 8, 1920, Harry Lamb, the officer at the British high commissioner's office responsible for making arrest recommendations, expressed his frustration over the unsatisfactory pace of the proceedings and the weakness of the available evidence. Not one of the Malta prisoners, he wrote, "was arrested on any evidence in the legal sense." No real dossiers existed. "It is safe to say that very few 'dossiers' as they now stand would not be marked 'no case' by a practical [practiced?] lawyer." The information available amounted to a prima facie case, but no more than that. In an implicit rejection of the authenticity of the Talaat Pasha telegrams contained in the Andonian-Naim book, Lamb noted the need for "Turkish official information, e.g. orders or instructions issued by the Central Government or the Provincial Administrations etc."[197]

The Turkish historian Bilal Simsir has argued that because the Turkish capital was under Allied occupation "all Ottoman State archives were easily accessible to the British authorities in Istanbul." Yet nothing incriminatory turned up.[198] The same argument was made more recently by the Turkish ambassador in Washington. The British appointed an Armenian, Haig Kazarian, to conduct a thorough examination of documentary evidence in the Ottoman archives, yet he was unable to discover evidence of complicity in massacres. "Proof could not be found because the acts complained of had not been committed."[199]

Armenian sources corroborate one part of this argument. Haigazn Kazarian indeed served as interpreter and archivist for the British occupation authority. According to the editor of the *Armenian Review,* he was given access to the Turkish government archives. However, the editor's claim that Kazarian "found a large number of highly valuable documents on the Turkish plan of extermination of the Armenians" is wrong,[200] for none of the material contained in Kazarian's book *Tseghasban Turkeh* (The Genocidal Turk), published in Armenian in Beirut in 1968 and excerpted in several issues of the *Armenian Review,* supports the charge of complicity by the Ottoman government or any other plan of extermination.

More importantly for the issue at hand, it is not clear how much access Kazarian or any other British employee actually had. According to the documentary record, the British never were able to search the

Turkish archives fully; nor did they have access to the evidence used by the Turkish courts-martial. British high commissioner Horace Rumbold noted with regret on March 16, 1921, that "since the Treaty [of Sèvres] has not yet come into force no sort of pressure could be brought on the Turkish Government or officials. Consequently no Turkish official documents are available." Rumbold went on to describe the difficulty of obtaining other evidence. Because of the lack of public security, travel to Constantinople was impossible, and therefore very few witnesses had come forward. "Of the male Armenian eye-witnesses to the massacres few indeed survive and among them there are practically no men of any education who are refugees in Constantinople." Those witnesses who had come forward had almost all done so under the promise of secrecy, because they feared for the safety of their relatives who might still be alive in Anatolia. "Up to the present," Rumbold concluded, "the Armenian Patriarchate has been the principal channel through which information has been obtained."[201]

An examination of the voluminous file listing the "accusations" against individual Malta detainees reveals the weakness of the legal case against them. For example, a note in the chart of Abbas Halim Pasha, minister of public works in 1915, stated: "No specific accusation has been made. He was a member of the cabinet which ordered the deportations entailing the massacre of hundreds of thousands of Christians."[202] Several other ministers and CUP officials similarly found themselves as prisoners of the British simply on account of the office they had held. Ziya Gökalp had been a member of the CUP central committee; the military court in Constantinople that had tried him had produced no evidence whatever implicating him in any wrongdoing, yet he wound up in Malta accused of "atrocities." The source of this accusation was not identified.[203] Ahmed Muammer Bey, the *vali* of Sivas, was also accused of atrocities, in his case on the basis of incriminating telegrams that his dossier referred to as "alleged to be translations of Turkish official telegrams."[204] Several dossiers include documents from the Andonian-Naim book.

Practically all of the information in the dossiers had come from Armenian sources, who, under the trauma of the deportations and massacres, were inclined to accept almost any allegation of Turkish guilt. Even the processing of the information in the Armenian-Greek section of the office of the high commissioner was in Armenian hands. Until he was no longer needed in November 1920, the head clerk and keeper of records in the section was an Armenian named A. Fenerdjian.[205] As mentioned earlier, another archivist was Haigazn Kazarian. For good reason none of the information laboriously collected by the section was considered legal evidence admissible before a British court of law.

In their search for evidence the British turned to the United States. On March 31, 1921, British ambassador A. Geddes in Washington was asked to contact the State Department and find out whether the U.S. government was in possession of any information that might be of value.[206] But on June 1 the ambassador reported his failure to find anything suitable. "I have made several inquiries at the State Department and to-day I am informed that while they are in possession of a large number of documents concerning Armenian deportations and massacres, these refer rather to events connected with perpetration of crimes than to persons implicated....From the description I am doubtful these documents are likely to prove useful as evidence in prosecuting Turks confined in Malta."[207] On July 13, after an embassy staff member had personally examined "a selection of reports from United States Consuls on the subject of the atrocities committed during the recent war" and had checked the files for any mention of forty-five Malta detainees accused of outrages against Armenians and other Christians, the ambassador sent a follow-up report, which again was negative:

> I regret to inform Your Lordship that there was nothing therein which could be used as evidence against the Turks who are being detained for trial at Malta. The reports seen, while furnishing full accounts of the atrocities committed, made mention, however, of only two names of the Turkish officials in question—those of Sabit Bey and Suleiman Faik Pasha—and in these cases were confined to personal opinions of these officials on the part of the writer, no concrete facts being given which could constitute satisfactory incriminating evidence.

American officials, the ambassador wrote, had expressed the wish that no information supplied by them be employed in a court of law. However, he added, this stipulation was really irrelevant, for "the reports in the possession of the Department of State do not appear in any case to contain evidence against these Turks which would be useful even for the purpose of corroborating information already in the possession of His Majesty's Government."[208]

The Turkish detainees on Malta repeatedly appealed to the governor of the island for their release. A petition of May 12, 1921, signed by forty-four of the prisoners, claimed that they had been the victims of "intrigues and denunciations" by political rivals and "Armenians and

Greeks of suspicious character who wanted to sell their services to the invaders in capacities of spies, secret agents, and interpreters."[209] What finally brought about the release of all of the prisoners was the shrewd maneuvering of Mustapha Kemal. After the victory of the nationalists in parliamentary elections and their successes against the French in Cilicia, on March 16, 1920, the Allies had taken full control of Constantinople and had detained prominent politicians and intellectuals considered to be sympathizers of the nationalist movement. "It is a good thing that we should arrest people from time to time," noted W. S. Edmonds in a foreign office minute of May 3, 1920, "for it will keep alive the wholesome effect of the occupation."[210] The Kemalists retaliated by seizing several British officers, including Lt. Col. Alfred Rawlinson, the brother of Lord Henry Rawlinson, commander-in-chief in India, and twenty-five other British soldiers and nationals. From this point on the Britons in Turkish custody came to drive British policy on the matter of the Malta detainees.[211]

Lengthy negotiations ensued to arrange a mutual release of prisoners. A partial exchange took place in May and June, but the release of the rest of the prisoners was still not resolved. For a time the British sought to exempt from release the eight detainees charged with mistreating British prisoners of war as well as those accused of atrocities against Christians; but as the negotiations dragged on pressure mounted for a deal that would free all Malta prisoners in exchange for all prisoners held by the nationalists. Lord Rawlinson asked the Foreign Office to save his brother, and the War Office as well as the governor of Malta supported this plea. There was fear that the British prisoners would not survive another harsh winter in captivity. The idea of holding a trial of Turks responsible for massacres of Armenians now was all but abandoned. A Foreign Office minute of July 20, 1921, noted: "We shall have to think twice trying the Turks. To do so might expose our people to barbarous reprisals."[212] On September 6 sixteen detainees escaped from Malta, thus further weakening British bargaining power. By September 20 both the Foreign Office and the law officers had agreed to an "all for all" exchange, for it was clear that the nationalists would settle for nothing less. On November 1 fifty-three Turkish captives were exchanged for the remaining British hostages.[213]

In the eyes of most Turkish authors the release of the prisoners of Malta accused of crimes against the Armenians supports their denial of Turkish responsibility for such crimes. "For once," write Orel and Yuca, "justice triumphed over propaganda."[214] Dadrian, however, speaks of "retributive justice [that] gave way to expediency of political accommodation."[215] The release of the Malta prisoners, writes Levon Marashlian, "was no indication of their innocence."[216]

Both sides, I believe, are correct in part. There can be little doubt that the main reason for the final release of the Turkish captives was the desire to obtain the freedom of the British hostages, and one can certainly call that a triumph of expediency. Nonetheless, it is a fact that the British were unable to find legal evidence against those alleged to have been involved in the Armenian massacres, and this outcome is not insignificant. Practically all of the relevant information available to them came from the Armenian patriarchate, hardly a disinterested party, and the British certainly were acting judiciously when they dismissed allegations such as those contained in the Naim-Andonian book as of no use in establishing the guilt or innocence of their prisoners.

"What the victorious Allies lacked," argues Dadrian, "was not so much evidence as probative evidence warranting the conviction of a criminal implicated by it."[217] Implicit in this appraisal is the view that the writing of history involves different standards of proof than a court trial, and this is certainly a correct observation. Still, the historian, too, cannot rely simply on allegations of guilt unsubstantiated by either authenticated documentary evidence or the testimony of credible and impartial witnesses. The failure of the British to locate evidence that could stand up in a court of law does not establish the innocence of the Malta prisoners, but neither can it be dismissed as unimportant. The occurrence of large-scale massacres is not disputed by anyone but a few Turkish historians who probably know better. At issue is the question of whether the Turkish officials imprisoned on the island of Malta are to be considered responsible for these massacres, and here the burden of proof is on the Armenians. As I see it, so far they have not been able to put forth evidence that could convince either a legal tribunal or a disinterested student of the history of these tragic events.

Part III

HISTORICAL RECONSTRUCTION
What We Know and What We Do Not Know

Chapter 8

The Sources

Despite the widespread destruction or disappearance of Turkish documents at the end of World War I, the sources available for a historical reconstruction of the tragic events of 1915–16 are extensive. During the 1980s the Turkish government began the release of archival materials; and since then both Turkish and Armenian authors have searched for and publicized a large quantity of documents. We have the reports of American, German, and Austrian consular officials as well as the testimony of Protestant missionaries who witnessed the deportations in Anatolia. Many members of the German military mission have composed recollections. Last but not least, numerous Armenian survivors of the deportations have written their memoirs. All this yields a rich mosaic of information, and in many instances it is possible to augment or confirm the trustworthiness of reports by checking a source against one or more other sources. Regrettably, though not surprisingly, the information available is of varied reliability, and some aspects of the events in question are better illuminated than others. In what follows I review the usefulness and significance of the most important primary sources available for the analysis of the deportations and massacres.[1]

TURKISH ARCHIVES

Because of the renewed interest in the Armenian massacres during the last twenty years and the demands of Western scholars for access to Turkish documentary evidence, the Turkish government in 1982 began the transliteration (into modern Turkish) and the publication of documents relating to the Armenian question. Three volumes of documents have also been translated into English and published in 1982–83 and 1989.[2] The quality of the translation is poor, and the publication had a pronounced political motive. As the editor noted in the introduction to volume 2 of the series:

> Documents published herein again reveal in a catalogue the Armenian
> atrocities and massacres perpetuated on Turkish people during the First
> World War years. The documents also very explicitly demonstrate the
> just and fair treatment accorded by the Ottoman administration to all
> citizens, irrespective of their religion, race or any other consideration.[3]

The documents released focus almost exclusively on Armenian rebellious activities. Hardly any documents are included on the relocations
or the confiscation of Armenian property.

In January 1989 the Turkish foreign minister announced that the
Turkish archives would be opened—primarily, it was said, in order
to render ineffective the Armenian accusations of genocide. He also
promised to make archival material on the treatment of the Armenians available to Western repositories on microfilm. At the time of
this announcement only 9 percent of the documents had been catalogued, which made it difficult for potential users to know what could
be found in the opened archives. Scholars everywhere welcomed this
decision, though some expressed concern about the partisan posture of
the historians entrusted with the task of administering the new program and feared that documents damaging to Turkey's official view of
the deportations might be removed.[4] Dadrian argues that the delay in
opening the archives was not due to ineptness but rather provided the
opportunity "to sanitize the records."[5]

The manner in which access to the archives has been implemented
since 1989 has not stilled these concerns. The American researcher Ara
Sarafian, for example, in 1991–92 was able to work for seven months in
several Turkish archives but complained that he was denied access to
files seen by other researchers sympathetic to the Turkish point of view,
such as Stanford Shaw, Justin McCarthy, and Kemal Karpat.[6] Ismet
Binark, the director of the state archives, denied that Sarafian had been
treated differently than other researchers;[7] and after a second visit in
January 1995 Sarafian reported that he "did not encounter any difficulties in gaining access to the catalogued materials and was allowed
to see documents which had been withheld during my earlier research
trips." Still, Sarafian continued to argue, "partisan authors are granted
exclusive and privileged access to such collections years before these
materials are made available for the scrutiny of other scholars," thus
creating "a two tier system" that impeded scholarship.[8] The director
of state archives, given the last word, again disputed Sarafian's charges
and suggested that "the cause of his dissatisfaction might rather be

that he, being of Armenian origin, cannot find evidence for his biased thesis."9

The affair ended in the summer of 1995 when Sarafian, as he relates it, was again refused access to records cited previously by Turkish authors and was assaulted by a guard. Threatened with expulsion, Sarafian left Turkey soon thereafter and was informed a bit later by colleagues that he had been expelled in absentia. His German colleague Hilmar Kaiser was also summarily expelled on "disciplinary grounds." The Turkish authorities, Sarafian charged, "are now committed to a semblance of an open-archives policy while restricting access to critical scholars and encouraging partisans to prop up the Turkish nationalist agenda."10 I have not seen the Turkish version of the events leading up to the expulsions of Sarafian and Kaiser.

The Turkish General Staff has published a 27-volume history documenting the role of the Ottoman army in the First World War, which is said to be "comprehensive and reliable."11 In the early 1970s Dyer had been able to work extensively in the historical archive of the Turkish general staff in Ankara. However, in 1996 Zürcher noted that the archives of the Turkish general staff "are almost completely closed to foreigners (and to most Turkish scholars as well)."12 Erikson was given access to this archive but was less than enthusiastic about the general state of affairs regarding access to Turkish documents. "Only a fraction of the massive Turkish archival holdings are available to researchers, and these are carefully controlled by the Turkish authorities."13 This appears to be a fair assessment of the current situation.

THE POLITICAL ARCHIVE OF THE GERMAN FOREIGN MINISTRY

The archive of the German foreign ministry is fully catalogued, and all of its holdings are open to researchers. The Political Archive contains the records of the German embassy in Turkey as well as the reports of the German consuls in Anatolia, materials representing one of the most important sources for the events of 1915–16. Some of the information in the consular reports was supplied by Armenian informants, but much of what the consuls wrote is based on their own personal observations.

In 1919 the German missionary and Orientalist Johannes Lepsius (1858–1925) published a collection of 444 documents from the archive of the German foreign ministry under the title *Deutschland und Armenien*

1914–1918: Sammlung diplomatischer Aktenstücke (Germany and Armenia 1914–1918: Collection of Diplomatic Documents).[14] Lepsius was a well-known friend of the Armenians, who already had written a book in 1897 protesting the massacres of Armenians under Abdul Hamid during the 1890s.[15] In July–August of 1915 he spent three weeks in Constantinople as well as several weeks in Sofia and Bucharest, where he collected material about the most recent massacres. A year later he brought out his book *Bericht über die Lage des armenischen Volkes in der Türkei* (Report on the Situation of the Armenian People in Turkey).[16] As a result of protests by the Turkish government and to please its ally, the German censor limited the number of copies that could be sold and eventually prohibited the further printing and distribution of the book. In 1918 Lepsius asked the German foreign ministry to be given access to the ministry's files in order to inquire into the truth of the accusation made by the Allies as well as many Armenians and Turks that Germany was responsible for the deportation and massacres of the Armenians during the world war. The German foreign ministry, which had intended to publish a white paper on this subject, readily agreed; the result was the collection of 444 documents published by Lepsius a year later. Lepsius was promised access to all documentary material in the foreign ministry and the right to select whatever documents he considered appropriate for inclusion in his book.[17]

It has been known for some time that the text of some of the documents included in the collection published by Lepsius in 1919 differed from the originals kept in the archive of the foreign ministry. In 1998 Wolfgang Gust published on the Internet a revised edition of the Lepsius book in which omissions and alterations were marked.[18] The discrepancies turned out to be far more extensive than hitherto assumed; only a few of the 444 documents corresponded fully to the originals. It appears that Lepsius was given only doctored copies of the documents and that most of the changes were made by pro-Turkish officials in the foreign ministry. Some additional alterations were made by Lepsius himself, who besides being a friend of the Armenians was also a German patriot.[19] Researchers who seek to read the full version of these important German diplomatic documents therefore must consult them in the archive of the German foreign ministry or in the Gust edition, though even the original documents do not resolve all discrepancies. Thus, for example, in the case of a report by two Danish Red Cross nurses on their trip from Erzinjan to Sivas we read in one version that they had seen about a hundred Armenian laborers lined up next to a slope, and this observation is followed by the sentence "We knew what would happen next." Another version of the same document reads: "We knew what would happen next, but did not see it [*Wir wussten was nun geschehen würde, sahen es aber nicht*]."[20] These two documents are not in the Lepsius collection; they reveal the extent to which German officials manipulated documentary evidence.

Authors in the Armenian camp consider the archival holdings of the German foreign ministry especially significant. In this abundant documentation, writes Dadrian, "the Armenian genocide is elevated to its highest degree of incontestability."[21] The German records, I would agree, are indeed very valuable, and Dadrian is correct in noting that many German diplomats considered the deportation of the Armenian community tantamount to annihilation. These records, especially the consular reports from Anatolia, help establish the terrible suffering of the deported Armenians and the occurrence of massacres. But, contrary to Armenian claims, they do not prove the responsibility of the central government in Constantinople for these killings (see chapter 10).

OTHER GERMAN EYEWITNESSES

As a crucial ally Germany maintained a large military mission in Turkey that at all times had a sizable presence in Anatolia and Mesopotamia. Some of these officers commanded or were staff officers of Turkish army units. Others had administrative assignments, such as on the Baghdad railway; military physicians sought to improve Turkish sanitation and medical services. In all of these positions German officers, though not proficient in the Turkish language and dependent on interpreters, were in an excellent position to observe the course of the Armenian deportations; and their reports, to be found in the archive of the German Foreign Ministry, contain much valuable information.

After the end of the war some of these officers published memoirs. The best known of these military authors are Colmar von der Goltz, Friedrich Kress von Kressenstein, Otto Liman von Sanders, Ludwig Schraudenbach, and Theodor Wiegand, as well as the Austrian military attaché Joseph Pomiankowski. All of these books represent important sources for the wartime deportations.

In contrast, the work of the writer and poet Armin T. Wegner, who has been called the genocide's "leading eyewitness,"[22] has been found to be untrustworthy. Serving as a young lieutenant in a volunteer sanitation unit, Wegner had learned of the deportations and massacres.

On journeys in 1915 and 1916 between Baghdad and Aleppo Wegner observed the terrible suffering of the deportees and was able to take photographs, despite orders forbidding the taking of pictures. Wegner conveyed this information to Lepsius and Walter Rathenau, later to become foreign minister; but the publication of Wegner's findings ran into difficulties in wartime Germany and did not take place until 1919 and 1920.[23] In January 1919 he also addressed an open letter to President Woodrow Wilson, in which he pleaded for the creation of an Armenian state in order to make up for the cruel fate of the Armenians and find a just solution of the Armenian question. The following excerpt from his letter to the American president is an example of what Tessa Hofmann, a generally sympathetic critic, has called a mode of description characterized by "pathos and passionate exaggeration."[24]

> Children cried themselves to death, men threw themselves to their death on the rocks while women threw their own children into wells and pregnant mothers leapt singing into the Euphrates. They died all the deaths of the world, the death of all the centuries. I saw men gone mad, feeding on their own excrement, women cooking their newborn children, young girls cutting open the still warm corpses of their mothers to search their guts for the gold they had swallowed out of fear of the thieving gendarmes.[25]

Wegner was a poet, Hofmann has noted, and was prone to "a highly dramatized self-absorption."[26] But Wegner's work on the Armenian tragedy suffers not only from excessive pathos and exaggeration. In 1993 the German scholar Martin Tamcke brought out a detailed critical examination of Wegner's writings on the deportations. Tamcke compared Wegner's published work with the original diary on which it was based, which had become available after his death in 1978. This comparison revealed numerous discrepancies as well as important differences of substance when contrasted with other available accounts of conditions in the Mesopotamian camps. Tamcke concluded that Wegner certainly did not deserve the title "chief eye-witness of the genocide," which had been bestowed on him by the Armenians and their friends. Wegner's published work, Tamcke wrote, could not be considered an authentic source on the Armenian deportation and belonged not to history but to "the realm of legends."[27]

THE BRITISH BLUE BOOK "THE TREATMENT OF ARMENIANS IN THE OTTOMAN EMPIRE"

In 1916 the British government published a parliamentary Blue Book on the treatment of the Armenians in Ottoman Turkey in 1915–16.[28] The work was authored by Lord James Bryce, a long-time friend of the Armenians, and Arnold Toynbee, a young Oxford historian and clerk in the newly formed Department of Information located at Wellington House. Both men had previously written on war atrocities. Lord Bryce was the author of the *Report of the Committee on Alleged German Outrages,* published in 1915, which has been called "in itself one of the worst atrocities of the war."[29] Toynbee had written a pamphlet on *Armenian Atrocities: The Murder of a Nation,* which was also issued in 1915.[30] The large work that he and Bryce compiled in 1916 contained 149 documents as well as historical and statistical background information on the Armenians in the Ottoman Empire. Most of the documentary material had come from American sources: the U.S. Department of State and the American Board of Commissioners for Foreign Missions (ABCFM).[31] At the time of publication in 1916 many of the persons reporting on the Armenian atrocities were still residing in Turkey, so their names and many of their places of residence were withheld. A confidential key to the names and places was published separately.[32]

Turkish authors have dismissed the Bryce-Toynbee volume as wartime propaganda. Gürün calls the Blue Book "a massacre story," typical of British efforts to spread "rumours of Armenian massacres" and consisting of documents of unproven accuracy "collected from Armenian sources or from people sympathetic to Armenians from second or third hand."[33] Enver Ziya Karal refers to the British work as "nothing more than one-sided propaganda."[34] Authors such as Sarafian, however, believe that the Blue Book possesses "a serious documentary quality because of its explicit presentation of data and careful analysis."[35]

It is known that the British government commissioned the compilation of Turkish atrocities against the Armenians for propaganda purposes, especially with regard to American public opinion. In October 1915 the Foreign Office asked G. Buchanan in Petrograd to inquire as to whether there existed "any photographs of Armenian atrocities or Armenian refugees," since "good use might be made of them in America."[36] As Toynbee recalled many years later, the Russian armies had committed barbarities against their Jewish population, which had been exploited by the Germans. The British government, worried that the influential American Jewish community might turn against the Allied cause and strengthen the anti-British camp in the United States, decided that "some counter-action must be taken quickly"; fortunately, suitable ammunition had become available. "If Russian barbarities were telling against Britain and France, would not Turkish barbarities tell against Germany and Austria-Hungary? This line of reasoning in Whitehall," Toynbee concluded, "lay behind H.M.G.'s application to Lord Bryce to produce a Blue Book on what the Turks had been doing to the Armenians."37 At a time of a desperate military need, writes Akaby Nassibian, the propagation of information about the Armenian deportations and massacres became an "aspect of British policy and a means, in the hands of the sophisticated Foreign office, for diminishing American sympathies for the Central powers."38 The British Blue Book, observes Sarafian, "is an excellent example of the use of American reports for anti-Turkish propaganda."39

Toynbee later expressed the view that both he and Lord Bryce had been unaware of the political purpose of the British government. If it had been known to them, "I hardly think that either Lord Bryce or I would have been able to do the job that H.M.G. had assigned to us in the complete good faith in which we did, in fact, carry it out. Lord Bryce's concern, and mine, was to establish the facts and to make them public, in the hope that eventually some action might be taken in the light of them."40 In a private letter written in 1966 Toynbee acknowledged that "the British Government's motive in asking Lord Bryce to compile the Blue Book was propaganda. But Lord Bryce's motive in undertaking it, and mine in working on it for him, was to make the truth known."41

In the final analysis, of course, the importance of the British Blue Book for historical knowledge must be judged irrespective of the motive that produced it, and in this respect it appears that both the Turkish and the Armenian sides overstate their case. The documentary materials of the Blue Book can neither be dismissed out of hand as propaganda nor (considered by themselves) be regarded as conclusive historical evidence. The accounts reproduced in the Blue Book contain important details about the deportations and massacres; contrary to the assurance of Lord Bryce that "most of them are narratives by eyewitnesses,"42 however, the majority of the enormities described appear to be based on hearsay.43

In his preface Lord Bryce noted that facts "of the same, or of a very similar, nature occurring in different places, are deposed to by differ-

ent and independent witnesses" and that therefore there was every reason to believe that "the massacres and deportations were carried out
under general orders proceeding from Constantinople."[44] This conclusion is unwarranted. First, the deportations in fact did not proceed in
the same way everywhere. Second, while nobody denies that the deportations were ordered by the central government in Constantinople, the
Blue Book contains no evidence proving the responsibility of that government for the massacres that did occur. The collection of materials
assembled by Bryce and Toynbee thus is important, but it is hardly an
"exemplary academic exercise" and "a solid milestone in the historiography of the Armenian Genocide," as Sarafian has argued.[45]

AMERICAN ARCHIVES

After the United States had declared war on Germany on April 6, 1917,
Turkey severed its diplomatic relations with America and U.S. diplomats and consuls had to leave the country. Until this time American
diplomatic personnel were at their posts in Turkey and thus were able
to witness the Armenian deportations. The State Department, in turn,
shared reports on the Armenian situation with the Reverend James
L. Barton, the chairman of the American Board of Commissioners for
Foreign Missions, who published accounts of the deportations and massacres in order to raise funds for the surviving victims. The reports of
the American diplomats on the events of 1915–16 are available at the
National Archives at College Park, Maryland, and have also been published in a carefully prepared edition by Ara Sarafian.[46]

The most valuable of the consular reports is the testimony of Leslie A. Davis, the American consul in Harput. A career foreign service
officer since 1912, Davis arrived in Harput in March of 1914 and left in
May 1917. He thus was an eyewitness to the deportations at a location
that was an important transit point for deportation convoys from eastern Anatolia. We have his individual dispatches as well as a final report
of 132 pages, dated February 9, 1918, prepared for the State Department after his return to the United States. Davis did not know Turkish,
and his reports draw on Turkish and Armenian informants as well as
on information provided to him by other foreign residents in Harput.
Still, he made repeated efforts to find out for himself what was going
on. Of special importance are accounts of his visits to several mass
execution sites, one of the few such reports available from any source.[47]

The American ambassador in Constantinople from November 1913 until February 1916 was Henry Morgenthau, a real-estate developer and chairman of Woodrow Wilson's 1912 presidential campaign. After his return to the United States, Morgenthau received permission to publish his memoirs. Several chapters of *Ambassador Morgenthau's Story*, published in 1918, deal with the Armenian deportations and massacres.[48] Morgenthau's book draws on the reports he received from American consuls and missionaries in Anatolia as well as on his own personal contacts in Constantinople. Armenians consider Morgenthau's book one of the key documents proving the Armenian genocide. Morgenthau, writes Dadrian, "emphatically confirms the genocidal intentions of the leaders of the Young Turk regime and equally emphatically affirms the reality of the intended genocidal outcome."[49]

In 1990 the pro-Turkish American historian Heath Lowry published a critical appraisal of Morgenthau's memoir. Lowry drew attention to Morgenthau's declared desire to help win a victory for the war policy of the U.S. government. In a letter to President Wilson, written on November 26, 1917, Morgenthau had expressed his discouragement at the amount of opposition and indifference to the war and proposed authoring a book that would help bring about a change in this situation:

> I am considering writing a book in which I would lay bare, not only Germany's permeation of Turkey and the Balkans, but that system as it appears in every country of the world. For in Turkey we see the evil spirit of Germany at its worst—culminating at last in the greatest crime of all ages, the horrible massacre of helpless Armenians and Syrians. This particular detail of the story and Germany's abettance of the same, I feel positive will appeal to the mass of Americans in small towns and country districts as no other aspect of the war could, and convince them of the necessity of carrying the war to a victorious conclusion.[50]

Lowry argues that Morgenthau's propagandistic purpose to foster public support for the war effort explains the exaggerations and distortions of the book. Lowry compared *Ambassador Morgenthau's Story* to the sources on which it is based (Morgenthau's Constantinople diary, his dispatches to Washington, as well as letters to his family) and found numerous discrepancies between the version of events recorded in these sources and the description of the same meetings and discussions narrated in the book.

I checked some of these alleged differences and found them to be real. The memoir is characterized by a pronounced anti-German outlook, which, as also noticed by Ralph Cook,[51] does not appear in his diplomatic reports. Indeed, as Morgenthau notes in his diary, in early 1916 on his way back to the United States he was told by undersecretary Arthur Zimmermann in Berlin that "I was the only American ambassador who was not antagonistic to the German government."[52] The diary records Talaat telling Morgenthau in May 1915 of his order to protect the deportees and to punish those who mistreated them,[53] but this kind of detail, favorable to the Turks, is omitted from the book. The published memoir portrays Talaat Pasha as the principal villain of the story, calling him "bloodthirsty and ferocious,"[54] when in fact Morgenthau had good relations with the Ottoman minister of the interior. On November 14, 1914, Morgenthau wrote secretary of state Robert Lansing that he had been able "to maintain the most cordial and almost intimate relations with Talaat and Enver, the Ministers of the Interior and of War,"[55] and the diary reveals that these good relations continued all through his tenure as ambassador. Morgenthau's entry for August 30, 1915, describing a meeting with the minister of the interior, is typical of many such observations: "He [Talaat] was in a very conciliatory mood and agreed to do most of the things that I asked." According to the diary, Enver told Morgenthau on November 5, 1915, that he appreciated the Americans' kind attitude toward them and that they "were ready to do most anything for me." Morgenthau not only saw Talaat and Enver on frequent official occasions but also invited them for meals at his home and went riding with them in the countryside. Much of the talk during these outings was frivolous banter.

The book records long conversations put into quotation marks, which include purported statements made by Turkish or German officials; however, with few exceptions, no such verbatim comments appear in the sources utilized by Morgenthau. The use of this literary device, designed to make the words put into the mouths of the various players more believable, apparently was the brainchild of the journalist Burton J. Hendrick, who ghost-wrote the book and received a share of the royalties. Morgenthau, who knew neither Turkish nor French, also relied heavily on the assistance of his Armenian secretary, Hagop S. Hagopian, who followed him to the United States and lived with him while the book was under preparation. Another key figure in the writing of the book was Morgenthau's interpreter in Constantinople, Arshag K.

Schmavonian. The memoir, Lowry concludes, was less a personal memoir than "a memoir by committee as it were," a work that bears "only a cursory relationship to what was actually experienced by Henry Morgenthau during his tenure in Turkey."[56]

Dadrian concedes that Morgenthau "may have erred in some respects, blundered in other respects, and in the description of some events in his book he may have submitted to the impulses of his ghost-writer to embellish certain points, and yielded to the pressures of a superior at one point or other." Still, he maintains, Morgenthau's central message—the occurrence of the Armenian genocide—is the same in his wartime reports and in the memoir, and this key element is confirmed by other American diplomats.[57] Dadrian is correct in maintaining that Morgenthau's propagandistic motive does not necessarily invalidate the argument he is making; nor, of course, does it have a bearing on the significance of the consular and missionary reports on which it draws. Both he and Lowry agree that Morgenthau's wartime dispatches and reports sent to Washington are the more important material on which to base any pertinent study of the events in question. Morgenthau's memoir, one is inclined to conclude, is a popular and rather imperfect summary of Morgenthau's experience in Turkey and of even less reliable assistance in resolving the question of the Armenian genocide. It has been given an importance that it does not deserve.

Some American consular officials were considered to be too close to the Armenians by their superiors. The chargé d'affaires of the American embassy, Philip Hoffman, on September 15, 1916, communicated to the secretary of state in Washington his impression that Jesse Jackson in Aleppo, because of his "long and constant association with the seemingly hopeless Armenian situation, may at times unconsciously over-accentuate certain phases of that situation." His views, therefore, were not shared by "all well-informed Americans in the country." Nevertheless, Hoffmann added, Jackson's judgment was good, and the information received from him was "most valuable."[58] The judgment "most valuable" can probably stand as a general summary appraisal of the reports rendered by American consular personnel in Anatolia.

MISSIONARY REPORTS

During the course of the nineteenth century Protestant missionaries had established stations in a large number of Anatolian towns. The most active group was sponsored by the American Board of Commissioners for Foreign Missions (ABCFM), which by the beginning of the twentieth century had placed nearly 145 missionaries and 800 native workers managing numerous churches, hospitals, and schools. Other American Protestant denominations sponsoring missions were the Presbyterian Church, the Methodist Episcopal Church, and the American Baptist Missionary Union.[59] German missionaries were sent to Turkey by the Deutsche Orient-Mission (German Mission for the Orient), headed by Johannes Lepsius, and by the Deutsche Hilfsbund für Christliches Liebeswerk im Orient (German League of Assistance for Works of Christian Charity in the Orient), founded in 1896. The missionaries sent regular reports to their respective headquarters; many of them kept diaries and wrote memoirs about their years of service in Turkey. The writings of these missionaries represent another important source for the history of the deportations in 1915–16.

The archive of the ABCFM is located in the Houghton Library of Harvard University. In 1917 James L. Barton, the head of the ABCFM, sent a circular survey to American missionaries who had been forced to leave Anatolia after the rupture of diplomatic relations with Turkey. In this survey Barton solicited descriptive statements about the persecution of Christians in the Ottoman Empire, which he submitted to "The Inquiry," a research group organized by Col. Edward M. House at the request of President Wilson to investigate geographical, economic, historical, and political problems that would become important for the work of the anticipated peace conference. Twenty-two of the missionary reports in Barton's survey were first-person accounts of the deportations, and twenty-one of these were published in 1998 under the editorship of Ara Sarafian.[60] The report of Henry H. Riggs, because of its length, was brought out as a separate volume.[61] Barton had asked the missionaries to distinguish between their own observations and what they had heard from others but believed to be true, and some of the responses paid attention to this distinction. Other materials collected by "The Inquiry," including a large number of missionary reports of considerable importance, can be consulted at the National Archives.[62]

In a publication sponsored by the Assembly of Turkish American Associations, Justin and Carolyn McCarthy have called the American missionaries prejudiced and biased. "Missionary accounts of the troubles of the 1890s or of World War I," they write, "did not mention the part of the Armenian revolutionaries or the massacres of Muslims....From their accounts one would think that all was well for the Muslims and only the Armenians had troubles."[63] This appraisal has some merit but is also somewhat overdrawn. The reports of the missionaries did not ignore the suffering of the Muslim population. At the same time, it must be acknowledged that the strong commitment of the missionaries to the Armenian cause made many of their writings less than objective and often led them to include half-truths.[64] In their zeal to help the Armenians they many times reported as facts events that they could not possibly have observed in person. Mary L. Graffam, principal of the girls' high school at Sivas, was one of the few missionaries who truthfully insisted that she had written "only what I have seen and know to be true." Hence, for example, when speaking of the fate of Armenian men who had been taken from a convoy she was accompanying, she acknowledged that the situation was unclear and constituted "a profound mystery. I have talked with many Turks, and I cannot make up my mind what to believe."[65]

The picture of the Muslims that the missionaries presented frequently conformed to the centuries-old image of "the terrible Turk," while Armenians were regularly depicted as innocent victims and Christian heroes who could do no wrong. When Armenian men were arrested in Bitlis, for example, Grace Knapp wrote that in one house, "according to the patriarchal custom of the country, there were ten guns which were used with telling effect against the police."[66] One would not know from this account that Bitlis province was one of the strongholds of the Armenian revolutionary movement and at the time of the Russian offensive in the spring of 1915 was the scene of prolonged fighting between Armenian guerrillas and Turkish troops. In the eyes of the missionaries, when Armenians used guns it was always strictly for self-defense, while Turkish troops using force were usually described as engaged in murderous activities.

ARMENIAN SURVIVOR TESTIMONY

At the time of the deportations foreign missionaries and the diplomatic representatives of the European powers considered the accounts of Armenians who had managed to escape from the convoys an important source of information, and there is no reason to question this appraisal. And yet the reception of these reports was often uncritical. There prevailed a strong inclination to believe anything the suffering Armenians were saying and to discount Turkish explanations. Some of the recipients of this information were aware of the Levantine tendency to exaggerate and therefore realized that not everything that was told them by their Armenian informants could be regarded as the complete truth. In a report on Armenian deaths dated September 23, 1913, the British consul in Erzurum noted "the Armenian tendency to blatant exaggeration."[67] The German missionary Hans Bauernfeind related in his diary entry for July 23, 1915, how several of his Armenian pupils had told him stories of robberies that they had witnessed, "even though with the exaggeration typical of this country."[68] The American consular agent in Damascus, Greg Young, on September 20, 1915, reported hearing numerous stories of cruelty on the part of Turkish guards, seizure of young women, selling of children, and the like and commented that he was convinced that "many of the worst stories that are circulating are much exaggerated." Still, he added, "there are some which I must credit."[69] The German missionary Anna von Dorbeller noted that people in the Middle East were in the habit of using imprecise language. "Assertions such as 'I have not eaten for three days,' etc., are regularly used by both Turks and Armenians, not to mention clumsy lies."[70] According to Arnold Toynbee, "Oriental arithmetic is notoriously inexact," and there is much "unconscious exaggeration" and "purposeful misrepresentation."[71] Some of these observations can be written off as stereotypes that are no more valid than the picture of the "terrible Turk," but others probably contain at least an element of truth.

The German consul in Trebizond, Heinrich Bergfeld, was able to track down one of the many false stories that flourished in a time of great stress and uncertainty. Soon after the first convoy of Armenians had left Trebizond rumors spread that the deportees had been murdered right after leaving the town and that the river Deirmendere, running parallel to the road taken by an Armenian convoy, was full of corpses. Bergfeld noted that the most fantastic accusations against the Turks had become highly popular in the town. However, as the stories about the masses of corpses in the river became ever more frequent and hardened into definite assertions, he decided to check out their veracity. On July 17, accompanied by the American consul as a neutral witness, he rode for four hours along the river but found only one dead body. Inasmuch as the river contained very little water and was split into numerous small and shallow branches, he concluded that it would have been quite impossible for a large quantity of corpses to be carried by the river and swept out to sea. In the meantime news was also received that the first group of deportees had reached Erzinjan without losing a single person.[72] Bergfeld served in Turkey for eight years and spoke the Turkish language. His credibility is enhanced by his documented intercessions on behalf of the expelled Armenians; later on he did not hesitate to report the murder of other deportees.

The reliability of the Armenian accounts that reached the diplomatic corps was further weakened by their need to be translated by interpreters, who almost always were Armenians. The American consul in Beirut, Mr. Hollis, who served there from 1911 to 1917, complained in a report rendered after he had left Turkey about the inordinate and inappropriate influence of the Armenian dragoman at the American embassy in Constantinople, Mr. Schmavonian. Hollis felt that he "did not always have the American point of view." This situation was not unique. Armenian functionaries in Constantinople, the American official wrote, "no matter for what Government they worked had a reputation throughout the Near East of being extremely slippery and much given to intrigue." Their loyalty to the government they served was not to be taken for granted, he noted, and this opinion was shared by his German colleague in Beirut.[73]

As the war ended eyewitness reports of the terrible fate of the Turkish Armenian community received wide publicity throughout the Western world, but much of this reporting lacked accuracy of detail or historical context. American high commissioner Mark Bristol noted on March 30, 1920, that Armenian propaganda flooding Europe and America "with a one-sided report of crimes, outrages and massacres, which are inaccurate, exaggerated and distorted with claims and statistics that are deceptive and misleading." Any information favorable to the Turkish side was being suppressed or distorted.[74] The validity of Bristol's views has been attacked by the accusation that he was a bigot and anti-Semite, but he was hardly the only one to make such observations at that time. The British author Marmaduke Pickthall, for example, noted the same anti-Turkish bias and spoke of Armenians' displaying a "pose of lamblike innocence before the sentimental peoples of the West."[75]

The Armenian Aram Andonian, the editor/author of the previously discussed *Memoirs of Naim Bey,* apparently was one of the first systematically to collect eyewitness accounts of the deportations and massacres. He gathered this testimony from survivors in Aleppo between the summer of 1915 and the winter of 1918–19, and in 1928 he deposited this material in the Bibliothèque Nubar in Paris. Some of these accounts were translated into French and published in a special issue of the *Revue d'Histoire Arménienne Contemporaine* in 1998, edited by Raymond H. Kévorkian. These accounts, wrote Andonian, were not always exact and included some exaggerations, but the reports nevertheless were important for the historian.[76]

During the last forty years we have seen the publication of numerous memoirs by survivors or the children of survivors as well as books that are based on such recollections. There also exist several thousand Armenian-language publications (memoirs, historical studies, collections of documents), many of which have been translated into Western languages. One group of works deals with the armed struggle of the Dashnaks and Hunchaks. These books tell of audacious and heroic assaults waged by Armenian guerrillas against their Turkish oppressors, while at the same time, paradoxically, stressing the strictly defensive aims of the Armenian fighters. The Armenian military commander General Andranik is given the title "the Armenian Garibaldi," and the books include pictures of heavily armed and ferocious-looking *fedayees*.[77] Many of these books throw an interesting light on the mode of operation of the Armenian revolutionary movement.

Some of the memoirs of survivors contain details of importance for historical inquiry, while others merely repeat the standard version, expected by the committed Armenian audience, without adding any significant new facts. The same holds true for what have been called "compatriotic studies"—books commissioned by compatriotic unions, whose members are survivors or descendants of survivors from various regions of Turkey, and written by educated individuals, though not necessarily trained historians.[78] Many of these books tell of identical Turkish atrocities occurring in different places, such as riveting red-hot iron horseshoes to the feet of Armenian victims and making them parade through the towns. Some of these works also contain gruesome photographs depicting scenes of mass executions or mounds of skulls and bones.

After 1965, the fiftieth anniversary of what Armenians call the beginning of the genocide, Donald and Lorna Miller started an oral history project, "Women and Children of the Armenian Genocide," which by the early 1990s had accumulated at least 2,400 formal interviews. Another 850 interviews were done for documentary films. An oral history collection focusing on Cilicia and edited by Paren Kazanjian was published in 1989.[79] Turkish critics have alleged that the aged survivors have been coached by their Armenian nationalist interviewers to relate tales of horror "regarding the so-called massacres during World War I," stories that are of no use whatsoever for historical research.[80] The Millers have denied any manipulation and have explained the specificity of the survivors' recall in terms of the exceptional and horrible nature of the events described. "Such memories are not easily forgotten. Indeed, they seem to be burnt irrevocably in the consciousness of survivors."[81] Actually, according to current empirical research, memory suffers as a result of traumatic events. Under conditions of great stress people are poorer perceivers, because stress causes a narrowing of attention.[82] This finding does not mean that the horrible events described by Armenian survivors are all invented; nor does it justify the habit of some Turkish historians to speak of "so-called massacres." It does mean that survivor accounts, like all other historical evidence, must be analyzed carefully and critically.

The most basic problem regarding any survivor testimony—whether recorded soon after the events in question or much later—is of course that such recollections do not so much reproduce reality or reconstruct history as present a version of reality in tune with the survivor's personality, perceptions, and experiences. The passage of time is especially corrosive in its effects, and it is for this reason that historians prefer contemporary sources to recollections produced many years later. Human memory has been compared to a rewritable compact disk that is continually being rewritten. It is influenced by information gained from reading or hearing the stories of others.[83] Not surprisingly, therefore, such recollections involve discrepancies, obvious afterthoughts, and contradictions. Some survivors describe their Turkish neighbors as helpful; others condemn the entire Turkish people. Some gendarmes accompanying the deportees are depicted as good-natured; in other accounts all of the guards, because they are Turks, are bloodthirsty fiends. Some survivors who were tiny children in 1915 "recall" that interior minister Talaat Pasha ordered the deportations in that year in order to destroy the entire Turkish Armenian community.

It recently became known that a few alleged Jewish Holocaust survivor accounts are outright fraudulent. These are the cases of Binjamin Wilkomirski (the author of the initially highly praised *Fragments: Memories of a Wartime Childhood*) and Deli Strummer, who over several years lectured on her "experiences" as a Nazi camp inmate until she was exposed as a fraud who had systematically invented events that had never taken place.[84] Yet such occurrences, deplorable as they are, do not destroy the utility of survivor testimony. It is no offense to such testimony, the well-known Holocaust scholar Christopher Browning has written, "to accept their fallibility as witnesses....It is no act of disrespect to subject survivor testimonies to the same critical analysis that we would the conflicting and fallible testimony of other historical witnesses, even as we recognize that the survivors have lived through events that we cannot even remotely imagine on the basis of our own personal experiences."[85] Such a respectful but critical approach means comparing and checking the accounts of survivors against all other available sources, and, above all, always pressing the question: was the survivor in a position to know what he or she claims to recall and know? Approached in this way, survivor testimony is another valuable type of evidence that can help throw light on the tragic events of 1915–16.

Chapter 9

The Deportation Decision

Our knowledge of the decision-making process in the Young Turk regime regarding the deportation of the Armenian community in the early summer of 1915 is severely hampered by the loss or destruction of important Turkish documents. There is much talk in the literature about the decisive role of the triumvirate of Enver, Talaat, and Djemal in the Committee of Union and Progress, but in fact the evidence to support this version of events is spotty. The inner workings of the CUP, Feroz Ahmad has correctly noted, "remain a mystery."[1] Some initiatives in the chain of decisions leading up to the deportations appear to have come from top members of the CUP central committee, others from the ranks of the military. None of the available evidence refers to a program of physical annihilation.

ANTECEDENTS

During the night of April 24, 1915 (April 11 according to the Ottoman calendar), while the Allies were landing at Gallipoli, several hundred Armenian community leaders—deputies, politicians, ministers, journalists, physicians, and others—were taken into custody in Constantinople. One Turkish historian speaks of 2,345 arrests.[2] The subsequent fate of these detainees is not clear. It appears that many were killed or deported and never returned. The Armenians consider this date the beginning of the program of genocide. The Turks speak of the arrest of revolutionaries and security measures that had become necessary as a result of the Armenian revolt. Morgenthau, who entertained Talaat for dinner that evening, was told by the minister that the government was prepared to crush all possible attempts at revolution. They had arrested a large number of Armenians, and "they intended to put them among Turks in the interior where they can do no harm."[3]

On April 24 Minister of the Interior Talaat also sent telegrams to the governors of provinces and districts where Armenian rebellious activities were underway, in which he ordered them to close down all Armenian revolutionary organizations and to arrest their leaders:

> Once again, especially at a time when the state is engaged in war, the most recent rebellions which have occurred in Zeitun, Bitlis, Sivas and Van have demonstrated the continuing attempts of the Armenian committees to obtain, through their revolutionary and political organizations, an independent administration for themselves in Ottoman territory. These rebellions and the decision of the Dashnak Committee, after the outbreak of war, immediately to incite the Armenians in Russia against us, and to have the Armenians in the Ottoman state rebel with all their force when the Ottoman army was at its weakest, are all acts of treason which would affect the life and future of the country....Naturally, as the Ottoman government will never condone the continuation of such operations and attempts, which constitute a matter of life and death for itself,...it has felt the necessity to promptly close down all such political organizations.
>
> You are therefore ordered to close down immediately all branches, within your province, of the Hinchak, Dashnak, and similar committees; to confiscate the files and documents found in their branch headquarters, and ensure that they are neither lost nor destroyed; to immediately arrest all the leaders and prominent members of the committees, together with such other Armenians as are known by the Government to be dangerous; further to gather up those Armenians whose presence in one area is considered to be inappropriate, and to transfer them to other parts of the province or sanjak [district], so as not to give them the opportunity to engage in harmful acts; to begin the process of searching for hidden weapons; and to maintain all contacts with the [military] commanders in order to be prepared to meet any possible counter-actions.

All those arrested were to be turned over to the military courts. The order was not to be implemented "in such a manner as will cause mutual killings on the part of the Muslim and Armenian elements of the population."[4]

THE DEPORTATION DECREE

The order of April 24 authorized the relocation of dangerous elements. The suggestion for a wider program of deportations appears to have

152 ♦ THE ARMENIAN MASSACRES IN OTTOMAN TURKEY

come from Enver Pasha, the acting commander-in-chief of the army, who on May 2 proposed to the minister of the interior that in view of the continuing revolutionary activities around Lake Van "this population should be removed from this area, and that this nest of rebellion be broken up." He made a suggestion "to expel the Armenians in question to Russia, or to relocate them and their families in other regions of Anatolia."[5] The formal decision to extend the deportations to the larger Armenian community apparently was made on May 26, even though orders to this effect were sent out by Talaat already on May 23.[6]

On May 26 Talaat Pasha sent the following communication to the grand vizier:

> Because some of the Armenians who are living near the war zones have obstructed the activities of the Imperial Ottoman Army, which has been entrusted with defending the frontiers against the country's enemies; because they impede the movements of provisions and troops; because they have made common cause with the enemy; and especially because they have attacked the military forces within the country, the innocent population, and the Ottoman cities and towns, killing and plundering; and because they have even dared to supply the enemy navy with provisions and to reveal the location of our fortified places to them; and because it is necessary the rebellious elements of this kind should be removed from the area of military activities and the villages which are the bases and shelter for these rebels should be vacated, certain measures are being adopted, among which is the deportation of the Armenians from the Van, Bitlis, Erzerum vilayets; the *livas* ["counties"] of Adana, Mersin, Kozan, Jebelibereket, except for the cities of Adana, Sis and Mersin; the Marash sanjak, except for Marash itself; and the Iskenderum, Beylan, Jisr-I Shuur, and Antakya districts of the Aleppo vilayet, except for the administrative city of each. It is being announced that the Armenians are to be sent to the following places: Mosul vilayet except for the northern area bordering on the Van vilayet, Zor sanjak, southern Urfa except for the city of Urfa itself, eastern and southeastern Aleppo vilayet, and the eastern part of the Syrian vilayet.[7]

On May 26 the Turkish High Command also sent a message to the ministry of the interior that insisted on several points:

> for settling the Armenians to ensure that pockets of rebellion do not reappear:

a) the Armenian population must not exceed 10 per cent of the tribal and Muslim population in the areas where Armenians will be settled;

b) each of the villages which the Armenians will found must not exceed 50 houses;

c) the migrant Armenian families must not be allowed to change residence even for reasons of travel or transport.[8]

A day later, on May 27, the Turkish cabinet adopted the "Provisional Law concerning the Measures to Be Taken by the Military Authorities against Those Who Oppose the Operations of the Government during Wartime." The measure was called a provisional law because it was adopted at a time when the parliament was not in session, a procedure authorized by a wartime enabling act. The parliament ratified the law when it reconvened on September 15. The text of the provisional law was published in the official gazette, *Takvim-i Vekayi,* on June 1:

Article 1. In time of war, the Army, Army Corps, and Divisional Commanders, their Deputies, and the Independent Commanders, are authorized and compelled to crush in the most severe way, and to eradicate all signs of aggression and resistance by military force, should they encounter any opposition, armed resistance and aggression by the population, to operations and measures relating to orders issued by the Government for the defence of the country and the maintenance of order.

Article 2. The Army, Army Corps, and Divisional Commanders are authorized to transfer and relocate the populations of villages and towns, either individually or collectively, in response to military needs, or in response to any signs of treachery or betrayal.

Article 3. This provisional law will come into effect when it is published.

Article 4. The Acting Commander-in-Chief and the Minister of War is [*sic*] responsible for the implementation of the articles of this law.[9]

On May 30 the cabinet approved a set of fifteen regulations for the implementation of the deportation law. Local administrators were given the responsibility to arrange for the transportation of the deportees (art. 1). The Armenians to be transferred had the right to take along their movable properties and animals (art. 2). Local administrations en route

were to protect the "lives and properties of Armenians to be transferred" to their new settlements and to provide "board and lodging"
during the journey (art. 3). The Armenians were to be settled in locations designated by the government. "Due attention will be paid to
establishing the villages in places which suit public health conditions,
agriculture and construction" (art. 4). The new villages and towns were
to be "at least 25 kilometers away from the Baghdad railroad and from
other railroad links" (art. 6). Other articles of the decree dealt with the
financing of the resettlement, the allocation and distribution of land as
well as tools and instruments, arrangements for boarding and housing,
and the like.¹⁰

Another set of thirty-four regulations issued on June 10 dealt with
the land and property of the Armenians "sent elsewhere as a result of
the state of war and the extraordinary political situation." Specially
formed commissions and assigned officials were to see to it that "all
buildings with furniture and other objects belonging to the Armenians" were sealed and taken under protection (art. 2). The value of
the goods taken under protection was to be registered, and the goods
themselves were to be sent to convenient storage places (art. 3). Goods
that could spoil were to be auctioned; the "result of the sale will be
preserved in the name of the owner" (art. 5). Pictures and holy books
found at the churches were to be registered and later sent to "the places
where the population is resettled" (art. 6). The migrants (Muslim refugees) to be resettled in evacuated Armenian villages and houses were
to be held responsible for any damage to the houses and fruit trees (art.
13). Other provisions of the decree regulated the administrative structure of the commissions for abandoned property.¹¹

Turkish and pro-Turkish Western historians such as Stanford Shaw
and Ezel Kural Shaw have cited these regulations as proof of the benevolent intentions of the Ottoman government. Neither in the decree of
May 30 nor in any other such orders, writes Salahi Sonyel, "is there
any mention of 'massacre' or 'genocide'; on the contrary, in every one
of them strict instructions are given that the Armenians should be
taken to their destination and allowed to set up new abodes there." The
documents "include strict and explicit rules about the safeguarding
of the life and property of the relocated Armenians."¹² According to
Mim Kemal Öke, "When the Unionist government decided to transport Armenians from the Russian border to the interior of the country,
it took certain measures to ensure the safety of the lives and property
of the emigrants. The sick, women and children were to be sent by rail,

and others on mules or on foot. They had to be provided with food and medicines. Special registers were kept on the debts and credits of the relocated Armenians."13 As the Turkish Foreign Policy Institute has put it, "great care was taken to make certain that the Armenians were treated carefully and compassionately as they were deported."14

Unfortunately, published decrees are not self-executing. The regulations of May 30 and June 10 gave the deportation law a modicum of fairness, but hardly any of these rules were implemented; and the actual course of the deportations and resettlement bore little resemblance to the procedures outlined in the law. Even the generally pro-Turkish Justin McCarthy in his most recent book acknowledges that the good intentions affirmed in the regulations "were seldom carried out."15 The railroad that according to Öke's account was to transport the sick, women, and children from the Russian border to the interior did not exist. By the time the convoys reached the Baghdad railway near the Mediterranean coast large numbers of deportees had perished of starvation or disease or had been killed. The Ministry of War as well as the Department for the Settlement of Tribes and Immigrants and the Department for Public Security, both in the Ministry of the Interior, were given oversight over the deportations, but these agencies were never able or willing to enforce the regulations issued in their name. Given what we know about the workings of the Ottoman bureaucracy, it is probably fair to say that the momentous task of relocating several hundred thousand people in a short span of time and over a totally inadequate system of transportation was well beyond the ability of any Turkish government agency. For all practical purposes, as a recent study points out correctly, there "was no central headquarters in overall charge of the deportation....There is nothing in the record to indicate that the military, the Ministry of the Interior, and local officials coordinated their efforts to alleviate the horrible conditions suffered by many of the deportees." The "critically flawed organizational command structure" provided and guaranteed "the mechanism for the deaths of many deportees enroute" as well as at several of their places of resettlement.16

The Reasons for the Deportation Order

Practically all Armenian authors consider the deportations a cloak for the intended destruction of the Armenian population. The Turkish side has argued that the deportations became necessary because of the treasonable conduct of the Armenian population and the threat that the Armenian rebellion represented to the survival of the country at a time of grave military crisis. The deportation of the Ottoman Armenians, Talaat Pasha wrote in his posthumous memoirs, was not the result of "a previously prepared scheme" but was made necessary by the rebellious activities of "strong Armenian bandit forces," armed and equipped by Russia, in the rear of the Turkish army on the Caucasus front. "All these Armenian bandits were helped by the native Armenians. When they were pursued by the Turkish gendarmes, the Armenian villages were a refuge for them."[17] According to an official Turkish publication, "The primary intent of the Ottoman order to deport Armenians was to deny support to the guerilla bands" and to remove the Armenians from railroads, war zones, and other strategic locations. "Equally obviously, the Ottomans intended that the Armenian population be diluted so that the 'critical mass' of Armenian population would be too low for revolution."[18] Recent Turkish experience with other Christian minorities in the Balkans, writes Roderic Davison, "had aroused an extreme sensitivity to revolt and territorial loss."[19] Enver explained to Ambassador Morgenthau on several occasions that it had taken only twenty to make a revolution (presumably a reference to the Young Turk seizure of power in 1908) and that the government therefore had to act forcefully against the Armenian community, intent upon independence.[20]

The decisive factor in the deportation decision is said to have been the successful rebellion in the city of Van, which Turkish forces had been forced to yield to Russian troops on May 17. The German naval attaché Hans Humann, a close confidant of Enver, told Morgenthau on August 17, 1915, that Enver initially had been willing to give the Armenians the opportunity to demonstrate their loyalty and had been inclined to moderation. After the events at Van, however, Enver had to yield to the pressure of the army, "who insisted upon feeling sure that their back was protected." The result was the decision to deport the Armenian community to a place where they could do no harm.[21] "The idea of collectively relocating the Armenian population," write two Turkish historians, "was born out of the Van rebellion."[22]

The Turkish notion that the empire faced the threat of a general insurrection by its Armenian minority is questionable (see chapter 7). However, fears that the guerrilla warfare waged by Armenian revolutionaries, occurring at the time of the serious military setbacks in the winter and spring of 1915, threatened the very lifelines of the empire had more basis in fact and appear to have been crucial factors in the deportation decision. The offensive of the Turkish Third Army in the Caucasus had ended in disastrous failure accompanied by crippling losses, and Russian forces were advancing into Anatolia. The attack of the Fourth Army against Egypt had been stopped at the Suez Canal, and there was concern about an Allied landing in the Gulf of Alexandretta (today's Iskenderun). The British had taken Basra in Mesopotamia and were moving toward Baghdad. The Allies had launched their assaults on the Dardanelles and the Gallipoli peninsula. Fearing the fall of the capital, the Turks made preparations to evacuate the sultan and the treasury from Constantinople. The larger context of the deportation decision, Suny points out, was the Turkish perception of an "imminent collapse of the empire" and the sense of "desperation and defeat" on the part of the Ottoman government.[23] "A mixture of frustration and anxiety," acknowledges Dadrian, "began to grip the Ittihad leaders and the Armenian issue was pushed onto center-stage, assuming as it did pivotal significance for subsequent party and state policy."[24] The strategic dilemmas of early May 1915, Erickson concludes, "caused a major shift in the philosophical and practical basis of the government's policy toward the Armenians" and led the Young Turks to decide on the radical policy of removing the Armenians from most of Anatolia.[25]

Feelings of revenge for the part played by Russian-Armenian volunteers in the defeat of the Caucasus campaign and retaliation for the subversion carried out by Armenian revolutionaries may also have played a role. The American intelligence agent Lewis Einstein noted in his diary on July 4, 1915: "They are taking it out on peaceful people, because of Armenian volunteers with the Russian armies at Van, and in the Caucasus." Talaat, he wrote on July 15, has declared openly that "the persecution is revenge for the defeat at Sarakymish, the Turkish expulsion from Azerbaidjan, and the occupation of Van, all of which he lays at the Armenian door."[26] The Austrian military plenipotentiary Joseph Pomiankowski mentions the "boundless fury and vengefulness" of Enver and Talaat, who attributed the failure of the Caucasus offensive to the Armenian rebellion.[27] An Armenian source reports that during the retreat of the defeated Caucasus army Enver met the Dashnak leader Murad and told him: "Be assured. You will be punished severely."[28] A Turkish author suggests that Enver used the Armenians "as a convenient scapegoat" to cover up the extent of the disaster in the Caucasus campaign.[29] None of these reports are confirmed by documentary evidence, but coming from diverse sources they might be considered plausible. It surely would have been only all too human for the

Young Turk leadership to be extremely angry at what they perceived to be the Armenian perfidy toward the Turkish nation.

The deportation decision may also have been motivated in part by the desire of the Young Turks to solve the long-standing, festering Armenian problem once and for all. On June 17, 1915, German ambassador Hans Freiherr von Wangenheim reported to Berlin on a recent conversation between his embassy official Mordtmann and Talaat Pasha. The Turkish minister of the interior, Wangenheim wrote, had openly acknowledged that the Porte wanted to use the war in order to make a clean sweep of its internal enemies—the Christians—without being harassed by the diplomatic interventions of foreigners ("mit ihren inneren Feinden—den einheimischen Christen—gründlich aufzuräumen").30 The Armenian patriarch, Wangenheim continued in his dispatch, was of the opinion that the expulsion of the Armenian population aimed to achieve not merely the temporary neutralization of the Armenian population but their expulsion from Turkey and their extermination, and the phrase "make a clean sweep" can indeed be interpreted as confirming such a murderous intention. However, other statements by Talaat Pasha and the actual chain of events make a different reading of these words more convincing.

It would appear that the "clean sweep" that Talaat and the other Young Turk leaders sought to achieve was the permanent removal of the Armenians from their position in the heartland of Turkey. Speaking in the cabinet, Talaat justified the deportation of the Armenians in these terms: "We have to create a Turkish block, free of foreign elements, which in the future will never again give the European big powers the opportunity to interfere in the internal affairs of Turkey."31 The Armenians, Talaat told Ambassador Morgenthau in August 1915, had enriched themselves at the expense of the Turks, they had sought to establish a separate state, and they had encouraged the nation's enemies. The authorities therefore "would take care of the Armenians at Zor [Der-el-Zor in eastern Syria] and elsewhere but they did not want them in Anatolia."32 This statement gains credibility because at the time when Talaat spoke with Morgenthau the Armenians deported to Der-el-Zor were indeed treated reasonably well. Armenians living in the Arab provinces of the Turkish empire were spared deportation, a historian of the Armenians in Jerusalem has pointed out correctly, precisely "because these areas were not inhabited by Turks and the presence or absence of a large Armenian population could not have affected Turkish assertion of political rights over those territories."33 The notion of a solid "Turkish block" also fits into the Pan-Turanian ideology, which had considerable attraction for the Young Turk leaders.

Finally, the deportation of the Armenian community helped solve the problem of relocating the large number of Muslim refugees from the lost Turkish provinces in the Balkans and Tripoli as well as the new wave of refugees from the battle zone in the Caucasus. The Austrian military plenipotentiary Pomiankowski was told by Grand Vizier Said Halim Pasha in August 1915 that, in addition to security concerns, the deportations had been carried out in order to take care of the Muslim refugees.[34] German consul Max Erwin von Scheubner-Richter in Erzurum reported in May that villages cleared of Armenians were settled by *mohadjirs* (refugees from the villages in the battle zone), who appropriated the property of the deportees. Perhaps, he surmised, this was the purpose of the deportations.[35]

As Suny has correctly pointed out, historians at this point can do no more than sketch out the political and intellectual atmosphere in which the deportation decision was made. "To understand why it occurred, why the government initiated the arrests and deportations and allowed the murders to go on for months requires knowledge of the decision-making within the highest government circles that historians do not yet have."[36] The Turkish archives may hold additional information, but I am not overly optimistic that we will ever gain definitive knowledge of the chain of events leading up the Armenian tragedy.

THE GERMAN ROLE

At the time of the deportations, there were many inside and outside of Turkey who attributed the displacement of the Armenian community to a German initiative. The American missionaries Ussher and Knapp, for example, voiced this view with great assurance in a book published in 1917: "That the deportations were planned by the Prussian Government cannot be doubted by any one who has had first-hand knowledge concerning them."[37] This conclusion was not based on firsthand knowledge of the decision-making process, which the missionaries could not have had; it was probably rooted in their belief in the ineptitude of the Turks, who, they were convinced, could not have planned and carried out such a scheme on their own. Allied propaganda during the war also frequently charged that the Germans originated and actively abetted the Armenian persecution.[38] The historian Ulrich Trumpener, in the first full scholarly examination of the German-Turkish relationship during World War I, concluded in 1968, however, that "the wartime persecution of the Ottoman Armenians was neither instigated nor welcomed by the German Government."[39]

With regard to the massacres and other crimes that accompanied the deportations, there is overwhelming archival evidence that the German government, while accepting the military necessity of the relocations, repeatedly intervened with the Porte in order to achieve a more humane implementation. Many German consular officials attempted to alleviate the harsh treatment of the deportees, and the German government even provided funds to German missionaries for their relief efforts. In order not to endanger the military alliance with Turkey, all of these interventions were carried out without publicity. To do more was seen as jeopardizing Germany's southeastern flank and risking German lives. The German press was even forbidden to write about the Armenian suffering, to the chagrin of friends of the Armenians such as Lepsius, and this policy of political expediency or *Realpolitik* was the subject of much criticism then and later.

During the last fifteen years several authors have revived the notion of German responsibility for the relocations. In a book published in 1989, Artem Ohandjanian argued that Germany had suggested the persecution of the Armenians.[40] A more specific charge was put forth in a Swiss dissertation by Christoph Dinkel, published as an article in 1991. The deportations, he wrote, were "not a purely Turkish 'solution' but were proposed and demanded" by German officers, who considered them necessary irrespective of their consequences. At least one such officer, Lt. Col. Otto von Feldmann, is quoted as acknowledging that he and others at times were forced to advise that "certain areas to the rear of the Turkish army be cleared of Armenians."[41] Such advice, it is important to note, did not involve the deportation of the entire Armenian community.

The most far-reaching accusations of German complicity have been made by Dadrian in a book devoted to this subject published in 1996. German officers, he concludes, "who one way or another participated in consultations or deliberations leading up to the decision to deport the Armenians are liable to the charge of co-conspirators, especially Marshal Wilhelm Leopold Colmar Freiherr von der Goltz and Lieutenant Colonel Feldmann."[42] As discussed above, Feldmann at the most can be held responsible for some local relocations. The same holds true for Lt. Col. Böttrich, head of the Ottoman General Staff's railway department. In the case of Marshal von der Goltz, an advisor to Enver,

Dadrian's charge is even less valid. As Hilmar Kaiser has pointed out in a review of Dadrian's book, Dadrian misinterprets the affidavits of three Armenian survivors and ignores accounts showing that Goltz was involved in rescuing Assyrian Christians in the Tur Abdin mountains. There is no evidence suggesting that Goltz had an initiating role in the deportation decision in the spring of 1915, though he may not have opposed it. He probably was one of many German officers who, as Kaiser puts it, "stood by or looked the other way." Kaiser concludes that Dadrian's book "leaves the reader with a rather unbalanced impression of German responsibility in the Armenian Genocide." Material that does not support Dadrian's theses is ignored. A crucial document is misquoted. Kaiser warns serious scholars against "accepting Dadrian's statements at face value."[43] Another reviewer finds likewise that the book is "based on circumstantial and often dubious evidence" and that the author "has simply failed to make his case."[44] According to Donald Bloxham, the accusations leveled by Dadrian "are often simply unfounded," and he concludes: "The idea of a German role in the formation of the genocidal policy...has no basis in the available documentation."[45]

Chapter 10

The Course of the Deportations

Turkish archives should contain extensive materials about the work of local officials who arranged the deportations and of the commissions in charge of abandoned Armenian property, but very little of this material has so far become available. Fortunately, as a result of the presence of German, Austrian, and American consular officials in Anatolia, Syria, and Mesopotamia, we know quite a lot about how the deportation decision was implemented. The reports of these officials (preserved in the archives of their respective countries), read together with the writings of European missionaries who also were eyewitnesses, complement each other well. At the same time, we have only limited knowledge about certain crucial aspects of the deportation process, such as the massacres. Chapter 12 examines what we know and do not know about these mass-killings. This chapter discusses the course of the deportations in several key locations.

ERZURUM

The manner in which the deportations of the Armenians were carried out varied greatly from place to place. Toynbee speaks of "remarkable differences of practice," which he correctly ascribes "to the good or bad will of the local officials."[1] Geographical factors also played an important role in accounting for these differences. For example, the city of Erzurum was located in eastern Anatolia and therefore at a great distance from the place of destination in Syria, which undoubtedly contributed to the heavy death toll for this particular group of deportees. It meant a longer exposure to the depredations of Kurdish robbers as well as a vastly more difficult problem of obtaining food and other necessities of life for the long trek, most of it on foot.

The total Armenian population of the province of Erzurum was about a hundred and twenty-five thousand, of whom around twenty thousand lived in the city of Erzurum. In early June 1915 Gen. Mahmud

Kamil Pasha, commander of the Turkish Third Army, ordered the deportation of all Armenians from the villages of the province. According to the German vice-consul, Max Erwin von Scheubner-Richter, this measure was carried out in an "unnecessarily ruthless and cruel manner." Thousands of women and children for a time were encamped in the open outside the city of Erzurum without food. Scheubner-Richter distributed a large quantity of bread to alleviate the hunger. About fifty miles from the town, near Mamahatun, the deportees were attacked by Kurds and Turkish irregulars. Despite the known insecurity on the roads, Kamil Pasha had failed to provide an adequate escort for the deportees. The government acknowledged, Scheubner-Richter reported, that three thousand to four thousand had been killed.[2]

The Ministry of the Interior reacted to this massacre in a message dated June 14. "The province of Erzurum has informed us that a convoy of 500 Armenians who were evacuated from Erzurum has been killed by tribes between Erzurum and Erzinjan....Incidents resulting in such killings will not be allowed to occur. For this reason it is absolutely necessary that every possible measure is taken to protect the Armenians against attacks by tribes and villagers, and that those who attempt murder and violence are severely punished."[3] At the same time, Consul Scheubner-Richter protested the killings to the authorities in Erzurum and demanded a humane implementation of the deportations.

When the deportations from the city of Erzurum itself got underway about two weeks later, the situation had improved somewhat. The first group of about five hundred deportees, Scheubner-Richter wrote, lost fourteen persons. At his suggestion the second group had been accompanied by one hundred gendarmes. Still, part of the group, especially men, had been separated and were feared killed. The remaining Armenians from Erzurum, deported in several convoys, reached Erzinjan safely.[4] A German Red Cross physician in Erzinjan, Dr. Neukirch, confirmed that the most recent later deportees from Erzurum looked far better than earlier groups. They were accompanied by a large number of gendarmes under the command of officers, and the exiles had large ox-carts with their belongings and even cattle. During the first weeks of the deportations there had been serious abuses, but now the program proceeded "in a relatively orderly manner according to oriental conditions." There had been no new massacres.[5]

Neukirch gave much of the credit for these improvements to the *vali* of Erzurum, Tahsin Bey. The American consul in Trebizond, Oscar

Heizer, also described the *vali* as "a very reasonable man." On a visit to Erzurum the governor told him that "in carrying out the orders to expel the Armenians from Erzurum he had used his best endeavors to protect them on the road and had given them 15 days to dispose of their goods and make arrangements to leave. They were not prohibited from selling or dispensing of their property and some families went with five or more ox carts loaded with their household goods and provisions. The Missionaries confirm this."[6] Scheubner-Richter, too, spoke well of the Turkish governor. The *vali* had made efforts to protect the Armenians, had provided ox-carts to needy families, and for families without males had arranged the discharge of men from the labor battalions so that they could accompany their families.[7]

Still, as the *vali* told Scheubner-Richter, his reach was limited. He never had enough gendarmes, and he could not provide security for the entire route. Hence new massacres appear to have taken place at the entry to the Kamakh gorge of the Euphrates River after the deportees from Erzurum had left the Erzinjan area. It is not clear whose responsibility it was to provide security at this point. Among the victims at this chokepoint were also Armenians deported from Erzinjan. The attackers were said to have been brigands, probably Kurds, but some survivors also implicated their Turkish escort.[8] Two Danish Red Cross nurses who worked in a hospital in Erzinjan reported that Turkish troops sent into the gorge in order to punish the Kurds killed all the survivors they encountered. The soldiers were said to have bragged about the slaughter.[9] The reliability of these reports is difficult to judge. The two nurses identify their Turkish cook as confirming "rumors"; they also mention that two Armenian teachers survived to tell of the massacres, but it is not clear whether they actually spoke to these women. Scheubner-Richter speaks of "credible" sources who charged that Turkish soldiers or gendarmes had participated in the killings.[10]

According to the German consul, a small number of militants in the Erzurum CUP branch were responsible for the travail of the deportees. They had preached hatred of the Armenians, accusing them of being in league with Turkey's enemies, and thus had created a climate of opinion conducive to massacres. In a report dated July 9 Scheubner-Richter spoke of a committee composed of the chief of police, Chulussi Bey; the head of the local CUP branch, Hilmi Bey; CUP central committee member Behaeddin Sakir; and several others who functioned as "an ominous parallel government." This group had been able to thwart the basically well-meaning intentions of the government, and these people probably were responsible for the harsh measures and the massacres.[11] The important role played by these CUP radicals is confirmed in one of the last dispatches of the British consul in Erzurum, J. H. Monahan, sent out on October 14, 1914. Monahan wrote that Hilmi Bey and the recently arrived Sakir "are virtually governing the Vilayet." Both men followed "a policy of Turkish Moslem chauvinism." He also mentioned the widespread belief in the province that the government was "arming Moslems who are not of military age to serve as a sort of militia reserve in the event of war."[12] It is possible that this militia participated in some of the massacres that we know took place during the Armenian deportation.

The tug of war in Erzurum between the constituted authorities and the CUP radicals is reflected in the way in which exemptions from the deportation order were handled. As a result of prodding by the German ambassador and other diplomats, on June 9 the government had given orders that "the transfer of those working for the military, as well as helpless women, be postponed."[13] On July 11 Scheubner-Richter confirmed that the *vali* was adhering to this policy.[14] But little more than two weeks later, on July 28, the German consul reported that Gen. Mahmud Kamil Pasha, commander of the Turkish Third Army, had given orders for the deportation of all of the remaining Armenians in the city. Women and the sick were asked to surrender their previously issued permissions to stay and were driven out on the roads, "facing a sure death." The *vali,* he wrote, was powerless to prevent these harsh actions.[15] An unknown number of Protestant and Catholic Armenians were able to remain in Erzurum even after July 28, indicating that the *vali* was not always the loser in this contest. American consul Heizer, who visited the city on August 17, was told by the *vali* that "he had received instructions from Constantinople to allow the Protestants and Catholics to remain where they were for the present."[16]

The deportation route for the Armenians of Erzurum and for many others from eastern Anatolia went through the city of Harput. The testimony of American missionaries in Harput, who tried to help the deportees, throws additional light on the tribulations of the Erzurum Armenians. The most informative account is by Henry H. Riggs, president of Euphrates College, who was born in Turkey and was fluent in both Turkish and Armenian. We also have reports by the American consul in Harput, Leslie A. Davis, a career foreign service officer who had come to Harput in 1914.

Riggs noted that there was "some variety in the experiences of the various parties" that reached Harput. Some reported that "their guards had actually taken good care of them, even providing food as well as protection, of course in exchange for heavy payments of money." Some of the convoys from Erzurum and Erzinjan, in particular, "arrived in Harput in comparative safety, a large percentage of men being among them." Other parties, however, had very different experiences:

> One party of wealthy Armenians from the city of Erzroum arrived during these days, among whom were several persons who were known to us. These people had been sent by the vali of Erzroum in the care of guards who apparently had orders to protect their charges from harm. There were many indications that that vali really tried to send his people to their destination in safety. After some days of travel, however, this party was set upon by brigands (whether bona fide brigands or agents of the government was not clear from the stories of these women). The guards put up a formal resistance, but were soon put to flight. The Armenian men of the party, however, offered a real and stubborn resistance, with the result that some of the brigands were wounded, and all of the Armenian men were killed. One boy, who took part in that fight, escaped, and afterwards returned to the caravan and reached Harpoot dressed as a woman.
>
> Resistance overcome, the brigands turned to work their will upon the defenseless women and children. All were stripped of their clothing. Then some of the brigands seized the most beautiful of the young women, threw them on their horses, and galloped away; while the rest stopped to gather up the booty. At last, the women, naked and terror-stricken, were left alone with their children, and when the attacking party were well out of the way, the guards returned from their hiding places, and succeeded in requisitioning from a nearby village enough clothing of some sort to make it possible for the women to continue their journey.[17]

Davis gives a very similar account. The American consul was able to talk with a group of deportees from Erzurum, "many of whom belonged to the wealthiest and best families of that city," but who now were in a wretched condition:

> They stopped at an abandoned schoolhouse just outside of the town where I saw them about an hour after their arrival. I had not supposed that I should be allowed to approach them but was able to talk with

some of them at a spring on the opposite side of the road which they were permitted to visit. They told me something of their experiences on the journey. They had left Erzurum more than a month before with horses, mules, money and personal effects. On the way all the men of the party had been butchered by Kurds before their eyes, while the women had been robbed of everything they carried and most of their clothes. They said that some of them had been left absolutely naked, but that the gendarmes who accompanied them and who pretended to have been unable to stop the Kurds had helped them to obtain clothes from some of the native women in the villages through which they passed. Consequently, many of them were dressed in peasants' clothes. They were sick and worn out with their journey, after the untold hardships which they had suffered, and wished to remain in Mamouret-ul-Aziz.[18]

Through the intervention of Davis some of these women were allowed to stay in Harput, but most of the deportees had to continue their journey of woe or, too weak to proceed, were left behind to die. Their camp, Davis wrote on July 24, "is a scene from the Inferno" that beggared all description. "The dead and dying are everywhere." Children were seen weeping over the dead body of their mother, while others with bloated bodies were lying in the sun. All were in the last stages of their misery waiting for death to come to their relief. Some food was distributed, but most of these people were too far gone to need food. Dead bodies were left to rot, "with the result that the air is made fetid with the stench from them and from the human filth that is all around. They are finally disposed of by the gendarmes digging one hole right in the midst of the encampment and throwing them all in together."[19]

According to the American missionary Tacy Atkinson, the Turkish administrator of the Red Crescent hospital in Harput told her on July 19 that he had six hundred of the sick Armenian exiles in his hospital. Their death rate was twenty-five patients a day.[20] It is impossible to say how accurate these numbers are, for this good man also asserted that one and a half million Armenians had been killed during the "last few weeks," a figure that he could not have known and that surely was wildly inflated. We do know that most of those reaching Harput were there only a day or so and then were pushed on.

We have no reliable information about the fate of the Erzurum Armenians after they left Harput. An undeterminable number were among the thousands of deportees who were killed a short distance from Harput.

HARPUT

The city of Harput (today's Elazig) and its twin Mezreh (also known as Mamouret-ul-Aziz), about two miles away, were in the *vilayet* of Mamouret-ul-Aziz. Both the seat of the provincial government and the American consulate were in Mezreh. The province had about a hundred thousand Armenians. Because of the very large number of Armenian deportees (from both within and outside the *vilayet*) who were killed here, Consul Davis called it the "slaughterhouse vilayet." When Davis first used this term in a dispatch of September 7, 1915, to Ambassador Morgenthau he acknowledged that he had "not seen the actual killing" but said that the massacres had been confirmed by survivors and by the gendarmes themselves.[21] Several weeks later Davis, after receiving a tip, discovered thousands of bodies about five hours' riding distance from Harput. Ironically, as Richard Hovannisian has pointed out, a large number of Armenian women and children also escaped deportation from the "slaughterhouse province" through religious conversion and adoption by Muslim families.[22] We know much about events in this province; but many questions, including the ultimate responsibility for the massacres, remain unanswered.

In May 1915, prior to the start of the deportations, the authorities in Harput began to mount systematic searches for arms in Armenian shops and homes in the twin cities and the surrounding villages. According to a Turkish Red Book issued in 1916, they found more than five thousand rifles and revolvers and large quantities of dynamite. Many of the men in the volunteer battalions fighting with the Russians were said to have come from the province of Mamouret-ul-Aziz.[23] The police made a great show of any weapon found or surrendered, which helped create a climate of suspicion, fear, and hostility among the Muslim population. The Danish missionary Maria Jacobsen noted in her diary on June 6 that the government had found some buried bombs and that many Armenians had been arrested. "It is thought that this will have serious consequences for the Armenians in the district. It is sad that so many innocent must suffer on account of the thoughtlessness of the revolutionaries. Unfortunately there are quite a lot of the latter, especially among the young men."[24] Consul Davis relates that one of the American missionaries, Dr. Herbert Atkinson, "found several revolvers and a large number of cartridges among the effects of an Armenian boy who had been in his employ in the Hospital but had recently been arrested and was then in prison."[25] The German missionary Johannes Ehmann reported that the authorities acted especially harshly against members of the Dashnak and Hunchak organizations, even though little compromising material had been discovered. The majority of the Armenians were loyal and, he thought, would welcome the dissolution of these groups.[26]

As Davis saw it, by June the arrests had created a "reign of terror." The authorities made little distinction between those involved in the revolutionary movement and people who were entirely innocent. Several hundred Armenian men had been seized, including nearly every person of importance. Almost all of them were being tortured in order to reveal hidden weapons and seditious plots. "Professor Lulejian, one of the professors in Euphrates College, whom I afterwards hid for some weeks in the attic of the Consulate, related to me how he had been beaten with a stick by the Kaimakam of Harput himself. He also described to me the sufferings of others whom he had seen tortured."[27] The missionaries, writes Riggs, at first were skeptical about the rumor that the arrested men were being tortured in prison, "though eventually we were forced to believe it....Persons passing the prison at night reported hearing the groans and shrieks coming from the victims." Several men succumbed to the suffering and died. "At least three of the members of our college faculty, after passing through the ordeal of torture, were seen before their death by Americans or other reliable witnesses, so that there is no doubt as to what they passed through."[28] One professor managed to smuggle out a note addressed to the American missionaries in which he asked for poison for himself and several other prisoners, "saying they could no longer stand the torturing and they wanted to die."[29]

In early July the authorities began to empty the prisons. Batches of men were taken away at night and were never heard of again. It soon became known that they had all been killed. Consul Davis had the opportunity to talk to a pharmacist, one of the few who managed to escape from a massacre and was being hidden at the American hospital. The men, numbering about eight hundred, had been tied together in groups of fourteen and marched out of town before daybreak so as not to be seen by the inhabitants. Under heavy guard they were taken to a ravine several hours' marching time from Harput and then shot by the gendarmes. Those not killed in that way were dispatched with knives and bayonets. Davis wrote that several others who also had escaped "confirmed the story as it was first told to me."[30] Riggs noted that there was no reason to doubt the pharmacist's story, "for not only was he himself a young man of unimpeachable integrity, but the details of the horrid story were fully verified by the testimony of Kurds who had seen some of the other fugitives before they were overtaken and butchered by the pursuing gendarmes."[31]

On June 26 the authorities announced that all Armenians would have to leave the twin cities within five days. Consul Davis, four American missionaries, the German missionary Ehmann, and an Austrian employed by the Ottoman Bank went to see the *vali* to plead for an extension of time so that the Armenians could prepare themselves for the difficult journey, but the governor rejected the idea. He also turned down the request of the missionaries to accompany the deportees. The *vali* promised to provide wagons and protection, but Davis and the missionaries were convinced that most of the deportees would lose their lives. By whatever route one left Harput, Davis wrote a few days later, it was necessary to carry all provisions for the journey. Much of the journey was through the desert, uninhabitable for people or beasts, where there was no water. This was especially the case on the road to Aleppo. Since not enough wagons and horses were available, most of the people would have to travel on foot and therefore would not be able to carry enough food or water for a journey that would last at least two weeks. "Under the most favorable conditions the journey is a very fatiguing one (I am speaking from experience, as I traversed that route twice last summer on my attempted trip to America and my return to Harpout). For people traveling as these Armenians who are going into exile will be obliged to travel it is certain death for by far the greater part of them." There also were the dangers from bands of pillaging Kurds. "It is quite possible," Davis surmised, "that the men may be killed, the more attractive women carried off as slaves, and the other women and children left to perish in the desert."[32]

Despite the original deadline of five days, there were numerous delays in the execution of the expulsion order. The authorities needed time to come up with some ox-carts and donkeys, though most of the people had to leave on foot carrying their baggage on their back and their small children in their arms. Another reason for delay, Riggs wrote, "was that apparently the government was making an effort to keep some sort of a record of the people deported. This, with the notoriously inefficient Turkish officials with their red tape and their bribery, took more time than had been allowed. To consider the claims to exemption and—if such a phrase could be used—to systematize the deportation and the exemptions, took time." The Turks also wanted to give the population the chance to buy the household goods and stock in trade of the deportees at ridiculously cheap prices. "For this purpose it was desirable to keep the Armenians in the constant expectation of being sent away within a day or two, so that haste might drive them to sell their goods at any prices they could at the moment command."[33]

Arrests continued during this time of delay, and the people waiting to hear their fate had the horror of seeing the convoys of Armenians from other parts of Anatolia pass through Harput. The missionaries, Riggs relates, at times visited the transit camp in order to distribute some bread, though this "effort really only added to the aggregate misery because the little that we could do did not suffice to even mitigate the pangs of hunger of the few who got a bit of bread; and it seemed to add another hopeless heartbreak to those multitudes outside the inner circle who could get nothing." The missionaries, Riggs writes, were not the only visitors to that camp:

> Each time I went there I saw others wandering about among the exiles. Turkish men, and sometimes women too, looking for slaves. There were plenty of candidates, for the experiences of the journey had broken the spirits of many a woman and girl who had bravely started out, choosing death rather than the slavery of the harem. So when these Turkish men walked about and looked for likely looking girls, they not infrequently found ready victims among those whose sufferings had made any fate seem like a blessed release. Sometimes these hunters led off little children who were gladly given up by their mothers, or some had lost their mothers already and went dumb and uncomprehending to their new homes. Some of the men and women whom I saw leading away these little slaves seemed to treat them kindly, and I fancied that their motives were not altogether sordid. They really seemed to pity the sufferers whom they were rescuing from such misery.[34]

Davis reports that he saw Armenian mothers sell their children for a few piasters. Turkish officers and others brought along their doctors to examine the prettiest girls, whom they had selected for their harems.[35]

On July 24 Davis informed Morgenthau that twelve thousand to fifteen thousand Armenians had been expelled from the twin cities of Harput and Mezreh. "Possibly 1,000 or 1,500 remain with permission or through bribery or in hiding."[36] The last group of Armenians forced to leave Harput was sent away on July 31. Some Armenian young women agreed to marry Turks. "They were willing to accept this proposition," recalled the American missionary Mary W. Riggs, "in order to save their own families and in a few cases it seemed successful, but in some it seemed to be in vain. Their people were carried away even after they had sacrificed themselves for their safety."[37]

The number of deportees from the twin cities who survived the hardships and dangers of the journey is not known. The German consul in Aleppo, Dr. Walter Rössler, reported on August 7 that a group of 120 deportees from villages in the province of Mamouret-ul-Aziz had reached the city after losing 88 persons: 24 of the men and 12 of the women had been killed; 29 young women and girls and 10 boys had been abducted; 10 persons were missing, and nothing was known about their fate (he does not account for the other 3). Rössler noted that several groups had suffered even worse casualties.[38] Ms. Frearson, a foreign resident who passed Aleppo on her way to Egypt in September, was told that of one party from Harput that numbered 5,000 only 213 reached Aleppo.[39] The accuracy of these statistics, compiled by Armenians in Aleppo, cannot be confirmed; but from all we know about this particular deportation route they probably are pretty much on target.

Some of the deportees did reach their places of resettlement in eastern Syria; others found refuge in Aleppo. Davis reports that in the fall of 1915 "communications began to be received from these exiles who had arrived at different places. Some had left money with the missionaries, some with Armenians who had been exempted from deportation, some with Turks, and one or two with me. They now sent for their deposits, and during the next year we received many telegrams and letters asking for them.... These telegrams came every day or two for a while, some of them asking for the deposits of as many as ten or fifteen different persons."[40]

In a few cases Davis himself rode out to some of the villages to collect money deposited there. In response to inquiries and in order to learn of conditions in the countryside, he also visited many Armenian villages, which he found deserted and in ruins. On the way he frequently saw corpses and shallow graves. One day Davis was told by a Turk that he had seen thousands of bodies around Lake Göljük (today called Lake Hazar), about twenty miles southeast of Harput near the road to Diarbekir, and he offered to take the consul to these places. Subsequently Davis undertook three trips on horseback to the area around the lake. The first trip was made in late September, many weeks after the last groups of deportees had left Harput. On the second of these rides into the countryside he was accompanied by another American, the missionary Dr. Herbert Atkinson. Davis took photographs that were recovered by Susan Blair many years later; some of them are included in her edition of Davis's report, entitled *The Slaughterhouse Province.*

There were dead bodies even on the outskirts of the town, Davis later wrote of his first trip. Some had been covered with a few shovelfuls of earth; most of them had been partially eaten by dogs. When they left the road to Diarbekir they saw hundreds of dead bodies scattered over the plain. "Nearly all of them were those of women and children. It was obvious that they must have been killed, as so many could not have died from disease or exhaustion. They lay quite near a Kurdish village, which was known as Kurdemlik, and I afterwards learned that the Kurds of this village had killed most of these people." A woman who was left for dead and found her way back to Harput described what had happened. Another survivor was a young woman who had been taken by one of the Kurds and kept in Kurdemlik for several months but eventually managed to escape and returned to Harput. Some of the bodies had been burned, and Davis was told that this was done in order to find any gold that the Armenians might have swallowed.[41]

Davis and his Turkish guide then rode along the lake for about two hours. "The banks of the lake for most of this distance are high and steep, while at frequent intervals there are deep valleys, almost like pockets. In most of these valleys there were dead bodies and from the top of the cliffs which extended between them we saw hundreds of bodies and many bones in the water below." It appeared that many had been pushed over the cliffs and killed in that way. In one valley Davis estimated that there were fifteen hundred bodies, but the stench was so great that they decided not to enter it. Nearly all of the bodies were naked. He later was told that the victims had been forced to take off their clothing before being killed, because Muslims consider clothes taken from a dead body to be defiled.[42] Riggs reports that this clothing was offered for sale in the Mezreh market "in great heaps."[43] Davis, too, in a dispatch to Morgenthau of December 30, 1915, mentions the sale of great quantities of such clothing that continued for many days. "I am told that that the same thing took place in the other towns of this Vilayet. I saw it going on here myself. One can hardly imagine anything so sordid or gruesome."[44]

A few weeks later Dr. Herbert Atkinson of the American hospital expressed the wish to make this trip with Davis, and the two men set out on October 24. Dr. Atkinson's wife, Tacy, mentioned the departure in her diary but gave no details. In a note added to the diary in 1924 she wrote: "The story of this trip I did not dare to write. They saw about ten thousand bodies."[45] Riggs, too, who was unable to accompany Davis and Atkinson on "their hideous ride" and was told of their findings after their return, withheld their names when he composed his report for "The Inquiry" in 1918. "I do not consider it wise to mention their names, but if I should name them it would be sufficient to make even that unbelievable report undeniable, even if I had not myself seen the photographs of the unspeakably ghastly scenes that they had passed through."[46]

Davis's second trip, accompanied by Dr. Atkinson, yielded more horrors. One group of several hundred corpses consisted of women and children only. All of the bodies were naked, and many of them showed signs of brutal mutilation. On the second day, on a path alongside the lake, they encountered "bodies and skeletons everywhere. Many of the bones were bleached and dry, showing that they had been there since early summer." In one large valley they estimated that there were no less than two thousand bodies. They also found some personal effects of the victims, including passports, which showed that the people were from Erzurum and other places. "We estimated that in the course of our ride around the lake, and actually within the space of twenty-four hours, we had seen the remains of not less than ten thousand Armenians who had been killed around Lake Geoljik."[47]

Davis acknowledged that his count of bodies was "approximate" but added that if anything it was too low. On subsequent rides in the direction of Lake Göljük "I nearly always discovered skeletons and bones in great numbers in the new places that I visited, even as recently as a few weeks before I left Harput."[48] Based on information that Davis was able to gather, most of the killing had been done by Kurds. An old Kurd whom he met near a Kurdish village that overlooked the lake told him that "gendarmes had brought a party of about two thousand Armenians there some twenty days before and had made the Kurds from the neighboring villages come and kill them." He later was told of a system of agreements under which "the Kurds were to pay the gendarmes a certain fixed sum—a few hundred pounds, or more, depending on circumstances—and were to have for themselves whatever they found on the bodies of the Armenians in excess of that sum."[49]

Riggs believed that the *vali* of Harput, Sabit Bey, had much to answer for. "Whether, as Sabit Bey pretended, his actions were under coercion from his superiors, or whether this wholesale butchery was but part of the perfidy and gratuitous cruelty of which we had such abundant examples in his local dealings, may perhaps some day be made clear."[50] The German missionary Johannes Ehmann, however, expressed the view that the *vali* had responded favorably to German interventions on behalf of the Armenians.[51] After the armistice of 1918 Sabit Bey is said to have been interrogated by an examining magistrate,[52] but he was never charged. In April 1919 the Greek delegation submitted a list of Turkish officials implicated in the deportation and massacre of the Armenian population to the Commission on Responsibilities of the Paris Peace Conference, in which Sabit Bey was named as most responsible for the atrocities committed in his province against Armenians from his *vilayet* as well as from other provinces.[53] Sabit's name also appeared on a list of several hundred Turkish officials accused of being responsible for atrocities against the Armenians prepared by the Armenian Revolutionary Organization in late 1918.[54]

When the British sought the help of the American State Department in obtaining evidence against the prisoners held on Malta, the name of Sabit Bey surfaced as one of those implicated in crimes against the Armenians. But as the British embassy in Washington informed the Foreign Office on July 13, 1921, the case against the *vali* of Harput rested on "personal opinions" on the part of the writer who described the atrocities, "no concrete facts being given which could constitute satisfactory incriminating evidence."[55] After the government of Kemal Pasha had appointed Sabit Bey governor of Erzurum, British High Commissioner Rumbold brought up the charges against the former *vali* of Harput on a visit to the minister of foreign affairs, but he was told that "Sabit Bey had been maligned."[56] No evidence to resolve this matter exists, and the role of Sabit Bey in the massacres remains unclear.

Despite periodic searches, some Armenians were able to avoid deportation. It was a capital offense to hide Armenians, but here and there Turks took the risk—for financial or other reasons. Maria Jacobsen reports that on October 3, 1915, Riggs went to the nearby village of Hoghe, where he found a hundred women and children "hidden by friendly Turks for high payment."[57] Most members of the family of Krikor Zahigian, a teacher in another village twenty-five miles north of Harput, survived through bribery.[58] Armenian artisans played an essential role in the life of the city; without them there was nobody to fix watches and doorlocks or make modern clothes and shoes. At the urging of influential Turks, some Armenian skilled workers therefore were allowed to stay; bribes, writes Riggs, helped to add "doubtful names to

176 ❖ THE ARMENIAN MASSACRES IN OTTOMAN TURKEY

the list of exempted tradesmen."[59] Finally, as a result of the intervention of foreign diplomats, in August the Porte decided to exempt Catholic and Protestant Armenians from the deportation decree.[60] These
orders reached Harput after most of these non-Gregorian Armenians
had already been deported; and even later, as Davis writes, "the gendarmes paid little attention to the different classes of people, rounding
them up and sending them away indiscriminately."[61] According to the
American missionary Dr. Ruth Parmelee, a few Protestants escaped
deportation and were able to stay.[62]

On December 30, 1915, Davis reported that of the original
Armenian population of a hundred thousand in the province "there
are probably not more than four thousand left." Some were Armenians
from villages who had sought shelter in the twin cities. There also were
said to be a great many Armenians hiding among the Kurds in the
Dersim, but it was impossible to estimate the number with any accuracy. "There may be five hundred or there may be a thousand in all."[63]
The helping hand of the heterodox Alevi Dersim Kurds, independent-
minded mountaineers living north of Harput and traditionally friendly
toward Christians, stands in sharp contrast to the massacres carried out
by other Kurds in the province. The refuge they provided for many
hapless Armenians is confirmed by other sources. Riggs writes that the
Dersim Kurds "often took advantage of the situation to extort heavy
pay from those who could pay for this protection. But in other cases,
and especially when the fugitives were penniless, the Kurds not only
protected them without compensation, but even shared their meager
living with those thus thrust upon them as guests or neighbors."[64]
After the advance of the Russians in the spring of 1916, many of the
sheltered Armenians were smuggled into Russian-occupied territory
and thus to safety. The Kurdish historian Kamal Ahmad states that
more than five thousand Armenians were given refuge by the Dersim Kurds;[65] while this number has no independent confirmation, it is
undisputed that the Dersim Kurds saved many lives. A regular underground network arranged for the crossing of the Euphrates River and
for transportation to the mountain villages. According to Ruth Parmelee, "the Turkish authorities knew about these flights and very likely
received bribes to close their eyes to it all."[66] The Armenian survivor
Alice Shipley describes how she left Harput on August 2, 1916, guided
by three Kurds and, fleeing through the Caucasus, eventually reached
England.[67]

The other way of escaping deportation was to renounce Christianity and to accept Islam. "Whole families turned Moslem," writes the American missionary Isabelle Harley. "Some mothers sacrificed one or two daughters to Moslem husbands in order to save themselves and the rest of their children. In some cases it succeeded and in other cases it did not."68 The Turks resorted to pressure and incentives to obtain Armenian women. Maria Jacobsen relates how they told them: "'If you are sent away, you will be attacked on the road by the Kurds, who will rob you of everything. You will lose your children, and you will be either captured or killed yourselves. For your children's sake—surrender here.' With all this talk there is many a mother who cannot resist."69 Some of the women and girls who thus entered Turkish families were treated fairly well; others suffered greatly. The total number of conversions and adoptions is not known. It is said to have been high.

The last deportation from the province of Mamouret-ul-Aziz took place in November of 1915. Thereafter the Armenian population began to increase again. Large numbers of deported Armenians managed to escape from the convoys, and by the spring of 1916 the American missionaries in Harput were giving out bread rations to about five thousand people. "That represented really the limit of our ability," writes Riggs, "and we were extremely glad when as summer came on, quite a large number of these people were able to find work here and there so as to diminish slightly the number of whom we were obliged to care." The people who came back to Harput were "pitiable objects. Physically they were, the most of them, emaciated beyond description, but the most pitiable part of their plight was the moral and mental condition into which they had fallen."70 Due to the large increase in prices and the general shortage of food, Maria Jacobsen noted in her diary on January 7, 1917, there is "a steady stream of new arrivals who up to now have been living in either Turkish or Kurdish villages or Turkish homes. Now that living costs are so high, they are being sent away without anything, so they come to us."71 In a letter dated June 21, 1917, and published in a German missionary journal, Ehmann gave the figure of seven thousand Armenians living in Harput and Mezreh.72 Riggs attributed the improved situation in part to a new military governor, "a man of remarkable refinement and a man of kindly and sympathetic temperament." Something like twenty-five thousand widows and orphans, Riggs estimated, were now living in the province. The German mission in Harput, headed by Ehmann, alone took care of about seven hundred orphans.73

A province that earlier had been known as the slaughterhouse province thus had become a place of relative security for its Armenian population. The lot of the survivors was still extremely difficult, especially after the break of diplomatic relations between the United States and Turkey in the spring of 1917 ended the flow of American relief funds. However, the deportations at least had finally stopped.

TREBIZOND

Estimates of the Armenian population in the city of Trebizond (today's Trabzon) range between six thousand and ten thousand. The Armenian community in the city had an active revolutionary organization. Local Armenians told the Austrian consul in January 1914 that the Russians were supplying arms to the revolutionaries and had promised to intervene once an uprising was underway. A search for weapons conducted in March 1914 yielded a large number of rifles and led to arrests.[74] On the whole, though, as German consul Dr. Heinrich Bergfeld noted, the searches of houses had been carried out with consideration. He had been told this by the Armenians themselves. The fact that the Armenians enjoyed full security, Bergfeld added, was all the more remarkable since the Armenians made no secret of their sympathy for the Allies and spread the most ridiculous rumors, such as the fall of the Dardanelles and of Constantinople.[75]

On June 24, 1915, the leaders of the local Dashnak organization were arrested and sent into the interior.[76] According to other reports by the American consul in Trebizond, Oscar Heizer, and a surviving resident of the city, these men were put on a boat and later drowned.[77] Two days later, on June 26, 1915, a proclamation was posted in Trebizond notifying the Armenians that, with the exception of the sick, they would have to leave the city within five days (i.e., on July 1). The preamble of the proclamation accused the Armenians of having attempted to destroy the peace and security of the Ottoman state and spoke of Armenian organizations that had made common cause with the enemy. "Therefore, as a measure to be applied until the conclusion of the war, the Armenians have to be sent away to places which have been prepared in the interior of vilayets." The expelled could take along articles of their movable property. "Because their exile is only temporary, their landed property, and the effects which they will be unable to take with them will be taken care of under the supervision of the Government, and stored in closed and protected buildings." Several provisions dealt with the well-being and safety of the deportees:

To assure their comfort during this journey, hans [inns] and suitable buildings have been prepared, and everything has been done for their safe arrival at their places of temporary residence, without their being subjected to any kind of attack or affronts.

The guards will use their weapons against those who make any attempts of attack or affront the life, honor, and property of one or more of a number of Armenians, and such persons as are taken alive will be sent to the Court Martial and executed....

As the Armenians are not allowed to carry any firearms or cutting weapons, they shall deliver to the authorities every sort of arms, revolvers, daggers, bombs, etc., which they have concealed in their places of residence or elsewhere. A lot of such weapons and other things have been reported to the Government, and if their owners allow themselves to be misled and the weapons are afterwards found by the Government, they will be under heavy responsibility and receive severe punishment.

The proclamation ended with a call to officials on the road to render all "possible assistance to the Armenians."[78]

Consul Heizer described the despair of the Armenian community produced by the proclamation. He also voiced his own fears for the fate of the deportees. "At the present time there are no means of transportation available. All horses, wagons and vehicles have been requisitioned for military purposes and the only way for these people to go is on foot, a journey of sixty days or more." Given the heat of the summer, women, children, and old men could not be expect to survive. "Even a strong man without the necessary outfit and food would be likely to perish on such a trip." Heizer added that he therefore had joined the Austrian consul in a plea to the government in Constantinople to secure a withdrawal of the order or achieve at least a modification that would spare the old men, women, and children.[79]

The German consul wrote his ambassador with a similar plea. The *vali* had assured him that the execution of the deportation order, even in the case of Armenian resistance, would be handled by the authorities exclusively and that the local CUP committee or other private persons would not be allowed to interfere. This meant that the occurrence of excesses was unlikely. Still, the movement of thousands of people over hundreds of kilometers on roads that lacked adequate shelter and food and were contaminated by typhus was sure to cause enormous numbers of victims, especially among women and children. "I am absolutely no friend of the Armenians," Bergfeld wrote; but he felt obligated to point

out the dangerous consequences that would follow this mass deportation (affecting about thirty thousand persons in the *vilayet* of Trebizond) from the point of view of humanity and the prestige of Germany.
The *vali* had promised him that he would provide full security until
Erzinjan but that he could not be responsible for the fate of the deportees outside his area of jurisdiction.[80]

These diplomatic interventions appear to have had some success.
Bergfeld reported on June 29 that the *vali* had informed the Porte of
his decision to exempt, for the time being, Catholic Armenians, widows, orphans, old men, and pregnant women.[81] Heizer confirmed these
exemptions in a dispatch a day later. He noted that, together with
his German and Austrian colleagues, he was continuing his efforts on
behalf of women and children generally.[82] By July 7, Heizer informed
Morgenthau, 5,200 Armenians had been sent away. "The children,
when the parents so desired, were left behind and placed in large houses
in different parts of the city. There are approximately three thousand
such children retained in these houses called by the Turks 'Orphanages.' Girls up to 15 years or age inclusive, and boys to 10 years of age
inclusive are accepted; those over these ages are compelled to go with
their parents."[83] A survivor has described how he was taken to one of
these orphanages and was told by the gendarme guarding the institution not to be afraid.[84]

Soon, however, some of the exemptions were revoked. Heizer
reported on July 10 that Catholic Armenians, the aged, and widows
had been deported with the rest of the Armenian population, "the only
exception being some of those in government employ, children, pregnant women, and sick persons who were placed in hospitals to be sent
as soon as they were able to go."[85] Heizer attributed the new, more
ruthless policy to the influence of the head of the local CUP organization, Nail Bey, who seemed to be the real authority in the town.
This man had also ended the plan to keep children in orphanages. The
boys were now being distributed among the farmers, and the girls were
given to Muslim families. "The best looking of the older girls who
were retained as care takers in these orphanages are kept in houses for
the pleasure of members of the gang which seems to rule affairs here. I
hear on good authority that a member of the Committee of Union and
Progress here has ten of the handsome girls in a house in the central
part of the city for the use of himself and friends."[86] This CUP member
was identified by Heizer in a later report as Nail Bey, who was said to
have returned to his home "ladened with gold and jewelry which was
his share of the plunder."[87]

Nail's departure appears not to have been voluntary. In a dispatch of August 27 Bergfeld informed Berlin that the *vali* had succeeded in having Nail Bey recalled. Unfortunately, he added, the other officials in town were little better: "with rare exceptions they enrich themselves shamelessly from the emptying of the Armenian houses."[88] Altogether, he concluded on September 9, little could be expected from the *vali,* who was powerless in any contest with the CUP.[89]

Soon after the first convoy of Armenians had left Trebizond a rumor spread that the deportees had all been murdered right after leaving the town and that the river Deirmendere, running parallel to the route of the convoy, was full of corpses. As mentioned in chapter 8, Bergfeld and Heizer checked out this rumor by riding for several hours along the river and found it to be false. Meanwhile word had been received that this convoy had safely reached Erzinjan. "I therefore consider all rumors about misdeeds against the Armenians deported from Trebizond as unfounded," Bergfeld wrote on July 25, "and am inclined to assume that the Armenians who died on the way have perished as a result of suicide or disease."[90] A month later Bergfeld reported that several Armenians who had received the permission of the *vali* to stay had been murdered right outside the city.[91]

We have little firsthand and verifiable information on the fate of the bulk of the Armenians deported from Trebizond. The Austrian consul in Damascus reported the arrival of a group of deportees from Trebizond who had reached the Syrian city after many tribulations. Half of them had perished during the long trek on foot.[92] Several sources speak of Armenians being drowned in the Black Sea. "A number of lighters," Heizer wrote on July 28, "have been loaded with people at different times and sent off towards Samsoun. It is generally believed that such persons were drowned....A number of such caiques have left Trebizond loaded with men and usually the caiques return empty after a few hours."[93] In a report filed after the war had ended Heizer tells of children who were loaded on boats, taken out to sea, and then thrown overboard. "I myself saw where 16 bodies were washed ashore and buried by a Greek woman near the Italian Monastery."[94] Austrian consul Ernst von Kwiatkowski concluded on July 31 that on "the basis of conformable information there can be no doubt, that a large number of local Armenians have been killed on the route while others (women and children) have been taken out to the sea on barges that were sunk."[95] In a report dated September 4 Kwiatkowski gave the number of these victims of drowning as "several hundred Armenian women, children and old men."[96]

Consul Bergfeld does not mention any drownings; and Ara Sarafian, not given to minimizing Turkish misdeeds, after reviewing the state of the evidence similarly rejects the thesis of mass drownings.[97] On May 22, 1919, a Turkish court-martial condemned both the *vali* of Trebizond, Djemal Azmi Bey, and the CUP functionary Nail Bey to death in absentia for using the deportations as a cloak for the massacre of the Armenian population. Among other crimes, the accused were said to have been responsible for the drowning of women and children.[98] One or both of these men may well have been guilty of the offenses charged, but in view of the serious problems of due process afflicting these trials these sentences cannot be regarded as proof.

Heizer speaks of "a reliable witness" who relayed information on the killing of a group of forty-five Armenians from a village about two hours from Trebizond.[99] From Samsun, a coastal town also in the province of Trebizond, the American consular agent W. Peter reported on the basis of "a reliable source" that the Armenians deported from Samsun had safely reached Amassia. "In Amassia, the women were separated from men, these were bound in groups of five and carried away at night, no one knows where." Peter also had received details of other killings from an inspector of the public debt. He very much had wanted to go to Amassia, he wrote, in order to see for himself what had really happened, "but the Caimakam had his eye on me. I do not know that one can believe everything one is told, and it seems rather curious that none of my friends from the interior have reported these things to me."[100] A survivor from Samsun describes how a convoy that included Armenians from Samsun when passing through the province of Harput was repeatedly attacked by Kurds, who seized girls and stole clothing, blankets, and so forth. The gendarmes accompanying the convoy failed to provide protection.[101] Most of the information in these accounts agrees with what we know to have happened to other deportees from eastern and central Anatolia. The Armenians of some convoys got through unmolested, while others were robbed and murdered. Some of the gendarmes protected their charges, while others made deals with attackers and shared the booty. The men in many instances were separated from the women and never heard of again. The state of knowledge does not allow us to determine the fate of each and every group of deportees from a particular location, but the general pattern unfortunately is all too confirmed.

CILICIA: MERSINA, ADANA, MARASH

The deportations from Cilicia involved a smaller loss of life than those from eastern or central Anatolia. First, many of the deportees were transported by rail and thus were spared the agony of long treks on foot. As an American relief worker noted, "the distance between Cilicia and the Syrian wasteland was considerably shorter, and, although many thousands died in a blistering exile, at least half of the deportees from Cilicia still clung to life when the world war ended."[102] Second, while some of the convoys from Cilicia were attacked by brigands, the deportees did not have to cross the main Kurdish territory; and we know of no large-scale massacres during the deportations from Cilicia. Finally, many of the Armenians from Cilicia were acculturated to Turkish custom and spoke Turkish as their first language. This, coupled with their generally better economic situation, meant that they had an easier time making or obtaining through bribery ameliorative arrangements, such as getting carriages and carts or provisions for the journey. Miss Frearson, a foreign resident in Aintab who was on her way to Egypt, met a convoy of deportees from Adana and Mersina near Aleppo. The refugees, she noted in a report that was published in the British Blue Book of 1916, had ox-carts, mules, donkeys, and a few horses and "looked so much better off in every way than any refugees we had seen that they hardly seemed like refugees at all. There were many more men than usual among them."[103] Not all the Armenians deported from Cilicia were as fortunate as this particular group; but compared with the fate of the exiles from eastern and central Anatolia the lot of the Cilician Armenians was indeed decidedly better.

The town of Mersina, located on the Mediterranean coast and with a population of about eighteen hundred Armenians, was initially exempt from the deportation decree.[104] On August 5, however, the order was received to expel the entire Armenian community. The American consul in Mersina, Edward I. Nathan, reported to Ambassador Morgenthau two days later that the deportation order "appears to have been hastened by the operations of some bands of Armenian outlaws who are said to have attacked villages near the border of this vilayet and Marash. The vali has gone to the scene of the alleged outrages. The coincidental arrival of six British and French warships at Alexandretta several days ago is stated to be connected with this matter."[105] The Turks may or may not have known of the assurances given by Boghos Nubar to the British that the Armenians in Cilicia were ready to give them their "perfect and total support."[106] With the British offensive at the Dardanelles bogged down, it was feared that the Allies would open a second front by landing troops at Alexandretta or Mersina. "The Turks," wrote the American intelligence agent Lewis Einstein in his diary on July 17, 1915, "are particularly anxious to be rid of those Armenians along the Cilician coast lest they should give aid to the English."[107]

The Armenians expelled from Mersina were sent to nearby Adana. The city of Adana, too, at first had been exempt from the deportation decree, but tensions there were high. The police were making house to house searches for weapons, and the prisons were full. Three Armenians accused of giving signals to the British fleet were hanged. On May 28 Consul Nathan reported that several hundred expelled Armenians had been stopped after leaving the city, "and in many instances permitted to return to Adana. The nervousness in Adana has consequently somewhat abated as further deportations have also been indefinitely postponed."[108]

During the following weeks the Armenians in Adana were left worrying about what would become of them. The German consul, Eugen Büge, noted that the authorities seemed to derive pleasure from issuing deportation orders and then revoking them. "Numerous families have been brought to Adana and anxiously await their fate. Entire armies of Armenians are camped out, without protection against sun and dust, at the stations of the Baghdad Railway."[109] On September 11 Nathan informed Morgenthau that since August 30 over six thousand Armenians had been deported from the city of Adana "without any special regard for the exception supposedly given to Catholics and Protestants." The local CUP branch, a rabid anti-Armenian organization, was pushing for the deportation of all remaining Armenians.[110] The *vali*, Consul Büge wrote on September 2, had declared that the orders of the ministry meant nothing to him; he alone was going to decide what to do with the local Armenians.[111]

As mentioned earlier, in the middle of August Talaat Pasha had issued orders to the provincial authorities, including those in Adana, to exempt families of soldiers, artisans, and Catholic and Protestant Armenians. These instructions had been reaffirmed at the end of August. Büge now told Ambassador Hohenlohe that these orders constituted "a bold deception," since they had been superseded by a second order conveyed by a special emissary, Ali Munif Bey. The deportations continued unabated.[112] Nathan in Mersina also attributed the increased severity to the arrival of Ali Munif, whom he identified as an official belonging to the foreign ministry.[113] William Chambers (a longtime Canadian missionary in Adana), in a report dated December 3, 1915, and publicized in the British Blue Book of 1916, speaks of a special emissary from the CUP in Constantinople.[114] How Büge, Nathan, and Chambers (an enemy alien) were able to obtain this kind of inside information is not known. Most likely it came from one common source.

Hohenlohe rejected the accusation of deception. It would appear, he wrote to Berlin, that the authorities in the provinces were under the domination of irresponsible local CUP leaders who failed to obey the orders of the central government and organized the excesses against the Armenians. He had been told by the Ministry of the Interior that the alleged special emissary had been an official on the way to a new post who had stayed a few days in Adana but had not carried out any official mission there.[115] On September 15 Hohenlohe informed Büge that Talaat had promised to order Adana to observe the exemptions.[116] It appears that the new instructions were disobeyed once again, but there exists no credible evidence to resolve the question of whether someone in Constantinople wanted them disregarded or whether it was the local CUP leadership that prevented their implementation.

During the week beginning September 19, Nathan informed Morgenthau, the population of Adana became extremely agitated over reports that an Allied landing was imminent. There was talk of burning Adana, and thousands of Muslims and their families abandoned the city for the interior:

> Naturally one of the first results of the above fears was a general rush to complete the deportation of the Armenians from Adana. The number of Armenians sent from that city now totals about 25,000 and this is in addition to the many thousands coming from the north that pass through. The misery, suffering and hardships endured by these people are indescribable. Deaths are innumerable. Hundreds of children are constantly being abandoned by their parents who cannot bear to see them suffer or who have not the strength to look after them. Many are simply left by the roadside and cases of their being thrown from railroad cars are reported. Petty cruelty by police and officials increase the sad plight of these people. Conditions in this vicinity are reported as moderate in comparison with those between Osmanie and Aleppo where the congested masses and lack of facilities render the problem of feeding and transporting these people an impossible task. Catholic and Protestant Armenians continue to be deported and the measures are applied also in the towns like Hadjin.[117]

About five weeks later, cooler heads had again asserted themselves in Adana. Whether this change was brought about by a successful intervention of the central government or resulted from a local power struggle is not known. Nathan reported on October 30 that "three rabid members of the Union and Progress Committee of Adana were expelled from that city because of the manner in which they were hounding the Armenians out of the city."[118] On November 6 Nathan was able to inform Morgenthau that an order to stop further deportations had been received.[119] The documentary record ends here, and we have no further reliable information about the situation in Adana. It appears that by the time the deportations finally ended the majority of Armenians in that city had already been sent away.

The total Armenian population in the *sancak* (district) of Marash was about thirty thousand. The deportation decree of May 23, 1915, provided for the relocation of the Armenians in the villages of the district but exempted those in the capital city.[120] During the month of April there were house to house searches for weapons in the city of Marash, and by May 12 about two hundred heads of prominent families had been arrested. On June 14 the Reverend John E. Merrill (president of Central Turkey College in Aintab, who had visited Marash) reported to the American consul in Aleppo that so far only seven or eight men had been deported. The governor, who had a good reputation, had assured him that nobody would be deported without specific charges against him.[121]

Little information is available about events during the following months. It appears that the issue of the Protestant Armenians also caused confusion in Marash. According to a message from Consul Rössler in Aleppo to the German ambassador dated August 28, the Protestants first had been sent away but after an intervention by the minister of the interior were allowed to return to Marash.[122] Aram Janikian was in this group and recalls that three hours after leaving Marash they were told that they could go back.[123] After this episode there appear to have been no more deportations. In March 1916 the German missionary Paula Schäfer reported that the remaining seven thousand or so Armenians in Marash were in dire straits because the Muslims refused to sell them food.[124]

A major crisis was precipitated in the spring of 1916 after the arrest of several Armenians who were found to be in possession of new English weapons. Their interrogation led to the discovery of an arms depot in Aleppo. Djemal Pasha thereupon commanded the deportation of all of the remaining Armenians in Marash, though the execution of this order appears to have been limited to 120 families.[125] Additional groups of families were exiled during the rest of 1916, yet a sizable number of Armenians were able to stay in Marash until the end of the war. The survivor Krikor Kaloustian told the American relief worker Stanley Kerr that "six thousand Armenians remained unmolested in the city throughout the war."[126] Levon G. Bilezkian gives the figure of 8,000 who "were allowed to stay in the city for one reason or another." Some were important craftsmen, like his own father, who made uniforms for the Turkish military.[127] A German study published in 1989 speaks of 6,000 who stayed in Marash.[128]

THE BAGHDAD RAILWAY ROUTE

Armenians from towns and villages located on or near the Baghdad railway were usually transported by rail, though in many instances those without money to pay had to go on foot. The railroad had only one track, however, so the trains made up of overcrowded cattle cars filled with deportees had to compete with the transport of troops and war supplies. This meant frequent delays and prolonged stays at various points along the railway, where the exiles had to wait in the open for the next available transport. Huge camps thus developed that were devoid of adequate sanitary facilities and in which large numbers died from exhaustion, lack of sufficient food, and epidemic diseases such as typhus. Also, two unfinished tunnels on the Baghdad railway north of Aleppo meant than some of the route had to be done on foot, and these forced marches of several days took a further toll in lives.[129]

One of the first big bottlenecks was at Konia. Dr. William S. Dodd, an American missionary in Konia, described the scene around the railroad station there:

> There were, at one time, 45,000 lying out in the fields with no provision for their food or shelter. The sanitary conditions were, of course, of the very lowest, and can only be described as horrible; women, men, girls and children, could be seen anywhere partly dressed, and the stench from the whole region was so great that the Turks of the city complained to the Government that their health was endangered by the wind from these encampments. The death rate was very great but I have no means of estimating it....Around about the encampment, I saw men and women lying in ditches half-filled with mud and water gasping out their last breath, some conscious and some unconscious. The scantiness of the

water supply added to their sufferings....There were instances, not a few, of which I have testimony from eye-witnesses, of women at the railway station selling their children, usually the girls, but some boys also, to Turks, for prices as low as half a dollar. The motives for this were undoubtedly mixed, less mouths to feed, and a little more money gained, but also the hope that the children in Turkish houses might at least escape some of the miseries that the rest were suffering.[130]

A report by another doctor, Wilfred M. Post of the American hospital in Konia, painted a very similar picture. Many of the people encamped in the fields were "lying out in the open with no protection from the scorching sun by day and from the dew and dampness at night. This state of affairs produces a vast number of cases of malaria and dysentery, and also of heat prostration, and one cannot walk a few paces through the camp without seeing sick lying everywhere, especially children." At night the deportees were no longer molested as much as earlier, but, Dr. Post explained, this was probably chiefly because "a vast assemblage of sickly and half-starved people is naturally comparatively safe from molestation."[131] A friendly and decent *vali* allowed the missionaries to distribute food and money, but of course their ability to help this vast mass of exiles was limited. "Friendless and desolate bands of Armenians wandered up and down the streets carrying what remained of their rugs, lace, jewelry and other possessions endeavoring to sell them for bread and for transportation on the railroad in order to avoid the whip and club of the gendarmes if they had to go afoot."[132]

Another huge encampment was at Bozanti, at the foot of the Taurus mountains. The local inhabitants were suffering from bread shortages, and even those deportees with means therefore could not buy any bread. An American businessman, Walter M. Geddes, who passed there on a trip to Smyrna from Aleppo, relates encountering a woman who had been in Bozanti for two days and had been unable to obtain anything to eat except what travelers had given her. From Bozanti an uncompleted tunnel necessitated a track of forty-seven miles on foot; only a few could still afford carriages or carts. Geddes described the pitiful sights he witnessed when traveling the same route in October 1915:

> There seems to be no end to the caravan which moves over the mountain range from Bozanti south. Throughout the day from sunrise to sunset, the road as far as one can see, is crowded with these exiles. Just outside

Tarsus I saw a dead woman lying by the roadside and further on passed two more dead women, one of whom was being carried by two gendarmes away from the roadside to be buried. Her legs and arms were so emaciated that the bones were nearly through her flesh and her face was swollen and purple from exposure. Further along I saw two gendarmes carrying a dead child between them from the road where they had dug a grave. Many of these soldiers and gendarmes who follow the caravan have spades and as soon as an Armenian dies, they take the corpse away from the roadside and bury it.[133]

By the time Dr. Post passed Bozanti a month later, the vast encampment had emptied out and only about two hundred and fifty exiles remained. They were too poor to hire conveyances, while their women and children were too feeble to make the journey on foot. "About two-thirds of the people had wretched tents of some description, and the rest had no shelter all. They had sold what had not been stolen from them, and many were half naked. All were famished and wretched; a large number were sick, and I counted five corpses in half-an-hour....The Government sends some bread to them from time to time, but with no regularity....The valley was strewn with graves, and many of them had been torn open by dogs and the bodies eaten."[134]

In and around Osmania farther east yet another unfinished tunnel had led to the creation of several additional large encampments, which at one time held as many as seventy thousand deportees waiting to continue their journey. Kress von Kressenstein, chief of staff of Djemal Pasha's Fourth Army, spoke of "wretchedness and misery that defies all description."[135] Writing in early November 1915, Consul Nathan attributed the terrible sanitary conditions in these camps in part to overcrowding but largely also to "the imperfect burials of corpses of victims of starvation and disease....The feeding problem is completely neglected and will become worse in the future as even the regular population is beginning to suffer because of a scarcity of wheat."[136] Paula Schäfer visited the camps at about the same time. The half-starved exiles, she related in a report to the German embassy in Constantinople, hurled themselves on the bread that she distributed; several times she was almost torn from her horse. A serious epidemic of typhus had broken out, and every third tent held a person with the disease. "Unburied women and children were lying in the ditches. The Turkish officials in Osmania were very helpful and I was able to achieve much; some abuses were obviated. I was given carriages to collect the dying and bring them into town."[137]

On December 1 Paula Schäfer was in the large encampment at Islahia, near the other end of the unfinished tunnel, where the Baghdad railway to Aleppo resumed. Again she distributed bread. This camp, she wrote, was the worst yet. "Right at the entrance lay a heap of unburied corpses, I counted thirty-five; at another place twenty-two, next to tents of persons who suffered from severe dysentery. The dirt in and around the tents is indescribable....The people fought like wolves for the bread and there were unpleasant scenes."138

The transit camp near the railroad station of Katma was considered one of the most infamous sites of its kind. In September 1915 it is said to have held twenty thousand deportees. Consul Rössler, who visited the camp, reported that due to the lack of hygiene conditions there were simply indescribable.139 A survivor speaks of the atmosphere filled with the sound of cursing, crying, and sighing. "There is a terrible stink that tears every one's nose. Everywhere is [?] covered with unburned, rotten human waste, corpses etc. Besides that, ten thousand people have left their filth, and have contaminated the whole area, and it is not possible not to choke."140 Typhus, dysentery, and cholera were rampant, and corpses were lying everywhere.

On September 5 the Ministry of the Interior sent orders to the governor of Aleppo that "the Armenians who have accumulated in the [railway] stations be transferred as soon as possible to the pre-determined areas of settlement, that they be provided with food, and that special care be taken to protect them from attack." A large sum of money, it was promised, would be sent from the funds for immigrants; and "if it is not sufficient, another appropriation should be requested."141 But, of course, like so many other promises of good treatment made by the bureaucrats in Constantinople, this order remained largely a dead letter. As Consul Rössler put it succinctly in a dispatch to Berlin on July 31, "the government organizationally is not up to the task of carrying out the deportations."142

Typhus, dysentery, and even cholera spread from the sick deportees to the general population, to the workers on the railroad, and to the troops. A German unit near Islahia at one time counted 25 percent of its total strength struck down by disease, and many died. The entire route from Bozanti to Aleppo became infested, thus threatening this essential military supply line, and by November an epidemic of typhus had broken out in Aleppo itself. Djemal Pasha commanded energetic remedial measures; but, as Kress von Kressenstein recalled, these efforts were frustrated by the incompetence of the local authorities and the laziness and indolence of the gendarmes. By early November 1915 a hundred and fifty to two hundred Muslim inhabitants of Aleppo were dying of typhus every day.[143]

ALEPPO

In 1914 the city of Aleppo, in today's Syria, had a population of about twenty-two thousand Armenians; about fifty thousand Armenians lived in the province of Aleppo. Most of the Armenians in the province were deported, but except for six or seven families those in the city of Aleppo itself were not interfered with. Aleppo was thus one of the three large Turkish cities—the others being Constantinople and Smyrna (today's Istanbul and Izmir)—that did not experience a full-scale deportation program. The exemption for Aleppo was contained in the deportation decree sent out by the minister of the interior, Talaat Pasha, on May 23.[144] The government never explained why these exemptions were made.

Aleppo was at the junction of several important routes taken by the deportation convoys. Armenians from towns such as Brusa and Konia along the Baghdad railway were coming to Aleppo from the northwest on the still unfinished railroad. Armenians from various places in Cilicia were using branches of that same railroad. From the northeast, through Urfa, a road converged on Aleppo from Diarbekir. That was the route taken by the deportees from Erzurum and Harput. Most of these exiles usually spent a few days in Aleppo or in transit camps located around the city. From Aleppo the exiles were shipped by rail eastward to Ras-ul-Ain and south to Hama, Homs, and Damascus and several locations in Palestine. Others were sent on foot toward Der-el-Zor in eastern Syria.

American, German, and Austrian consular officials as well as foreign residents have given us descriptions of the deportees as they arrived in Aleppo and of conditions in the encampments in and around the city. A steady stream of deportees was pouring into Aleppo, reported the American consul Jesse B. Jackson to Ambassador Morgenthau on June 5, 1915. "Several expeditions have arrived here and have been taken care of locally by the sympathizing Armenian population of this city. A few days rest in the churches and schools, where they fill all rooms, courts, balconies and even cover the roofs." Then they were forced to continue.[145] By late September more than thirty thousand had arrived by rail and at least a hundred thousand on foot. The deportees,

Jackson wrote Morgenthau on September 29, were utterly worn out; all were "sparsely clad and some naked from the treatment by their escorts and the despoiling depopulation en route. It is extremely rare to find a family intact that has come any considerable distance, invariably all having lost members from disease and fatigue, young girls and boys carried off by hostile tribesmen," and the men separated from their families and killed. "The exhausted condition of the victims is further proven by the death of a hundred or more daily of those arriving in the city."[146] The convoys of deportees were in such dreadful shape, Consul Rössler reported on September 27, that Djemal Pasha had issued an order strictly forbidding the taking of photographs. Taking pictures of Armenians was to be regarded as the unauthorized photographing of military objects.[147] Djemal Pasha did a lot for the exiles who came through his province, but he also was a patriot intent upon preventing anything that might harm the Turkish war effort.

The deportees able to move on were sent on their way, leaving behind the emaciated and sick, who were too weak to stand on their feet. Dr. Martin Niepage, a German teacher in Aleppo, described the horrible conditions of these exiles in a report that the German consul forwarded to the German embassy on October 19 (together with pictures he had taken himself):

> In dilapidated caravanseries (hans) I found quantities of dead, many corpses being half-decomposed, and others, still living, among them, who were soon to breathe their last. In other yards I found quantities of sick and starving people whom no one was looking after. In the neighborhood of the German Technical School, at which I am employed as a higher grade teacher, there were four such hans, with seven or eight hundred exiles dying of starvation....In the mornings our school children, on their way through the narrow streets, had to push past the two-wheeled ox-carts, on which every day from eight to ten rigid corpses, without coffin or shroud, were carried away, their arms and legs trailing out of the vehicle.[148]

Vice-Consul Hermann Hoffmann requested that Dr. Niepage's report be forwarded to the Foreign Ministry and added that "the conditions described, as I verified personally, correspond to the facts."[149] The report was also signed by two fellow teachers, Dr. E. Gräter and Marie Spiecker, as well as by the director of the school, Huber, who added this comment: "My colleague Dr. Niepage's report is not at all exaggerated. For weeks we have been living here in an atmosphere poisoned with sickness and the stench of corpses. Only the hope of speedy relief makes it possible for us to carry on our work."[150] After excerpts from the Niepage report (with the names of Spiecker and Huber withheld) had appeared in the British Blue Book of 1916 and in the *Journal de Genève* on August 17, 1916, Djemal Pasha told Consul Rössler that he intended to court-martial Niepage and Gräter. Some time later police appeared at the school and inquired about the two men. By that time both had left the city, however, and Rössler suggested to Berlin that they be warned against returning to Aleppo.[151]

An Armenian from Sivas, who was nine years old at the time and reached Aleppo with his family, describes a very similar scene:

> The refugees poured into the narrow streets; some were directed into large buildings, some settled in the corners of irregular streets and my clan landed in a *khan*. This had a large courtyard, with rooms all around it and a well in the centre, the only source of water for men or beasts. My family settled in the corner of one room filled with people with just enough space to lie straight. The typhus struck every family in the *khan*. If in any room there was someone who had the strength to draw water from the contaminated well, he took charge of the needs of the others. Each day a horse-drawn wagon entered the courtyard, the driver and helper entered the rooms, picked up the dead, loaded the bodies on the wagon and drove away. Some days the same wagon made three trips, each trip carrying at least a dozen bodies.[152]

According to Consul Rössler, at the beginning of September the average daily death toll of the deportees in Aleppo was 25, by the middle of the month it had reached 60, and on September 26 it was 110. "Thoughtlessness, lack of foresight, the harshness of the authorities and the brutality of the lower governing bodies combine and lead to a situation in which the exiled Armenians are not treated like human beings."[153] By the end of October, after the outbreak of typhus had reached epidemic proportions, 200 of the exiles in Aleppo were dying every day.[154] The situation was similar in the several camps around the city. The distribution of food was irregular and clearly insufficient. Jackson visited each of these sites once or twice a week and distributed food and money. At Karlukh, a small village just north of Aleppo, the authorities had provided a few tents; but the great majority of the exiles were exposed to the burning sun and later in the season to rain and snow. In their weakened condition "hundreds [were] dying from disease and exposure."[155]

Several thousand deportees managed to go into hiding, sheltered by the Armenian inhabitants of Aleppo, and their number grew steadily as more Armenians escaped and made their way to the city from the places of resettlement. The police conducted periodic sweeps of the city, and those caught without a residency permit were arrested and sent away. Vice-Consul Hoffmann reported on August 29, 1916, that some eight hundred such nonlocal Armenians had been deported so far.[156] The illegals in Aleppo were aided by a network of support organized by the Reverend Hovhannes Eskijian, a young Armenian Protestant minister. Women, girls, and boys under the age of fourteen were placed as servants in Christian, Jewish, and even Muslim homes. For others jobs were found in an army hospital. Under the guidance of another Protestant minister, the Reverend Aaron Shiradjian, several houses were rented to set up orphanages. Some of the orphans sheltered there had been abandoned by their parents, who hoped to save them in this way. The contributions of wealthy Armenians in Aleppo and of American and Swiss charities helped defray the cost of the orphanages.[157]

The official Turkish position was that no foreigners were to provide help to the deportees, because this might make the Armenians expect foreign intervention on their behalf and encourage more treasonable conduct. On January 30, 1916, Talaat Pasha ordered an investigation of allegations that Armenians in America "are at present sending large amounts of money for the needs of the Armenians living in the Ottoman Empire, and that these funds are being distributed through secret channels."[158] However, as conditions worsened the government relented somewhat and tolerated a de facto aid program.

A key figure in channeling funds to the relief effort was the Constantinople-based treasurer of the American missions in Turkey, William W. Peet, who had good relations with the German embassy and therefore was able to send the relief workers money through the German consulate in Aleppo.[159] Other funds were forwarded through Consul Jackson. In the fall of 1915 Peet had met Sister Beatrice Rohner, a Swiss missionary with the German League of Assistance for Works of Christian Charity in the Orient (known as the Hilfsbund); and at his suggestion she had agreed to head the relief work in Aleppo. During the first two months of 1916 Sister Rohner was sent 500 pounds a week to be spent on the needs of the Armenian deportees.[160] The activities of Sister Rohner, who had come to Turkey in 1899 and was a woman of great energy and organizational talent, expanded very quickly. The reports rendered by her to the German embassy were (and are) an important source of information about the fate of the deportees.

With the help of Kress von Kressenstein, Djemal Pasha's chief of staff, the Turkish commander was prevailed upon in December 1915 to allow an aid program for orphans. The orphanage run by Sister Rohner eventually had 850 children; because it was regarded as a quasi-official institution, the local authorities for a time provided food and clothing. After the Reverend Eskijian died of typhus in March 1916, Sister Rohner took over some of the institutions set up by him and by June 1916 cared for 1,400 orphans. The adroit missionary, helped by local Armenians, also was able to find jobs for about ten thousand Armenian men and women in several large factories newly set up to manufacture cloth, uniforms, and bedding for the Turkish army. Finally, continuing an activity started by Eskijian, Sister Rohner sent much-needed money to the Armenians left in Cilicia as well as to the exiles in Mesopotamia and Syria. Most of the relocated Armenians there were starving, and the money distributed with the help of trusted messengers enabled at least some of the exiles to buy food. More money would save many more lives, Sister Rohner wrote in a report on her relief work for the first five months of 1916, but funds were never sufficient to meet all needs.[161]

In September 1916 an Armenian conveying money to the exiles in eastern Syria was arrested and after beatings revealed the source and destination of the cash he was carrying on his person.[162] Sister Rohner therefore had to relinquish the distribution of American money, and this task was taken over by Consul Jackson, who had been involved in general relief work for some time. Using the mail, friendly businesspeople, and local bankers, Jackson was able to send funds to many in need. According to Rössler, the Turkish authorities knew and approved of this aid program.[163] In Aleppo itself Armenian churches used American money to support about nine thousand exiles on the relief list.[164] After Turkey severed diplomatic relations with the United States in April 1917, American relief funds were sent to a Swiss businessman in Aleppo, Emil Zollinger, a dedicated philanthropist.[165]

German money, too, became available in support of the Armenians. Starting in October 1915, Ambassador Metternich repeatedly sent money to Rössler.[166] Consul Hoffmann in Alexandretta used official funds "in several cases of special misfortune," and the foreign ministry authorized the embassy to reimburse him.[167] In November

1916 the foreign ministry deposited 15,000 marks directly into the bank account of the Hilfsbund. The director of the mission, Friedrich Schuchardt, was told that this money had been provided to the foreign ministry by "friends of the Armenians" to help alleviate their misery; he was asked not to tell anyone about either the origin of these funds or the mediating role of the ministry.[168]

Sister Rohner's work suffered a serious setback in February 1917 when the authorities began to remove children from her care and take them to government orphanages in the Lebanon and other locations in Anatolia in order raise them as patriotic Muslims. For a short time she was able to continue to provide much-needed help for the many thousands of needy Armenians in Aleppo, where her relief payments benefited twenty thousand exiles.[169] She suffered a nervous breakdown a month later, however, and eventually returned to Germany.

Rössler blamed Djemal Pasha for the removal of the Armenian orphans. A more recent work puts the responsibility on a new *vali*.[170] Some Armenians, going beyond the issue of the orphans, charge Djemal (the viceroy of Syria, Lebanon, and Palestine) with the death of thousands of deportees. An Armenian reference work calls him "part of the unholy triumvirate that were responsible for the wholesale massacre of the Armenians." His assassination on July 25, 1922, is called an "execution."[171] Kazarian includes Djemal Pasha among the 160 Turks he considers most responsible for the atrocities against the Armenians.[172] In contrast, a survivor whose family was allowed to stay in Aleppo refers to Djemal Pasha as "a great man," who was "responsible for the saving of half-a-million Armenians in the part of Turkey subject to his control."[173] As already mentioned, Dadrian thinks that Djemal Pasha dissented from the genocidal agenda of the CUP top leadership and "tried to resist and discourage the attendant massacres."[174]

In a 1919 article and in his memoirs published in 1922, Djemal Pasha sought to justify his role in the Armenian deportations. He had an aversion, he wrote, to telling of the help that he had rendered, especially to widows and orphans. "It seems to me as though in doing so I am reflecting on the moral value of these actions which were prompted only by feelings of humanity." But since a court set up by the new government in Constantinople had gone so far as condemning him to death for allegedly ordering banishments and massacres, he felt entitled to tell what had really taken place. Djemal stated that he had nothing to do with the decision to deport the Armenian community: "I am equally innocent of ordering any massacres; I have even prevented them and caused all possible help to be given to all emigrants at the time of the deportations."[175]

The record, for the most part, bears out Djemal Pasha's claims. As early as March 29, 1915, Djemal Pasha had threatened trial by court-martial for anyone who attacked Armenians (see chapter 7). On July 8 Rössler reported that Djemal "has recently again given strict orders aiming at the prevention of massacres of Armenians, and he has proposed to the government that it issue the same orders for the area under the jurisdiction of the 3rd Army [in eastern and central Anatolia]."[176] That these orders were not just empty words is proven by the hanging, directed by Djemal, of several officers responsible for massacres.

The testimony of persons on the spot also confirms Djemal's efforts to provide relief for the deportees. Rössler reported on July 27, 1915, that Djemal Pasha had ordered an increase in the amount of money made available for food.[177] The German consul in Damascus, Dr. Julius Loytved Hardegg, noted in a message of May 30, 1916, that for about six weeks a system of support for the Armenians, set up by Djemal Pasha, had been functioning in his city.[178] Kress von Kressenstein observed that some of these measures were sabotaged by lower echelons; food supposed to be distributed to the Armenians was stolen and sold by corrupt officials. Nonetheless, the German officer was firm in his conviction that Djemal Pasha and his staff were sincere in their endeavors to moderate the hardships experienced by the exiles.[179]

According to the Austrian military plenipotentiary Joseph Pomiankowski, Djemal Pasha condemned both the deportations and massacres.[180] This is correct insofar as the decision to send the Armenians to the Syrian desert is concerned. Djemal wrote that he was furious at the use of the Baghdad railway, which interfered with the shipment of troops and supplies for the attack on Egypt. "I considered it more expedient to settle the Armenians in the interior of the provinces of Konia, Angora and Kastamuni." When his views were overruled, Djemal did his best to direct the deportees to Syria and Lebanon. He was convinced that the deportation to Mesopotamia was bound to cause great distress; and he therefore thought it better "to bring a large number of them into the Syrian vilayets of Beirut and Aleppo; I succeeded in obtaining the desired permission after I had made vigorous representations to Constantinople. In this way I was actually able to bring nearly 150,000 Armenians to these vilayets."[181] Djemal Pasha's efforts to this effect and other improvements in the lot of the deported Armenians achieved by the viceroy are confirmed by the German ambassador, Paul von

Wolff-Metternich, who calls Djemal one of those Turks ashamed at the way in which the deportations had been carried out.[182] Djemal Pasha's interventions on behalf of the Armenians are said to have earned him the nickname "Pasha of Armenia."[183]

The plight of the Armenians also arose in connection with Djemal Pasha's offer in December 1915 to march on Constantinople and overthrow the Ottoman government. The documentary record does not reveal all of the events in this affair, one of the more bizarre episodes of World War I, but we do know that Djemal used Dashnak officials to contact the Russians and British and propose a separate peace. The offer envisaged an independent Asiatic Turkey governed by Djemal Pasha as sultan and consisting of several autonomous provinces, one of them being Armenia. He also promised to take immediate steps to protect and feed the Armenians. Russia, which was to get control over Constantinople and the Dardanelles, was sympathetic to the proposal, but France rejected it. The French had their own territorial ambitions in the Middle East, which they were unwilling to forego.[184]

URFA

In 1914 the district of Urfa (province of Aleppo) had a population of about eighteen thousand Armenians. The most important sources for the events in the city of Urfa are the writings of a longtime Swiss missionary, Jakob Künzler, who had arrived in Urfa in late 1899 and had become fluent in both Turkish and Armenian. In addition, we have a book by the Armenian Protestant minister Ephraim Jernazian, who served as chief interpreter for the provincial authorities. Useful information is also provided by the German missionary Bruno Eckart and by the British citizen Henry W. Glockler, who was interned in Urfa.

The outbreak of war strained relations between Muslims and Armenians in Urfa. The Christian population made no secret of its hopes for a victory of the Allies. Large numbers of Armenian conscripts deserted. By April 1915 the authorities had started searches in Armenian homes for weapons and seditious literature, and the first arrests had taken place. The fall of Van in mid-May led to threats against the Armenian community.[185] A month later the American missionary F. H. Leslie reported that a reign of terror had begun in the city. "Daily the police are searching the houses of the Armenians for weapons, and, not finding any, they are taking the best and the most honourable men and imprisoning them; some of them they are exiling, and others they are torturing with red hot irons to make them reveal the supposedly concealed weapons." The young Armenian men were getting restless, and there was talk of resistance, but most of the Armenians were loyal to the government. "There is no revolutionary organization here; there may be thirty or forty men of revolutionary beliefs, but there has been no propaganda and no organization."[186]

In the early summer of 1915 the majority of the Armenian community was indeed opposed to any attempt at active resistance; but, contrary to Leslie's assurances, the city did have an active revolutionary organization, headed by Mugerditch Yotneghparian, a daredevil guerrilla leader. Jernazian describes his exploits:

> While arrests and harassments continued, Mgrdich, although restrained from starting a direct armed protest, kept his promise to go into hiding and do what he must. With a handful of young guerillas he kept up a stream of acts of sabotage, providing the only active defense against governmental persecutions. Stories of his daring and resourceful deeds were on everyone's lips. He continued to acquire supplies, weapons, and ammunition for the inevitable battle. With ingenious plans, clever disguises, and bold, dramatic action, he soon became notorious for his activities in Urfa and elsewhere, even as far as Diarbakir and Aleppo.[187]

By the end of June the local authorities were making energetic efforts to catch Mugerditch and his band, and the guerrillas took refuge in caves near the Armenian village of Garmudj (Germüs), just outside of Urfa. Turkish gendarmes and soldiers laid siege to the caves, but, according to Jernazian, Mugerditch and his men were able to escape the trap. The governor claimed that thirty-five guerrillas had been captured.[188] Künzler reports that Armenian craftsmen in Urfa were busily engaged in manufacturing hand grenades in preparation for the battle that was expected to take place sooner or later.[189]

The clash at Garmudj worsened the situation for the Armenian population of Urfa. There were more arrests and reports of torture in the prison in order to obtain information about hidden arms. Meanwhile long caravans of Armenians deported from Erzurum and Harput were passing through the city. There were straggling lines of old men, dazed women, and emaciated children, but no younger men. "As the different parties were brought in," writes Glockler, "they were lodged in khans, in the city, amidst indescribable filth and often without food or water, except what their guards chose to procure for them at extortionate rates." Many died before their turn came to move on; others were bought from the guards and taken as servants into Muslim homes. Local Armenians tried to help the deportees by bringing them clothing and food, for by the time they reached Urfa most of the exiles had been robbed of all their possessions. It often happened, reports Glockler, that "soon after one of these dismal processions had passed out of sight among the hills, we would hear repeated shots fired from that direction. This meant that those who were too sick or weary to drag themselves any further had been put out of their misery so as not to impede the march."[190] Künzler states that on trips into the countryside he found everywhere corpses that had been covered with some earth but had been dragged out by roving animals.[191]

On August 10 two men in officer's uniform, Cerkez Ahmed Bey and Galatali Halil Bey, arrived in Urfa from Diarbekir. The two officers were said to be delegates of the CUP and, over the objections of the local authorities, took over the handling of the local Armenian population. They collected ransom for imprisoned notables but failed to release them and instead had them killed. Both Eckart and Künzler report that prisoners were taken out on the road to Diarbekir and killed shortly after leaving Urfa.[192] According to Glockler, the Armenian members of parliament Krikor Zohrab and Vartkes Seringulian met their end in this way.[193] Cerkez Ahmed and Galatali Halil were later arrested on orders issued by Djemal Pasha, tried for the murder of the two deputies and other atrocities against Armenians, and hanged (see chapter 7).

During a search for arms on August 19 an Armenian deserter opened fire on the policemen, and two of them were killed. The American vice-consul in Aleppo, Samuel Edelman, happened to be in Urfa on that day and later described what happened next. The killing of the policemen "was the spark that inflamed the Kurdish population to fury and arming themselves with any available weapon at hand including cudgels and iron pikes, a rush was made on the Armenian quarter. All who fell into their hands were slaughtered without mercy, this was followed by the looting of Armenian shops." The total number of slain, Edelman reported, was not known, but two hundred and fifty was a conservative estimate. "Despite their intense hatred of the Armenians, the police did their duty well, but their numbers were totally out of proportion in handling the mob."[194] By the next morning order was finally restored. Eckart and Künzler state that the two CUP delegates had given the order to massacre the unbelievers.[195]

Mugerditch for some time had been urging the Armenians of Urfa to start armed resistance, and by the end of August he finally prevailed. The Armenians, writes Jernazian, had now "realized that the pitiable condition of the Armenian refugees from other cities could be theirs, too....Almost all of the influential people who had always opposed the decision to resist in the past were already dead." Just at this point, Jernazian relates, an order arrived from Constantinople to stop the deportations. The order in question must have been the directive of August 29, which stated that "aside from those who have already been transferred and relocated, no additional Armenians are to be removed."[196] Jernazian informed Mugerditch of this order and inquired whether he might not wish to postpone the uprising, but the guerrilla leader rejected the idea. Jernazian quotes him saying: "Badveli, the people refused to defend themselves at the right time. Now I don't care whether this is the wrong time or not." The next Turkish aggression against the Armenians of Urfa was going to be resisted on the spot.[197] It is not known whether the Armenian community at large was informed of the directive commanding an end to the deportations.

The battle for Urfa began on September 29 after a police patrol had entered the Armenian quarter to investigate shots fired during the previous night, apparently by drunks at a party. When the police attempted to enter the house from which the shots had been heard they were fired upon and had to retreat. Reinforcements were called, but they also were met with heavy fire and suffered casualties. Church bells rang to signal the start of the uprising. According to a long-existing plan, barricades were set up around the Armenian quarter. The Armenians, writes Jernazian, had "resolved to die honorably rather than submit to being trapped and slaughtered."[198] Led by the charismatic Mugerditch, the resistance of the Armenian fighters in the heavily fortified stone houses lasted sixteen days and was finally broken only with the help of a newly arrived contingent of six thousand Turkish troops equipped with heavy artillery. The chief of staff of the Turkish general in command of these troops was the German officer Eberhard Count Wolffskeel von Reichenberg, who several times himself commanded the attackers. He is the only German officer known personally to have participated in the killing of Armenians.[199] Jernazian's statement that Eckart, "being a trained artilleryman," directed the fire of the heavy guns and thus provided the Turks with "invaluable aid" in their siege is false. The missionary Eckart had never served in an artillery unit and has an exemplary record of helping the Armenians.[200] The origin

of this allegation, which perhaps confuses Eckhart with von Reichenberg, is not known.

The surrender of the rebels took place on October 16. Mugerditch,
who had been wounded several days earlier, committed suicide in order
not to fall into the hands of the Turks. Others are said to have shot
their wives, children, and then themselves. According to Künzler, several Armenian men and women committed acts of betrayal by pointing out hiding places. This was understandable, he contends, because a
large majority of the Armenians had opposed the uprising but had been
forced to endure the ill-fated rebellion. "Betrayal was their revenge."[201]
The fighters who surrendered were executed. Prisoners in one large
batch, writes Glockler, "were marched off to a neighboring ravine and
shot. Another lot of about a hundred, they tied together and shot to
death against the Mission wall."[202] Still others were tried by court-martial and then were hanged in groups of five, six, or seven in different
quarters of the city. According to the Turkish commander, his losses in
the suppression of the uprising were twenty killed and fifty wounded;
Consul Rössler spoke of fifty dead and about a hundred and twenty-
five wounded.[203] As soon as the fighting had ended, Glockler reports,
Kurdish men, women, and children swarmed in from the neighboring
villages and began to loot the Armenian houses. They even stripped
the dead bodies of the clothing they wore.[204]

Those who clearly had not belonged to the revolutionaries and the
women and children were spared. Most of these were deported and
are said to have died on the way to Ras-ul-ain, southeast of Urfa.[205]
The inhabitants of Armenian village of Garmudj near Urfa, which had
not participated in the uprising, were also deported in late October.[206]
Consul Jackson notes that not one of those deported from Urfa was
ever heard of again, "though I sent a trustworthy Mohammedan on a
five weeks journey throughout the interior into which they had disappeared to make a diligent search for any of the survivors, and I personally made many inquiries to that end. Without a doubt they suffered
the fate of their fellow townsmen when at a safe distance from the city,
and their bones lie bleaching in the sun and sands of the vast Mesopotamian desert."[207] Whether the Armenians of Urfa might have been
able to avert this horrible outcome if they had refrained from staging a
rebellion will never be known.

Little more than a year later a large number of Armenians were
again living in Urfa. Finding themselves without pharmacists, bakers, tanners, shoemakers, weavers, or other artisans and merchants,

the people of Urfa petitioned Djemal Pasha for relief. He ordered that twenty-five hundred such persons and their families be released from the Armenian camp at Rakka, south of and about three days' travel away from Urfa.[208] Rössler reported in February 1917 that these craftsmen were living in Urfa "relatively well and safely."[209] Jernazian calls them "forced laborers" but acknowledges that they were able to move freely during off-duty hours.[210] When he left the country in May 1917, Jackson writes, over six thousand Armenians were back in the city, though, according to Künzler, they were under pressure to convert.[211] Künzler also took care of about twenty-five hundred Armenian orphans as well as more than two thousand women and children who had been in hiding and needed help. During the winter of 1917–18 food in Urfa was in such short supply that many died of starvation.[212] After the war had ended, in the summer of 1919, the number of Armenians in Urfa was estimated to be "several thousand." The Swiss relief worker making this report noted that some children taken into Muslim homes and girls married to Muslims were reluctant to be "liberated" and preferred to stay where they were.[213]

CONSTANTINOPLE AND SMYRNA

The Armenian population of Constantinople (today's Istanbul) in 1915 has been variously estimated to have ranged between seventy thousand and a hundred and sixty thousand. During the night of April 24, 1915, while the Allies were landing at the Dardanelles, several hundred leading citizens were arrested and deported, and there were subsequent deportations of thousands of Armenians caught without a residence permit. The permanent Armenian population of the capital, however, was never subjected to a mass deportation program and survived the war largely intact.

On June 15, 1915, the government hanged twenty Hunchak leaders. The men had been accused of involvement in a plot to assassinate Talaat (decided at a Hunchak conference in Constanza, Rumania, in 1913), though in fact they had opposed the plan. It appears that the Hunchaks in Constantinople had failed to denounce the presence of two assassins, who were caught in 1914, and the government now used this abortive plot in order to highlight the unreliability of the entire Armenian community.[214]

Despite agitation against the Armenians that continued for many months the Armenians of Constantinople were not deported. Some attribute this fact to the presence of a large number of foreign diplomats and merchants in the capital.[215] Lepsius argues that it was Germany that prevented the deportation.[216] Whatever the real reasons for the decision to spare this large group of Armenians, it is certainly significant in regard to the alleged intent of the Young Turks to destroy and exterminate the entire Armenian population. As a recent student of the subject has written: "Could anyone conceive of Hitler allowing the Jews of Berlin to continue living in Berlin while he implemented his genocide against them elsewhere?"[217]

About thirteen thousand Armenians lived in Smyrna (today's Izmir), and many of them belonged to the richest and most influential people in that city. In the early summer of 1915 the authorities conducted searches for weapons and there were some arrests, but otherwise the situation was fairly normal. In July a court-martial condemned seven Armenians to be hanged for an offense allegedly committed in 1909, and this sentence prompted a vigorous show of protest from the diplomatic corps as well as from prominent local Turks. The American consul in Smyrna, George Horton, informed Ambassador Morgenthau: "This is a peaceful community; up till now we have had no massacres, serious plotting or wholesale hanging, and the spectacle of seven Armenians being hanged, generally believed to be innocent, will be a thing not at all salutary for Smyrna from any point of view."[218] Morgenthau thereupon intervened with Enver, and his efforts on behalf of the condemned men were successful. On August 25 the government announced that, acting upon an imperial pardon, the sentence had been changed to fifteen years' imprisonment at hard labor.[219] The *vali* of Smyrna, Rahmi Bey, continued to have the reputation of being a moderate and opposed to the deportations.[220]

Following the appearance of pro-Allied leaflets in several parts of the city in early November, about twenty-five hundred Armenians were arrested, but most of them were soon freed again.[221] A year later, in November 1916, weapons and bombs were found buried in an Armenian cemetery. This led to the arrest and deportation of three hundred Armenians. Since the bombs hailed from the time of Abdul Hamid and since most of those arrested were rich people, the Austrian consul noted, it would appear that this was an instance of blackmail.[222] As it happened, Marshal Otto Liman von Sanders, the German commander of the Turkish Fifth Army and the head of the German military mission, was in Smyrna on an inspection trip that day, and the German consul there informed him of what had happened. Subsequent inquiries revealed that the deportation had been carried out by the police in the most brutal manner and that even old women and sick children had not been spared. Liman von Sanders thereupon sent a message to the *vali* that demanded the immediate end of such relocations. In the event that the *vali* failed to obey, Liman von Sanders was prepared to use troops under his command to prevent further deportations. The relocation order, he wrote in a report filed on November 17, had created great excitement in the city; and he was unwilling to tolerate such measures, which jeopardized the military security of a city threatened by enemy attack.[223]

The *vali* obeyed the order. Before Liman von Sanders left Smyrna, Rahmi Bey reaffirmed to the German marshal once again that he personally was opposed to the deportations and promised that there would be no recurrence. A few days later Liman von Sanders was informed in writing that those Armenians found innocent would be allowed to return to Smyrna.[224] According to one account, in order to appease the authorities in Constantinople, the *vali* "was forced to deport Armenian revolutionary party leaders from the city."[225] The German consul reported in the spring of 1917 that the Armenians in the province of Aidin (with Smyrna as the capital) for the most part had not been deported and that any distress was due to the lack of food, which created a difficult situation, especially for the poorer Armenians.[226] Indeed there were no further deportations. "Until the war ended," a survivor recalls, "the comparatively few Armenians in the Vilayet of Aidin were left in more or less of [*sic*] peace."[227]

The End of the Deportations

The deportation of the Armenian community did not end at a definite date. Beginning in late August 1915 the government repeatedly issued orders that no further Armenians were to be deported; but these orders apparently were seldom obeyed, thus necessitating the promulgation of further such decrees. The same holds true for the various exemptions granted to Protestant and Catholic Armenians as well as to the families of soldiers, doctors, and other important professions and crafts. Here, too, we know that these decrees were frequently ignored.

On August 29, 1915, Minister of the Interior Talaat communicated the following decree to all of the provinces:

> The only goal which the Government hopes to attain by the removal of the Armenians from their places of residence, and their transfer to

specified areas, is the prevention of their activities against the Government, and to put them in a position where they will be unable to pursue their dreams of establishing an Armenian Government....In addition, it is the wish of the Government that, aside from those who have already been transferred and relocated, no additional Armenians are to be removed. As has been previously announced, the families of soldiers, artisans in the necessary proportion, and the Protestant and Catholic Armenians, are not to be transferred.228

However, this order ended neither the deportations nor the disregard of the exemption for Protestants and Catholics. The endeavors of various diplomatic representatives to help the Armenians therefore continued. On November 8 the Austrian ambassador, Johann Markgraf von Pallavicini, spoke with the Turkish foreign minister, Halil Bey, and once again protested "in the most serious and forceful manner" against the persecution of the Armenians. The minister assured him, Pallavicini reported to Vienna, that the government had decided to end the relocation of the Armenians. For those who already were in Syria the government would find shelter and sustenance. An official had been sent out to implement this decision.229 About three weeks later the German ambassador met with Enver Pasha, Halil Bey, and Djemal Pasha to discuss the "Armenian horrors." Metternich emphasized that anxiety and indignation had spread in Germany, and in response Enver and Halil affirmed that the Porte planned no further deportations. Unfortunately, Metternich wrote Berlin, Turkish promises that they would undertake no new deportations were "worthless."230

Talaat Pasha gave the same pledge in a meeting with the German ambassador on December 18. Just returned from Anatolia, Talaat told Metternich that he had taken "far-reaching measures" for the feeding of the relocated Armenians; offenses against the property and life of the Armenians were being severely punished. At that moment no relocations were taking place anywhere, and the government sought to alleviate the problems that had developed in the wake of the deportations. As far as possible, Catholic and Protestant Armenians, who on the whole had not participated in revolutionary activities, would be allowed to return to their regular places of residence.231

Actual practice, of course, did not conform to these assurances in terms of either the adequate feeding of the deportees or the end of compulsory relocations. When informed of an incident that had involved the deportation of twenty-seven families in February 1916, Talaat reprimanded the offending official. General relocations, he pointed out on March 12, were to have ended; and "transfer was to be restricted to those individuals with close ties to the committees [the Dashnaks and Hunchaks], and those whose treachery has been ascertained by the Government."[232] Three days later, on March 15, Talaat sent a message to all the governors that reaffirmed what should have been operating procedure since August 1915: "Owing to administrative and military considerations it has been determined that from this time forward the transfer of Armenians will cease. It is ordered that from this time forward no Armenians, other than those already relocated, will be transferred for any reason."[233]

That the exception for dangerous individuals had created a new loophole and excuse for deportations was acknowledged by Halil Bey in a meeting with Metternich on March 21, 1916. Local officials out of exaggerated zeal had misinterpreted the order permitting the relocation of "unruly elements" and had deported large groups of Armenians. An order had now been issued that in Konia, Angora, Aintap, and Marash, the scene of new deportations, no Armenians at all were to be relocated.[234] Yet this new order also did not put an end to the deportations, and on October 24 Talaat had to issue still another instruction: "As the transfer of Armenians is revoked, it is no longer appropriate to dispatch convoys of Armenians who are to be transferred and relocated. Therefore, if investigations have determined that there are dangerous individuals who should be transferred, we are to be promptly notified of their names and total number."[235]

On February 4, 1917, Talaat Pasha was elevated to the post of grand vizier. In a declaration before parliament some days later the new head of government affirmed the equality of all nationalities in the Ottoman state, a formula that was seen as a repudiation of the extremist wing of the CUP. In a personal talk with the German ambassador, Richard von Kühlmann, Talaat confirmed that in the matter of the non-Turkish nationalities he intended to steer a new course. He had met with the Catholic and Gregorian patriarch and had assured them that the legal rights of the Armenian population would not be infringed upon. "If at all possible amends should be made for what the previous government had been forced to do because of military necessities. Orders to this effect had been sent to all the provincial authorities."[236] The Austrian ambassador was told by Djavid Bey, the new finance minister, that the persecution of the Armenians had been a great mistake and a crime and that the new government was determined not only to abandon this policy but make up for it to the best of its ability.[237]

Unfortunately and not surprisingly, the ability of the central government to influence events in the provinces remained limited. At a time of increasingly grave shortages of food and other essential commodities, the lot of the surviving Armenians continued to be dismal. In many places pressure to convert persisted. But the deportations for all practical purposes had finally come to an end, and there was even talk of an amnesty that would allow the deportees to return to their homes.[238] Before these measures could be realized Turkey suffered decisive military defeats and had to sign an armistice. Many Armenians now drifted back to their old communities, only to find their houses either plundered or occupied by Muslim refugees and face starvation. At the end of the war even the capital, which throughout the war had enjoyed relatively good supplies of food, experienced near-famine conditions. An American who lived in Constantinople reports that the misery of the people was unconcealed, and people were collapsing in the streets.[239] The deportations had exacted a huge death toll, and the once flourishing Armenian community in Turkey had ceased to exist.

Chapter 11

Resettlement

According to the deportation orders of May 1915 the Armenians were to be settled in the southern parts of the province of Mosul, the district of Urfa (with the exception of the provincial capital), and the district of Zor. Most of these destinations were in the eastern part of Syria. Local officials were instructed to protect the lives and property of the deportees passing through and to provide them food and shelter. Once they arrived in the resettlement areas, the Armenians were to be "relocated in accordance with local existing conditions, either in houses which they will build in existing towns and villages, or in newly founded villages, which will be located in areas to be determined by the government."[1] According to the implementing regulations approved on May 30, attention was to be paid "to establishing the villages in places which will suit public health conditions, agriculture and construction." When needed, the government was to provide funds for the construction of houses, operating capital, and tools for those engaged in agriculture and crafts. "Each family to be resettled will be allocated appropriate land, taking into account their previous economic conditions and their present needs."[2] Unfortunately, hardly any of these fair-sounding provisions for resettlement were implemented. The majority of the deportees ended up in inhospitable arid areas, and hardly any of them received help to start a new life of self-sufficiency. An uncounted number of the exiles never reached their destination in the resettlement zones and perished of starvation or disease or were killed on the way.

RAS-UL-AIN

The camp of Ras-ul-Ain was located in an oasis populated by Circassians, about 250 miles northeast of Aleppo. A branch of the Baghdad railway that eventually was to reach Mosul led to the oasis and ended there. The camp of Ras-ul-Ain appears to have been a transit camp on the way to Der-el-Zor, but the inmates stayed there for quite a while under conditions somewhat less horrible than in the other transit camps along the Euphrates (see the discussion below). They also probably were in better condition on arrival because they did not have to get there on foot. The first transports of Armenians arrived in early July 1915. Beginning in late October, for a time, groups of exiles arrived from Aleppo every day, and by February 1916 the Armenian population of Ras-ul-Ain was estimated to be about twenty thousand.[3]

According to a survivor, most of the time the guards left the camp inmates alone, and those with money could go out and buy food in the marketplace.[4] Others had to depend on an erratic distribution of bread that was never sufficient to meet all needs. A German engineer reported a "flourishing trade in girls" conducted by the gendarmes. For an appropriate sum of money it was possible to acquire girls or women for a limited time or for keeps.[5] Sanitary conditions were extremely poor, and soon dysentery and typhus were taking their toll. A German officer noted that hundreds were dying daily.[6]

In the spring of 1916 the camp of Ras-ul-Ain still held about fourteen thousand exiles. On April 6 reports reached Aleppo of massacres involving the population of the camp. A German emissary sent there by Consul Rössler spent several days in the area to investigate the situation and reported on his return that he had found only two thousand survivors. The others had been taken out of the camp in groups of three hundred to five hundred each day over the course of the preceding month and killed. The corpses had been thrown into a river. The killers were said to have been Circassians, but the prevailing view, Rössler wrote to Berlin, was that they had acted on orders. The *kaimakam,* too, claimed to have followed orders.[7]

Whether the massacres had indeed been perpetrated on command from above, and, if so, on whose command, will probably never be known. Those perpetrating the killings had an obvious interest in pleading superior orders. Two Arab officers who deserted from the Turkish army and reached England implicated the Kurds who served as gendarmes guarding the camp. The Kurds, too, were said to have acted on orders from above.[8] A German missionary who visited Ras-ul-Ain in June of 1917 found only a handful of impoverished Armenian women and children and two craftsmen. He thought that the motive for the killings had been greed. The huts of the Circassians, he reported, were crammed with the possessions of the murdered Armenians.[9]

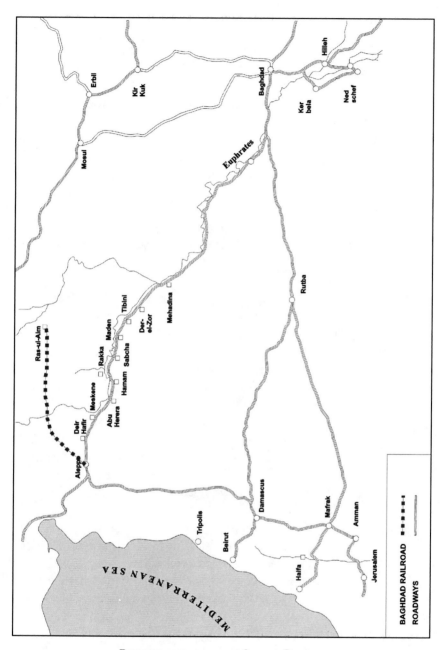

RESETTLEMENT IN THE SYRIAN DESERT

"THE ROUTE OF HORRORS"

The largest concentration of deported and resettled Armenians was in Der-el-Zor, about 270 miles southeast of Aleppo. Some exiles reached Der-el-Zor by boat on the Euphrates, but most of the deportees got there by means of a long and difficult trek on foot through the Syrian desert. The German consular official Wilhelm Litten, going from Baghdad to Aleppo, traveled this route in January–February of 1916 and in his report to Rössler called it "The Route of Horrors." The numerous corpses along the way revealed what had happened here. Some, from early convoys, had become skeletons; others were naked bodies whose clothing had been torn away by robbers; while still others, who had died very recently, were lying on or by the side of the road fully clothed, with faces distorted by their suffering. He also saw a large convoy of new deportees driven forward by gendarmes who carried whips. Weakened by hunger, disease, and pain, Litten wrote, the laggards among the exiles staggered on. Those who failed to catch up risked their life: the way stations with water were about forty miles apart, and many of the deportees did not have enough food or water to last even the three days of walking that it took to get from one station to the next. At some stations no food was available at all. Those able to survive the trek through the desert, Litten predicted, would die later because of the shortage of food and the spread of typhus.[10]

An employee of the Vacuum Oil Company of New York, Auguste Bernau, who was sent by Consul Jackson to distribute relief, traveled the same route in September of that year and reported very similar conditions. All along the road to Der-el-Zor he had seen graves containing the remains of Armenians who had failed to outlast the rigors of the long trek. His journey had left him with an "impression of horror," which it was difficult to convey. "Everywhere you see emaciated and wan faces, wandering skeletons, lurking for all kinds of diseases and victim moreover to hunger." He observed women searching in the dung of horses for not yet digested barley seeds on which they fed. When he gave them some bread, they stuffed it voraciously into their mouths amid hiccups and epileptic tremblings. What he had seen and heard, Bernau wrote, "surpasses all imagination. Speaking of 'thousand and one horrors' is very little in this case."[11]

A large number of deportees destined for resettlement in Der-el-Zor were to be found in encampments all along the Euphrates. "Those who have some money left," Bernau reported, "are incessantly exploited by their guards, who under threats of sending them further on, take from them gradually their last resources, and when these resources are exhausted, they put these threats into execution." Bernau estimated that there were about fifteen thousand deportees in these transit camps, who, "ill-treated by the authorities, put in an impossible position to provide for their food, are gradually dying of hunger." Unless substantial relief funds reached these exiles, he concluded, "these unfortunate people are doomed."[12]

The camp at Meskene, about seventy miles east of Aleppo, was fairly typical of these transit camps. When Litten came through Meskene in early February 1916 he found an encampment of more than two thousand tents and about ten thousand persons. He saw no latrines, and all around the camp there was a wide belt of excrements and garbage.[13] An emissary of Sister Rohner, sent to the encampments along the Euphrates to distribute money, returned from there on June 20 and reported seeing thirty-five hundred deportees and more than a hundred orphans. A few had found work as bakers, coachmen, and so forth, but most of the exiles were forced to beg, since the government did not distribute any food. Every tent contained sick and dying persons. Those who did not manage to obtain any bread through begging lived on grass, which they cooked and ate. "Many hundreds of the sick," the emissary reported, "lie in the open without tents or blankets under the burning sun." He was able to gather a hundred children in a tent, had them bathed and their ragged clothes washed, and left money to feed them a daily soup and bread. Ten days later the children were sent on toward Der-el-Zor, where the emissary found only two still alive. The others had perished on the route.[14]

Bernau, who passed Meskene in September of the same year, described the camp as a place at which thousands arrive, but which most do not leave alive. He estimated that there were about forty-five hundred deportees in Meskene.

> These are but living fantoms. Their superintendents distribute to them sparingly and very irregularly a piece of bread. Sometimes three or four days pass when these famished people who have nothing to eat but this piece of bread, receive absolutely nothing. A dreadful dysentery makes numerous victims among them, especially among the children. These latter fall ravenously upon all that come under their hands, they eat herbs, earth and even their excrement. I saw, under a tent of five or six square meters, about 450 orphans pele mele in dirt and vermin. These

poor children receive 150 grams of bread a day, sometimes and this is more often the case, they remain two days without eating anything.[15]

Bernau related that, according to information he had been able to obtain in Meskene, "nearly 60,000 Armenians are buried there, carried off by hunger, by privations of all sorts, by intestinal diseases and typhus which is the result. As far as the eye can reach mounds are seen containing 200 to 300 corpses buried in the ground pele mele, women, children and old people belonging to different families." Rössler learned from two different sources that the number of Armenian exiles buried in Meskene was 55,000.[16] Seven months later, on February 14, 1917, Rössler reported to Berlin that an emissary of the American consulate (who had just returned from a trip undertaken for the purpose of distributing money) had informed him of the most recent conditions in the camps along the Euphrates. Some of the deportees were now being used for the purpose of building roads, bridges, and houses. In Meskene six hundred deportees were thus employed, while another three hundred were there without work and in the most miserable shape.[17]

Conditions were somewhat better in Rakka, a town on the left bank of the Euphrates, in which a sizable number of Armenians were allowed to stay and which therefore can be considered a place of resettlement. In February 1916 some ten thousand Armenians were said to be living in Rakka and the surrounding villages.[18] Some Armenian artisans were able to open shops in the town; an Armenian baker even provided bread to the military garrison in the town.[19] Bernau reported in September 1916 that "5 to 6000 Armenians, mostly women and children, are scattered in the different quarters of the town, and live in groups of 50 to 60 in houses which the kindness of the governor has procured for the most poor." Armenian women and children could be seen begging in the streets. On the right bank of the Euphrates, opposite Rakka, was a transit camp of some thousand deportees who lived in tents and were famished.[20] "The more enterprising among us," recalls an Armenian from Erzurum, "were able to skip away to Aleppo and other places by means of the usual bribe."[21]

By February 1917 the situation of the exiles in Rakka had seriously deteriorated. Bernau, who once again had visited Rakka to distribute aid, reported that the town itself now experienced hunger and that the government therefore had almost completely stopped distributing food to the deportees. An epidemic of typhus had broken out among the exiles, living crowded into close quarters, and twenty were dying every day.[22] When the Swiss missionary Künzler visited Rakka in April he found there six thousand exiles in "a hopeless situation."[23] He informed Rössler about what he had seen, and the German consul relayed this information to Berlin. Since sufficient funds to alleviate this crisis were not available, Rössler wrote, the six thousand Armenians in Rakka for the most part would have to starve to death. The persons leading the aid program had decided that they would use the limited money at their disposal to help those deportees who had a chance to survive. In places like Rakka any help provided would result merely in prolonging the agony of the exiles by a few days or weeks.[24]

Help for the Armenians at Rakka came from an unexpected quarter. In December 1916 Djemal Pasha had ordered that twenty-five hundred Armenian artisans and their families be sent to Urfa (see chapter 10). During the summer of 1917 another large group of deportees was taken from Rakka to Urfa to do road work, for which they received a daily ration of bread. In a report to Rössler submitted on December 9 Künzler noted that the number of Armenians left at Rakka was now down to about a thousand. He had been back to Rakka in August, and the misery of those left behind was beyond description. "I can only say that seeing it was almost more than my nerves could stand."[25]

DER-EL-ZOR

For about a year the final destination of the Armenian deportees sent to Mesopotamia was the district of Der-el-Zor. We have contradictory figures about the number of exiles settled there. Consul Jackson in Aleppo reported in early February 1916 that some three hundred thousand Armenian exiles had been settled in Der-el-Zor and the surrounding villages; but in a dispatch of September 10, 1916, Jackson gives the figure of thirty thousand. In a report composed about two years later after his return to the United States Jackson speaks of "about 60,000 collected at Deir-el-Zor."[26] In March 1916 Consul Rössler gave the number of Armenians there as forty thousand, a figure accepted by a contemporary author.[27] A German military chaplain, who was in Der-el-Zor in April 1916, also speaks of forty thousand Armenians there.[28] According to an Armenian survivor, a hundred and eighty thousand exiles arrived in Der-el-Zor between June 1915 and May 1916.[29] Some of these figures refer to the exiles in the city of Der-el-Zor proper while others include the entire district, which may explain the discrepancies. A considerable number of deportees are known to have been settled in the general vicinity of the city of Der-el-Zor but further downstream on the Euphrates. Still, even when interpreting the figures in this way, we are left with a large disparity.

For about a year the exiles in Der-el-Zor were treated relatively well. The *mutassarif* (governor) of Der-el-Zor, Ali Suat Bey, was a decent and educated man who spoke English and French and did what he could with the limited means at his disposal. He scattered the Armenians on farmlands, built homes for them, and sought to provide food, clothing, and medical care.[30] On September 26, 1915, as Ambassador Morgenthau recorded in his diary, Zenop Bezjian, the representative of the Armenian Protestants, called on him and asked for help for the various camps of the deportees. At the same time Morgenthau was surprised to learn from his conversation with Bezjian that the "Armenians at *Zor* were fairly satisfied; that they have already settled down to business and are earning their livings."[31] Of course, the good intentions of Suat Bey were not sufficient to solve all problems created by the huge influx of largely destitute people. An Armenian priest sent to Der-el-Zor by the Catholicos of Sis to look into conditions there reported back that most of the more than fifteen thousand exiles who had arrived by the middle of July were still living in the open without adequate shelter and that there was not enough food.[32] Rössler heard from a military physician, who had visited Der-el-Zor in November, about a continuing shortage of vegetables and bread. The three hospitals in the town were overcrowded; according to the municipal doctor, the daily death toll was 150 to 200. Many others were dying in the tent camp outside the town.[33] Yet Rössler felt that the *mutassarif* was "doing everything in his power to relieve the misery."[34]

In April 1916 the situation got drastically worse. The original deportation orders had included the provision that the relocated Armenians were not to exceed 10 percent of the Muslim population among which they were to be resettled. As Rössler reported on April 27, the *mutassarif* of Der-el-Zor had now been reminded of this provision and had been ordered to reduce the Armenian population accordingly. The Armenians above the quota were to be sent to Mosul, located northeast of Der-el-Zor in today's Iraq. The German consul feared that this meant the expulsion of at least thirteen thousand persons. Those exiles who escaped the depredations of the Bedouins and Kurds, he wrote, would perish on this new trek as a result of starvation and disease.[35]

The expulsion of thousands of Armenians from Der-el-Zor has generally been blamed on the new *mutassarif,* Zeki Bey, who was appointed, it is said, to replace the too lenient Suat Bey. In fact several convoys of Armenians had already been forced to leave Der-el-Zor weeks before the arrival of Zeki Bey. An emissary of Sister Rohner, who spent six weeks in Der-el-Zor and by June 20 was back in Aleppo, reported that during the time he was in Der-el-Zor twelve thousand new exiles arrived there and "large convoys were sent away to Mosul every day." Those who could pay were able to get residency permits; all others had to move on.[36] We do know that two convoys left Der-el-Zor on April 15 and that twenty-five hundred exiles arrived in Mosul on May 22.[37]

On July 12 the Ministry of the Interior ordered a halt to further deportations to Der-el-Zor because the Armenians there had exceeded 10 percent of the Muslim population.[38] On July 17 Zeki Bey had the leading figures among the exiles at Der-el-Zor (priests, lawyers, etc.) arrested.[39] All others were ordered to leave, but none of these convoys reached their destination. It appears that practically all of these deportees either succumbed to the severe desert conditions encountered on this route of about 350 miles or were murdered near the river Khabar a short distance from Der-el-Zor. Survivors named Kurdish gendarmes, Circassians, Chechens, and Arabs as the killers.[40] Jackson writes that a "systematic search was made of each person before the murders and whatever money or article of value they possessed was taken from them by order of the governor who personally took charge of the loot. The actual murderers were permitted to profit by whatever clothing or other things found on the corpses, and many articles of clothing were recognized in Deir-el-Zor thereafter in the possession of these brigands and others to whom they were sold."[41] Three German officers who passed through the area along the Khabar in April 1917 encountered large quantities of skeletons; many of the skulls had bullet holes. Local inhabitants spoke of twelve thousand Armenians who were said to have been slaughtered there.[42]

Whether these killings were indeed carried out on the orders of Zeki Bey is not clear. The Circassians and Chechens living along the Khabar River had a reputation of being fanatic Muslims, and they may have acted on their own initiative. It is undisputed that large numbers of Armenian exiles lost their lives at this location. Rössler estimated that more than thirty thousand deportees were killed during the months of July and August. Thereafter only a few Armenian artisans and children were left at Der-el-Zor. According to Rössler the total number of Armenians still alive between Meskene and Der-el-Zor had been reduced by the end of August 1916 to a mere fifteen thousand.[43]

A German officer, Ludwig Schraudenbach, who passed through Der-el-Zor in early 1917, reports hearing of horrible atrocities committed on the orders of Zeki Bey. Children were said to have been tied between wooden boards and set on fire. Schraudenbach's account makes it clear that he heard of but did not see any of these outrages. Dadrian leaves out this important qualification and refers to these allegations as fact.[44]

THE *Vilayet* OF DAMASCUS

Due to the intervention of Djemal Pasha more than one hundred thousand Armenians were sent to the province of Damascus rather than to the Syrian desert (see chapter 10). Most of these deportees could use the railroad. Many men with means bribed the authorities and thus were able to rent quarters in the major cities (Hama, Homs, and Damascus), where they made themselves useful as artisans or traders. At times there was pressure to convert, and the exiles in southern Syria experienced losses due to shortages of food and epidemics. There were no massacres, however, and large numbers of these deportees survived.

The Austrian consul in Damascus, Dr. Karl Ranzi, reported on September 24, 1915, that to date some twenty-two thousand Armenians had come through the city. The Turkish authorities had let it be known that the exiles would receive shelter and arable land to settle on; but so far, Ranzi wrote, this had been granted only to one group, who had been put into homes prepared for Muslim refugees. While in Damascus the Armenians had been under guard, but quite a few had managed to escape and had found refuge with local Armenians.[45]

Some five months later Ranzi noted a change for the better in the situation of the exiles. While previously the deportees had been sent to the southern thinly populated areas east of the Jordan, they now also were being sent to more populated parts of the province, and some had even been kept in Damascus. Many exiles had found work in agriculture and with the railroad. The subsistence allowance paid to them had been raised. Credit for these improvements, the consul wrote, was generally given to Djemal Pasha. In a declaration publicized in all the newspapers, Djemal had recently stated that the removal of the Armenians was necessary for reasons of state but that the life, honor, and property of the relocated were under the protection of the government. The fulfillment of this obligation was a matter of moral integrity.[46]

During the winter of 1915–16 Syria and Lebanon experienced a severe shortage of food as well as an epidemic of typhus, and the situation of the deportees took a turn for the worse. A survivor who had been sent to Amman (today's Jordan) reports that typhus killed most members of his family and "wiped out hundreds of lives daily."[47] A German officer was told by a gendarme that the Armenian exiles at Petra (Jordan) had food for one day and then suffered hunger for the next twenty days. The officer was so moved by what he had seen that he left the Armenians two sacks of barley.[48]

In March 1916 Djemal Pasha organized an aid program for the Armenians that was headed by Hussein Kasim Bey, the former *vali* of Saloniki and Aleppo. Loytved Hardegg, the German consul in Damascus, reported on May 30 that Kasim Bey had provided bread, had established a delousing and bathing facility together with a hospital, and had found work for many of the exiles. About seven hundred widows and orphans had been sent to Hama, where they were given work in a knitting factory. Unfortunately, Hardegg wrote, Kasim Bey threatened to resign his office because he was not given enough funds to help the approximately sixty thousand Armenians in Syria and Palestine and local authorities not only did not support his measures but opposed them. Kasim Bey also was greatly upset about the deportations to Mesopotamia, which he regarded as an attempt to exterminate the Armenians. Hardegg suggested that the Swiss charity program send money to the Turkish official, who was an honorable man and in whom he had complete confidence.[49]

There is no information on whether Kasim Bey made good on his threat to resign the directorship of the aid program, but we do know that the anti-Armenian attitude of the local authorities continued. During the course of the year 1916, both the German and the Austrian consul wrote of increasing pressure on the Armenians to convert, which was especially strong in the villages. In the towns, where many of the exiles had been able to practice their crafts and therefore were relatively better off, they were being threatened with expulsion to the villages. The poor among the deportees were told that they would lose their subsistence allowance unless they converted to Islam. Austrian consul Ranzi noted that large numbers of Armenians were yielding to these threats. The terrible fate that had overtaken them had broken their spirit and had weakened their strength to resist.[50]

One of the last archival references to the exiles in the province of Damascus is a dispatch from Hardegg dated March 23, 1917. The Armenians had gone through hard times, the German consul wrote. It was difficult to get exact figures, but he feared that some thirty thousand deportees had lost their lives. Only about 10 percent of the exiles could be considered self-sufficient, and at least fifteen thousand depended on outside help. The situation for artisans in the towns recently had improved somewhat.[51] All in all and despite many difficulties, as a recent author has noted, the Armenians deported to southern Syria "survived in surprising numbers." It is now estimated that 20,000 out of 132,000 died, a sadly large number but a far better ratio than among the deportees to the eastern part of the province.[52] The overall number of deaths is discussed in chapter 13.

Chapter 12

Who Were the Perpetrators of the Massacres?

Our knowledge of who committed the mass killings of Armenians that accompanied the deportations of 1915–16 is woefully incomplete. The dead cannot speak, and survivors often were too traumatized to have firm recollections of what had happened to them. One of the most important clues is geographic. Practically all of the known massacres were carried out in eastern and central areas of Anatolia inhabited by Kurds or in places of resettlement populated by Circassians such as Ras-ul-Ain and around Der-el-Zor. There were no massacres in Cilicia or in Syria south of Aleppo or in Palestine. Most of the references to the killers by contemporary witnesses involve Kurds, Circassians, brigands, irregulars, and the gendarmes accompanying the convoys. Gendarmes are also implicated in the murders of Armenians arrested before the beginning of the deportations. None of the observers on the scene as much as mentions the Special Organization, which the courts-martial of 1919–20, Dadrian, and a few other authors contend was the agent of the state-sponsored exterminatory process.

THE ROLE OF THE KURDS

Relations between Armenians and Kurds had been strained and hostile for many decades, but the year 1914 brought new tensions. The rights granted the Armenians under the reform agreement signed by the Ottoman government under the threat of Russian intervention were seen by both Turks and Kurds as the opening wedge for Armenian independence. Turkey's declaration of a "holy war" on November 13 denounced England and France as infidel nations and enemies of Islam. Even though the declaration was not aimed against the empire's Christians it nevertheless encouraged religious fanaticism. Finally, the continuing activities of the Armenian revolutionary movement created

fears of the establishment of Armenian hegemony in the contested territories of eastern and central Anatolia. Kurdish farmers were afraid of
losing their lands, and these concerns were exploited and cultivated by
Ottoman propaganda, especially after the beginning of the war and
the Russian offensive of 1914. The Armenians, it was said, had made
common cause with the Russians. Unless the Kurds actively helped the
Turks against the Russians and their Armenian allies, in the event of a
Russian victory they could expect a terrible vengeance for the wrongs
they had inflicted on the Armenians in the past.[1] Kurdish depredations
against the Armenian population received a new license.

The Ottoman government had never been able to establish full
security for the Anatolian countryside; conditions on the roads were
especially bad in the eastern territories, where the Kurds had a reputation for being ardent robbers and brigands. An English traveler who
journeyed through this area in 1913 noted that "highway robbery takes
place with impunity even under the walls of the large towns."[2] After
the outbreak of war Ottoman troops and soon even gendarmerie units
left for the front, and the imperfect protection formerly provided by
the presence of these forces came to an end. Kurdish bands now could
operate with relative impunity. Security on the roads also suffered
from the presence of tens of thousands of deserters. It is estimated that
by the summer of 1916 there were fifty thousand deserters from the
Turkish Third Army alone. "They roamed the countryside, living off
the land and turning into robber bands."[3] It is possible that some of the
attacks on Armenian convoys were carried out by such deserters from
the Turkish army.

The Kurds had always looked upon the Armenians as their natural prey; the Armenian deportations became for some of them a welcome opportunity to gather booty and seize women. Many Armenians
in the convoys were known to carry large sums of money and gold.
Wartime conscription had taken most of the younger men and had left
Armenian girls and women without much protection. The few men in
the convoys were usually killed first, and Kurdish tribesmen then could
plunder and kidnap with little risk. With their religious fanaticism
enhanced by government anti-Christian propaganda or simply out of
greed for the clothing of the victims, the Kurds often murdered even
women and children. They may have caused the greatest toll of lives
by stealing the Armenians' money; in view of the little food that was
provided to the deportees, without money to buy provisions the exiles
were condemned to starvation and death.[4]

Survivor accounts of the massacres often implicate "irregulars" or "volunteers," and this term probably refers to Kurdish irregular forces, especially the Hamidiye units established by Sultan Abdul Hamid in 1891. After the Young Turks had deposed the sultan in 1908, they reorganized these Kurdish volunteer forces and renamed them "tribal regiments" or "tribal cavalry." Some of these units, loosely attached to the regular army, fought in the Balkan wars and later against the Russians in the battle for the Caucasus. Others, motivated by fear of an Armenian state and greed for material gain, participated in the Armenian massacres with "contemptible success."[5]

In some sources the Kurdish volunteer tribal cavalry is called the "tribal militia" or just "militia."[6] Many of the massacres in Diarbekir are said to have been perpetrated by such a militia, brought into the city specifically for this purpose.[7] The Danish missionary in Harput, Maria Jacobsen, noted in her diary the arrival in the town of four hundred "Kurdish volunteers." These men, she wrote on March 16, 1916, "look and behave like wild animals....Their greatest pleasure and occasion for celebration is when there is a massacre, and it is these Kurds who have been used to kill our many friends."[8]

In the Van area Kurdish militiamen are accused of perpetrating atrocities against Armenian villagers. This militia, an Armenian deputy charged in a memorandum submitted to the Turkish cabinet in February 1915, was reinforced by Kurdish criminals released from jail and by armed Kurdish deserters.[9] The militia units were usually organized by local authorities, often under the influence of militants in the CUP clubs. The German and British consuls attributed much of the violence against the Armenians in that city to the role of this ominous parallel government (see chapter 10).

According to some authors, the Kurds who massacred deportees did so at the behest of the Ottoman government. The Kurdish brigands are said to have been "put into active duty by the Turkish government."[10] Kurdish writers share this view. The Ottoman rulers, writes the Kurdish historian Kamal Madhar Ahmad, employed the Kurds "as a tool." The Kurds had nothing to do with the organization of the massacres, and "most of them had their hands smeared with blood by government instigation or outright coercion." Many of them were motivated by "blind religious intolerance" and "strove to earn God's 'blessing' through participating in the liquidation of the 'infidels.'" The Kurds also suffered from "backwardness and harsh economic conditions." Hence "there were simple-minded and poor Kurds who wanted to share in looting the Armenians."[11]

It is true that Turkish gendarmes and Kurds often cooperated in arranging for massacres and the looting of Armenian convoys, but the idea that the Kurds were coerced to kill the Armenians is not supported by any evidence. The astute George Hepworth noted that the Kurds "love a gun, a sword, a dagger, and are exceedingly reckless in the use of these weapons, especially when the victim is unarmed." Killing was not seen as a crime, and brutality was rampant. "If the man in their way happened to be an Armenian, and especially if he had valuables on his person, they made quick work with him, and did not suffer from any compunctions whatever."[12] These lines were written in 1898, but little, if anything, had changed by the time of World War I. Some Kurds, notably the Alevi Kurds in the Dersim mountains, sheltered Armenians. Nonetheless, it appears that in 1915–16 many Kurds were active and willing participants in the massacres of Armenians, primarily because of the desire for booty. There was no need to incite or coerce them.

THE WARTIME GENDARMERIE

The Turkish gendarmes were known to be ignorant, corrupt, and poorly trained. Their performance had shown some improvement after the Young Turk revolution of 1908, but they were still led by practically uneducated officers.[13] A British police instructor who spent six weeks on an inspection tour in eastern Anatolia in 1913 reported that the gendarmes were paid irregularly and sometimes not at all for months on end.[14] Missionary Henry Riggs wrote that the gendarmes had a reputation for extortion and violence. Decent men would generally not enter this service, "which is ordinarily recruited from the lowest classes of the population." The outbreak of war worsened this situation:

> The Turks were desperately short of men, and the gendarmes, with some sort of training and experience with arms, were the first and most valuable reserve. So the trained gendarmes, bad as they were, had gone to meet the first onslaught of the Russian armies and were replaced by sevenfold more the children of hell than themselves. An order came from Constantinople...to the effect that any convict who could accept service as a gendarme should be given his liberty. Needless to say, they all volunteered, the prisons were soon emptied, and the force of gendarmes was

speedily brought up to full strength by the enlistment of the worst criminals in the country—hardened wretches whom even the Turkish government had found it necessary to restrain from their careers of murder, plunder and worse.[15]

The enlistment of the convicts did not in fact end the shortage of gendarmes. An Austrian officer reported from Bitlis that the *vali* there also complained that he did not have enough gendarmes to accompany the Armenian convoys.[16] Foreign minister Halil Bey told Ambassador Morgenthau on November 12, 1915, that he did not have "sufficient gendarmes and soldiers" for escort duty.[17] Riggs's description of the consequences of taking hardened convicts into the gendarmerie is nonetheless correct. It is likely that these were the men who in many towns murdered the Armenians arrested in the spring of 1915 and who later played an equally nefarious role during the deportations. Some gendarmes, as survivor accounts confirm, were kind and protected their charges, but the majority appear to have been callous and corrupt.

Liman von Sanders, the former head of the German military mission, who testified at the trial of the assassin of Talaat Pasha in Berlin in 1921, also attributed many of the outrages against the Armenians to the wartime gendarmerie. The deportations, he stated, "fell into the worst possible hands." After the gendarmerie had been enrolled in the fighting forces, "a relief gendarmerie was created that was certainly not made up of the best elements. Some of them were brigands and the rest were unemployed. These circumstances should be borne in mind when we are talking about the atrocities committed in the Armenian convoys."[18] Other observers confirm the ignoble role played by the wartime gendarmes. The Swedish missionary in Mush, Alma Johannsen, describes how "vagrants who could not find any other employment were being recruited as gendarmes and then had the right to do whatever they wanted. The outcome is one long sequence of cruelty and inhumanity."[19]

In a conversation with Ambassador Morgenthau, foreign minister Halil Bey acknowledged that "the gendarmes that had been assigned to act as escort to the deported Armenians, committed some of the worst crimes against them."[20] From the testimony of survivors and witnesses on the scene we know that this included killing, rape, extortion, and collusion with the rapacious Kurds. A survivor of the massacres near Harput told Consul Davis that "the gendarmes sold them in groups of fifty or a hundred to the Kurds who were to kill them and could have whatever they could find on them."[21] In his summary report composed in 1918 after his return to the United States Davis mentions additional details that he learned a bit later. The gendarmes would bring a large group of Armenians to a valley or some other convenient place, summon the Kurds from nearby villages, and order them

> to kill the Armenians, telling the Kurds they could make money in this way but would have trouble if they refused. An agreement was then made by which the Kurds were to pay the gendarmes a certain fixed sum—a few hundred pounds or more, depending on circumstances— and were to have for themselves whatever was found on the bodies of the Armenians in excess of that sum. As I heard this explanation a number of times, I think such a system was employed quite generally in that region and perhaps in other parts of Turkey as well.[22]

It is doubtful that the Kurds needed to be threatened in order to enter into such a deal. This particular detail probably came from the Kurds, who told Davis of these events and who wanted to be seen as acting under quasi-orders. The basic facts of the scheme are mentioned by others. A former Ottoman official who spent twenty-two days in a Turkish jail was told by a Kurdish fellow inmate that gendarmes in Harput sold more than fifty thousand Armenian deportees to a Kurdish chief with orders to kill them and share all of their possessions with the gendarmes.[23] A survivor tells how before reaching Aleppo her convoy was sold by the gendarmes to mountaineers, presumably Kurds, who then proceeded to rob and rape the deportees.[24] The Kurdish historian Kamal Madhar Ahmad also speaks of Kurdish *aghas* (lords) who bought Armenian convoys from the gendarmes.[25] The German vice-consul in Alexandretta, Hermann Hoffmann, relates that gendarmes sold pretty girls and women to Kurds.[26] The "delivery [of deportees] to the Kurds by the gendarmes accompanying the convoys" is also reported by Consul Jackson in Aleppo.[27]

CIRCASSIANS, CHETTES, AND "SIMILAR SCUM"

After the Circassians had been subjugated by Russia in 1862, large numbers of them were deported under horrendous conditions to Turkey. Their hatred of Christians was strong, which accounts for their pronounced hostility toward the Armenians. The Circassians often were recruited for police work. Many of the *zaptiye* (policemen) in the towns were Circassians.[28]

Circassians were involved in the massacre of exiles in Ras-ul-Ain and Der-el-Zor (see chapter 11). Consul Rössler in Aleppo reported on July 27, 1915, that the authorities had recruited "Circassian volunteers" and had directed them against the Armenians.[29] In another dispatch he speaks of a turf fight between Circassians and Kurds in the Urfa region, who came into conflict with each other over the plundering of the Armenians.[30] We have no further details about the role of the Circassians.

The picture is even more murky with regard to the *chettes*. In a report to the German military mission in Constantinople, the German officer Stange speaks of the murder of Armenian deportees from the province of Erzurum by "so-called Chettes (volunteers), Aschirets [tribesmen], and similar scum."[31] Stange equates the *chettes* with volunteers but does not explain who these volunteers are. Consul Scheubner-Richter in Erzurum, on whose reporting Stange draws, defines the *chettes* as "mounted Turkish volunteers,"[32] perhaps meaning Kurds. Consul Davis in Harput blames the killing of deportees on Kurds, gendarmes, and "companies of armed 'tchetehs' (convicts) who have been released from prison for the purpose of murdering the Armenian exiles."[33] A few pages later in the same report Davis suggests that the *chettes* are brigands who prey upon all travelers, not just Armenians. "The roads are filled with bands of Kurds and 'tchetehs' who have been turned loose on travelers and it is a matter of little importance to them whom they rob and kill. I understand that many Turks have been killed while traveling. It seems as though there is a great danger of these people getting beyond all control and overrunning the country."[34]

Armenian survivors give different descriptions of the *chettes*. Mrs. Papazian, wife of an Armenian photographer in Erzurum, relates how her convoy was "beset by Chetas or guerilla soldiers," who killed her husband and baby.[35] Another survivor from the Smyrna region states that the *chettes* were "men who belonged to the Turkish militia, feared to a certain extent by the civilian population as it was into their hands that much of the 'law and order' was given." They were drawn mostly from "the lawless elements of mountain people."[36] The equation of the *chettes* with Turkish militia can also be found in the dossiers of suspected war criminals compiled after the war by the office of the British high commissioner in Constantinople. One Shevki Bey of Diarbekir is accused of having been an "Officer of Militia i.e. Tchetes." The militia is described as "a sort of volunteer force organized specially for the purpose [of massacres]. It was officered by local notables. The rank and file were recruited from the worst elements including released criminals from local prisons."[37]

Authors who have written about the period of World War I have put forth their own descriptions. Former ambassador Morgenthau speaks of "Chétés or brigands."[38] The *chettes* of 1915, Toynbee maintains, were brigands out for loot, reinforced by released convicts, who were organized and armed by the authorities in order to "accomplish results which they desired to see accomplished but preferred not to obtain openly for themselves."[39] A more recent author defines the *chettes* as bands of Turkish irregulars.[40] These different descriptions of the *chettes* do not completely contradict each other and overlap to some degree. The common element is that the *chettes* were irregulars who (no matter how recruited, directed, or composed) participated in the robbing and killing of Armenian deportees.

THE FATE OF THE LABOR BATTALIONS

Until 1908 Armenians were barred from military service; but soon after the Young Turk revolution the Armenians, now treated as equal citizens, became subject to conscription like other Turks. This meant that they had to serve in the military or pay an exemption tax (*bedel*). The general mobilization of August 1914 resulted in the drafting of most able-bodied Armenian males nineteen to forty-five years old into the army, but their service as regular soldiers did not last very long. The brutal treatment of all recruits resulted in a generally high rate of desertion, and the number of Armenian deserters appears to have been especially large. Some Armenian soldiers joined guerrilla bands or went over to the Russians. Unsure of the loyalty of the Armenians, the government therefore began to disarm the Armenian soldiers and put them into labor battalions (*amele tabouri*). This decision apparently was made in September 1914. The British consul in Erzurum reported on October 14, 1914, that "in the last two to three weeks many Armenian soldiers have been permanently disarmed and put to spade work.... The government are doubtful of the willingness of the Armenian soldiers to fight Russia."[41]

The process of disarming the Armenian soldiers took several months. On February 25, 1915, the Turkish High Command reminded the commanders of the Third and Fourth Army that Armenians were not to be employed in any military unit, including the gendarmerie.[42]

On July 25, 1915, another order from the commander-in-chief took note of the relocation of the Armenian population. "For this reason, it is necessary to take strict measures against Armenian soldiers enrolled in the Labour battalions, so that they cannot disturb the local security. They must be watched closely."[43]

The treatment of the Armenian soldier-laborers was harsh. At a time of general food shortages the provisioning of the Armenians had low priority. A survivor recalls working twelve hour days with little food.[44] A Jewish doctor treated Armenians sent to the Sinai desert to build roads and railway tracks and noted their high mortality. "Without clothing, poor supplies or no supplies at all, limited food, without proper sanitary conditions, all this quickly decimated some battalions by 30 percent. There were days in which tens and even hundreds would die in a single day. A typhoid fever epidemic ravaged them. By the end of March [1916] there was, in effect, no longer a single labor battalion in the desert."[45] According to an official German source, the labor battalions in the Beersheba desert were the worst hit by the typhus epidemic.[46] The Latin American soldier of fortune Nogales reports that the Turkish officers stole the rations and lived in grand style, while their laborers died of starvation and disease.[47] There was pressure to convert, and those who hesitated were threatened with deportation.[48]

We have several reports of massacres of Armenians serving in the labor battalions. About six hundred men working on a road construction project near Urfa were murdered in August 1915. Two missionaries and an Englishman interned in Urfa were told of this event by a survivor of the massacre, carried out by Circassians and gendarmes.[49] Consul Rössler in Aleppo heard of this mass killing from a different source.[50] Other Armenians, who had been transporting grain for the army at Mush and Bitlis, were killed near Harput. According to Consul Davis, "some of them resisted and a few escaped, but most of them were killed. I have seen their dead bodies alongside of the road just outside of the town."[51] Consul Heizer in Trebizond was told of the massacre of 180 Armenian laborers by a soldier who had participated in burying the bodies, all which had been stripped of their clothing.[52] The Austrian consul in Trebizond reported the killing of 132 soldier-laborers during the same month.[53] The massacre near Urfa was instigated by two Turkish officers subsequently tried and convicted by a court-martial convened by Djemal Pasha. In most other cases we do not know who was responsible for the killings.

We have no information on how many Armenians in the labor bat-talions died of hunger and disease and how many were killed.[54] A Ger-man missionary states that as a rule the laborers were killed after they had finished their construction project, but he provides no details.[55] "Numbers of Armenian males," writes Erickson, "remained alive as the Turkish Army continued to use Armenian manpower in its labor battalions until the end of the war."[56] The Swiss missionary Künzler speaks of several hundred Armenian soldiers returning to Urfa after the armistice, and these may have been members of labor battalions.[57] According to Sarkis Atamian, large numbers of Armenians escaped service in the labor battalions, joined guerrilla forces, and engaged in numerous skirmishes and battles with the Turks.[58]

The Baghdad railway employed about eight hundred skilled Arme-nians, while more than eight thousand Armenians in labor battalions were used in construction work, especially in the completion of the tunnels. The men were housed in tents and primitive huts. Food was of poor quality and was distributed irregularly. Because large numbers of infected persons passed along the railway route the workers suffered a high rate of disease, especially typhus.[59]

For more than a year the railway workers were exempt from depor-tation; but in June 1916 local officials in Adana, under the pressure of a rabid anti-Armenian CUP branch, ordered the deportation of thou-sands of Armenian railroad workers and their families. Interior Minis-ter Talaat reaffirmed the exemption order on August 4,[60] but the local officials disregarded it. The tug of war over the fate of the Armenian workers continued until the end of the war. The German engineers directing the construction sought to keep their workers, and they were supported by the directors of the railway company. Humanitarian con-siderations also played a role. At least one highly placed German offi-cer, however, supported the deportations, which seriously hampered the construction effort and for a time brought all work to a halt. It was the government's realization of the disastrous consequences of this policy for a crucial military supply line that saved at least a part of the Armenian employees and construction workers.[61]

Many of the deported railroad workers succumbed to the hard-ship of the journey or were killed. On July 10, 1916, Consul Rössler forwarded to his ambassador the story of a convoy that had started out with 1,000 deportees but was down to only 623 persons at the time when the Armenian composing the report managed to escape.[62] Künzler saw this convoy come through Urfa and reports that the young railroad workers were killed soon after leaving the town.[63] The archives of the Turkish General Staff are said to contain reports on the Armenian labor battalions,[64] but so far these files they have not been systematically studied by Western historians.

THE POWER OF LOCAL OFFICIALS

Some of the killings are said to have been organized by CUP fanatics, who in certain towns formed a kind of shadow government. We know that in many cases local officials disregarded instructions received from Constantinople or interpreted orders of the central government in an especially harsh manner. An admonition to take all necessary measures to maintain order or punish all rebels with the utmost severity thus could easily lead to massacres. Some of these officials were Muslims who had been forced to flee from the Balkans or Russia and therefore hated all Christians with great vehemence.[65]

The important role played by local CUP branches was already apparent before the outbreak of war. In a dispatch of February 25, 1914, the German consul in Trebizond, Dr. Heinrich Bergfeld, noted that every official sought first of all to find out what the local CUP committee thought. If the wishes of these men contradicted orders received from the central government, then these orders were disregarded.[66] With respect to the deportations this situation often meant that exemptions or ameliorations granted by Constantinople were ignored. Ambassador Hohenlohe reported to Berlin in September 1915 that promises for improvements in the lot of the Armenians made by Talaat most likely would remain unobserved because of the arbitrary actions of the local authorities in the provinces, over which the central government had little or no control.[67] About a year later, a dispatch by an American embassy official similarly noted the destructive role of the local CUP organizations, who carried out deportations without instructions from the central government and excused these activities as "measures of local necessity."[68] In his memoirs Otto Liman von Sanders, the head of the German military mission, saw conditions in the same light. "In the execution of the expulsions many of the terrible and damnable cases of ruthlessness may unquestionably be ascribed to the minor officials whose personal hatred and rapacity gave the measures ordered from above an enhancement of harshness that was not intended."[69]

The local hotheads did not always prevail. Three particularly rabid CUP members were expelled from Adana because of the way in which they had hounded the Armenians from the city (see chapter 10). There were other such cases, but in many instances the disputes between moderates and radicals in the provinces appear to have ended with the victory of the militants. Reports that these fanatical elements at times organized massacres therefore have credibility even if the documentation for them is meager.

Chapter 13

The Number of Victims

The number of Armenians who were killed or perished during the deportations of 1915–16 can only be estimated, because no death statistics for this period exist. One can compare the size of the Armenian population before World War I with the number of survivors at the end of the war, but such a comparison cannot yield precise figures either. For one thing, the size of the Armenian community in 1914 itself is controversial. More importantly, the number of Armenians who survived the tribulations of the war period can also be fixed only approximately, and there is no way of separating the number of Armenians who died as a result of starvation or disease from those who were killed. The Muslim population also suffered a very large death toll from famine and epidemics; a certain number of Armenians therefore undoubtedly would have died from these same causes even if they had not been deported. Still, it is probably safe to conclude that as a result of being removed from their homes the number of Armenians who lost their life was far higher than it otherwise would have been. We know that many of the deportees perished as a direct result of the deprivations incurred during the long marches through inhospitable terrain and due to the terrible conditions in many of the settlement sites.

Finally, an undeterminable number of Armenians lost their lives as a result of the guerrilla war waged by Armenian revolutionaries. Some of this fighting may be considered a defensive reaction to the threat of deportation. Other armed engagements, however, especially in the eastern provinces of Anatolia, were offensive in nature, designed to help the Russian invaders. It is therefore not obvious that the losses incurred in this warfare should be included in a tabulation of Armenian victims of the Young Turk regime. While we can arrive at an estimate of the total Armenian death toll, probably a very high percentage of the resultant figure—but clearly not all of it—is due to deliberate Turkish malfeasance.

THE SIZE OF THE PREWAR ARMENIAN POPULATION

Both the Turkish government and the Armenian patriarchate compiled statistics for the population of the empire, and each side challenged the accuracy of the statistics prepared by the other. Official Turkish figures were said to have undercounted the Armenian population, while the Armenian figures were seen as exaggerating the number of Armenians and minimizing the Muslim population. Both Turks and Armenians accused each other of misusing population statistics for political purposes.

The last Ottoman census was carried out in 1904–5 and is considered reasonably reliable by most students of the subject. The statistics for 1914, important for the calculation of Armenian losses, were based on reports sent to the census department in Istanbul every three months by provincial registrars. These reports included the number of births, deaths, and changes of address in each district of the province. The census department, in turn, used these reports to update the census and issue new tables at the end of each year.[1] The major shortcoming of this system was the undercount of women and children as well as underreporting due to factors such as the isolation of some groups of the population, difficulties of communication, and the resistance of some subjects to the census. The demographer Kemal Karpat maintains that the Muslim population was undercounted more often than the Christian groups: it included nomadic people such as the Kurds, while the Christian population was more settled and therefore more easily accessible.[2] Armenian authors have argued that the Armenians, especially in the eastern provinces, were undercounted because they sought to evade military service or the military exemption tax as well as the payment of ecclesiastical taxes. They therefore avoided registration.[3]

The Armenian position is supported by a study prepared in 1919 by a British delegate to the Paris peace conference, who faulted the Ottoman statistics of 1914 for a substantial understatement of the non-Muslim population.[4] However, the statistics of the Armenian patriarchate have also come in for criticism. The patriarchate's figures, the demographer Justin McCarthy argues, were more or less informed guesses, which consistently undercounted the Muslim population. This undercount of Muslims "met the political aims of those who desired Armenian independence."[5] McCarthy and Karpat stress that only the statistics of the government were compiled by making an actual count of the population. The undercounts that did occur were not deliberate deception, involved errors happening in all developing countries, and can be compensated for. Using the raw Ottoman statistics as a base, McCarthy has compiled figures that correct for the undercount of women and children. Karpat suggests a margin of error of 6 to 12 percent for both Muslims and non-Muslims in remote regions.

Demographers on both sides agree that the raw numbers for the Armenian population presented by the Ottoman government and the Armenian patriarchate require correction, but there is no agreement by how much. Nonspecialists in the Armenian camp, seeking to buttress Armenian territorial claims and claiming a high number of Armenians killed during the deportations, therefore have felt free to go well beyond the official raw statistics, and some have put forth prewar population figures as high as 3,000,000 Armenians.[6] Pro-Turkish writers, in contrast, who want to minimize the Armenian presence in eastern Anatolia and the number of Armenian victims, have generally accepted the raw Ottoman figures for 1914: 1,294,851 Armenians in the empire.[7] The discrepancy between these two sets of numbers is more than 1,500,000.

If we limit ourselves to official statistics and the corrected figures produced by demographers and similarly qualified authors, the discrepancy is a bit smaller but still substantial:

Raw Ottoman statistic for 1914	1,294,851[8]
McCarthy (1991)	1,735,920[9]
Patriarchate (1910 and 1912)	1,973,950[10]
Marashlian (1991)	1,944,230[11]
Karajian (1972)	2,500,000[12]

Most historians have accepted figures for the prewar Armenian population that remain below 2,000,000. Toynbee in 1916 estimated it at between 1,600,000 and 2,000,000.[13] An article by Charles J. F. Dowsett (*Encyclopaedia Britannica,* 1967) speaks of 1,750,000 Armenians.[14] Hovannisian acknowledges that Armenians have exaggerated the number of Armenians and minimized the number of Muslims, while the Turks have done the opposite. He concludes that the true size of the prewar Armenian population is probably between 1,500,000 and 2,000,000.[15] Malcolm E. Yapp and Erik Zürcher place the Armenian population of Anatolia at 1,500,000, which would put the total number of Armenians in all of the Ottoman Empire at about 1,750,000.[16] I am inclined to accept this figure.

THE NUMBER OF SURVIVORS

We do not know the number of Armenians who were deported. According to the American military mission to Armenia, led by Maj. Gen. James G. Harbord, the "official reports of the Turkish government show 1,100,000 as having been deported."[17] But the document (issued in 1920) does not further identify these "official reports," and none have ever been discovered. A British memorandum on relief needs dated October 30, 1918, speaks of the deportation of "over 1,000,000 Armenians."[18] The Turkish historian Salahi Sonyel gives the figure of about 800,000 deported Armenians.[19] Raymond Kévorkian works with the figure of 870,000 deported to Syria.[20] And Boghos Nubar, the head of the Armenian delegation to the Paris peace conference, stated in 1918 that the number of deported was 600,000 to 700,000.[21] None of these authors base their counts on authoritative sources. In a recent publication the Turkish historian Yusuf Halacoglu invokes Ottoman documents to support his figure of 438,758 persons "relocated,"[22] but there is reason to question the completeness of this count. The same author claims that no Armenians were deported from Urfa, but numerous sources make it clear that this is not the case.

We also do not know how many persons survived the hardships of the deportation. It is possible to arrive at some estimates by using available information such as the number of exiles who were supported by aid organizations after the war and the number of Armenians who took refuge in neighboring countries. It is known that a surprisingly large number of Armenians managed to find shelter with friendly Turks, while others were exempted from deportation because of their needed skills or because they bribed Turkish officials. A good number of exiles were able to escape from the convoys or the places of resettlement and found refuge in cities such as Aleppo and Constantinople or drifted back to where they had come from. Children were often left near mission stations or given to the missionaries for protection. A survivor recalls that in the town where he was employed as a goldsmith "almost every Turkish household kept one or two young Armenian women, some as maids, others for their harems."[23] This appears to have been a not uncommon situation, but we do not know how many Armenians were thus able to avoid deportation.

Contentions that large numbers of Armenians survived the ordeal of the deportations are supported by an unexpected source. During the last year of the war and at the ensuing peace conference in Paris the

Armenians put forth their claims for an independent state, a reward for their contribution to the Allied war effort and in line with Wilsonian principles. As the Allies soon began to realize, however, this demand for Armenian self-determination conflicted with the right of self-determination of the Turks and Kurds, who outnumbered the Armenians in much of the large expanse of Turkish territory that the Armenians were claiming. The Armenians had never constituted a majority in these provinces, and the deportations had further reduced their number. The Armenian National Delegation headed by Boghos Nubar therefore began a concerted effort to lower the claims of Armenian losses and to stress the number of survivors.

It was wrong to assume, Boghos Nubar stated in a memorandum of May 24, 1917, handed to the Allies, that not enough Armenians were left in Turkey to form an independent nation. "Notwithstanding the large number of victims of massacres and deportations, most of the Armenians have been able to escape or survive extermination."[24] In an official communication to the French government composed at the end of 1918 Boghos Nubar provided details to support this conclusion. It was believed, he wrote, that there were about 250,000 Armenian refugees in the Caucasus, 40,000 in Persia, 80,000 in Syria and Palestine, and 20,000 in the Mosul-Baghdad area. This meant that a total of 390,000 Armenian exiles waited to return to their homes in Anatolia, and this figure did not take into account other survivors whose whereabouts were still unknown.[25]

The historian Albert Lybyer, writing in 1922, took a dim view of these diplomatic maneuvers of the Armenians. "Pitiful attempts were made to minimize the terrible losses of the nation by deportation and massacre, in the vain attempt to prove that there existed enough Armenians to receive and rule so large a country."[26] Still, despite the opportunistic motive, the numbers cited by Boghos Nubar are not all wrong. For example, his figure of 250,000 survivors in the Caucasus is similar to the number of 300,000 Armenians who were aided by the American relief effort there in 1917 (though this figure may have included an unknown number of needy Russian Armenians).[27] William L. Westermann, the American delegate at the Paris peace conference and chief of the delegation's Near Eastern division, gave an even higher figure: 400,000 Armenian refugees in Russian Armenia.[28] Similarly, while Boghos Nubar spoke of 80,000 Armenians alive in Syria and Palestine, other sources cite still higher numbers. After an inspection tour, James Barton (the head of the American Board of Commissioners for Foreign

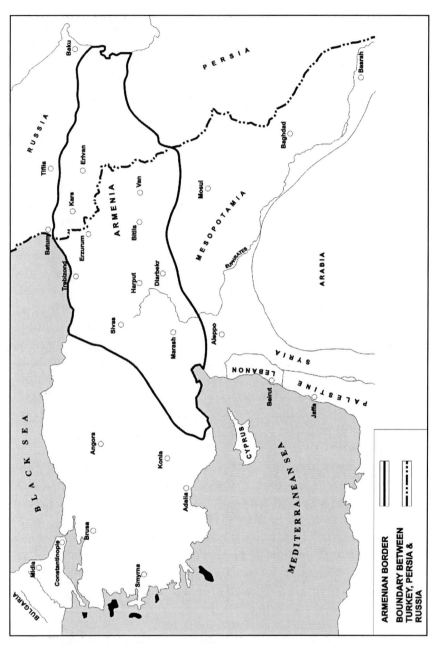

BOUNDARIES OF ARMENIA AS CLAIMED AT THE PARIS PEACE CONFERENCE (1919)

Missions) in April 1919 reported to the American peace delegation in Paris that there were 100,000 Armenian refugees in the Aleppo and Damascus districts waiting to return to their homes.29 The American relief official Stanley Kerr writes that at "the time of the Armistice the Allied commanders in Syria found some two hundred thousand Armenians who had survived the 1915 deportations but were on the verge of starvation." Some 170,000 of these were eventually repatriated and returned to their abode in Cilicia and other parts of Western Anatolia.30

We have several other estimates of the total number of Armenians alive at the end of the war. George Montgomery (an American official at the Paris peace conference in charge of Western Asia) provided a detailed tabulation of Armenians alive in Turkey in 1919, which amounted to 594,000. In addition he reported 450,000 Armenians in the Caucasus and 60,000 in Persia, for a total of 1,104,000. The source of these figures was given as Aleppo, but we have no further details about who compiled the tabulation.31 A very similar number, 1,250,000 Armenian survivors, was put forth by the Armenian National Council of Constantinople in 1919. This figure was said to include Armenians who had converted.32

In 1921 the German missionary Johannes Lepsius published a compilation of Armenians still alive in Turkey and in the Caucasus, which yielded a total of 650,000 survivors.33 His figures were for 1921, by which time a large number of Turkish Armenians had left Turkey for various countries in the Middle East, Europe, and the United States. We have no exact figures for Armenian emigration during this period. But we do know that by 1920 some 10,000 Armenian refugees had arrived in Palestine,34 by 1925 well over 200,000 Turkish Armenians had found refuge in the Arab lands under French and British mandate,35 and by 1925 more than 30,000 had emigrated to France and close to 100,000 to the United States.36 In order to render Lepsius's figure comparable to those compiled in 1919 one would have to adjust it by several hundred thousand; but without knowing the number of Armenian emigrants during the 1919–21 period such a correction is impossible. If we were to take the average of these four sets of figures, including the uncorrected numbers of Lepsius, we would arrive at the number of 948,500 survivors. Without Lepsius's numbers the average of the other three sets yields a total of 1,108,000 Armenian survivors, which is probably the better of the two figures.

An Estimate of the Losses

By deducting the number of survivors from the Armenian prewar population we get an idea of the magnitude of the losses suffered by the Armenian community of Turkey during World War I. According to the numbers I have accepted (1,750,000 prewar population and 1,108,000 survivors), the death toll comes to about 642,000 lives or 37 percent of the prewar population.

The following list of Armenian losses given by various authors reveals wide discrepancies, though the disparity would be reduced if the loss of life were to be expressed in percentages—most of those who cite large losses also give higher numbers for the prewar population and vice versa.

Halacoglu (2002)	56,612[37]
Gürün (1985)	300,000[38]
Sonyel (1987)	300,000[39]
Ötke (1989)	600,000[40]
Toynbee (1916)	600,000[41]
McCarthy and McCarthy (1989)	almost 600,000[42]
Kévorkian (1998)	630,000[43]
Courbage and Fargues (1997)	688,000[44]
Steinbach (1996)	700,000 (600,000–800,000)[45]
Zürcher (1997)	700,000 (600,000–800,000)[46]
Morgenthau (1918)	800,000 (600,000–1,000,000)[47]
Suny (1998)	800,000 (600,000–1,000,000)[48]
Ottoman Ministry of Interior (1919)	800,000[49]
Lepsius (1919)	1,000,000[50]
Ternon (1981)	1,200,000[51]
Dadrian (1999)	1,350,000 (1,200,000–1,500,000)[52]
Kazarian (1977)	1,500,000[53]
Karajian (1972)	2,070,037[54]

Some of these authors have based their numbers on research in the sources; others have put forth what they consider to be a reasonable figure. However, even the most careful research, it must be stressed, cannot yield anything but estimates, for we know neither the exact number of the prewar population nor the precise number of the survivors. It should also be noted again that there exists no way of separating out the Armenian deaths due to guerrilla warfare or due to starvation and disease among those who escaped deportation—causes of death that also took the lives of many Muslims. We also do not know how many Armenians were forced to convert. Relying on the reports of well-placed commentators in different parts of the empire, Sarafian estimates that between 5 and 10 percent of Ottoman Armenians were converted and absorbed in Muslim households during 1915.[55] Some of these converts returned to the fold after the war; but many others did not, and these persons simply disappeared from the statistics.

In the final analysis, these uncertainties and the great disparities in the estimates of deaths probably do not matter much. The question of whether my figure of 642,000 Armenian lives lost is more or less accurate than the figures of other authors reproduced above loses its pertinence in the face of the incredible human tragedy that lies behind these statistics. Turkish and pro-Turkish authors correctly stress that the Armenians were not the only ones to suffer horribly and that Muslims, too, lost their life in large numbers during World War I. According to Justin McCarthy, the death rate of Muslims in eastern Anatolia alone "is well beyond that of most of the great disasters in world history, such as the Thirty Years War and the Black Death."[56] Still, none of this can compare or compensate for the special calamity of the Armenians, who lost not only their lives but also their existence as an organized ethnic community.

There is also an important difference between deaths lost as a result of natural causes such as famine and epidemics—blows of fortune that afflicted Muslims and Christians alike—and deaths due to deliberate killing—the massacres that were the lot of many thousands of Armenians during the deportations. The large-scale killing of noncombatants that occurred during the fighting in eastern Anatolia was also deliberate; but inasmuch as this intercommunal warfare involved reciprocal excesses that took the lives of both Muslims and Christians (each group gave as good as it got) it cannot be equated with the murder of the hapless Armenian deportees. Muslim refugees also suffered greatly, but their movement westward for the most part was at their own pace rather than under the lash of gendarmes; the agonizing deaths of Armenian women and children during the long marches through the desert find no parallel among the adversities experienced by the Turkish population. Due to famine, epidemics, and warfare, the people of Turkey, both Muslims and Christians, experienced a mortality rate far worse than that of any other country during the First World War; but the sad fate of the Armenians will always stand out as a special tragedy.

Part IV

THE STATE OF THE CONTROVERSY

Chapter 14

Conclusion: The Question of Premeditation

In previous chapters of this book I have discussed the reasons for the deportation of the Armenian community in Turkey, the way in which this relocation was implemented, and its often deadly consequences. In this concluding chapter I focus on the key question of whether the Young Turk regime deliberately set out to destroy the Armenians and on the issue of responsibility for the large loss of life that took place. Although Armenians and Turks and their respective supporters have put forth conflicting explanations for the horrendous death toll, I believe that an alternative explanation has better support in the historical evidence.

A SPECTRUM OF VIEWS

Practically all defenders of the Armenian cause believe that the World War I deportation of the Armenians carried out by the Ottoman government represented a state-sponsored plan of annihilation. Dadrian argues, for example, that a vast corpus of archival and other evidence documents "a deliberate scheme of extermination carried out under the guise of deportation, a course of action beyond the realm of feasibility without the complicity of the central authorities."[1] In view of the large number of victims, deportation is held to have been merely a euphemism for extermination. The Young Turk regime aimed at the destruction of an entire people and thus is guilty of the crime of genocide. By calling this attempted annihilation a case of genocide, I should point out, one makes this act a crime under international law; but the use of this legal nomenclature does not add any material facts important for the history of these events.

The great majority of pro-Armenian authors writing about the deportations also maintain that plans for the destruction of the Armenian community in Turkey were made well ahead of the events of 1915 and thus provide further proof of premeditation. The Armenian genocide is seen as "the culmination of the protracted Turko-Armenian conflict, a conflict that did not lend itself to a mutual accommodation or a peaceful resolution."[2] The Ottoman government, it is argued, used the opportunity of war in order to solve the Armenian problem once and for all. The planned character of this scheme of physical destruction is held proven by the pattern of identical events at many different locations: "a systematic program to annihilate Armenians in the Ottoman empire."[3] In the eyes of some Armenians these actions are also seen as manifestations of the Turkish national character: "massacre, outrage and devastation have always been congenial to the Turks." By his conduct during the First World War, the Turk proved that "he is as cruel and brutal as he was when he first swooped down as the scourge of God in Asia Minor one thousand years ago."[4]

In 1915 Toynbee argued that all "this horror, both the concerted crime and its local embellishments, was inflicted upon the Armenians without a shadow of provocation,"[5] and since then numerous other non-Armenian authors have lined up behind the Armenian position. In the absence of Turkish documentary evidence that proves the complicity of the Ottoman government, these writers, too, find the fact of premeditation established by the actual results, which are seen to be of an exterminatory character. It cannot be doubted, write Gerard Chaliand and Yves Ternon, that the central government had an overall extermination plan:

> There was nothing to justify a universal deportation order. It is impossible to describe as regrettable excesses or over-enthusiasm the criminal acts of which the population, the bands of brigands, the Kurdish tribes and the gendarmes responsible for protecting the convoys were guilty during the journey of deportation. One order would have been enough to put an end to the carnage. This order was never given because the carnage was deliberate. The only conclusion that can be drawn from these events is that the genocide was deliberate policy.[6]

Leo Kuper finds "a systematic pattern of massacre" that proves the culpability of the Turkish government. There were, he acknowledges, some local variations. "In some areas the civilian population were murdered outright. In other areas, the movement of civilians bore more nearly the semblance of a genuine deportation: and there might be some possibility of conversion. But the overall pattern of massacre and deportation, and the thoroughgoing elimination of Armenians from their traditional homelands, are clear evidence of genocidal intent."[7]

According to Christopher Walker, the immense testimony of suffering and death that is available can lead only to one conclusion. If "we accept that the massacres and brutal deportations occurred, and were carried out with the ferocity which the witnesses describe, then these facts point inevitably to government responsibility." The extensive evidence "presents an overwhelming case for affirming that a planned genocide of the Armenian people took place in the Ottoman Empire in 1915–16."[8] Whether the Young Turks from the beginning had a premeditated master plan of slaughter is immaterial, two recent scholars maintain. "It must have occurred to the Young Turk leadership that the destruction of such a pervasive national movement would inevitably entail suffering on an enormous scale, and that the forceful relocation of almost an entire people to a remote, alien, and hostile environment amid a general war was tantamount to a collective death sentence. In the end, whatever their initial intention, the Ottomans' actions constituted nothing short of genocide."[9]

The idea that the deportations were a cloak for massacre and that the real intent of the Young Turk regime was to destroy the Armenian community can also be found in the reports of some members of the diplomatic corps who witnessed the events of 1915–16. In the eyes of Consul Jackson in Aleppo, the Ottoman government inflicted daily outrages "upon a defenseless and inoffensive people that demand nothing more than to be given a chance to eke out at the best a miserable existence....It is without doubt a carefully planned scheme to thoroughly extinguish the Armenian race."[10] The element of premeditation was also accepted by Ambassador Morgenthau, who called the deportations into the arid and hostile wastes of the Ottoman Empire an "attempt to exterminate a race."[11] Some German officials took the same view and used very similar language. Ambassador Wangenheim drew attention to the fact that the deportations included provinces that were not threatened by hostile invasion at the time. "This fact and the manner in which the relocation is being implemented reveal that the real aim of the government is the destruction of the Armenian race in the Ottoman empire."[12]

To this day the Turkish side strongly denies that the Ottoman regime sought the destruction of the Armenians. The removal of the Armenians from certain regions, it is argued, was a measure dictated by imperative military necessity. The Armenian revolutionaries threatened the rear of the Turkish army in all parts of the empire and were supported and fed by the local population. In these circumstances it was impossible to limit the relocation to one area or to sort out the guilty from the innocent. The Turkish historian Salahi Sonyel acknowledges the loss of life:

> Out of about 700,000 Armenians who were relocated until early 1917, some lives were lost as a result of large-scale military and guerilla activities then going on in the areas through which they passed, as well as the general insecurity and blood-feuds which some tribal forces sought to carry out as the convoys passed through their territories. In addition, the relocation and resettlement of the Armenians took place at a time when the Ottoman Empire was suffering from extreme shortages of food, medicine, and other supplies as well as from large-scale plague and famine. A number of them also died because of disease, climatic conditions, difficulties of travel, or illegal actions of some officers. Many more died as a result of their rebellion, during fights in revolts.[13]

What took place in Turkey during World War I, writes another Turkish historian, "was not a 'massacre' but a deportation." During this relocation many lives were unfortunately lost, but the government could not provide better conditions; and, in any event, Armenian casualties were no greater in percentage than those of the Turks. Armenian nationalists and later British and French intelligence services distorted these events by spreading "throughout the world the stories of imaginary 'massacres' for the sake of their own political purposes."[14] The experience of the Armenians, argue the Shaws, was undoubtedly terrible, but it was part of a tragedy that engulfed all the people of the empire. It was not the result of "a conscious effort to exterminate any of these groups."[15] During the intercommunal fighting in Anatolia Armenians murdered Muslims and Muslims murdered Armenians. "What passed between the Armenians and the Turks was not genocide; it was war."[16] According to the German scholar Christian Gerlach, the loss of life was the result of the disastrous food situation and the rapacity of robbers who waylaid the convoys. The fate of the deportees, while terrible, Gerlach concludes, does not support the idea of a centrally planned scheme of annihilation.[17]

Some students of the subject have taken a position that lies somewhere between the claim of a premeditated plan of extermination and the flat denial that any massacres occurred. According to Ronald Suny, the uprooting and deportation of the Armenians in eastern Anatolia was equivalent to the murder of a people, to genocide, but it is important to see this decision in its proper historical setting, in "the context of imminent collapse of the empire in 1915." It was not part of a widespread and popular exterminationist mentality. "Rather than a long-planned and carefully orchestrated program of extermination the Armenian Genocide was more a vengeful and determined act of suppression that turned into an opportunistic policy to rid Anatolia of Armenians once and for all, eliminate the wedge that they provided for foreign intervention in the region, and open the way for the fantastic dream of a Turanian empire." In the brutal context of war this policy "became a massive campaign of murder, the first genocide of the twentieth century. Social hostilities between Armenians and Turks, Kurds and Armenians, fed the mass killings, which the state encouraged (or at least did little to discourage)." Suny stresses that he remains "unconvinced that there was premeditation and prewar initiation of plans for genocide as Dadrian has often argued."[18] A similar position is taken by Hilmar Kaiser and Donald Bloxham.[19]

Another group of scholars has acknowledged that the Ottoman government was justified in ordering the deportation but has argued that the implementation of this program was unnecessarily cruel. "The existence of a separate Armenian population of from 500,000 to 600,000 in the rear of the Eastern army," writes the Turkish historian Ahmed Emin Yalman, "including thousands of organized revolutionaries and daring fighters well armed with modern rifles, constituted a great military danger. Some measures of precaution were certainly justified"; but the actual action taken can be seen as "not being commensurate with military necessity."[20] According to the British historian Andrew Mango, the government, affected by fear of Armenian subversion, "sought both to repress uprisings and to preempt them through deportations. It did so with a heavy hand, and large numbers of Armenians perished." However, there was "no official policy of extermination....Deportations and massacres were linked in fact, but all the evidence produced so far suggests that they were not linked in intention."[21]

In a letter written in 1966 to an Armenian author Toynbee stated that in view of the Russian invasion of northeastern Turkey and the fear that the Armenian minority was a fifth column it would have been legitimate to deport the Armenians. But the ways in which the relocations were carried out "were so inhuman that they were bound to cause wholesale mortality, as they did."[22] Because the Armenians hoped for an Allied victory and some Armenians even collaborated with the advancing Russian armies, James Willis writes, the leaders of the Young Turks "had some justification for moving against the Armenians." It is evident, however, that "the punishment meted out to the Armenians was completely out of proportion to the offense. Subversion by some Armenians gave the Young Turks an excuse to carry out a nationalist program designed to rid their country once and for all of a troublesome minority problem."[23] The generally pro-Turkish McCarthys, relying on the benefit of hindsight, even acknowledge that "Armenians in central Anatolia did not provide enough of a threat to justify the drastic action of deportation."[24]

CRITIQUE

No authentic documentary evidence exists to prove the culpability of the central government of Turkey for the massacres of 1915–16. It is also significant that not one of the many thousands of officials who would have been involved in so far-reaching a scheme as a premeditated plan to destroy the Armenians has ever come forth to reveal the plot. The order for the Final Solution of the Jewish Question also is not embodied in a written record, but the major elements of the decision-making process leading up to the annihilation of the Jews can be reconstructed from events, court testimony that has been subject to cross-examination, and a rich store of authentic documents. Barring the unlikely discovery of some new sensational documents in the Turkish archives, it is safe to say that no such evidence exists for the events of 1915–16.

In the absence of this kind of proof, the Armenian side has relied upon materials of highly questionable authenticity, such as Andonian's *Memoirs of Naim Bey* or copies of alleged documents used by the Turkish military tribunals after the end of the war. Armenians have also invoked the exterminatory consequences of the deportations; but this argument (as suggested in chapter 5) rests on a logical fallacy and ignores the huge loss of life among Turkish civilians, soldiers, and prisoners-of-war due to sheer incompetence, neglect, starvation, and disease. All of these groups also experienced a huge death toll that surely cannot be explained in terms of a Young Turk plan of annihilation.

As noted earlier, some foreign diplomats also charged that the real aim of the Ottoman regime was to bring about the extermination of the Armenian people. Given the very large number of deaths and the observed complicity of many local officials in the murders, it is not surprising that not a few diplomats, like other eyewitnesses on the scene, concluded that the high death toll was an intended outcome of the deportations. Still, well-informed as many consular officials were about the horrible events unfolding before their eyes, their insight into the mindset and the real intentions of the Young Turk leadership was necessarily limited to hunches and speculation. Their assertions of the existence of a scheme of annihilation were indeed merely assertions.

The argument that the deportations in reality constituted a premeditated program of extermination of the Armenians of Turkey is difficult to square with many aspects and characteristics of the relocations. I mention here just a few of the most important:

1. The large Armenian communities of Constantinople, Smyrna, and Aleppo were spared deportation and—apart from tribulations such as hunger and epidemics that also afflicted the Muslim population of these cities—survived the war largely intact. The argument that the Turks refrained from deporting the Armenians in these cities in order to avoid unfavorable publicity is invalid, for the world heard of the deportations and accompanying massacres in the provinces almost as soon as they took place. Adverse publicity was not avoided by sparing the Armenians of these three important cities. These exemptions are analogous to Adolf Hitler failing to include the Jews of Berlin, Cologne, and Munich in the Final Solution.

2. The trek on foot that took so many lives was imposed only on the Armenians in eastern and central Anatolia, a part of the country that had no railroads. Although the one-spur Baghdad railway was overburdened with the transport of troops and supplies, the deportees from the western provinces and Cilicia who had the money were allowed to purchase tickets for travel by rail and thus were spared at least some of the tribulations of the deportation process. If, as is often alleged, the intent was to subject the exiles to a forced march until they died of exhaustion, why was this punishment not imposed on all of the deportees?

3. Many authors have pointed to the alleged basic uniformity of procedure characterizing the deportations and massacres as proof of the responsibility of the central government in Constantinople for these events. In fact, as we have seen, the deportations and resettlement exhibited a great deal of variation that depended on factors such as geography and the attitude of local officials.

In the absence of a large Kurdish population no massacres took place in Cilicia, and a substantial part of the Armenian exiles sent to southern Syria and Palestine survived. Some convoys from eastern Anatolia were robbed and massacred, while others arrived at their destination almost intact. Some of the exiles were given food here and there, while others were left to fend for themselves and often died of starvation. Some gendarmes accompanying the convoys protected their charges, while others sold them to Kurds, who pillaged and murdered them. In some places Protestant and Catholic Armenians as well as artisans were exempted from deportation, while in others all Armenians irrespective of creed and local necessity were sent away. Many of the deportees succumbed to the harsh conditions in the places of resettlement or were massacred there; others were able to survive by making themselves useful as skilled workers or traders. In some locations large numbers of Armenians were allowed, or even forced, to convert, while in others conversion did not purchase exemption from deportation or assure survival.

All these differences in treatment and outcomes are difficult to reconcile with a premeditated program of total annihilation. To question the existence of a deliberate scheme of destruction is not to deny the horrendous suffering of the Armenian exiles or the frequent occurrence of massacres. The Turkish side, which seeks to dismiss the mass killings as "excesses" or "intercommunal warfare" and often speaks of "so-called massacres," therefore is distorting the historical record. In order to exculpate the Ottoman government from blame for the large number of deaths that accompanied the deportations it is not enough to point to that government's many decrees and orders that commanded protection and compassionate treatment of the deportees. But if these events represented neither a plan of extermination nor simply the effects of natural causes and the unfortunate occurrence of excesses, what does account for the large loss of life during the deportations?

AN ALTERNATIVE EXPLANATION

I start with the assumption that the various decrees issued by the government in Constantinople dealing with the deportation and its implementation are genuine and were issued in good faith. The Ottoman government, I am inclined to believe, wanted to arrange an orderly process but did not have the means to do so. The momentous task of relocating several hundred thousand people in a short span of time and over a highly primitive system of transportation was simply beyond the ability of the Ottoman bureaucracy. Neither existing institutions nor the officials were up to the task. Moreover, the deportation and resettlement of the Armenians took place as the country experienced severe food shortages and under totally inadequate conditions of sanitation that soon led to large-scale epidemics. I have described the disastrous results of this situation for the civilian population and the military in chapter 5, when I discussed the issue of so-called genocidal consequences. Under conditions of Ottoman misrule, it was possible for the country to suffer an incredibly high death toll without a premeditated plan of annihilation. If we add that the deportations took place at a time of great insecurity in the countryside and that large numbers of deportees had to pass areas inhabited by hostile Kurds or settle amid equally rapacious Circassians, against whom the authorities failed to provide adequate protection, we have sketched out the crucial context for the human disaster that ensued.

Many contemporary observers on the scene saw the tragedy in this light. The incompetence and the inefficiency of the Ottoman bureaucracy are a constant theme in the reports that have been preserved, though the logistical problem of moving and feeding so many people probably would have been highly challenging even for a more capable government apparatus. "The lack of proper transportation facilities," Consul Nathan in Mersina wrote to Ambassador Morgenthau on September 27, 1915, "is the most important factor in causing the misery." The inadequate number of carts and carriages forces many deportees to travel on foot. Furthermore, the government failed to solve the problem of feeding the exiles. "Thus at Osmanie where for the past few weeks there have always been from forty to sixty thousand people the food supply is scarcely enough for one third of that number so that all are either on short rations or without food. This is responsible for the illness which prevails and the numerous deaths which are reported."[25]

Consul Rössler in Aleppo shared this view. In June 1914, before the outbreak of war, Rössler told his government that the authorities were incapable of handling the resettlement of Muslim refugees from Tripoli and the Balkans. These refugees had to live in mosques and created a threat to public order.[26] The care for the Armenian deportees now constituted another bureaucratic fiasco. Despite the order of the Porte to feed the exiles, he informed his ambassador on September 14, the majority of them would gradually starve to death, "since the Turks are incapable of solving the organizational task of mass-feeding." Even if the officials had been full of goodwill, the challenge of providing food for the masses of destitute exiles was simply beyond their capability.[27] Or as the American missionary Kate Ainslee put it, "A government that is not able to feed even its soldiers, how is it to obey the beautiful paper instructions and see that the people are well fed and lack of nothing?"[28]

According to the American journalist George Schreiner, who observed the misery of thousands of women, children, and decrepit men en route in the Taurus mountains, "Turkish ineptness, more than intentional brutality, was responsible for the hardships the Armenians were subjected to."[29] The importance of the chaos that accompanied the expulsions was also stressed by the governor of Diarbekir, Resid Bey. In a memoir composed shortly before his suicide in 1919, Resid Bey argued that the disorganization of the state authorities was so pronounced that an orderly deportation became impossible.[30]

A lengthy memorandum on the Armenian question drawn up by the German embassy official Von Hoesch, probably in 1916, argued the same position. The authorities, he wrote, had been unprepared for the deportations and therefore had failed to provide food and protection for the exiles. However, given the large number to be relocated and the lack of competence on the part of officials available for this task, the outcome would not have been any different even if more time had been available. The central government, the German official maintained, was unable to enforce a uniform policy, and the way the deportations were handled therefore depended on the attitude of military or civilian authorities in the provinces. Some officials, such as Djemal Pasha, sought to alleviate the hardships of the exiles, but others were extremely hostile to the Armenians and abandoned the deportees to the violence of Kurds or Circassians. The government in Constantinople did not approve of these developments but did not do enough to prevent them either. The harsh climate, the long distances to be traversed on foot, and the arbitrariness of local officials all contributed to the human catastrophe that ensued.[31]

Writing more recently, Edward Erickson has similarly concluded that the relocation of the Armenian population was fated to end in disaster. He has too benevolent a view of the Turkish officer corps, but the rest of his observations on the challenges presented by the deportations are on target.

Administratively such a scheme wildly exceeded Turkish capabilities. Even had the Turks been inclined to treat the Armenians kindly, they simply did not have the transportation and logistical means necessary with which to conduct population transfers on such a grand scale. Military transportation, which received top priority, illustrates this point, when first-class infantry units typically would lose a quarter of their strength to disease, inadequate rations, and poor hygiene while traveling through the empire. This routinely happened to regiments and divisions that were well equipped and composed of healthy young men, commanded by officers concerned with their well-being. Once again, in a pattern which would be repeated through 1918, Enver Pasa's plans hinged on nonexistent capabilities that guaranteed inevitable failure.[32]

Consul Rössler took the position that the Ottoman government would have to shoulder the responsibility for the disaster that had resulted from the lack of foresight, the malfeasance of the implementing authorities, and the general anarchy in the eastern provinces. The government was to be blamed, for it had sent the exiles into this chaotic situation.[33] Morgenthau similarly rejected the Turkish excuse that not enough troops had been available to protect the deportees. "If that is true, they had no right to deport them, because they knew they would be pillaged and murdered on the way unless properly protected."[34]

The argument that the Ottoman regime should have refrained from deporting the Armenians unless it could guarantee the smooth working of the relocation exaggerates the farsightedness of the Young Turk leadership. It assumes that these men were aware of the human catastrophe that would ensue, and this assumption is probably mistaken. If Enver could delude himself in 1914 that he would be able to wage a successful campaign against Russia in the Caucasus mountains in the dead of winter without adequate provisions and clothing for his soldiers—a military disaster that resulted in the death of more than seventy thousand men out of an original army of ninety thousand—he undoubtedly could have had equally strong illusions and misconceptions about the ability of his bureaucracy to accomplish the deportation of the Armenian community without too many problems. The prevailing indifference to human misery and the acceptance of the dispensability of human lives probably also played a role. A government as callous about the suffering of its own population as was the Ottoman regime could hardly be expected to be very concerned about the possible calamity that would result from deporting its Armenian population, rightly or wrongly suspected of treason.

The conclusions of Gwynne Dyer, a researcher with extensive immersion in the Ottoman archives, in my view are more on the mark. Given the state of the evidence from Ottoman sources, Dyer maintains, it is impossible to prove conclusively that the Young Turk regime did not initiate a program of deliberate genocide in the spring of 1915, "but it seems to me most improbable that this was the case. Such a programme requires a degree of calculation and foresight which was almost entirely absent in all the other actions of the C.U.P. government in the war." Dyer does not regard Talaat, Enver, and their associates as cruel and savage dictators who ruthlessly exploited a long-sought opportunity for a much-desired genocide. He sees them "not so much as evil men but as desperate, frightened, unsophisticated men struggling to keep their nation afloat in a crisis far graver than they had anticipated when they first entered the war (the Armenian decisions were taken at the height of the crisis of the Dardanelles), reacting to events rather than creating them, and not fully realizing the extent of the horrors they had set in motion in 'Turkish Armenia' until they were too deeply committed to withdraw."[35]

I believe that the evidence I have examined and presented in this book is in line with Dyer's appraisal made more than thirty years ago. We do not know how many Armenians perished as a result of starvation and disease and how many were killed by Kurds, seeking booty and women, or by fanatic Muslims, who regarded the Armenians as infidels and traitors. For all of these occurrences the incompetent Ottoman regime bears some indirect responsibility. But there is a difference between ineptness, even ineptness that has tragic and far-reaching consequences, and the premeditated murder of a people. As we have seen, the government also badly mishandled its wounded soldiers, refugees, and prisoners of war, but one would hesitate to consider these acts of neglect and callousness a crime of equal magnitude as deliberate killing. Even the fact that some fanatic Young Turk officials welcomed the death of large numbers of Armenians is not the same as intentionally seeking and causing such deaths.

It is impossible to ignore the horrors to which the Armenians were subjected, but it is important to see these terrible events in their proper historical context. The order for the deportation of the Armenian community was issued at a time of great insecurity, not to say panic, which made any calm calculation of possible consequences difficult and unlikely. Any full discussion of the events of 1915–16 also cannot ignore the impact of the loss of Van and the displacement of large numbers of Muslims in eastern Anatolia, who were forced to flee for their lives in the face of the advancing Russian armies and their Armenian helpers. This dislocation sharply increased hostility toward the Armenians among the Muslim population of the empire and added to the tensions created by charges of Armenian treason. The fear that the Armenian population constituted a fifth column may have been exaggerated, but it did have some basis in fact. While the Armenians were victims, not all of them were innocent victims; and the disaster that overtook them therefore was not entirely unprovoked. Most importantly, while the Ottoman government bears responsibility for the deportations that got badly out of hand, the blame for the massacres that took place must be put primarily on those who did the actual killing.

Epilogue

The Politicization of History

The Treaty of Lausanne, signed on July 24, 1923, ended the dream of an Armenian state that would include the eastern provinces of Anatolia, the heartland of historic Armenia, and Cilicia. The setback was serious and deeply demoralizing. It was not until 1965, the fiftieth anniversary of what Armenians began to call the first genocide of the twentieth century, that Armenians in Soviet Armenia and in the worldwide diaspora started to focus new attention on the events of 1915–16. History became a tool to highlight the suffering and injustices suffered by the Armenian nation. At the same time, the Turkish side stepped up its efforts to deny the alleged genocide and to insist on its version of history. Since then both sides have used heavy-handed tactics to advance their cause and silence a full and impartial discussion of the issues in dispute. Both Turks and Armenians cite important documents out of context or simply ignore the historical setting altogether. A polemical and propagandistic style of writing now dominates the field and for the most part has displaced the search for historical truth.

THE CAMPAIGN FOR RECOGNITION OF THE GENOCIDE

The Turkish military tribunals of 1919–20 were unable to impose punishment upon the major figures of the Young Turk regime who had fled the country, the German government ignored Turkish demands for the extradition of the CUP leaders, and the Allies abandoned their efforts to bring to justice those responsible for the Armenian massacres. The result was a wave of private vengeance (organized by the Dashnak organization "Nemesis") that in quick succession took the lives of the best-known personages of the Young Turk regime. On March 15, 1921, Soghomon Tehlirian shot and killed Talaat Pasha, the former minister of the interior and the man most involved with the deportations, in Berlin. On December 5, 1921, Arshavir Shirakian assassinated Said Halim Pasha in Rome. On April 17, 1922, he killed Dr. Behaeddin

Sakir in Berlin. On July 25, 1922, Bedros Der Boghosian and Ardavesh Gevorgian shot Djemal Pasha in Tiflis. Finally, on August 4, 1922, Enver Pasha was killed under unclear circumstances in an ambush in Central Asia, probably by an Armenian.[1]

A new wave of assassinations began in the early 1970s, due to the failure of political efforts to achieve significant results for the Armenian cause. Radicalized young people in the Lebanon, influenced by the militancy of the Palestinian exiles and imbued with Marxist third-worldist ideas, now formed two new organizations: the Armenian Secret Army for the Liberation of Armenia (ASALA) and the Justice Commandos for the Armenian Genocide (JCAG); between 1973 and 1985 more than forty Turkish diplomats and other Turkish officials were killed all over the world. After the publication of Stanford Shaw and Ezel Kural Shaw's *History of the Ottoman Empire and Modern Turkey* in 1977, their house was bombed and severely damaged. Members of the ASALA, who accused the Dashnaks of having betrayed the original ardor of the Armenian revolution, also assassinated Dashnak political leaders. By the mid-1980s, after a particularly bloody attack at the Orly airport in 1983, a series of violent internal disputes and splits over tactics, and signs of waning support in the Armenian community, the organizations disbanded and the assassinations came to an end.[2] "Like the cold war polarization on the issue of Soviet Armenia," Suny has noted, "so the harsh choice between politics and revolutionary warfare divided Armenians rather than bringing them together."[3]

During the last thirty years Armenians have made major efforts to get various parliamentary bodies to remember and commemorate the victims of the massacres of 1915–16 and to achieve the recognition of these killings as a case of genocide. Resolutions to this effect have been adopted by legislatures such as the Argentinean Senate, the Russian Duma, the Canadian House of Commons, the Belgian Senate, the European parliament at Strasbourg, and the French National Assembly. The French resolution, adopted on May 29, 1998, declared that "France publicly recognizes the Armenian genocide of 1915" but omitted any mention of the perpetrator. The U.S. House of Representatives on April 8, 1975, adopted a resolution designating April 24 as a "National Day of Remembrance of Man's Inhumanity to Man." The administration of Gerald Ford, protective of its North Atlantic Treaty Organization (NATO) ally Turkey, strongly opposed the resolution. It passed only after the reference to the victims of genocide, "especially those of Armenian ancestry who succumbed to the genocide perpetrated in

1915," omitted the words "in Turkey." Even as thus modified, the resolution failed to pass the Senate Judiciary Committee.[4]

In August 1982 the U.S. State Department explained its opposition
to official recognition of the Armenian genocide in this way: "Because
the historical record of the 1915 events is ambiguous, the Department
of State does not endorse allegations that the Turkish government committed a genocide against the Armenian people."[5] After this statement
had been criticized by Armenian-American organizations, the State
Department in the following issue of the *Department of State Bulletin*
denied that the earlier article "necessarily reflected the official position of the Department of State." Despite this disclaimer, however, in
actual fact the State Department has continued to use such arguments
in opposing all subsequent congressional resolutions that have sought
to recognize the Armenian genocide. At times the department has also
acknowledged that such a resolution would seriously damage the strate-
gically vital relationship between Turkey and the United States. There
can be little doubt that this is indeed the most important reason why
all U.S. administrations over many years have consistently objected to
the adoption of such a statement of recognition.[6]

Armenian authors have expressed regret that the demands of *Realpolitik* dominate the thinking and pronouncements of the U.S. government, but there are indeed far more important reasons why historians
and the entire scholarly community should object to letting politicians
decide historical questions. These reasons were articulated in an open
letter in 1985 to the members of the House of Representatives, which
was debating once again the issue of establishing a "National Day of
Remembrance of Man's Inhumanity to Man." The resolution in question singled out for special recognition "the one and one half million
people of Armenian ancestry who were victims of genocide perpetrated
in Turkey between 1915 and 1923." The open letter, published as a
large advertisement in the *New York Times* and *Washington Post* on May
19, 1985, was signed by sixty-nine academics who described themselves as specialists "in Turkish Ottoman, and Middle Eastern studies,"
among them such well-known scholars as Roderic Davison, J. C. Hurewitz, and Bernard Lewis.

Critics of this letter have pointed out that only four of the sixty-
nine signers could be considered experts on the specific period and
topic of Turkish policy toward the Armenians. They have also noted
that the ad was commissioned and paid for by the Assembly of Turkish
American Associations (an organization financed largely by the Turkish

government) and that forty of the signatories had received a total of sixty-five grants from the Institute of Turkish Studies (a semiofficial Turkish body in Washington, D.C.) and the American Research Institute in Ankara.[7] This information, while interesting, has no bearing on the validity of the arguments put forth by the sixty-nine scholars. Historical positions, like all scholarly findings, must be judged independently of their origin, motive, or consequences.

The open letter stated that the evidence so far available argued against genocide and pointed to "serious inter-communal warfare (perpetrated by Muslim and Christian irregular forces), complicated by disease, famine, suffering and massacres" as the causes of the large loss of life. After this rather one-sided view of the issues in contention, the letter proceeded to set forth more important and valid arguments by stressing that

> much more remains to be discovered before historians will be able to sort out precise responsibility between warring and innocent, and to identify the causes for the events which resulted in the death or removal of large numbers of the eastern population, Christians and Muslims alike.
>
> Statesmen and politicians make history, and scholars write it. For this process to work scholars must be given access to the written records of the statesmen and politicians of the past. To date, the relevant archives in the Soviet Union, Syria, Bulgaria and Turkey all remain, for the most part, closed to dispassionate historians. Until they become available the history of the Ottoman Empire in the period encompassed by H.J. Resolution 192 (1915–1923) cannot be adequately known.
>
> We believe that the proper position for the United States Congress to take on this and related issues, is to encourage full and open access to all historical archives, and not to make charges on historical events before they are fully understood. Such charges as those contained in H.J. Res. 192 would inevitably reflect unjustly upon the people of Turkey, and perhaps set back irreparably progress historians are just now beginning to achieve in understanding these tragic events.
>
> As the above comments illustrate, the history of the Ottoman-Armenians is much debated among scholars, many of whom do not agree with the historical assumptions embodied in the wording of H.J. Res. 192. By passing the resolution Congress will be attempting to determine by legislation which side of a historical question is correct. Such a resolution, based on historically questionable assumptions, can only damage the cause of honest historical enquiry, and damage the credibility of the American legislative process.[8]

Supporters of the Armenian cause have referred to the alleged Turkish genocide of the Armenians as an "established, incontrovertible historical fact,"[9] thus making it a closed issue similar to the Jewish Holocaust that would be questioned only by pseudo-historians such as Arthur Butz and Robert Faurisson. Yet the scholars who signed the Open Letter and who have questioned the appropriateness of the genocide label cannot be dismissed as a fringe group; they include some of the best-known experts on the history of Turkey. Even as strong a defender of the Armenian position as the historian Taner Akcam has acknowledged the difference between the generally accepted historical reality of the Holocaust and the issue of the Armenian massacres. "One cannot deal with this set of questions as with the National Socialist crimes and the 'Auschwitz lie,' which are settled unequivocally both historically and legally. With regard to the relations between Turks and Armenians we are miles away from such a situation."[10]

It is possible, of course, to use the word "genocide" not as a legal concept under the exclusive ownership of the experts but as a "term of moral opprobrium" that is now part of our common discourse. Applied in this way the word "genocide" would express "a 75-year old moral consensus that a grave moral evil had been perpetrated against the Armenian people by the Ottoman regime."[11] Yet we should remember that human history exhibits gradations or degrees of moral evil. We prejudge the precise nature of the evil suffered by the Ottoman Armenians by calling the deportations and massacres a case of genocide. With so much that is unknown about the workings of the Young Turk regime, it is highly presumptuous to cut off lines of inquiry that may end up putting some blame on others than just the "terrible Turk." To decide whether such conclusions are warranted is not the job of legislators but of historians. If we look to politicians for the confirmation of historical facts we may create more confusion than clarification. As a reviewer of the recently released moving picture *Ararat* has correctly put it: "If you turn the truth over to people who negotiate, you may end up with negotiated truth."[12]

PRESSURE TACTICS

Efforts by the Turkish government to prevent the airing of pro-Armenian views go back many decades. The novel *The Forty Days of Musa Dagh* by Franz Werfel, describing the heroic resistance of a small Armenian village on the Mediterranean coast to the threat of deportation, was published in Germany in 1933. When the Turkish government learned in November 1934 that Metro-Goldwyn-Mayer planned to produce a film based on the book, it conveyed to the State Department its displeasure over this project. The State Department in turn suggested to the film industry that the filming of Werfel's novel would be "detrimental to the cordial feelings between the two peoples." After the death of President Kemal Atatürk in November 1938, new rumors that the film would be made led to renewed pressure by the Turkish government and the State Department on the motion picture industry, and the project was abandoned for good.[13]

In 1980 a group of notables appointed by President Jimmy Carter began to plan a federal museum to commemorate the Jewish Holocaust, and the Turkish government immediately began a concerted campaign to keep any reference to the Armenians from being included in the exhibit. The U.S. government was threatened with unspecified repercussions, and individual members of the Holocaust Memorial Council came under similar pressure. Council member Hyman Bookbinder recalls receiving an invitation to a luncheon by the Turkish ambassador, who told him that the well-being of the Jewish community in Turkey might be threatened if the Armenian story was included in the museum.[14]

A 1982 academic conference in Tel Aviv on the Holocaust and genocide that was to include a discussion of the massacres of 1915–16 also drew the ire of the Turkish government. The Israeli government, "out of concern for the interests of Jews," sought the removal of the conference from Israel and also is said to have discouraged the attendance of invited participants. The conference did take place, but some of the scheduled speakers had withdrawn. When the Turkish pressure was publicized, the Turkish government disowned it as an unauthorized pronouncement by a Turkish official that might have been construed as a threat.[15] Almost twenty years later, in the spring of 2000, a similar dispute burdened the otherwise close political and military relations between Israel and Turkey. The Israeli minister of education, Yossi Sarid, told an Armenian audience in the Gregorian St. James church in Jerusalem on April 24 that he intended to include the genocide of the Armenians in the curriculum of Israeli schools. In retaliation the Turkish foreign ministry instructed all Turkish officials to boycott the celebration of Israeli independence day at the Israeli embassy in Ankara. That even Turkish military leaders stayed away from the festivities was seen as particularly significant.[16]

Turkish efforts to prevent the adoption of any commemoration of the Armenian massacres have continued. After the French parliament passed a law in early 2001 that recognized the killing of Armenians during World War I as genocide, the Turkish government canceled a $149-million deal to buy a spy satellite from the French firm Alcatel and excluded another French company from competing to sell Turkey tanks worth up to $7 billion.[17] When the United States Congress considered a similar resolution during the election campaign of 2000, Turkey threatened an economic boycott and alluded to measures that could have disrupted U.S. air operations over northern Iraq that use bases in Turkey. On November 15, 2000, the European parliament in Strasbourg, over angry reaction from Ankara, passed a resolution that called on Turkey to make "public recognition of the genocide" against the Armenians.[18]

Turkish historians have sought to damage the reputation of their Armenian adversaries by publicizing the service of Armenian volunteers in Hitler's armies. "During World War II, while the Turkish Government was giving asylum to many Jews from Hitler's tyranny," writes Sonyel, "anti-Semitism engulfed the Armenian circles in the Nazi-occupied territories....Armenian volunteers, under the wings of Hitler's Germany, were used in rounding up Jews and other 'undesirables' for the Nazi concentration camps."[19] Some of these charges are exaggerated, but the basic facts are correct. It is believed that eleven thousand Armenians from the Caucasus, motivated by hunger and anti-Russian sentiments more than by anti-Semitism, had joined the so-called Ostlegionen (eastern legions) of the German army by October 1944. They served in front-line units but, like other German troops, were also used for fighting partisans in the rear.[20] However, the wider implications of these condemnatory facts are not obvious. Some Dutch, Belgians, and French also served in the German army or the Waffen-SS, without thereby compromising an entire people.

Pro-Armenian authors, too, have tried to link their opponents to Hitler's Holocaust. "There is now some evidence to suggest," writes Dadrian, "that the impunity accorded the Turks in the aftermath of the World War I genocide by the rest of the world served to stimulate Hitler to embark upon his own initiatives of genocide."[21] Dadrian does not say what that evidence is, but he is probably thinking of a reference to the Armenian massacres that Hitler is said to have included in a speech before his generals on August 22, 1939. In the context of outlining Germany's need for *Lebensraum* (vital space) and the destruction of people standing in the way of this expansion, Hitler is supposed to have said: "Who still talks nowadays of the extermination of the Armenians?" This statement is frequently quoted to suggest that Hitler felt encouraged to pursue his plan to exterminate the Jews of Europe because the world did not punish the Ottoman Turks for their annihilation of the Armenians.

There are several problems with this charge. First, it is generally accepted that by August 1939 Hitler had not yet decided upon the destruction of the Jews, the Final Solution of the Jewish Question. The remark therefore can have referred only to the forthcoming ruthlessness of the military campaign against the Slavs and not to the destruction of the Jews.[22] More importantly, a controversy exists with regard to the authenticity of this reference to the Armenians. Without entering into the minutiae of this dispute, it must suffice to note here that we have no stenographic record of Hitler's speech on that day in 1939 but only five sets of notes taken by persons who heard the speech. Two of these versions were accepted as evidence by the Nuremberg Tribunal in 1945; the version containing the remark about the Armenians was not. The pro-Turkish historian Heath Lowry therefore speaks of "a spurious quotation,"[23] which probably overstates the significance of this action by the Nuremberg court. In a more thorough analysis of the speech the German historian Winfried Baumgart allows for the possibility that the sentence in question represents an embellishment of points made in the speech.[24] Other scholars have lined up on one side or the other of this controversy, which must be regarded as irresolvable.[25] The Armenian attempt to see in this purported remark by Hitler a link between the Armenian massacres and the Jewish Holocaust therefore stands on a shaky factual foundation.

Armenians in the diaspora have also made efforts to silence those who have questioned the appropriateness of the term "genocide" for the tragic events of 1915–16. The best-known of these attempts involves the eminent scholar of Islam Bernard Lewis. In his book *The Emergence of Modern Turkey,* first published in 1961, Lewis describes the unfortunate results of the Armenian nationalist movement that had sought to restore an independent Armenia in these words:

> For the Turks, the Armenian movement was the deadliest of all threats. From the conquered lands of the Serbs, Bulgars, Albanians, and Greeks, they could, however reluctantly, withdraw, abandoning distant provinces and bringing the Imperial frontier nearer home. But the Armenians,

stretching across Turkey-in-Asia from the Caucasian frontier to the Mediterranean coast, lay in the very heart of the Turkish homeland—and to
renounce these lands would have meant not the truncation, but the dissolution of the Turkish state. Turkish and Armenian villages, inextrica-
bly mixed, had for centuries lived in neighbourly association. Now a
desperate struggle between them began—a struggle between two nations
for the possession of a single homeland, that ended with the terrible holocaust of 1915, when a million and half Armenians perished.[26]

It appears that Lewis later became dissatisfied with the last sentence
that spoke of a "terrible holocaust" and one and a half million deaths.
In the third edition of the book he changed "holocaust" into "slaughter" and stated that "according to estimates, more than a million Armenians perished as well as an unknown number of Turks."[27]

On November 16, 1993, while in Paris for the publication of two
of his books translated into French, Lewis was interviewed by two journalists of *Le Monde* and was asked why the Turks continued to deny
the Armenian genocide. In his reply Lewis again spoke of two peoples
fighting over a single homeland and then added: "If we talk of genocide,
it implies there was a deliberate policy, a decision to blot out systematically the Armenian nation. That is quite doubtful. Turkish documents
prove an intent to banish, not to exterminate." When Lewis repeated
this argument on January 1, 1994, in a letter to *Le Monde* (in which he
stated: "There is no serious proof of a plan of the Ottoman government
aimed at the extermination of the Armenian nation"), the Forum of the
Armenian Associations of France took him to court. The civil suit was
based on article 1382 of the French Civil Code, which states: "Whoever
is guilty of causing harm must make reparation for it."[28]

The plaintiffs argued that Lewis had committed "a fault causing
very grievous prejudice to truthful memory, to the respect and to the
compassion due to the survivors and to their families." On June 21,
1995, the court found against Lewis, and imposed a token fine. The
court declared that it was beyond its competence to decide whether
the massacres between 1915 and 1917 constituted a crime of genocide. However, the judgment argued, Lewis had failed in his "duties
of objectivity" and had not fulfilled his responsibilities as a conscientious historian by "concealing the elements that were contrary to his
thesis." Only thus had he been able to affirm that there was no "serious
proof" of the Armenian genocide. The contrary elements that the court
enumerated referred to findings by bodies such as the European par-

liament, which had recognized the reality of the genocide.[29] Another suit against Lewis, brought by the Committee for the Defense of the Armenian Cause under the so-called Gayssot Act (which provides that punishment shall be imposed upon those who call into question the very existence of crimes against humanity), was dismissed. The court held that the Gayssot Act applied only to crimes committed by the Nazi regime between 1939 and 1945.[30]

The guilty verdict by the French court was severely criticized in the United States. The *Washington Post* editorialized that when a court punishes a scholar "for expressing an 'insulting' opinion on a historical matter, even when debate on the point in question has been raging worldwide for years, the absurdity and perniciousness of such laws is on full display."[31] The Armenian side, for its part, defended the decision by once again insisting on the established truth of the Armenian genocide, which was said to be beyond doubt. Anyone who denied this crime became an accessory to it. "In this context, denying that the genocide occurred takes the historian beyond the outer threshold of scholarship and make [*sic*] him or her an agent of the state....Acting as he did, Bernard Lewis became the active accomplice of a political fraud."[32] One pro-Armenian author even has suggested that denial of the Armenian genocide represents hate-speech and therefore should be illegal in the United States.[33] It appears that Lewis himself has not been intimidated by the affair, for he has continued to voice his views on this issue. Thus, for example, in a program on C-Span 2 on March 25, 2002, he once again reaffirmed his belief that the Armenian massacres in Ottoman Turkey were linked to the massive Armenian rebellion and therefore were not comparable to the treatment of the Jews under the Nazis.[34]

Americans of Armenian origin in the United States have actively sought the support of the intellectual community for their position, and they have had considerable success in this endeavor. On February 2, 1996, a group of "Concerned Scholars and Writers," organized by the Armenian Assembly of America, ran an advertisement in the *Chronicles of Higher Education* under the heading "Taking a Stand against the Turkish Government's Denial of the Armenian Genocide and Scholarly Corruption in the Academy." A slightly abbreviated version of this ad ran in the *New York Times* on April 24, 1998, under the more explicit headline "We Commemorate the Armenian Genocide of 1915 and Condemn the Turkish Government's Denial of This Crime against Humanity." The ads were signed by scholars with expertise on the

Jewish Holocaust, such as Yehuda Bauer, Helen Fein, and Raul Hilberg, and by scholars with specific knowledge of the events of 1915–16, such as Dadrian and Hovannisian. In addition the ads were subscribed to by many distinguished writers, among them Alfred Kazin, Arthur Miller, Joyce Carol Oates, and John Updike. Notably absent from the list of signers (100 in 1996 and 150 in 1998) were scholars of Turkish history or the Middle East.

The ads began by affirming the innocence of the defenseless Armenian victims:

> In the years 1915–1918 the Young Turk government of the Ottoman Empire carried out a systematic, premeditated genocide against the Armenian people—an unarmed Christian minority living under Turkish rule. Over a million Armenians were exterminated through direct killing, starvation, torture, and forced deportation marches....The Armenian Genocide is well documented by Ottoman court-martial records, an abundance of documents in official archives of nations around the world, the reports of missionaries and diplomats, especially from the United States, England, Germany, and Austria, the testimony of survivors, and eight decades of historical scholarship.

The advertisements then listed the various ways in which the Turkish government had sought to coerce the U.S. government and to influence public opinion in order to cleanse its image, including the funding of chairs of Turkish history at prestigious universities. This was followed by an indictment of genocide denial:

> When scholars deny genocide, their message is: murderers did not really murder; victims were not really killed; mass murder requires no confrontation, but should be ignored. Scholars who deny genocide lend their considerable authority to the acceptance of this ultimate human crime.... We denounce as intellectually and morally corrupt Turkey's manipulation of American institutions for the purpose of denying its genocide of the Armenians. We condemn fraudulent scholarship supported by the Turkish government and carried out in American universities....We advocate that U.S. government officials, scholars, and the media refer to the annihilation of the Armenians as genocide, and not use evasive or euphemistic terminology to appease the Turkish government.[35]

The text of the Armenian-sponsored ads involved not only simplification, which is usual in such cases, but also some distortion. The Armenian community in Turkey was not simply "an unarmed Christian minority," and it is not acceptable to discuss the events of 1915–16 without mentioning the fifth-column role of the Armenian revolutionaries. But the most serious issue raised by the ads was the attempt to coerce adherence to the views of the sponsors by accusing all those dissenting from this version of history of nefarious motives. The ads with justification condemned the Turkish government for its crude attempts "to censure scholarship about the Armenian Genocide" but then resorted to this very same tactic by suggesting that those who refused to call the mass killings genocide were seeking "to appease the Turkish government." The ads also admonished scholars to avoid "evasive terminology." This attempt to foreclose further scholarly investigation of the deportations and massacres by imposing a politically correct nomenclature unfortunately represents the very "scholarly corruption in the academy" that the ads claimed to denounce.

THE FUTURE OF TURKISH-ARMENIAN RELATIONS

As we enter the twenty-first century and approach the 100th anniversary of the beginning of the deportation of the Armenian community in the Ottoman Empire, the positions of both Turks and Armenians appear to be as frozen as ever. The Turkish government continues to maintain that apart from some unfortunate excesses nothing very untoward happened during the course of the Armenian deportations and that the large loss of life was the result primarily of disease, starvation, and intercommunal warfare. Some Armenians would be satisfied with an official statement by the Turkish government that it deeply regrets the great suffering of the Armenians during World War I. Yet many other Armenians still vehemently condemn the Turks for perpetrating a premeditated genocide, and for some of them the return of the Armenian homeland "is the only meaningful redress the Turks can make for the massacres."[36] This demand in turn causes the Turks to refuse to make even a limited admission of wrongdoing, for they fear that any concession would initiate a chain reaction, leading to sweeping demands for financial and even territorial restitution.[37]

But there are also more hopeful signs. Over the weekend of March 17–19, 2000, scholars from ten universities and research centers met at the University of Chicago as the Turkish-Armenian Workshop to discuss the controversial topic "Armenians and the End of the Ottoman Empire." Professor Ronald Suny of the University of Chicago, one of the conveners of the conference, opened the proceedings with remarks that noted their great significance:

This is a small, humble, and historic meeting—the first time that schol-ars of various nationalities, including Armenians and Turks, have gath-ered together to present papers and discuss in a scholarly fashion the fate of the peoples of the Ottoman Empire as that state declined and disinte-grated.... We do not expect full agreement, but we do expect serious and learned discussion. This is a first probe, an attempt to form a new schol-arly community inspired by liberal Ottomanism, tolerance of differences on the basis of equality and respect, rather than exclusivist and insular nationalism.

At the close of the meeting the participants agreed to continue their deliberations, and the workshop met again at the University of Michigan in 2002 and at the University of Minnesota in 2003. It is expected that papers from the proceedings will be published.[38]

And there is more. During the last few years Turkish historical scholarship has begun to reveal signs of a postnationalist phase in which the Armenian massacres are starting to find a place.[39] On the Armenian side, too, scholars such as Ara Sarafian and Ronald Suny have engaged in historical research without the usual propagandistic rhetoric. Between March 23 and 25, 2001, historians, jurists, and soci-ologists from Armenia, Turkey, Germany, and the United States met under the auspices of the Evangelical Academy, Mühlheim, Germany, to discuss the fateful events of 1915–18. The participants left the con-ference convinced that it was possible to overcome inherited prejudice and misunderstandings.[40] During the summer of 2001 a group of about 150 Armenian-Americans participated in a pilgrimage to Anatolia organized by the New York diocese of the Armenian Church of Amer-ica. The pilgrims followed the footsteps of St. Gregory and were well received during their 600-mile bus trip. "Everywhere we went," stated one of the participants on his return, "we had the opportunity to exchange words of hope that we can have an open dialogue and con-tinue our relationship and visits." It appears that the "years of mistrust and hatred will ease up and we will find a way to forgive."[41] A greater openness toward the Armenian problem has also developed in the Turk-ish media (daily newspapers and television), which have seen previously unimaginable discussions of the deportations and massacres.[42]

Yet progress toward better relations between Turks and Armenian is slow and has its setbacks. In July 2001 a group of prominent indi-viduals from Armenia and Turkey agreed to establish a reconciliation commission between the two countries. Turkey had broken diplomatic relations with Armenia after the start of the war between Armenia and Turkey's ally Azerbaijan almost a decade earlier. The Turkish-Armenian Reconciliation Commission also was to look at the events of 1915–16 and explore ways to close the gap between the contending positions.[43] However, the war in Iraq and the attempt to reopen the issue of the Armenian massacres doomed the reconciliation commission. Powerful groups in Armenia and in the Armenian diaspora are opposed to a fresh look at the historical record. "Even participating in such a research panel, say Armenians, would validate precisely the premise they reject: that there's any doubt that Armenians suffered genocide."[44] American Armenian scholars, interested in a less nationalistic and more objective view of Armenian history, have been charged by historians at Yerevan State University with promoting "pro-Turkish perspectives on the Armenian Genocide."[45] Turkish hard-liners, too, were opposed to the work of the reconciliation commission, and it disbanded without substantial accomplishments in April 2004.[46]

The willingness on the part of some Turkish historians to discuss the Armenian tragedy has come under attack. Denouncing the "enemy within," in October 2000 the influential columnist Emin Cölasan (writing for Turkey's largest daily, *Hürriyet*) deplored the lack of concord: "Until now we have been united as a nation against the genocide claims of the Armenians. But now distorted sounds are coming from our own ranks." Other public figures have voiced similar concerns about the new "traitors."[47]

As mentioned earlier, some Armenians use the word "genocide" not as a legal concept but as a term of moral opprobrium that castigates the deportation and its attending huge loss of life as a grave moral evil. Paradoxical as it may seem, this way of approaching the problem may offer a way out of the frozen positions. If the Armenians could be persuaded to forego resort to the legal concept of genocide as a systematic and premeditated program of the destruction of a people and be satisfied with a Turkish acknowledgment of sincere regret for the terrible suffering of the Armenian people during the First World War, a path might open toward reconciliation. The Turkish political scientist Sina Aksin has suggested such a move in an official Turkish publication. Both Turks and Armenians should "accept publicly the fact that they inflicted great wrong on each other."[48]

Turks and Armenians, the historian Selim Deringil has urged, should "step back from the was-it-genocide-or-not dialogue of the deaf, which only leads to mutual recrimination and is ultimately unproductive" and instead concentrate on historical research that seeks a "common project of knowledge." Ideally, Deringil writes, "the target should be a removal of the 'them' and 'us' as historians."[49] Suny has similarly indicated that he is frustrated "by the usual sterile debates about whether a genocide occurred or not and by the banality of analysis and explanation." He, too, has proposed more empirically grounded historical research.[50] Needless to say, the task of thus rescuing history from the grip and polemics of the politicians and nationalists is not an easy assignment. If and when it succeeds it may pave the way toward the reconciliation of Armenians and Turks and bring about the settlement of a conflict that has lasted all too long.

Abbreviations and Glossary

Botsch. K.	Botschaft Konstantinopel
Chette	Band of irregulars
CO	Colonial Office
CUP	Committee of Union and Progress
*Fedayee*s	Freedom fighters prepared to sacrifice themselves for the cause
FO	Foreign Office
Kaimakam	Head official of a district (*kaza*)
Kavass	Messenger of a consulate
Kaza	District
LC	Library of Congress
Mohadjir	Refugee
Mutassarif	Head official of a subprovince or county (*sancak*)
NA	National Archives
PA	Politisches Archiv des Auswärtigen Amtes
Porte	The Ottoman government
RG	Record Group
Sancak	Subprovince or county
Vali	Governor of a province (*vilayet*)
Vilayet	Province
Wk.	Weltkrieg
WO	War Office

Notes

Chapter 1. ARMENIANS IN THE OTTOMAN EMPIRE DURING THE NINETEENTH CENTURY

1. Roderic H. Davison, "Turkish Attitudes concerning Christian-Muslim Equality in the Nineteenth Century," *American Historical Review* 59 (1954): 855.

2. Ronald Grigor Suny, *Looking toward Ararat: Armenia in Modern History*, p. 101.

3. Vahakn N. Dadrian, *Warrant for Genocide: Key Elements of Turko-Armenian Conflict*, p. 39.

4. Jeremy Salt, *Imperialism, Evangelism and the Ottoman Armenians, 1878–1896*, p. 31.

5. Charles Eliot, *Turkey in Europe*, pp. 400–402. See also the observations of Selim Deringil in *The Well-Protected Domains: Ideology and Legitimation of Power in the Ottoman Empire 1876–1909*, pp. 128–29.

6. Ronald Grigor Suny, "Empire and Nation: Armenians, Turks and the End of the Ottoman Empire," *Armenian Forum* 1, no. 2 (Summer 1998): 33.

7. Quoted in Louise Nalbandian, *The Armenian Revolutionary Movement: The Development of Armenian Political Parties through the Nineteenth Century*, p. 27.

8. R. W. Seton-Watson, *Disraeli, Gladstone and the Eastern Question: A Study in Diplomacy and Party Politics*, p. 334.

9. George Douglas Campbell, Duke of Argyll, *Our Responsibilities for Turkey: Facts and Memories of Forty Years*, p. 68.

10. James Bryce, *Transcaucasia and Ararat: Being Notes of a Vacation Tour in the Autumn of 1876*, pp. 524, 523.

11. The German ambassador to Berlin, November 16, 1894, in Johannes Lepsius et al., eds., *Die grosse Politik der Europäischen Kabinette 1871–1914: Sammlung der diplomatischen Akten des Auswärtigen Amtes*, vol. 9, p. 203.

12. Stephen Duguid, "The Politics of Unity: Hamidian Policy in Eastern Anatolia," *Middle Eastern Studies* 9 (1973): 145.

13. Robert Olson, *The Emergence of Kurdish Nationalism and the Sheikh Said Rebellion, 1880–1925*, p. 10.

14. Nalbandian, *Armenian Revolutionary Movement*, p. 29.

Chapter 2. THE ARMENIAN REVOLUTIONARY MOVEMENT

1. William L. Langer, *The Diplomacy of Imperialism: 1890–1902*, vol. 1, p. 154.

2. Simon Vratzian, "The Armenian Revolution and the Armenian Revolutionary Federation," *Armenian Review* 3, no. 3 (Autumn 1950): 12.

3. Quoted in Sarkis Atamian, *The Armenian Community: The Historical Development of a Social and Ideological Conflict,* p. 96. Nalbandian, in *Armenian Revolutionary Movement,* summarizes this article thus: "The most opportune time to initiate the general rebellion for carrying out the immediate objective was when Turkey was engaged in war" (p. 111).

4. Anaide Ter Minassian, *Nationalism and Socialism in the Armenian Revolutionary Movement (1887–1912),* trans. A. M. Berrett, p. 12.

5. Quoted in Vratzian, "The Armenian Revolution," pp. 18–19.

6. Nalbandian, *Armenian Revolutionary Movement,* p. 172.

7. Vice-Consul Devey to Acting Consul Fitzmaurice, December 8, 1892, in *British Documents on Ottoman Armenians,* ed. Bilal N. Simsir, vol. 3, p. 147.

8. James G. Mandalian, ed. and trans., *Armenian Freedom Fighters: The Memoirs of Rouben der Minasian,* pp. 19–20.

9. Nalbandian, *Armenian Revolutionary Movement,* p. 119.

10. Eliot, *Turkey in Europe,* pp. 404–5. Langer in his *Diplomacy of Imperialism* calls Eliot "one of the best informed and most conscientious writers about modern Turkey" (vol. 1, p. 325).

11. Dadrian, *Warrant for Genocide,* p. 69.

12. Simsir, *British Documents on Ottoman Armenians,* vol. 3, p. 208.

13. Souren Aprahamian, *From Van to Detroit: Surviving the Armenian Genocide,* p. 16.

14. Atamian, *Armenian Community,* p. 276.

15. Mandalian, *Armenian Freedom Fighters,* pp. 55–56.

16. Edwin Munsell Bliss, *Turkish Cruelties upon the Armenian Christians,* p. 342.

17. Simsir, *British Documents on Ottoman Armenians,* vol. 3, p. 335.

18. Charles S. Hampton, acting consul in Erzurum, to Ambassador W. White, May 23, 1891, in ibid., p. 67.

19. Richard G. Hovannisian, *Armenia on the Road to Independence, 1918,* p. 27. Both the French and the British government published extensive accounts of the events of 1894 and the subsequent investigation. They are summarized by Yves Ternon, *The Armenians: History of a Genocide,* trans. Rouben C. Cholakian, pp. 75–77.

20. This view is accepted by Justin McCarthy in *Death and Exile: The Ethnic Cleansing of Ottoman Muslims, 1821–1922,* p. 119, as well as by Stanford J. Shaw and Ezel Kural Shaw, *History of the Ottoman Empire and Modern Turkey,* pp. 203–4.

21. Langer, *Diplomacy of Imperialism,* vol. 1, pp. 158, 164.

22. Justin McCarthy and Carolyn McCarthy, *Turks and Armenians: A Manual on the Armenian Question,* p. 42. The McCarthys' account fails to mention the increase in Kurdish violence that followed the establishment of the Hamidiye regiments in 1891; the Kurds did not need Armenian provocative attacks in order to be prepared to attack Armenian villages. See Duguid, "The Politics of Unity," p. 147; and Langer, *Diplomacy of Imperialism,* vol. 1, p. 160.

23. Richard G. Hovannisian, "The Critic's View: Beyond Revisionism," *International Journal of Middle East Studies* 9 (1978): 381.

24. Suny, *Looking toward Ararat,* pp. 98–99.

25. Robert Melson, "A Theoretical Inquiry into the Armenian Massacres of 1894–1896," *Comparative Studies in Society and History* 25 (1982): 495, 486.

26. Foreword to Robert F. Melson, *Revolution and Genocide: On the Origins of the Armenian Genocide and the Holocaust,* p. xi.

27. Letter by Cyrus Hamlin in the *Boston Congregationalist,* December 23, 1893, reprinted in U.S. Department of State, *Papers Relating to the Foreign Relations of the United States, 1895,* p. 1416.

28. Nalbandian, *Armenian Revolutionary Movement,* p. 110.

29. Simsir, *British Documents on Ottoman Armenians,* vol. 3, p. 203.

30. Robert Graves, *Storm Centres of the Near East: Personal Memories 1879–1929,* p. 139.

31. George H. Hepworth, *Through Armenia on Horseback,* p. 341.

32. Edwin Pears, *Forty Years in Constantinople: The Recollections of Sir Edwin Pears, 1873–1915,* p. 155.

33. Christopher J. Walker, *Armenia: The Survival of a Nation,* p. 135.

34. Simsir, *British Documents on Ottoman Armenians,* vol. 3, p. 251.

Chapter 3. THE MASSACRES OF 1894–96

1. Graves, *Storm Centres of the Near East,* p. 142.

2. Ertugrul Zekai Ökte, ed., *Ottoman Archives, Yildiz Collection: The Armenian Question, Talori Incidents,* p. 357. See also Jeremy Salt, "Britain, the Armenian Question and the Cause of Ottoman Reform: 1894–96," *Middle Eastern Studies* 26 (1990): 313, who largely accepts the Turkish account.

3. Memo of Ambassador Currie, November 1, 1894, in Simsir, *British Documents on Ottoman Armenians,* vol. 3, p. 395.

4. Bliss, *Turkish Cruelties upon the Armenian Christians,* p. 372.

5. The text of the report can be found in Simsir, *British Documents on Ottoman Armenians,* vol. 3, pp. 93–112. See also Ternon, *The Armenians,* p. 77.

6. Vahakn N. Dadrian, *The History of the Armenian Genocide: Ethnic Conflict from the Balkans to Anatolia to the Caucasus,* pp. 114–15.

7. Salt, *Imperialism, Evangelism and the Ottoman Armenians, 1878–1896,* p. 75.

8. Langer, *Diplomacy of Imperialism,* vol. 1, pp. 162–63; Hovannisian, *Armenia on the Road to Independence,* p. 27.

9. Simsir, *British Documents on Ottoman Armenians,* vol. 4, p. 24, vol. 3, p. 261.

10. Ambassador to Berlin, October 4, 1895, in Lepsius et al., *Die grosse Politik der Europäischen Kabinette 1871–1914,* vol. 9, p. 68.

11. Ambassador Currie report to London, October 11, 1895, in Simsir, *British Documents on Ottoman Armenians,* vol. 4, p. 298.

12. Bliss, *Turkish Cruelties upon the Armenian Christians,* pp. 408–9, 553.

13. Hepworth, *Through Armenia on Horseback,* pp. 56, 60, 63.

14. For the text see Simsir, *British Documents on Ottoman Armenians,* vol. 4, pp. 322–37.

15. Salt, *Imperialism, Evangelism and the Ottoman Armenians,* p. 101.

16. Vice-Consul Hampson to Consul Cumberbatch (Erzurum), October 29, 1895, in Simsir, *British Documents on Ottoman Armenians,* vol. 4, p. 533.

17. Embassy Constantinople to London, November 2, 1895, in ibid., vol. 4, p. 426.

18. Hepworth, *Through Armenia on Horseback,* p. 146.

19. Graves, *Storm Centres of the Near East,* p. 157.

20. Embassy Constantinople to London, November 2, 1895, in Simsir, *British Documents on Ottoman Armenians,* vol. 4, p. 427; Bliss, *Turkish Cruelties upon the Armenian Christians,* p. 423.

21. Duguid, "The Politics of Unity," p. 151.

22. The Turkish perspective on the uprising is given by Esat Uras, *The Armenians in History and the Armenian Question,* trans. Süheyla Artemel, pp. 746–47. A view tilted to the Armenian side can be found in Ternon, *The Armenians,* pp. 96–97. For a fairly balanced account by a contemporary observer, see the report of British consul Barnham in Aleppo, November 24, in Simsir, *British Documents on Ottoman Armenians,* vol. 4, pp. 634–35.

23. Salt, *Imperialism, Evangelism and the Ottoman Armenians,* pp. 106–7; and Dadrian, *History of the Armenian Genocide,* pp. 131–38.

24. Eliot, *Turkey in Europe,* p. 409; Sir P. Currie to the Foreign Office, December 19, 1895, in Simsir, *British Documents on Ottoman Armenians,* vol. 4, p. 660.

25. A detailed description of the plot is given by one of the leaders, then known as Armen Garo, in Garegin Pasdermadjian, *Bank Ottoman: Memoirs of Armen Garo,* trans. Haig T. Partizian, pp. 96–139.

26. Langer, *Diplomacy of Imperialism,* vol. 1, p. 325.

27. This is also the view of Eliot, *Turkey in Europe,* p. 412; and of George Washburn, the president of Robert College in Constantinople, in his memoir *Fifty Years in Constantinople and Recollections of Robert College,* pp. 246–47.

28. See his note of resignation in Lepsius et al., *Die Grosse Politik der Europäischen Kabinette,* vol. 12, part 1, pp. 30–37.

29. Graves, *Storm Centres of the Near East,* p. 161.

30. Kamuran Gürün, *The Armenian File: The Myth of Innocence Exposed,* p. 161; E. K. Sarkisian and R. G. Sahakian, *Vital Issues in Modern Armenian History: A Documented Exposé of Misrepresentation in Turkish Historiography,* trans. Elisha B. Chrakian, p. 18.

31. Gürün, *The Armenian File,* p. 161.

32. Hepworth, *Through Armenia on Horseback,* p. 344.

33. Lepsius et al., *Die Grosse Politik der Europäischen Kabinette,* vol. 10, p. 120.

34. Salt, *Imperialism, Evangelism and the Ottoman Armenians,* p. 105.

35. Hepworth, *Through Armenia on Horseback,* p. 324; Vice-Consul Hampson in Mush to Consul Cumberbatch in Erzurum, November 16, 1895, in Simsir, *British Documents on Ottoman Armenians,* vol. 4, p. 632.

36. Eliot, *Turkey in Europe,* p. 408.

37. Bliss, *Turkish Cruelties upon the Armenian Christians,* p. 477.

38. Ernest Jackh, *The Rising Crescent: Turkey Yesterday, Today, and Tomorrow,* p. 44.

39. Henry Morgenthau, *Ambassador Morgenthau's Story,* pp. 289–90.

40. Ternon, *The Armenians,* p. 92.

41. Vahakn N. Dadrian, "The Armenian Genocide and the Pitfalls of a 'Balanced' Analysis: A Response to Ronald Grigor Suny," *Armenian Forum* 1, no. 2 (Summer 1998): 75.

42. David Marshall Lang, *The Armenians: A People in Exile,* p. 1.

43. Eliot, *Turkey in Europe,* p. 407.

44. Hepworth, *Through Armenia on Horseback,* pp. 162, 173.

45. Lepsius et al., *Die grosse Politik der Europäischen Kabinette,* vol. 12, part 1, pp. 84–85, 103.

46. Simsir, *British Documents on Ottoman Armenians,* vol. 4, pp. 409, 639–40.

47. Sidney Whitman, *Turkish Memories,* p. 127.

48. Ardern Hulme-Beaman, *Twenty Years in the Near East,* pp. 304–5.

49. Hepworth, *Through Armenia on Horseback,* p. 157.

50. Bliss, *Turkish Cruelties upon the Armenian Christians,* p. 557.

51. Hepworth, *Through Armenia on Horseback,* pp. 295, 145–46.

Chapter 4. THE YOUNG TURKS TAKE POWER

1. James H. Tashjian, "The Armenian 'Dashnag' Party: A Brief Statement," *Armenian Review* 21, no. 4 (Winter 1968): 53.

2. Chalabian, *Revolutionary Figures,* p. 328; Vratzian, "The Armenian Revolution and the Armenian Revolutionary Federation," p. 27; Atamian, *Armenian Community,* p. 109.

3. Langer, *Diplomacy of Imperialism,* vol. 1, p. 350.

4. Atamian, *Armenian Community,* p. 109.

5. Aprahamian, *From Van to Detroit,* p. 21.

6. Tashjian, "The Armenian 'Dashnag' Party," p. 53.

7. Chalabian, *Revolutionary Figures,* p. 215.

8. W. A. Wigram and E. T. A. Wigram, *The Cradle of Mankind: Life in Eastern Kurdistan,* pp. 247–50.

9. Chalabian, *Revolutionary Figures,* p. 265.

10. Mandalian, *Armenian Freedom Fighters,* p. 142.

11. Atamian, *Armenian Community,* p. 277.

12. Edward Alexander, *A Crime of Vengeance: An Armenian Struggle for Justice,* p. 97; Richard G. Hovannisian, "The Armenian Question in the Ottoman Empire," *East European Quarterly* 6 (1972): 15; Salahi R. Sonyel, *The Ottoman Armenians: Victims of Great Power Diplomacy,* p. 261.

13. Ernest E. Ramsaur, Jr., *The Young Turks: Prelude to the Revolution of 1908,* pp. 70–75 (quotation on p. 70); Sükrü M. Hanioglu, *The Young Turks in Opposition,* pp. 195–97.

14. Feroz Ahmad, "Unionist Relations with the Greek, Armenian, and Jewish Communities of the Ottoman Empire, 1908–1914," in *Christians and Jews in the Ottoman Empire: The Functioning of a Plural Society,* ed. Benjamin Braude and Bernard Lewis, p. 419.

15. Pears, *Forty Years in Constantinople,* p. 298.

16. Ahmad, "Unionist Relations," pp. 420–21; Avedis K. Sanjian, *The Armenian Communities in Syria under Ottoman Dominion,* pp. 279–80.

17. Stephan H. Astourian, "Genocidal Process: Reflections on the Armeno-Turkish Polarization," in *The Armenian Genocide: History, Politics, Ethics,* ed. Richard G. Hovannisian, p. 67; Aykut Kansu, *Politics in Post-Revolutionary Turkey, 1908–1913,* pp. 124–25.

18. Sarkisian and Sahakian, *Vital Issues in Modern Armenian History,* p. 20.

19. Vahakn N. Dadrian, "The Convergent Roles of the State and Governmental Party in the Armenian Genocide," in *Studies in Comparative Genocide,* ed. Levon Chorbajian and George Shirinian, p. 102.

20. H. Charles Woods, *The Danger Zone of Europe: Changes and Problems in the Near East,* p. 76.

21. William M. Ramsay, *The Revolution in Constantinople and Turkey: A Diary,* p. 207.

22. Woods, *Danger Zone of Europe,* pp. 183–88; Kansu, *Politics in Post-Revolutionary Turkey,* pp. 144–46.

23. Hratch Dasnabedian, *History of the Armenian Revolutionary Federation Dashnaktsutiun 1890–1924,* pp. 87–91.

24. Quoted in Chalabian, *Revolutionary Figures,* p. 285.

25. Dasnabedian, *History of the Armenian Revolutionary Federation,* p. 103.

26. Erik J. Zürcher, *Turkey: A Modern History,* p. 137.

27. Suny, *Looking toward Ararat,* p. 108.

28. Dadrian, in his essay "The Convergent Roles of the State and Governmental Party in the Armenian Genocide," p. 114, calls Gökalp "one of the party chieftains in this exterminatory enterprise." On the ideology of the Young Turks prior to World War I, see the exchange involving Suny, Akarli, and Deringil in the *Armenian Forum* 1, no. 2 (Summer 1998): Ronald Grigor Suny, "Empire and Nation: Armenians, Turks and the End of the Ottoman Empire," pp. 17–51; Engin Deniz Akarli, "Particularities of History: A Response to Ronald Grigor Suny,"

pp. 53–64; and Selim Deringil, "In Search of a Way Forward: A Response to Ronald Grigor Suny," pp. 65–71. The role of Gökalp in the events of 1915 is discussed in more detail in chapter 5.

29. George W. Gawrych, "The Culture and Politics of Violence in Turkish Society, 1903–14," *Middle Eastern Studies* 22 (1986): 326–27.

30. Hovannisian, *Armenia on the Road to Independence,* pp. 30–31.

31. McCarthy, *Death and Exile,* p. 161; Dadrian, *Warrant for Genocide,* pp. 112–13.

32. See especially Gaidz F. Minassian, "Les relations entre le Comité Union et Progrès et la Fédération Révolutionnaire Arménienne à la veille de la Première Guerre Mondiale après les sources arméniennes," *Revue d'Histoire Arménienne Contemporaine* 1 (1995): 81–99.

33. Roderic H. Davison, "The Armenian Crisis, 1912–1914," *American Historical Review* 53 (1948): 499.

34. For details on this conspiracy, see Vahakn N. Dadrian, "The Secret Young-Turk Ittihadist Conference and the Decision for the World War I Genocide of the Armenians," *Holocaust and Genocide Studies* 7 (1993): 190.

35. Quoted from the memoirs of the patriarch by Dadrian, "The Armenian Genocide and the Pitfalls of a 'Balanced' Analysis," p. 78.

36. Serge D. Sazonov, *Fateful Years, 1909–1916: The Reminiscences of Serge Sazonov,* p. 141.

37. Richard G. Hovannisian, "The Armenian Question in the Ottoman Empire, 1876–1914," in *The Armenian People from Ancient to Modern Times,* ed. Richard G. Hovannisian, pp. 236–37; Sazonov, *Fateful Years,* p. 143.

38. Kamal Madhar Ahmad, *Kurdistan during the First World War,* trans. Ali Maher Ibrahim, p. 423, suggests that the Turkish reform proposal had been prepared several months earlier and reflected the desire of the CUP to solve the Armenian problem by way of reform. The question of the sincerity of the Ottoman offer of reform is probably more important than its timing.

39. Ibid., pp. 161–62.

40. Sazonov, *Fateful Years,* p. 144.

41. Hovannisian, "The Armenian Question in the Ottoman Empire," p. 237; Sazonov, *Fateful Years,* pp. 144–45.

42. Quoted in Ahmed Djemal Pasha, *Memories of a Turkish Statesman, 1913–1919,* p. 274. This work also includes the full text of the reform agreement (pp. 272–74).

43. Hovannisian, "The Armenian Question in the Ottoman Empire," p. 237.

44. Quoted in Hovannisian, *Armenia on the Road to Independence,* p. 38.

45. Ibid., pp. 38–39; Sonyel, *The Ottoman Armenians,* p. 284.

46. Ahmad, "Unionist Relations," p. 424.

47. Cf. Kurt Ziemke, *Die Neue Türkei: Politische Entwicklung 1914–1929,* p. 271.

Chapter 5. The Armenian Case (1): Genocidal Plans

1. Richard G. Hovannisian, ed., *Remembrance and Denial: The Case of the Armenian Genocide*, pp. 14-15.

2. Dadrian, *Warrant for Genocide*, p. 97.

3. In this chapter and in the following chapter, much of the time my discussion focuses on the work of Vahakn N. Dadrian, who is the best-known exponent of the premeditation thesis and who has been called the "foremost scholar of the Armenian Genocide" (Peter Balakian, *The Burning Tigris: The Armenian Genocide and America's Response*, p. xvii). Dadrian's approach, Malcolm E. Yapp has correctly noted in reviewing one of his recent books, "is not that of an historian trying to find out what happened and why but that of a lawyer assembling the case for the prosecution in an adversarial system" (review of *The History of the Armenian Genocide* by V. N. Dadrian, in *Middle Eastern Studies* 32 [1996]: 397). A German scholar, Hilmar Kaiser, who is generally supportive of the Armenian side and accepts the charge of genocide, has nevertheless pointed out the "selective use of sources" in another of Dadrian's books and has concluded that "serious scholars should be cautioned against accepting all of Dadrian's statements at face value" ("Germany and the Armenian Genocide: Reply to Vahakn N. Dadrian's Response," *Journal of the Society for Armenian Studies* 9 [1996-99]: 139-40). I have heeded this warning.

4. Dadrian, *Warrant for Genocide*, p. 95. Other attempts to link the mass killing of Armenians in World War I to the ideology of the Young Turks are made by Mihran Dabag, "Jungtürkische **Visionen und der Völkermord an den Armeniern,**" in *Genozid und Moderne*, ed. Mihran Dabag and Kristin Platt, vol. 1, pp. 152-205; and by Taner Akcam, *From Empire to Republic: Turkish Nationalism and the Armenian Genocide*, p. 150.

5. Great Britain, Foreign Office, *British Documents on the Origin of the War 1898-1914*, p. 208.

6. Jean Naslian, *Les mémoires des Mgr. Jean Naslian, évêque de Trébizonde*, p. 10 (n. 6), 148, 412, quoted in Vahakn N. Dadrian, "The Secret Young-Turk Ittihadist Conference and the Decision for the World War I Genocide of the Armenians," *Journal of Political and Military Sociology* 22 (1994): 194 (n. 14).

7. James H. Tashjian, "On a 'Statement' Condemning the Armenian Genocide of 1915-18 Attributed in Error to Mustafa Kemal, Later 'The Ataturk,'" *Armenian Review* 35 (1982): 228, 232-33; Ternon, *The Armenians*, p. 289 (n. 24).

8. Dadrian, "The Secret Young-Turk Ittihadist Conference," p. 179.

9. Ternon, *The Armenians*, p. 134.

10. Andrew Mango, "Understanding Turkey," *Middle Eastern Studies* 18 (1982): 212.

11. James Reid, "The Armenian Massacres in Ottoman and Turkish Historiography," *Armenian Review* 37, no. 1 (Spring 1984): 31.

12. Stephan H. Astourian, "Genocidal Process: Reflections on the Armeno-Turkish Polarization," in *The Armenian Genocide: History, Politics, Ethics,* ed. Richard G. Hovannisian, p. 69.

13. Balakian, *The Burning Tigris,* p. 163.

14. Haigazn K. Kazarian, "A Catalogue of Those Principally Responsible for the 1915–1918 Massacres," *Armenian Review* 29 (1976): 272.

15. Uriel Heyd, *Foundations of Turkish Nationalism: The Life and Teachings of Ziya Gökalp,* p. ix; Robert Devereux, preface to Ziya Gökalp, *The Principles of Turkism,* p. x.

16. Gökalp, *Principles of Turkism,* pp. 20, 28.

17. Taha Parla, *The Social and Political Thought of Ziya Gökalp, 1876–1924,* pp. 120, 19, 25–26.

18. Gotthard Jäschke, *Der Turanismus der Jungtürken: Zur Osmanischen Aussenpolitik im Weltkriege,* pp. 5, 8.

19. Introduction to Ziya Gökalp, *Turkish Nationalism and Western Civilization: Selected Essays,* trans. Niyazi Berkes, pp. 15, 8.

20. Heyd, *Foundations of Turkish Nationalism,* p. 129.

21. Dadrian, "The Convergent Roles of the State and Governmental Party in the Armenian Genocide," p. 114.

22. Heyd, *Foundations of Turkish Nationalism,* p. 36.

23. Robert Melson, "Provocation or Nationalism: A Critical Inquiry into the Armenian Genocide of 1915," in *The Armenian Genocide,* ed. Hovannisian, p. 76.

24. Heyd, *Foundations of Turkish Nationalism,* p. 35.

25. Parla, *Social and Political Thought of Ziya Gökalp,* p. 15. See also Niyazi Berkes, *The Development of Secularism in Turkey,* pp. 415–16.

26. Memo of C. E. Heathcote Smith, February 4, 1919, FO 371/4172/31307, pp. 384–86.

27. Dadrian, "The Secret Young-Turk Ittihadist Conference," p. 177.

28. Christopher J. Walker, "Letter to the Editor," *Middle Eastern Studies* 9 (1973): 376.

29. FO 371/4172/31307, pp. 388–89.

30. See, for example, Sir H. Lamb's minute of August 11, 1920, FO 371/6500/E3557.

31. Memo of Major Cameron, February 25, 1920, WO 32/5620/5897, p. 16.

32. Heck's memo (867.4016/409) is reproduced in the microfiche collection edited by Rouben Paul Adalian, *The Armenian Genocide in the United States Archives, 1915–1918,* fiche 95.

33. Dadrian, "The Secret Young-Turk Ittihadist Conference," p. 178.

34. Taner Akcam, *Armenien und der Völkermord: Die Istanbuler Prozesse und die türkische Nationalbewegung,* p. 163.

35. FO 371/4172/31307, p. 386.

36. Gwynne Dyer, "Letter to the Editor," *Middle Eastern Studies* 9 (1973): 378.

37. Ibid.

38. Sarkisian and Sahakian, *Vital Issues,* p. 32. See also Haigaz K. Kazarian, "Minutes of Secret Meetings Organizing the Turkish Genocide of Armenians," *Armenian Review* 18, no. 3 (Autumn 1965): 23.

39. Rifat, *Türkiye,* pp. 159–60, quoted in Sarkisian and Sahakian, *Vital Issues in Modern Armenian History,* p. 32.

40. Rifat, *Türkiye,* p. 148, quoted in ibid., p. 34.

41. Rifat, *Türkiye,* pp. 194–95, quoted in ibid., pp. 35–36.

42. Hovannisian, *Armenia on the Road to Independence,* p. 174 (n. 47). Hovannisian in the same place also accepts the authenticity of the equally dubious Andonian documents, which I discuss in the next chapter.

43. Walker, "Letter to the Editor," p. 376; Christopher J. Walker, "World War I and the Armenian Genocide," in *The Armenian People from Ancient to Modern Times,* ed. Richard G. Hovannisian, p. 247.

44. Florence Mazian, *Why Genocide?: The Armenian and Jewish Experiences in Perspective,* p. 61.

45. Ahmad, *Kurdistan during the First World War,* p. 165.

46. Dyer, "Letter to the Editor," pp. 379–82. See also Kansu, *Politics in Post-Revolutionary Turkey,* pp. 140, 184–85.

47. The text of an accord between the Dashnaks and the Kurdish National League "Hoybun" signed in 1927 is reproduced in Hamit Bozarslan, "Histoire des relations kurdo-arméniennes," in *Kurdistan und Europa: Einblicke in die kurdische Geschichte des 19. und 20. Jahrhunderts,* ed. Hans-Lukas Kieser, pp. 182–86.

48. Michael M. Gunter, *The Kurds in Turkey: A Political Dilemma,* p. 114.

49. Dyer, "Letter to the Editor," p. 382.

50. Dadrian, "The Convergent Roles of the State and Governmental Party," p. 100.

51. Suny, "Empire and Nation," p. 17, and "Reply to My Critics," p. 134.

52. Vahakn N. Dadrian, *German Responsibility in the Armenian Genocide: A Review of the Historical Evidence of German Complicity,* p. 118, and "The Naim-Andonian Documents on the World War I Destruction of Ottoman Armenians: The Anatomy of a Genocide," *International Journal of Middle East Studies* 18 (1986): 338. In his 1986 article Dadrian applies this conceptual framework to the authentication of documents that speak of a planned extermination, but in the 1996 book he uses the same approach to ascertain intent.

53. NA, RG 59, 867.00/720 (M 353, roll 6, fr. 70).

54. Morgenthau, *Ambassador Morgenthau's Story,* p. 186.

55. Morgenthau diary, LC, reel 5.

56. Theodor Wiegand, *Halbmond im letzten Viertel: Briefe und Reiseberichte aus der alten Türkei von Theodor und Marie Wiegand 1895 bis 1918,* pp. 193, 250.

57. Joseph Pomiankowski, *Der Zusammenbruch des Ottomanischen Reiches: Erinnerungen an die Türkei aus der Zeit des Weltkrieges,* p. 180.

58. Great Britain, Parliament, *The Treatment of Armenians in the Ottoman Empire: Documents Presented to Viscount Grey of Fallodon, Secretary of State for Foreign Affairs,* p. 667.

59. Ephraim K. Jernazian, *Judgment unto Truth: Witnessing the Armenian Genocide,* trans. Alice Haig, p. 99.

60. Carl Mühlmann, *Das Deutsch-Türkische Waffenbündnis im Weltkriege,* p. 132.

61. Ahmed Emin Yalman, *Turkey in My Time,* p. 251.

62. Erik Jan Zürcher, "Between Death and Desertion: The Experience of the Ottoman Soldier in World War I," *Turcica* 28 (1996): 250–52, 248–49.

63. Wiegand, *Halbmond im letzten Viertel,* p. 229.

64. Count Johann von Bernstorff, *Memoirs of Count Bernstorff,* trans. Eric Sutton, p. 201.

65. Otto Liman von Sanders, *Five Years in Turkey,* trans. Carl Reichmann, p. 243.

66. Report of A. Bernau in Ara Sarafian, comp., *United States Official Documents on the Armenian Genocide,* vol. 1, pp. 132, 134.

67. Hans Werner Neulen, *Adler und Halbmond: Das deutsch-türkische Bündnis 1914–1918,* pp. 55–56.

68. PA, T. 183/46, A8613 (fiche 7163).

69. Türkkaya Ataöv, *Deaths Caused by Disease in Relation to the Armenian Question,* p. 4.

70. Malcolm E. Yapp, *The Making of the Modern Near East, 1792–1923,* p. 269.

71. Clarence D. Ussher and Grace H. Knapp, *An American Physician in Turkey: A Narrative of Adventures in Peace and War,* p. 220.

72. Maria Jacobsen, *Diaries of a Danish Missionary: Harpoot, 1907–1919,* trans. Kristen Vind, p. 61.

73. Henry H. Riggs, *Days of Tragedy in Armenia: Personal Experiences in Harpoot, 1915–1917,* pp. 40–41. (This is the first printing of an account written in 1918.)

74. Ibid., p. 43.

75. James Kay Sutherland, *The Adventures of an Armenian Boy,* pp. 133–34.

76. Report of Leslie A. Davis, February 9, 1918, reprinted in Sarafian, *United States Official Documents on the Armenian Genocide,* vol. 3, pp. 98–99. For very similar descriptions, see Jacobsen, *Diaries of a Danish Missionary,* pp. 48, 52, 59, 161.

77. Ussher and Knapp, *An American Physician in Turkey,* p. 227.

78. Jacobsen, *Diaries of a Danish Missionary,* p. 172.

79. Hedwig von Mohl, "Erinnerungen an ein türkisches Lazarett im Weltkrieg," *Der Neue Orient* 8 (1920): 44.

80. Werner Steuber, *Arzt und Soldat in drei Erdteilen,* p. 281.

81. Quoted in Liman von Sanders, *Five Years in Turkey,* p. 49.

82. Victor Schilling, "Kriegshygienische Erfahrungen in der Türkei," in *Zwischen Kaukasus und Sinai: Jahrbuch des Bundes der Asienkämpfer,* vol. 2, p. 76.

83. Report of Davis to the State Department, February 9, 1918, in Sarafian, *United States Official Documents on the Armenian Genocide,* vol. 3, p. 50.

84. Jacobsen, *Diaries of a Danish Missionary,* p. 150.

85. Jakob Künzler, *Im Lande des Blutes und der Tränen: Erlebnisse in Mesopotamien während des Weltkrieges,* p. 64.

86. Helmut Becker, *Äskulap zwischen Reichsadler und Halbmond: Sanitätswesen und Seuchenbekämpfung im türkischen Reich während des ersten Weltkriegs,* p. 427.

87. Lewis Einstein, *Inside Constantinople: A Diplomatist's Diary during the Dardanelles Expedition, April–September, 1915,* p. 164.

88. Ellen Marie Lust-Okar, "Failure of Collaboration: Armenian Refugees in Syria," *Middle Eastern Studies* 32, no. 1 (January 1996): 57.

89. Edward J. Erickson, *Ordered to Die: A History of the Ottoman Army in the First World War,* pp. 211, 241.

90. Zürcher, "Between Death and Desertion," p. 245.

91. Sarkis Karayan, "An Inquiry into the Number and Causes of Turkish Human Losses during the First World War," *Armenian Review* 35 (1982): 286; Ahmed Emin Yalman, *Turkey in the World War,* pp. 252–53; Neulen, *Adler und Halbmond,* pp. 123–24.

92. Arnold T. Wilson, *Loyalties Mesopotamia, 1914–1917: A Personal and Historical Record,* p. 99; Erickson, *Ordered to Die,* p. 151.

93. Quoted in Edward Herbert Keeling, *Adventures in Turkey and Russia,* p. 42.

94. Becker, *Äskulap zwischen Reichsadler und Halbmond,* p. 297.

95. E. W. C. Sandes, *In Kut and Captivity with the 6th Indian Division,* p. 319.

Chapter 6. THE ARMENIAN CASE(2): THE IMPLEMENTATION OF GENOCIDE

1. Sinasi Orel and Süreyya Yuca, *The Talât Pasha 'Telegrams': Historical Fact or Armenian Fiction?* pp. 2–4.

2. Aram Andonian, comp., *The Memoirs of Naim Bey: Turkish Official Documents Relating to the Deportations and Massacres of Armenians,* pp. 51, 64, 50.

3. Ibid., pp. 62–63, 60, 62.

4. FO 371/1773/58131.

5. Report of December 1914, PA, Botsch. K./168 (Fiche 7243).

6. Louise Jenison Peet, *No Less Honor: The Biography of William Wheelock Peet,* p. 170. (This book, based on Peet's diaries and journals, is written in the form of an autobiography.)

7. Bernstorff, *Memoirs of Count Bernstorff,* p. 175.

8. Stephan H. Astourian, "The Armenian Genocide: An Interpretation," *History Teacher* 23 (1990): 116. See also Zaven M. Messerlian, *The Premeditated Nature of the Genocide Perpetrated on the Armenians,* pp. 43–45.

9. Lang, *The Armenians,* p. 27; Melson, *Revolution and Genocide,* p. 312 (n. 22).

10. Yves Ternon, "La qualité de la preuve: A propos des documents Andonian et de la petite phrase d'Hitler," in *L'actualité du génocide des Arméniens,* ed. Comité de Défense de la Cause Arménienne, p. 138. See also his *Enquête sur la négation d'un génocide.*

11. Gerard Chaliand and Yves Ternon, *The Armenians: From Genocide to Resistance,* trans. Tony Berrett, p. 93; Mary Mangigian Tarzian, *The Armenian Minority Problem 1914–1934: A Nation's Struggle for Security,* p. 65; Jean-Marie Carzou, *Un génocide exemplaire: Arménie 1915,* p. 248.

12. Tessa Hofmann, ed., *Der Völkermord an den Armeniern vor Gericht: Der Prozess Talaat Pasha,* p. 69. In his summation the prosecutor returned to the question of Talaat's guilt. Revolutionary upheavals, he pointed out, frequently bring forth forged documents. It therefore could not be concluded that the guilt of Talaat had been proven (p. 86).

13. Rössler's letter is reproduced in a book on the Tehlirian trial published by a Dashnak organization in Paris, Comité de Défense de la Cause Arménienne, entitled *Justicier du génocide arménien: Le procès de Tehlirian,* pp. 226–29. I have used the translation provided by Orel and Yuca, *The Talât Pasha 'Telegrams,'* p. 16.

14. This letter, addressed to an Armenian woman living in Switzerland, Dr. Mary Terzian, is reproduced in Comité de Défense de la Cause Arménienne, *Justicier du génocide arménien,* pp. 230–37. The discussion of the documents sent to Constantinople is on pp. 230–31.

15. Vahakn N. Dadrian, "The Naim-Andonian Documents on the World War I Destruction of the Ottoman Armenians: The Anatomy of a Genocide," *International Journal of Middle East Studies* 18 (1986): 317 (note e); Vatche Ghazarian, ed. and trans. *Boghos Nubar's Papers and the Armenian Question 1915–1918: Documents,* p. xvii.

16. Orel and Yuca, *The Talât Pasha 'Telegrams,'* p. 23.

17. Ibid., pp. 143–44, 39.

18. Ibid., pp. 25–26.

19. Aram Andonian, *Documents officiels concernant les massacres arméniens* (Paris, 1920), p. 14, quoted in Orel and Yuca, *The Talât Pasha 'Telegrams,'* p. 8.

20. Andonian quoted in ibid., p. 9.

21. Ibid.

22. Ibid., p. 5.

23. Andonian, *Documents officiels concernant les massacres arméniens,* p. 225, quoted in ibid., p. 7.

24. FO 371/6500/E3557, pp. 2, 6–8.

25. Andonian, *Documents officiels concernant les massacres arméniens,* p. 232, quoted in Orel and Yuca, *The Talât Pasha 'Telegrams,'* pp. 16–17.

26. Ibid., p. 39.

27. Dadrian, "The Naim-Andonian Documents," pp. 318–19, 340.

28. Ibid., pp. 323, 325, 340.

29. Michael M. Gunter, "Why Do the Turks Deny They Committed Genocide against the Armenians?" *Orient* (Leverkusen, Germany) 30 (1989): 492.

30. Walker, "World War I and the Armenian Genocide," p. 247.

31. Hilmar Kaiser, "The Baghdad Railway and the Armenian Genocide, 1915–1916: A Case Study of German Resistance and Complicity," in *Remembrance and Denial,* ed. Hovannisian, p. 108 (n. 78).

32. Wolfdieter Bihl, preface to Artem Ohandjanian, *Armenien: Der verschwiegene Völkermord,* p. 8.

33. Dadrian, *History of the Armenian Genocide* and *Warrant for Genocide.*

34. Michael M. Gunter, review article, *International Journal of Middle East Studies* 21 (1989): 422.

35. Zürcher, *Turkey: A Modern History,* p. 121.

36. Andrew Mango, "Turks and Kurds," *Middle Eastern Studies* 30 (1994): 985.

37. Vartkes Yeghiayan, *The Armenian Genocide and the Trials of the Young Turks,* p. i.

38. Examples are given in John S. Kirakossian, *The Armenian Genocide: The Young Turks before the Judgment of History,* trans. Shoshan Altunian, pp. 161–62.

39. FO 371/3411/210534, p. 334.

40. Akcam, *Armenien und der Völkermord,* pp. 88–92; Annette Höss, "The Trial of Perpetrators by the Turkish Military Tribunals: The Case of Yozgat," in *The Armenian Genocide,* ed. Hovannisian, pp. 210–11.

41. The full text of the declaration can be found in U.S. Department of State, *Papers Relating to the Foreign Relations of the United States, 1915: Supplement,* p. 981.

42. Akcam, *Armenien und der Völkermord,* p. 93.

43. Vahakn N. Dadrian, "The Documentation of the World War I Armenian Massacres in the Proceedings of the Turkish Military Tribunal," *International Journal of Middle East Studies* 23 (1991): 554.

44. Vahakn N. Dadrian, "The Turkish Military Tribunal's Prosecution of the Authors of the Armenian Genocide: Four Major Court-Martial Series," *Holocaust and Genocide Studies* 11 (1997): 31.

45. Cf. James B. Gidney, *A Mandate for Armenia,* p. 62.

46. NA, RG 59, 867.00/834 (M 353, roll 7, fr. 244).

47. National Congress of Turkey, *The Turco-Armenian Question: The Turkish Point of View,* pp. 79, 83. See also Kara Schemsi [pseudonym for Rechid Safet Bey], *Turcs et arméniens devant l'histoire: Nouveaux témoignages russes et turcs sur les atrocités arméniens de 1914 à 1918.*

48. FRUSA, "FRUSA's Documentation of the Appearance of the Ottoman Turkish Delegation before the Council of Four, Paris, June 17, 1919," *Armenian Review* 35 (1982): 72.

49. For a list of the trials, see Akcam, *Armenien und der Völkermord,* pp. 162–65.

50. FO 371/4172/31827, 32889, 35094; FO 371/4173/47293.

51. Quoted in Dadrian, *Warrant for Genocide,* p. 125.

52. Dadrian, "The Turkish Military Tribunal's Prosecution of the Authors of the Armenian Genocide," p. 45.

53. Quoted in Akcam, *Armenien und der Völkermord,* p. 204. The entire indictment of April 12, 1919, is reproduced there on pp. 192–207.

54. Quoted in Dadrian, "The Documentation of the World War I Armenian Massacres," p. 558.

55. The verdict is reproduced in Akcam, *Armenien und der Völkermord,* pp. 353–64.

56. Verdict of January 8, 1920, p. 4, quoted in Taner Akcam, ed., "The Proceedings of the Turkish Military Tribunal as published in *Takvim-i Vekayi,* 1919–1920," part 2. This mimeographed edition of the trial proceedings represents a German translation used by Akcam and deposited by him at the Armenian Research Center of the University of Michigan–Dearborn. Another selection from the transcripts of the trials is provided by Yeghiayan, *The Armenian Genocide and the Trials of the Young Turks.* However, this work represents a translation from the Turkish into Armenian and then into English. Moreover, the book is marred by omissions and sloppy dating.

57. Vahakn N. Dadrian, "The Role of the Special Organisation in the Armenian Genocide during the First World War," in *Minorities in Wartime: National and Racial Groupings in Europe, North America and Australia during the Two World Wars,* ed. Panikos Panayi, p. 74.

58. Calthorpe to Foreign Office, April 17, 1919, FO 371/4173/61185, p. 279.

59. NA, RG 59, 867.00/868 (M 353, roll 7, fr. 448).

60. Andonian, *Memoirs of Naim Bey,* p. 69.

61. James F. Willis, *Prologue to Nuremberg: The Politics and Diplomacy of Punishing War Criminals of the First World War,* p. 155.

62. The Greek atrocities were confirmed by an Allied commission of inquiry that rendered its report on October 14, 1919. See Laurence Evans, *United States Policy and the Partition of Turkey, 1914–1924,* p. 181; and the earlier work of Arnold J. Toynbee, *The Western Question in Greece and Turkey: A Study in the Contact of Civilizations,* p. 169. According to the American consul in Smyrna, George Horton, the Greek governor-general did impose severe punishment on those responsible for atrocities. See his *The Blight of Asia,* p. 76.

63. For a more detailed discussion of this chain of events, see Akcam, *Armenien und der Völkermord,* pp. 114–19.

64. Dadrian, "The Turkish Military Tribunal's Prosecution of the Authors of the Armenian Genocide," pp. 30–31, 50, 53.

65. Richard G. Hovannisian, "Denial of the Armenian Genocide in Comparison with Holocaust Denial," in *Remembrance and Denial,* p. 220.

66. Melson, *Revolution and Genocide,* p. 152.

67. Dadrian, "The Secret Young-Turk Ittihadist Conference," p. 191. The German memo is referred to in a revised version of this article published in the *Journal of Political and Military Sociology* 22 (1994): 188.

68. Artem Ohandjanian, comp., *Österreich-Armenien, 1872–1936: Faksimilesammlung diplomatischer Aktenstücke*, vol. 7, pp. 5011–12.

69. Stephen H. Longrigg, *Syria and Lebanon under French Mandate*, p. 51.

70. FO 371/474/118392, p. 267.

71. John M. Lindley, *"A Soldier Is Also a Citizen": The Controversy over Military Justice, 1917–1920*, p. 10.

72. U.S. Air Force ROTC, *Military Law*, pp. 4, 113.

73. "Rules for Military Tribunals," *New York Times*, March 21, 2002.

74. Yilmaz Altug, trans., *The Turkish Code of Criminal Procedure*, art. 232; Baki Kuru, "Law of Procedure," in *Introduction to Turkish Law*, ed. T. Ugrul Ansay and Don Wallace, pp. 177, 204. See also George Young, *Corps de droit ottoman*, vol. 7, pp. 226–300.

75. Vahakn N. Dadrian, "Genocide as a Problem of National and International Law: The World War I Armenian Case and Its Contemporary Legal Ramifications," *Yale Journal of International Law* 14 (1989): 297 (n. 286).

76. Akcam, "The Proceedings of the Turkish Military Tribunal," part 1, third session, pp. 24, 27.

77. NA, RG 59, 867.00/81 (M 820, roll 536, fr. 440).

78. Hikmet Sener, "A Comparison of the Turkish and American Military Systems of Nonjudicial Punishment," *Military Law Review* 27 (1965): 113.

79. Vahakn N. Dadrian, *The Key Elements in the Turkish Denial of the Armenian Genocide: A Case Study of Distortion and Falsification*, p. 27.

80. Quoted in Dadrian, "The Armenian Genocide and the Pitfalls of a 'Balanced' Analysis," p. 89. A somewhat different translation is given by Akcam, *Armenien und der Völkermord*, p. 204.

81. For the text of the indictment, see Akcam, *Armenien und der Völkermord*, pp. 192–207; the verdict of the Harput trial is reproduced in Haigazn K. Kazarian, "The Genocide of Kharpert's Armenians: A Turkish Judicial Document and Cipher Telegrams Pertaining to Kharpert," *Armenian Review* 19 (Spring 1966): 18–19.

82. Clarence R. Johnson, ed., *Constantinople Today, or the Pathfinder Survey of Constantinople: Study in Oriental Social Life*, p. 116; Nur Bilge Criss, *Istanbul under Allied Occupation, 1918–1923*, pp. 48–49.

83. Quoted in Dadrian, "A Textual Analysis of the Key Indictment of the Turkish Military Tribunal," p. 138.

84. Quoted in Akcam, *Armenien und der Völkermord*, p. 197.

85. See, for example, Gürün, *The Armenian File*, p. 232.

86. FO 371/4174/118377.

87. De Robeck to London, September 21, 1919, FO 371/4174/136069.

88. Dadrian, *Key Elements in the Turkish Denial of the Armenian Genocide,* p. 27.

89. Dadrian, *History of the Armenian Genocide,* pp. 236–37.

90. Ibid., p. 237. See also Dadrian, "The Role of the Special Organization," p. 51.

91. Philip H. Stoddard, "The Ottoman Government and the Arabs, 1911 to 1918: A Preliminary Study of the Teskilat-i Mahsusa," pp. 52–58, 1–2. Stoddard confirmed these points in an interview with me on March 12, 2001.

92. Jacob M. Landau, *Pan-Turkism in Turkey: From Irredentism to Cooperation,* p. 52.

93. Dogu Ergil, "A Reassessment: The Young Turks, Their Politics and Anti-Colonial Struggle," *Balkan Studies* 16, no. 2 (1975): 70–71 (n. 4).

94. Donald M. McKale, *War by Revolution: Germany and Great Britain in the Middle East in the Era of World War I,* p. 50.

95. Erik Jan Zürcher, *The Unionist Factor: The Role of the Committee of Union and Progress in the Turkish National Movement 1905–1926,* pp. 59, 84.

96. Quoted in Akcam, *Armenien und der Völkermord,* pp. 192–200.

97. Dadrian, "The Role of the Special Organization," p. 56.

98. It is worth noting that the use of convicts for military duty in wartime is not at all unprecedented, and that includes British and American practice. English literature of the eighteenth century is replete with stories about the use of men released from the nearest jail in order to fill up the ranks of sailors on British warships. It is estimated that during World War I 7,900 men convicted of serious offenses were released by U.S. courts on condition of being inducted into military service (U.S. Provost Marshal General, *Second Report of the Provost Marshal to the Secretary of War on the Operations of the Selective Service System to December 20, 1918,* p. 149). In World War II persons convicted of murder, rape, and other serious crimes were exempted from a similar release program, though there is anecdotal evidence that federal and military prisons did not always adhere to these rules.

99. Stange to the German military mission, Constantinople, August 23, 1915, PA, Botsch. K./170 (fiche 7254). This document can also be read in Johannes Lepsius, ed., *Deutschland und Armenien, 1914–1918: Sammlung diplomatischer Aktenstücke,* pp. 138–42. A reprint of this collection was published by Donat und Temmen (Bremen) in 1986.

100. Dadrian, "The Role of the Special Organization," p. 58.

101. Vahakn N. Dadrian, "The Role of Turkish Physicians in the World War I Genocide of Ottoman Armenians," *Holocaust and Genocide Studies* 1 (1986): 173.

102. Dadrian, *History of the Armenian Genocide,* p. 244 (n. 8).

103. Dadrian, "The Role of the Special Organization," p. 58.

104. Vahakn N. Dadrian, "Documentation of the Armenian Genocide in German and Austrian Sources," in *The Widening Circle of Genocide: A Critical Bibliographical Review,* ed. Israel W. Charny, vol. 3, p. 110.

105. Walter Nicolai, *The German Secret Service,* p. 138. See also Neulen, *Adler und Halbmond,* especially chapter 16: "German-Turkish Discords"; and Ulrich Trumpener, "Suez, Baku, Gallipoli: The Military Dimensions of the German-Ottoman Coalition, 1914–18," in *Coalition Warfare: An Uneasy Accord,* ed. Keith Neilson and Roy A. Prete, p. 40.

106. Report of the German intelligence agent Louis Mosel of March 3, 1915, PA, Wk. no. 11d, vol. 4 (R 21011), pp. 6–7; Wolfdieter Bihl, *Die Kaukasus Politik der Mittelmächte,* p. 67.

107. PA, Wk. no. 11d, vol. 9 (R 21016), p. 31; Felix Guse, *Die Kaukasusfront im Weltkrieg: Bis zum Frieden von Brest,* p. 38; Erikson, *Ordered to Die,* pp. 54–55. On the role of the Georgian volunteers, see William Edmond D. Allen and Paul Muratoff, *Caucasian Battlefields: A History of the Wars on the Turco-Caucasian Border, 1828–1921,* pp. 274–75; and Garegin Pasdermadjian [aka Armen Garo], *Armenia: A Leading Factor in the Winning of the War,* trans. A. Torossian, p. 4.

108. Paul Leverkuehn, *Posten auf ewiger Wache: Aus dem abenteuerlichen Leben des Max von Scheubner-Richter,* p. 33.

109. Philip H. Stoddard, prologue to Esref Kuscubasi, *The Turkish Battle at Khaybar,* trans. and ed. Philip H. Stoddard and H. Basri Danisman, pp. 21–32.

110. Vahakn N. Dadrian, "Ottoman Archives and Denial of the Armenian Genocide," in *The Armenian Genocide,* ed. Hovannisian, pp. 300–301.

111. Cemal Kutay, *Birinci Dünya Harbinde Teskilat-I Mahsusa ve Hayber'de Türk Cengi.*

112. At my request, two Turkish-speaking persons compared Dadrian's quotation with Kutay's original text, and they confirmed the deceptive juxtapositions of Esref's words.

113. Vahakn N. Dadrian, "The Complicity of the Party, the Government, and the Military: Select Parliamentary and Judicial Documents (Recently Uncovered and Obtained)," *Journal of Political and Military Sociology* 22 (1994): 60–61.

114. Ibid., pp. 59, 61, 33.

115. Akcam, "The Proceedings of the Turkish Military Tribunal," part 1, especially 5th and 6th session of the main trial.

116. Ibid., 5th session, pp. 58–59. Riza Bey characterized this scenario as a "conjecture" during the 7th session, p. 26.

117. Yalman, *Turkey in the World War,* p. 220.

118. Haigazn K. Kazarian, "Turkey Tries Its Chief Criminals: Indictment and Sentence Passed Down by Military Court of 1919," *Armenian Review* 24 (Winter 1971): 7–19, and "A Catalogue of Those Principally Responsible for the 1915–18 Massacres," p. 254.

119. Walker, "Letter to the Editor," *Middle Eastern Studies* 9 (1973): 376.

120. Dyer, "Letter to the Editor," *Middle Eastern Studies* 9 (1973): 379.

121. Richard G. Hovannisian, "The Question of Altruism during the Armenian Genocide of 1915," in *Embracing the Other: Philosophical, Psychological, and Historical Perspectives on Altruism,* ed. Pearl M. Oliner et al., p. 283.

122. Zürcher, *Turkey: A Modern History*, p. 121.

123. Akcam, *Armenien und der Völkermord*, p. 65.

124. Donald Bloxham, "Power Politics, Prejudice, Protest and Propaganda: A Reassessment of the German Role in the Armenian Genocide of World War I," in *Der Völkermord an den Armeniern*, ed. Hans-Lukas Kieser and Dominik J. Schaller, p. 220.

125. Edward J. Erickson, "The Turkish Official Military Histories of the First World War: A Bibliographical Essay," *Middle Eastern Studies* 39 (2003): 198 (n. 7).

126. Dadrian, *History of the Armenian Genocide*, pp. 384–85.

127. Dadrian, "The Complicity of the Party, the Government, and the Military," p. 85.

128. Quoted from the official transcript of the Ottoman Senate in ibid., p. 85.

129. Ibid.

Chapter 7. THE TURKISH POSITION

1. Cf. Gwynne Dyer, "Turkish 'Falsifiers' and Armenian 'Deceivers': Historiography and the Armenian Massacres," *Middle Eastern Studies* 12 (1976): 100–101; Fatma Müge Göcek, "Reconstructing the Turkish Historiography on the Armenian Massacres and Deaths of 1915," in *Looking Backward, Moving Forward: Confronting the Armenian Genocide*, ed. by Richard G. Hovannisian.

2. For a concise statement of the official Turkish position, see Center for Strategic Research, *Armenian Claims and Historical Facts*. The most recent formulations can be found in Salahi R. Sonyel, *The Great War and the Tragedy of Anatolia: Turks and Armenians in the Maelstrom of Major Powers;* and Yusuf Halacoglu, *Facts on the Relocation of Armenians (1914–1918)*. Another detailed defense, sponsored by the Assembly of Turkish American Associations, is McCarthy and McCarthy, *Turks and Armenians*.

3. The statement issued by the Armenian patriarch on November 10, 1914, is reprinted in Raymond H. Kévorkian, ed., "R. P. Yervant P'Erdahdjian: Evénements et faits observés à Constantinople par le vicariat [patriarcal] (1914–16)," *Revue d'Histoire Arménienne Contemporaine* 1 (1995): 250–51.

4. Hovannisian, *Armenia on the Road to Independence*, p. 42.

5. Dadrian, "The Secret Young-Turk Ittihadist Conference," p. 188.

6. Quoted in A. P. Hacobian, *Armenia and the War: An Armenian's Point of View with an Appeal to Britain and the Coming Peace Conference*, p. 83.

7. The text of this order is reproduced in Turkey, Prime Ministry, *Documents on Ottoman Armenians*, vol. 1, p. 2.

8. For examples of such reports, see ibid., vol. 2; and Orel and Yuca, *The Talât Pasha 'Telegrams,'* pp. 105–12.

9. The text of Directive 8682 is reprinted in Gürün, *The Armenian File*, pp. 205–6.

10. Quoted from the Ministry of Interior files in Orel and Yuca, *The Talât Pasha 'Telegrams,'* p. 108.

11. Turkey, Prime Ministry, *Documents on Ottoman Armenians,* vol. 2, p. 80.

12. Morgenthau to Washington, May 25, 1915, NA, RG 59, 867.4016/71 (M353, roll 43).

13. Justin McCarthy, *The Ottoman Turks: An Introductory History to 1923,* p. 364.

14. Yusuf Hikmet Bayur, *Türk Inkilabi Tarihi* (History of the Turkish Revolution), p. 4.

15. Deringil, "In Search of a Way Forward," p. 66.

16. Uras, *The Armenians in History,* p. 687. I have cited art. 6 in the paraphrase of Nalbandian, *Armenian Revolutionary Movement,* p. 111.

17. National Congress of Turkey, *The Turco-Armenian Question,* pp. 151–52, 79.

18. Dasnabedian, *History of the Armenian Revolutionary Federation,* p.113.

19. Chalabian, *Revolutionary Figures,* pp. 290–91.

20. Ohandjanian, *Österreich-Armenien,* vol. 6, p. 4563.

21. Scheubner-Richter to Berlin, August 10, 1915, PA, T. 183/39/A28584, p. 10 (fiche 7129).

22. André N. Mandelstam, *Das armenische Problem im Lichte des Völker- und Menschenrechts,* p. 36.

23. Kuckhoff to embassy, July 4, 1915, PA, T. 183/37/A2201 (fiche 7123).

24. Felix Guse, "Der Armenieraufstand 1915 und seine Folgen," *Wissen und Wehr* 6 (1925): 614.

25. Dadrian, "The Secret Young-Turk Ittihadist Conference," p. 189.

26. Dadrian, *German Responsibility in the Armenian Genocide,* p. 36.

27. Dadrian, *Key Elements in the Turkish Denial of the Armenian Genocide,* p. 12, and "The Armenian Question and the Wartime Fate of the Armenians as Documented by the Officials of the Ottoman Empire's World War I Allies: Germany and Austria-Hungary," *International Journal of Middle East Studies* 34 (2002): 67.

28. Erickson, *Ordered to Die,* p. 99.

29. Dyer, "Turkish 'Falsifiers' and Armenian 'Deceivers,'" p. 99.

30. FO 371/1773/34585.

31. Minassian, "Les relations entre le Comité Union et Progrès et la Fédération Révolutionnaire Arménienne," p. 96.

32. Käthe Ehrhold, *Flucht in die Heimat: Aus dem Kriegserlebnis deutscher Missionsschwestern in der asiatischen Türkei,* p. 9. See also the reports of such events cited by Johannes Lepsius, *Der Todesgang des armenischen Volkes: Bericht über das Schicksal des armenischen Volkes in der Türkei während des Weltkrieges,* p. 185; and by the French war correspondent Henry Barby in his *Au pays de l'épouvante: L'Arménie martyre,* pp. 229–32.

33. Turkey, Prime Ministry, *Documents on Ottoman Armenians,* vol. 1, p. 23.

34. McCarthy and McCarthy, *Turks and Armenians,* p. 49.

35. Onnig Mukhitarian, *An Account of the Glorious Struggle of Van-Vasbouragan,* trans. Samuels S. Tarpinian, pp. 3–4.

36. Rafael de Nogales, *Four Years beneath the Crescent,* trans. Muna Lee, p. 70.

37. Hovannisian, *Armenia on the Road to Independence,* p. 56.

38. Haig Gossoian, *The Epic Story of the Self-Defense of Armenians in the Historic City of Van,* trans. Samuels S. Tarpinian, p. 58.

39. Mukhitarian, *An Account of the Glorious Struggle of Van,* pp. 116–17. See also Aprahamian, *From Van to Detroit,* p. 61.

40. Ussher and Knapp, *An American Physician in Turkey,* p. 285.

41. John Otis Barrows, *In the Land of Ararat: A Sketch of the Life of Mrs. Elizabeth Freeman Barrows Ussher,* p. 145.

42. Ehrhold, *Flucht in die Heimat,* p. 15.

43. *Aspirations et agissements révolutionnaires des comités arméniens avant et après la proclamation de la Constitution Ottomane,* p. 394.

44. Ussher and Knapp, *An American Physician in Turkey,* p. 284.

45. Narrative of Y. K. Rushdouni in Great Britain, Parliament, *The Treatment of Armenians in the Ottoman Empire,* p. 70.

46. Unpublished memoirs of Johannes Spörri, quoted in Hans-Lukas Kieser, *Der verpasste Friede: Mission, Ethnie und Staat in den Ostprovinzen der Türkei, 1839– 1938,* p. 451 (n. 633).

47. Morgenthau, *Ambassador Morgenthau's Story,* p. 238.

48. McCarthy and McCarthy, *Turks and Armenians,* p. 49.

49. Assembly of Turkish American Associations, *Armenian Atrocities and Terrorism: Testimonies of Witnesses,* pp. 28, 41–42.

50. Sonyel, *The Ottoman Armenians,* p. 302.

51. See, for example, Garegin Pasdermadjian (aka Armen Garo), *Why Armenia Should Be Free: Armenia's Role in the Present War,* trans. A. Torossian, p. 23.

52. Dadrian, "The Armenian Question and the Wartime Fate of the Armenians," p. 69.

53. Morgenthau, *Ambassador Morgenthau's Story,* p. 199.

54. Allen and Muratoff, *Caucasian Battlefields,* p. 302 (n. 1).

55. Scheubner-Richter to Wangenheim, May 15, 1915, PA, Botsch. K./168 (fiche 7246); Scheubner-Richter to embassy, November 6, 1915, PA, Botsch. K./171 (fiche 7256).

56. Guse, "Der Armenieraufstand 1915," p. 614.

57. Dadrian, *Warrant for Genocide,* p. 116. The same position is defended by Anahide Ter Minassian, "Van 1915," *Guerres Mondiales et Conflits Contemporains* 39, no. 153 (January 1989). An English version can be found in Richard G. Hovannisian, ed., *Armenian Van/Vaspurakan,* pp. 209–44.

58. Ussher and Knapp, *An American Physician in Turkey,* p. 237, call it a murder on orders of the governor. Scheubner-Richter is not sure that the government

was implicated in this crime. Cf. Scheubner-Richter to Wangenheim, May 15, 1915, PA, Botsch. K./168 (fiche 7246).

59. Barrows, *In the Land of Ararat,* p. 128.

60. Grace Higley Knapp, *The Mission at Van: In Turkey in War Time,* p. 15.

61. M. N. Pokrowski, ed., *Die Internationalen Beziehungen im Zeitalter des Imperialismus: Dokumente aus den Archiven der Zarischen und der Provisorischen Regierung,* trans. Erich Boehme, vol. 7, part 2, p. 750.

62. C. F. Dixon-Johnson, *The Armenians,* p. 46.

63. Dyer, "Letter to the Editor," *Middle Eastern Studies* 9 (1973): 382.

64. Pasdermadjian, *Why Armenia Should Be Free,* p. 17.

65. Hovannisian, *Armenia on the Road to Independence,* p. 42.

66. Turkey, Prime Ministry, *Documents on Ottoman Armenians,* vol. 2, p. 44.

67. Ibid., p. 44.

68. Kapriel Serope Papazian, *Patriotism Perverted: A Discussion of the Deeds and Misdeeds of the Armenian Revolutionary Federation, the So-Called Dashnagtzoutune,* p. 39.

69. Yalman, *Turkey in the World War,* p. 218. See also Sonyel, *Ottoman Armenians,* p. 299.

70. Kévorkian, "R. P. Yervant P'Erdahdjian," p. 286.

71. Morgenthau to Secretary of State, November 18, 1915, NA, RG 59, 867.00/798 (M 353, roll 6).

72. Hovannisian, *Armenia on the Road to Independence,* pp. 44–45.

73. Lindy V. Avakian, *The Cross and the Crescent,* p. 34.

74. Antranig Chalabian, *General Andranik and the Armenian Revolutionary Movement,* p. 218.

75. Uras, *The Armenians in History,* p. 863.

76. Turkey, Prime Ministry, *Documents on Ottoman Armenians,* vol. 2, p. 80; Halacoglu, *Facts on the Relocation of Armenians,* p. 105.

77. Aprahamian, *From Van to Detroit,* p. 62.

78. Dadrian, "The Role of the Special Organization," p. 53.

79. Pasdermadjian, *Bank Ottoman,* p. 19.

80. Firuz Kazemzadeh, *The Struggle for Transcaucasia (1917–1921),* p. 26.

81. Liman von Sanders, *Five Years in Turkey,* p. 40.

82. The Turkish historian Salahi R. Sonyel asserts that according to Turkish documents "the blame for the great Turkish defeat by the Russians at Sarikamis, where 90,000 Turks perished, lies with the local Armenians who had acted as informers and saboteurs" (*Greco-Armenian Conspiracy against Turkey Revived,* p. 5). In his memoirs Pasdermadjian also stresses the important role of the Armenian volunteers in the Russian victory at Sarikamis. See his *Bank Ottoman,* p. 21.

83. Gabriel Korganoff, *La participation des Arméniens à la guerre mondiale sur la front du Caucasus (1914–1918),* p. 28; Hacobian, *Armenia and the War,* p. 86; Hovannisian, *Armenia on the Road to Independence,* p. 44.

84. Sonyel, *The Ottoman Armenians,* p. 305.

85. Atamian, *The Armenian Community,* pp. 100, 200.

86. Maurice Larcher, *La guerre turque dans la guerre mondiale,* p. 395.

87. Pasdermadjian, *Bank Ottoman,* pp. 27–28.

88. U.S. Department of State, *Papers Relating to the Foreign Relations of the United States, 1915: Supplement,* p. 982.

89. Arthur Beylerian, comp., *Les grandes puissances, l'Empire Ottoman, et les Arméniens dans les archives françaises (1914–1918),* p. 7.

90. Sir Edward Grey to the Army Council, March 1, 1915, FO 371/2484/22083.

91. Turkey, Prime Ministry, *Documents on Ottoman Armenians,* vol. 1, p. 53.

92. Levon Meguerditchian to Boghos Nubar, May 28, 1915, in Ghazarian, *Boghos Nubar's Papers,* p. 65.

93. George Abel Schreiner, *From Berlin to Baghdad: Behind the Scenes in the Near East,* p. 197.

94. Nerses S. Sarian, *I Shall Not Die: A Tribute to the Faithfulness of God,* p. 69.

95. Memo of February 3, 1915, in Ghazarian, *Boghos Nubar's Papers,* p. 5.

96. Büge to Wangenheim, March 13, 1915, in Wolfgang Gust, "Revidierte Ausgabe der von Johannes Lepsius 1919 unter dem Titel 'Deutschland und Armenien' herausgegebenen Sammlung diplomatischer Aktenstücke" (http://home.t-online.de/home/wolfgang.gust/ehome.htm), pp. 27–28.

97. Rössler to Berlin, May 10, 1915, PA, T. 183/37/A17735a (fiche 7120); report of Rev. William Chambers, December 1915, Great Britain, Parliament, *The Treatment of Armenians in the Ottoman Empire,* p. 502.

98. Sir H. Bax Ironside to the Foreign Office, March 4, 1915, FO 371/2484/25167; March 6, 1915, FO 371/2484/37609.

99. FO 371/2485/41444.

100. Ghazarian, *Boghos Nubar's Papers,* p. 203.

101. These arguments recur in numerous memos of the War Council and the Foreign Office. See, for example, FO 371/2484/28172; FO 371/2485/41444; CO 67/178/20859.

102. A. J. Barker, *The Neglected War: Mesopotamia 1914–1918,* p. 473.

103. FO 371/2488/172811.

104. Cf. Uras, *The Armenians in History,* p. 871; Djemal Pasha, *Memories of a Turkish Statesman,* p. 299.

105. See, for example, Boghos Nubar's memo of December 20, 1915, in Ghazarian, *Boghos Nubar's Papers,* pp. 302–3.

106. Ibid., p. 194.

107. Beylerian, *Les grandes puissances, l'Empire Ottoman, et les Arméniens,* pp. 170–71.

108. Boghos Nubar to the Armenian National Union of Egypt, October 6, 1916, in Ghazarian, *Boghos Nubar's Papers,* pp. 372–73.

109. Ibid., p. 417.

110. Mim Kemal Öke, "The Response of the Turkish Armenians to the 'Armenian Question,' 1919–1926," in *Armenians in the Ottoman Empire and Modern Turkey (1912–1926),* ed. Bogazici University, p. 81; Commander in Chief, Egyptian Expeditionary Force to British High Commissioner, April 15, 1919, FO 371/4165/79400. See also Toynbee, *The Western Question in Greece and Turkey,* p. 312; McCarthy, *Death and Exile,* pp. 204–5.

111. Ghazarian, *Boghos Nubar's Papers,* p. 332.

112. See Yigal Sheffey, *British Military Intelligence in the Palestine Campaign 1914–1918,* pp. 78–80; Lewen Weldon, *"Hard Lying": Eastern Mediterranean 1914–1919,* pp. 15, 20; Nicholas Z. Ajay, "Political Intrigue and Suppression in Lebanon during World War I," *International Journal of Middle East Studies* 5 (1974): 143.

113. Gidney, *A Mandate for Armenia,* pp. 74–75.

114. Quoted in Stephen Bonsal, *Suitors and Suppliants: The Little Nations at Versailles,* pp. 190–91.

115. Ertugrul Zekai Ökte, ed., *Ottoman Archives, Yildiz Collection: The Armenian Question, Talori Incidents,* p. 28.

116. Talaat Pasha, "Posthumous Memoirs of Talaat Pasha," *Current History* 15 (1921): 295. This article represents about fifty pages of the original manuscript and was made available for publication by Talaat's widow after his death at the hand of an Armenian assassin in Berlin. Some questions have been raised about the extent to which the full memoir published in 1946 was edited (see Dadrian, "The Armenian Genocide and the Pitfalls of a 'Balanced' Analysis," pp. 120–21). Suny accepts the authenticity of the excerpt published in 1921, and I concur in this assessment.

117. This document from the Turkish state archives is reproduced in an English translation in Dadrian, *Warrant for Genocide,* p. iv.

118. Morgenthau papers, reel 7, LC.

119. Director of service of installation and of the maintenance of emigrants in the name of the minister of the interior, August 28, 1915, FO 371/9158/E5523. A slightly different translation of this document is given in Salahi R. Sonyel, ed., *Displacement of the Armenians: Documents,* p. 11.

120. Quoted from the Ministry of Interior files in Orel and Yuca, *The Talât Pasha 'Telegrams,'* pp. 129–30.

121. Hohenlohe to Berlin, September 2, 1915, PA., Botsch. K./170 (fiche 7253).

122. Metternich to Berlin, December 18, 1915, ibid., T. 183/40/A 37207 (fiche 7136).

123. *Vérité sur le Mouvement Révolutionnaire Arménien et les mesures gouvernementales,* p. 14. I have used the English translation by Susan K. Blair, the editor of Leslie A. Davis, *The Slaughterhouse Province: An American Diplomat's Report on the Armenian Genocide, 1915–1917,* p. 194.

124. Beylerian, *Les grandes puissances, l'Empire Ottoman, et les Arméniens,* p. 206.

125. NA, 867.00/791 (M 353, roll 6, fr. 431).

126. Quoted in Gürün, *The Armenian File*, p. 214.

127. Ohandjanian, *Österreich-Armenien*, vol. 6, pp. 4722–23.

128. Büge to Hohenlohe, September 10, 1915, PA, Botsch. K./170 (fiche 7253).

129. Akcam, *Armenien und der Völkermord*, p. 6.

130. Hohenlohe to Berlin, September 25, 1915, PA, T. 183/39/A 28578 (fiche 7129).

131. PA, T. 183/36/A 11957 (fiche 7117).

132. Julius Loytved-Hardegg (Damascus) to embassy, November 17, 1915, PA, Botsch. K./171 (fiche 7256); Ahmed Djemal Pasha, "Zur Frage der Greuel in Armenien: Eine Rechtfertigungsschrift," *Frankfurter Zeitung*, September 3, 1919. (This article was also published in *Der Neue Orient* 6 [1919]: 120–22.) Dadrian ("The Role of the Special Organization," pp. 68–69) refers to the two officers as "Special Organization brigands." Other sources simply call them "brigands."

133. Rössler to Berlin, January 3, 1916, PA, T. 183/41/A2888 (fiche 7139).

134. Ohandjanian, *Österreich-Armenien*, vol. 7, p. 5020.

135. Dadrian, *Key Elements in the Turkish Denial of the Armenian Genocide*, p. 54 (n. 64).

136. Ibid.

137. *Vérité sur le Mouvement Révolutionnaire Arménien* (Blair translation), p. 194.

138. Gürün, *The Armenian File*, p. 213.

139. Yalman, *Turkey in the World War*, p. 221.

140. Dadrian, "The Armenian Genocide and the Pitfalls of a 'Balanced' Analysis," p. 123.

141. Sarafian, *United States Official Documents on the Armenian Genocide*, vol. 2, p. 102.

142. Talaat Pasha, "Posthumous Memoirs," p. 295.

143. The Austrian ambassador reported on November 13, 1915, that the *valis* of Brussa and Diarbekir had been dismissed because they had stolen the goods of deported Armenians. See Ohandjanian, *Österreich-Armenien*, vol. 6, p. 4870. The *vali* of Trebizond was dismissed on August 13, 1917, also apparently for profiting from the seizure of Armenian property. See FO 371/5089/E1347.

144. Assembly of Turkish American Associations, *Armenian Allegations: Myth and Reality, a Handbook of Facts and Documents*, p. xi.

145. Assembly of Turkish American Associations, *Armenian Atrocities and Terrorism*, p. 3.

146. Djemal Pasha, *Memories of a Turkish Statesman*, p. 281.

147. Mim Kemal Öke, *The Armenian Question 1914–1923*, p. 135.

148. Haig Shiroyan, *Smiling through the Tears*, p. 186.

149. Abraham H. Hartunian, *Neither to Laugh Nor to Weep: A Memoir of the Armenian Genocide*, trans. Vartan Hartunian, p. 58.

150. Stanley E. Kerr, *The Lions of Marash: Personal Experiences with American Near East Relief, 1919–1922,* p. 19.

151. Dyer, "Turkish 'Falsifiers' and Armenian 'Deceivers,'" p. 105.

152. Toynbee, *The Western Question in Greece and Turkey,* p. 354.

153. Assembly of Turkish American Associations, *Armenian Atrocities and Terrorism,* p. 51.

154. Turkey, Prime Ministry, *Documents on Ottoman Armenians,* vol. 1, p. 42.

155. Salahi R. Sonyel, "Turco-Armenian Relations and British Propaganda during the First World War," *Belleten* 58 (1994–95): 413.

156. Nogales, *Four Years beneath the Crescent,* p. 45.

157. Yalman, *Turkey in the World War,* p. 219.

158. Guse, "Der Armenieraufstand 1915," p. 613.

159. See, for example, National Congress of Turkey, *Documents relatifs aux atrocités commises par les Arméniens sur la population musulmane.* After the armistice the Turkish government exchanged military documents with the Russian government, and many of the Turkish charges of Armenian atrocities are based on these documents deposited in the Ministry of War.

160. Ohandjanian, *Österreich-Armenien,* vol. 6, p. 4675.

161. Main trial, 6th session, June 25, 1919, in Akcam, "The Proceedings of the Turkish Military Tribunal," part 2, p. 13.

162. Dadrian, "The Complicity of the Party, the Government, and the Military," p. 51.

163. NA, RG 59, 867.00/143 (M 820, roll 537, fr. 117).

164. Grace Higley Knapp, *The Tragedy of Bitlis,* p. 146.

165. Vatche Ghazarian, ed., *Village Remembered: The Armenians of Habousi,* pp. 111–12.

166. M. Philips Price, *War and Revolution in Asiatic Russia,* p. 141.

167. Stephen G. Svajian, *A Trip through Historic Armenia,* p. 523.

168. FO 371/4173/80976.

169. Larcher, *La guerre turque dans la guerre mondiale,* pp. 414–15.

170. Chalabian, *Revolutionary Figures,* p. 299.

171. Turkey, Prime Ministry, *Documents on Ottoman Armenians,* vol. 2, p. 137.

172. Commander of the Third Army, April 1, 1918, quoted in Orel and Yuca, *The Talât Pasha 'Telegrams,'* p. 138. Allegations of Armenian atrocities in Erzurum are also to be found in notes appended to a regimental history compiled by the Russian artillery officer Tverdokhlebov and published in 1919, probably in Constantinople, in Turkish, French, and English editions. A copy of the English translation is owned by the New York Public Library: *Notes of Superior Russian Officer on the Atrocities at Erzeroum: Drawn from the Memoirs of Lt.-Col. Tverdokhlebov.* The original Russian text is reproduced in Azmi Süslü, ed., *Russian View on the Atrocities Committed by the Armenians against the Turks,* pp. 105–56.

173. Yves Ternon, *The Armenian Cause,* trans. Anahid Apelian Mangouni, pp. 123–24.

174. The final report itself is lost and may have been suppressed because it ran counter to the then prevailing pro-Armenian sentiments in the United States. A copy of the draft report can be found in the National Archives (184.02102/5). The entire draft is reproduced in Justin McCarthy, "The Report of Niles and Sunderland: An American Investigation of Eastern Anatolia after World War I," *XI. Türk Tarih Kongresi* (Ankara, 1994), pp. 1809–52. The quoted passage is on p. 1850.

175. U.S. Congress, Senate, *Conditions in the Near East: Report of the American Military Mission to Armenia,* appendix, p. 9.

176. Harold Armstrong, *Turkey in Travail: The Birth of a New Nation,* p. 223.

177. McCarthy and McCarthy, *Turks and Armenians,* p. 51; Ökte, *Ottoman Archives,* p. 74.

178. Guse, "Der Armenieraufstand 1915," p. 614.

179. Report to the office of the prime minister, December 4, 1916, in Sarafian, *United States Official Documents on the Armenian Genocide,* vol. 1, p. 163. Sarafian correctly points out that Turkish authors (e.g., Gürün, *The Armenian File,* p. 214) mistakenly cite this report as proof of Turkish solicitude for the Armenian deportees but then errs in suggesting that "this document does seem to indicate that Ottoman authorities had the capacity for a massive transfer of population at this time, providing food, shelter, and medical care on the way" (p. 161). The report is simply a self-serving document put out by the Ottoman bureaucracy and proves nothing of the kind.

180. Yalman, *Turkey in the World War,* pp. 248–49.

181. Ohandjanian, *Österreich-Armenien,* vol. 7, p. 5307.

182. Riggs, *Days of Tragedy in Armenia,* p. 158.

183. Knapp, *The Tragedy of Bitlis,* p. 130.

184. Ernst J. Christoffel, *Zwischen Saat und Ernte: Aus der Arbeit der christlichen Blindenmission im Orient,* p. 141.

185. Werth report, April 20, 1916, PA, Wk. no. 11d/12 (R 21019).

186. McCarthy and McCarthy, *Turks and Armenians,* p. 223.

187. Dadrian, *Key Elements in the Turkish Denial of the Armenian Genocide,* p. 6.

188. Dadrian, "Ottoman Archives and Denial of the Armenian Genocide," in *The Armenian Genocide,* ed. Hovannisian, pp. 285–86.

189. Vigen Guroian, "Collective Responsibility and Official Excuse Making: The Case of the Turkish Genocide of the Armenians," in *The Armenian Genocide: A Perspective,* ed. Richard G. Hovannisian, p. 146.

190. Dadrian, "Ottoman Archives and Denial of the Armenian Genocide," p. 285.

191. Deringil, "In Search of a Way Forward," p. 71.

192. Orel and Yuca, *The Talât Pasha 'Telegrams,'* p. 99.

193. Willis, *Prologue to Nuremberg,* pp. 159–61. See also Bilal N. Simsir, *The Deportees of Malta and the Armenian Question.*

194. Quoted in Willis, *Prologue to Nuremberg,* p. 181.

195. See FO 371/6501/E3557.

196. FO 371/4174.

197. FO 371/6500/E3557.

198. Simsir, "The Deportees of Malta," p. 40.

199. Letter by Ambassador Baki Ilkin to a congressman, May 27, 1999, reprinted in Dadrian, *Key Elements in the Turkish Denial of the Armenian Genocide,* p. 64.

200. Editor's note to Haigazn K. Kazarian, "Unpublished Turkish Document No. 289 on the Deportations," *Armenian Review* 34 (1981): 195.

201. FO 371/6500/E3557.

202. Ibid.

203. On a list of detainees, dated December 6, 1919, Gökalp is one of sixteen persons "against whom specific charges of atrocities are alleged"; F.O. 371/4175/163689.

204. FO 371/6500/E3557.

205. FO 371/5089/14882.

206. FO 371/6500/E3557.

207. FO 371/6503/E6311.

208. FO 371/6504/E8519.

209. FO 371/6503/E6728.

210. FO 371/5089/E4056.

211. Willis, *Prologue to Nuremberg,* p. 159; Gary Jonathan Bass, *Stay the Hand of Vengeance: The Politics of War Crimes Tribunals,* p. 139.

212. FO 371/6503/E8225. For a chronology of the negotiations, see FO 371/6504/E9112.

213. Willis, *Prologue to Nuremberg,* p. 162.

214. Orel and Yuca, *The Talât Pasha 'Telegrams,'* p. 98.

215. Dadrian, *History of the Armenian Genocide,* pp. 310–11.

216. Levon Marashlian, "Finishing the Genocide: Cleansing Turkey of Armenian Survivors, 1920–1923," in *Remembrance and Denial,* ed. Hovannisian, p. 125.

217. Dadrian, "The Naim-Andonian Documents," p. 336.

Chapter 8. THE SOURCES

1. A good, though somewhat outdated, introductory bibliography of both primary and secondary sources is Richard G. Hovannisian, comp., *The Armenian Holocaust: A Bibliography Relating to the Deportations, Massacres and Dispersion of the Armenian People, 1915–1923.*

2. Turkey, Prime Ministry, *Documents on Ottoman Armenians*; Ökte, *Ottoman Archives*. The Turkish government website (www.mfa.gov.tr), under the link "Diplomatic archives," reproduces 272 documents on the Armenian question in the Turkish language with English abstracts.

3. Turkey, Prime Ministry, *Documents on Ottoman Armenians,* vol. 2, p. xi.

4. Speros Vryonis, Jr., *The Turkish State and History: Clio Meets the Grey Wolf,* pp. 104–5.

5. Dadrian, "Ottoman Archives and Denial of the Armenian Genocide," p. 303.

6. Ara Sarafian, "The Issue of Access to Ottoman Archives," *Zeitschrift für Türkeistudien* 6 (1993): 98.

7. Ismet Binark, "Letter to the Editor," *Zeitschrift für Türkeistudien* 7 (1994): 287–89.

8. Ara Sarafian, "Research Note: The Issue of Access to Ottoman Archives Revisited," *Zeitschrift für Türkeistudien* 7 (1994): 291.

9. Ismet Binark, "Comment," *Zeitschrift für Türkeistudien* 8 (1995): 267.

10. Ara Sarafian, "The Ottoman Archives Debate and the Armenian Genocide," *Armenian Forum* 2, no. 1 (Spring 1999): 43–44.

11. Erickson, "The Turkish Official Military Histories of the First World War," p. 190.

12. Zürcher, "Between Death and Desertion," p. 237.

13. Erikson, *Ordered to Die,* p. 96.

14. The book was published by the Tempelverlag in Potsdam. A reprint was brought out by Donat und Temmen in Bremen in 1986.

15. Johannes Lepsius, *Armenien und Europa: Eine Anklageschrift wider die christlichen Grossmächte und ein Aufruf an das christliche Deutschland.*

16. Published by the Tempelverlag in Potsdam in 1916. A French translation appeared in Paris in 1918.

17. Tessa Hofmann, "German Eyewitness Reports on the Genocide of the Armenians, 1915–16," in *A Crime of Silence: The Armenian Genocide,* ed. Permanent People's Tribunal, p. 63.

18. Gust, "Revidierte Ausgabe der von Johannes Lepsius 1919 unter dem Titel 'Deutschland und Armenien' herausgegebenen Sammlung diplomatischer Aktenstücke."

19. Wolfgang Gust, "Magisches Viereck: Johannes Lepsius, Deutschland und Armenien," enlarged version of lecture given in Berlin on September 25, 2001, pp. 2–10 (www.armenocide.de); Hofmann, *Der Völkermord an den Armeniern vor Gericht,* preface.

20. PA, Botsch. K./170 (fiche 7252), and PA, T. 183/44/A24663 (fiche 7152). The second version is the one that acknowledges that the two nurses did not actually see what happened.

21. Dadrian, *German Responsibility in the Armenian Genocide,* p. 4.

22. Hofmann, "German Eyewitness Reports on the Genocide of the Armenians," p. 65. In a 1996 publication cited below and in a conversation with me in Berlin in September 2001, Professor Hofmann acknowledged that her earlier appraisal had been too flattering and that Wegner's testimony was less than reliable.

23. The most important and best-known of these publications is Armin T. Wegner, *Der Weg ohne Heimkehr: Ein Martyrium in Briefen.*

24. Tessa Hofmann, *Armin T. Wegner: Writer, Eyewitness and Photographer of the Armenian Genocide,* p. 7.

25. Quoted in Hofmann, "German Eyewitness Reports on the Genocide of the Armenians," p. 66. The complete text of the letter, albeit in a different translation, can be found in Andonian, *Memoirs of Naim Bey,* pp. 72–84.

26. Hofmann, *Armin T. Wegner,* p. 7.

27. Martin Tamcke, *Armin T. Wegner und die Armenier: Anspruch und Wirklichkeit eines Augenzeugen,* p. 220. A table listing the discrepancies between the original diary and its published version as well as differences from other accounts (especially by Lepsius) can be found on pp. 242–45.

28. The original Blue Book carried the title *Miscellaneous No. 31 (1916).* The work was published commercially as *The Treatment of Armenians in the Ottoman Empire 1915–16: Documents Presented to Viscount Grey of Fallodon, Secretary of State for Foreign Affairs by Viscount Bryce* (London: n.p., 1916). This edition was reprinted in 1990 by J. C. and A. L. Fawcett in Astoria, New York.

29. Horace Peterson, *Propaganda for War: The Campaign against American Neutrality, 1914–1917,* p. 58. See also Gary S. Messinger, *British Propaganda and the State in the First World War,* p. 73.

30. Arnold J. Toynbee, *Armenian Atrocities: The Murder of a Nation.*

31. Ara Sarafian, "The Archival Trail: Authentication of *The Treatment of Armenians in the Ottoman Empire, 1915–16,*" in *Remembrance and Denial,* ed. Hovannisian, pp. 53–54. The main conduit for the transmission of this material was James L. Barton, the head of three organizations—the American Board of Commissioners for Foreign Missions, the Committee on Armenian Atrocities, and the American Committee for Armenian and Syrian Relief.

32. Great Britain, Parliamentary Papers, *Key to Names of Persons and Places Withheld from Publication in "The Treatment of Armenians in the Ottoman Empire, 1915–16."* A copy of this key can also be found in NA, RG 59, 867.4016/307. In 2000 the Gomidas Institute of Princeton, New Jersey, published an edition of the Blue Book, edited by Ara Sarafian, with all the names inserted.

33. Gürün, *The Armenian File,* pp. 219, 43.

34. Enver Ziya Karal, *Armenian Question (1878–1923),* trans. Sekip Engineri, p. 18.

35. Sarafian, "The Archival Trail," pp. 52.

36. Foreign Office to G. Buchanan, October 11, 1915, FO 371/24881/148680.

37. Arnold J. Toynbee, *Acquaintances,* p. 151. See also Michael L. Sanders and Philip M. Taylor, *British Propaganda during the First World War, 1914–18,* p. 178.

38. Akaby Nassibian, *Britain and the Armenian Question, 1915–1923,* p. 79.

39. Sarafian, *United States Official Documents on the Armenian Genocide,* vol. 1, p. xiv.

40. Toynbee, *Acquaintances,* p. 149.

41. Toynbee to Etmekjian, March 16, 1966, quoted in Lillian Etmekjian, "Toynbee, Turks, and Armenians," *Armenian Review* 37, no. 3 (Autumn 1984): 61.

42. Bryce to Grey, July 1, 1916, in Great Britain, Parliament, *The Treatment of Armenians in the Ottoman Empire,* p. xvi.

43. That is the conclusion of James Morgan Read, *Atrocity Propaganda: 1914–1919,* p. 221, with which I concur.

44. Great Britain, Parliament, *The Treatment of Armenians in the Ottoman Empire,* p. xxiii.

45. Sarafian, "The Archival Trail," p. 58.

46. NA, RG 59, 867.4016; Sarafian, *United States Official Documents on the Armenian Genocide.* See also Sarafian's article "The Paper Trail: The American State Department and the *Report of Committee on Armenian Atrocities,*" *Revue du Monde Arménienne Moderne et Contemporaine* 1 (1994).

47. Davis's reports can be found in vol. 3 of Sarafian, *United States Official Documents on the Armenian Genocide.* His final report is also published separately, edited by Susan Blair, as *The Slaughterhouse Province: An American Diplomat's Report on the Armenian Genocide, 1915–1917.*

48. Morgenthau, *Ambassador Morgenthau's Story.* The English edition is entitled *Secrets of the Bosphorus* (London: Hutchinson, 1918). The book was reprinted by the Gomidas Institute and republished in Ann Arbor, Michigan, in 2000. Another new edition, edited by Peter Balakian, was published by Wayne State University Press in 2003.

49. Dadrian, *Key Elements in the Turkish Denial of the Armenian Genocide,* p. 39.

50. Quoted in Heath W. Lowry, *The Story behind Ambassador Morgenthau's Story,* p. 2.

51. This point is also made by Ralph Elliot Cook, "The United States and the Armenian Question, 1894–1924," p. 129.

52. LC, Morgenthau diary, February 3, 1916, reel 5. The Gomidas Institute is planning to publish the diary under the title *American Diplomacy on the Bosphorus: The Diaries of Ambassador Morgenthau,* edited by Ara Sarafian.

53. LC, Morgenthau Papers, Morgenthau to Washington, May 2, 1915, reel 7.

54. Morgenthau, *Ambassador Morgenthau's Story,* p. 239.

55. LC, Morgenthau Papers, reel 7.

56. Lowry, *The Story behind Ambassador Morgenthau's Story,* pp. 23–24.

57. Dadrian, *Key Elements in the Turkish Denial of the Armenian Genocide,* pp. 38–39.

58. Sarafian, *United States Official Documents on the Armenian Genocide,* vol. 1, p. 124.

59. Suzanne Elizabeth Moravian, "Bearing Witness: The Missionary Archives as Evidence of the Armenian Genocide," in *The Armenian Genocide,* ed. Hovannisian, p. 104.

60. James L. Barton, comp., *"Turkish Atrocities": Statements of American Missionaries on the Destruction of Christian Communities in Ottoman Turkey, 1915–1917,* ed. Ara Sarafian.

61. Riggs, *Days of Tragedy in Armenia.*

62. NA, RG 256.2 (Microfilm Publication M1107).

63. McCarthy and McCarthy, *Turks and Armenians,* p. 73.

64. Cf. Edward Mead Earle, "American Missions in the Near East," *Foreign Affairs* 7 (1929): 417.

65. Great Britain, Parliament, *The Treatment of Armenians in the Ottoman Empire,* pp. 308, 306.

66. Knapp, *The Tragedy of Bitlis,* p. 53.

67. FO 371/1775/45736.

68. Tessa Hofmann and Méline Péhlivanian, "Malatia 1915: Carrefour des convois de déportés d'après le journal du missionaire allemand Hans Bauernfeind," in *L'Extermination des déportés arméniens ottomans dans les camps de concentration de Syrie-Mésopotamie (1915–1916): La deuxième phase du génocide,* ed. Raymond H. Kévorkian, p. 302.

69. Sarafian, *United States Official Documents on the Armenian Genocide,* vol. 1, pp. 82–83.

70. Deutscher Hilfsbund für christliches Liebeswerk, *1896–1921, 25 Jahre im Orient: Ein Gang durch die Arbeit des Deutschen Hilfsbundes für christliches Liebeswerk im Orient,* p. 62.

71. Great Britain, Parliament, *The Treatment of Armenians in the Ottoman Empire,* p. 648.

72. Bergfeld to Berlin, July 25, 1915, PA, T.183/38 (fiche 7124).

73. Hollis to the Secretary of State, February 2, 1920, NA, RG 59, 867.00/1115 (M353, roll 8, fr. 585).

74. Ibid., RG 59, 867.00/1190 (M 353, roll 8, fr. 847).

75. Marmaduke Pickthall, "Massacres and the Turks: The Other Side," *Foreign Affairs* (London) (July 1920, special supplement): xvi.

76. *Revue d'Histoire Arménienne Contemporaine* 2 (1996–998): 214.

77. Sarkis H. Kash, *Crime Unlimited,* pp. 48–49. For some other examples, see the literature cited at the beginning of Kash's chapter 4.

78. Levon Marashlian, *Politics and Demography: Armenians, Turks, and Kurds in the Ottoman Empire,* p. 61.

79. Paren Kazanjian, ed., *The Cilician Armenian Ordeal.*

80. Assembly of Turkish American Associations, *Setting the Record Straight on Armenian Propaganda against Turkey,* no pagination.

81. Donald E. Miller and Lorna Touryan Miller, *Survivors: An Oral History of the Armenian Genocide,* p. 28.

82. Elizabeth F. Loftus and James M. Doyle, *Eyewitness Testimony: Civil and Criminal,* pp. 21–31.

83. Timothy Garton Ash, "On the Frontier," *New York Review of Books,* November 7, 2002, p. 60.

84. Libby Copeland, "Survivor," *Washington Post,* September 24, 2000. On Wilkomirski, see Stefan Maechler, *The Wilkomirski Affair: A Study in Biographical Truth,* trans. John E. Woods.

85. Christopher R. Browning, *Nazi Policy, Jewish Workers, and German Killers,* p. 91.

Chapter 9. THE DEPORTATION DECISION

1. Feroz Ahmad, *The Young Turks: The Committee of Union and Progress in Turkish Politics 1908–1914,* p. 159.

2. Sonyel, *The Ottoman Armenians,* p. 299.

3. Morgenthau diary, April 24, 1915, LC, reel 5.

4. Quoted from the Prime Minister's Archives by Orel and Yuca, *The Talât Pasha 'Telegrams,'* pp. 113–14. A copy of this order was captured by British troops in Palestine in 1918 and, in a different translation, can be found in FO 371/4241/170751. Erickson mentions an order of Enver, also dated April 24, that "outlined a plan to evacuate the Armenian population from the region [of eastern Anatolia]" (*Ordered to Die,* pp. 100–101). According to this directive, the ratio of Armenians was to drop to 10 percent of the Turkish population. This order does not quite fit into the chronology of events known from other sources. On May 2 Enver still suggested only the evacuation of the Armenians around Lake Van.

5. Quoted from the Prime Minister's Archives by Orel and Yuca, *The Talât Pasha 'Telegrams,'* p. 116. This document, in a slightly different translation, is also included in Turkey, Prime Ministry, *Documents on Ottoman Armenians,* vol. 1, p. 71.

6. Several telegrams addressed to provincial governors and containing instructions on the mode of relocation are reproduced in Orel and Yuca, *The Talât Pasha 'Telegrams,'* pp. 117–19; and, in a different translation, in Gürün, *The Armenian File,* p. 210.

7. Quoted in Hovannisian, *Armenia on the Road to Independence,* p. 50. A longer version and different translation of this document is given by Kazarian, "Unpublished Turkish Document No. 289 on the Deportations," pp. 195–97. In this version Talaat considers it "imperative" that the danger of the "division and dismemberment" of the empire be "radically solved and eliminated" (p. 196). A large-scale program of relocation can appropriately be called a "radical solution."

Dadrian's interpretation, which sees in this phrase "the hint of 'a final solution'" and "a euphemism for genocide," is hardly self-evident (Dadrian, *Warrant for Genocide,* pp. 123–24).

8. Quoted from the archive of the chief-of-staff in Gürün, *The Armenian File,* p. 206.

9. Quoted in Orel and Yuca, *The Talât Pasha 'Telegrams,'* pp. 116–17.

10. Turkey, Prime Ministry, *Documents on Ottoman Armenians,* vol. 2, pp. 91–92. The decree is reprinted in Sarafian, *United States Official Documents on the Armenian Genocide,* vol. 1, pp. 170–71.

11. Turkey, Prime Ministry, *Documents on Ottoman Armenians,* vol. 1, pp. 76–80. This decree, too, is reprinted in Sarafian, *United States Official Documents on the Armenian Genocide,* vol. 1, pp. 172–76.

12. Sonyel, *The Ottoman Armenians,* p. 300.

13. Mim Kemal Öke, "The Response of the Turkish Armenians to the 'Armenian Question,' 1919–1926," in *Armenians in the Ottoman Empire and Modern Turkey (1912–1926),* ed. Bogazici University, p. 76. See also Stanford J. Shaw and Ezel Kural Shaw, "The Authors Respond [to criticism of their book *History of the Ottoman Empire and Modern Turkey,* vol. 2]," *International Journal of Middle East Studies* 9 (1978): 395–96.

14. Foreign Policy Institute, "The Turkish Argument: The Armenian Issue in Nine Questions and Answers," in *A Crime of Silence,* ed. Permanent People's Tribunal, p. 154.

15. Justin McCarthy, *The Ottoman Peoples and the End of Empire,* p. 111.

16. Erickson, *Ordered to Die,* pp. 102–3.

17. Talaat Pasha, "Posthumous Memoirs of Talaat Pasha," p. 294.

18. McCarthy and McCarthy, *Turks and Armenians,* p. 52.

19. Roderic H. Davison, *Turkey,* p. 118.

20. Morgenthau diary, October 18, 1915, LC, reel 5.

21. Ibid., August 17, 1915.

22. Orel and Yuca, *The Talât Pasha 'Telegrams,'* p. 115.

23. Suny, "Empire and Nation," pp. 46, 48.

24. Dadrian, "The Secret Young-Turk Ittihadist Conference," p. 189.

25. Erickson, *Ordered to Die,* p. 101.

26. Einstein, *Inside Constantinople,* pp. 160–61, 176.

27. Pomiankowski, *Der Zusammenbruch des Ottomanischen Reiches,* p. 147.

28. Chalabian, *Revolutionary Figures,* p. 290.

29. Suhnaz Yilmaz, "An Ottoman Warrior Abroad: Enver Pasha as an Expatriate," *Middle Eastern Studies* 35, no. 4 (October 1999): 47.

30. PA, T. 183/37 (fiche 7122).

31. The statement was made to German embassy counselor Konstantin Freiherr von Neurath by foreign minister Said Halim Pasha. See Neurath's dispatch of November 5, 1915, PA, T. 159 no. 2/14 (R 13799).

32. Quoted from Morgenthau's diary entry of August 8, 1915, in Lowry, *The Story behind Ambassador Morgenthau's Story,* p. 49.

33. Victor Azarya, *The Armenian Quarter of Jerusalem: Urban Life behind Monastery Walls,* p. 42.

34. Pomiankowski, *Der Zusammenbruch des Ottomanischen Reiches,* p. 161.

35. Scheubner-Richter to Ambassador Wangenheim, May 22, 1915, PA, Botsch. K./169 (fiche 7247).

36. Suny, "Empire and Nation," p. 46.

37. Ussher and Knapp, *An American Physician in Turkey,* p. 207.

38. See, for example, J. Selden Willmore, *The Great Crime and Its Moral,* p. 145.

39. Ulrich Trumpener, *Germany and the Ottoman Empire: 1914–1918,* p. 204.

40. Ohandjanian, *Armenien,* p. 221.

41. *Deutsche Allgemeine Zeitung,* June 30, 1921, quoted in Christoph Dinkel, "German Officers and the Armenian Genocide," *Armenian Review* 44, no. 1 (Spring 1991): 96.

42. Dadrian, *German Responsibility in the Armenian Genocide,* p. 185.

43. Hilmar Kaiser, "Germany and the Armenian Genocide: A Review Essay," *Journal of the Society for Armenian Studies* 8 (1995–97): 133–35, 142, and Kaiser's reply to Dadrian's response in *Journal of the Society for Armenian Studies* 9 (1996–99): 137.

44. Clive Foss, book review, *Institute for the Study of Genocide Newsletter* 19 (Fall 1997): 14, 16.

45. Donald Bloxham, "Power Politics, Prejudice, Protest and Propaganda," p. 234.

Chapter 10. THE COURSE OF THE DEPORTATIONS

1. Great Britain, Parliament, *The Treatment of Armenians in the Ottoman Empire,* p. 653.

2. Scheubner-Richter to Ambassador Hohenlohe-Waldenburg, May 18, 1915 (probably old calendar), Botsch. K./168 (fiche 7245) and August 5, 1915, PA, T. 183/39/A28584 (fiche 7129).

3. Quoted from Ministry of the Interior files by Gürün, *The Armenian File,* p. 211.

4. Scheubner-Richter to Hohenlohe, August 5, 1915, PA, T. 183/39/A28584 (fiche 7129), and June 22, 1915, Botsch. K./169 (fiche 7248).

5. Dr. Neukirch report of August 5, 1915, in Wolfgang Gust, "Revidierte Ausgabe der von Johannes Lepsius 1919 unter dem Titel 'Deutschland und Armenien' herausgegebenen Sammlung diplomatischer Aktenstücke," p. 167.

6. Heizer to Morgenthau, September 25, 1915, in Sarafian, *United States Official Documents on the Armenian Genocide,* vol. 2, pp. 46, 44.

7. Scheubner-Richter to Hohenlohe, August 5, 1915, PA, T. 183/39/A28584 (fiche 7129).

8. Ibid.; see also the report of A. S. Safrastian of March 15, 1916, in Great Britain, Parliament, *The Treatment of Armenians in the Ottoman Empire,* p. 238.

9. Undated report, PA, T. 183/44/A24663 (fiche 7152).

10. Scheubner-Richter to Hohenlohe, August 5, 1915, PA, T. 183/39/A28584 (fiche 7129).

11. Scheubner-Richter to Wangenheim, July 9, 1915, PA, Botsch. K./169 (fiche 7249).

12. FO 371/2146/70602.

13. Quoted from the Ministry of the Interior archive in Orel and Yuca, *The Talât Pasha 'Telegrams,'* p. 119.

14. PA, Botsch. K./ 96 (fiche 7205).

15. PA, Botsch. K./170 (fiche 7251).

16. Heizer to Morgenthau, September 25, 1915, in Sarafian, *United States Official Documents on the Armenian Genocide,* vol. 2, p. 45. An order of the minister of the interior to this effect, dated August 15, is reprinted in Orel and Yuca, *The Talât Pasha 'Telegrams,'* p. 122.

17. Riggs, *Days of Tragedy in Armenia,* pp. 120, 138.

18. Davis report of February 9, 1918, in Sarafian, *United States Official Documents on the Armenian Genocide,* vol. 3, pp. 63–64. This is a summary report prepared by Davis for the State Department after his return to the United States in 1917 that combines into a single narrative material from his dispatches sent out at the time of the events in question.

19. Davis to Morgenthau, July 24, 1915, in Sarafian, *United States Official Documents on the Armenian Genocide,* vol. 3, pp. 21–22.

20. Tacy Atkinson, *"The German, the Turk and the Devil Made a Triple Alliance": Harpoot Diaries, 1908–1917,* p. 47.

21. Sarafian, *United States Official Documents on the Armenian Genocide,* vol. 3, p. 143.

22. Hovannisian, "The Question of Altruism," p. 289.

23. See the relevant excerpts from *Aspirations et agissements révolutionnaires,* in Davis, *The Slaughterhouse Province,* pp. 195–96.

24. Jacobsen, *Diaries of a Danish Missionary,* p. 67.

25. Davis report of February 9, 1918, in Sarafian, *United States Official Documents on the Armenian Genocide,* vol. 3, p. 52.

26. Ehmann to Wangenheim, May 18, 1915, PA, Botsch. K./169 (fiche 7247).

27. Davis report of February 9, 1918, in Sarafian, *United States Official Documents on the Armenian Genocide,* vol. 3, p. 55.

28. Riggs, *Days of Tragedy in Armenia,* p. 48.

29. Statement of Dr. Tacy Atkinson in Barton, *"Turkish Atrocities,"* p. 40. This episode is also mentioned by Isabelle Harley (printed in the same collection, p. 65), and by Riggs, *Days of Tragedy in Armenia,* p. 48.

30. Davis report of February 9, 1918 in Sarafian, *United States Official Documents on the Armenian Genocide,* vol. 3, pp. 66–67.

31. Riggs, *Days of Tragedy in Armenia,* p. 124.

32. Davis to Morgenthau, June 30, 1915, in Sarafian, *United States Official Documents on the Armenian Genocide,* vol. 3, p. 4.

33. Riggs, *Days of Tragedy in Armenia,* pp. 118–19.

34. Ibid., pp. 148–49.

35. Davis report of February 9, 1918 in Sarafian, *United States Official Documents on the Armenian Genocide,* vol. 3, p. 79.

36. Sarafian, *United States Official Documents on the Armenian Genocide,* vol. 3, p. 19.

37. Barton, *"Turkish Atrocities,"* p. 32.

38. PA, T. 183/38/A 24905 (fiche 7125).

39. Great Britain, Parliament, *The Treatment of Armenians in the Ottoman Empire,* p. 543.

40. Davis report of February 9, 1918, in Sarafian, *United States Official Documents on the Armenian Genocide,* vol. 3, pp. 97–98.

41. Ibid., p. 84. The woman who lived to tell of the massacre is also mentioned in Atkinson, *"The German, the Turk and the Devil Made a Triple Alliance,"* p. 62.

42. Davis report of February 9, 1918, in Sarafian, *United States Official Documents on the Armenian Genocide,* vol. 3, pp. 84–86.

43. Riggs, *Days of Tragedy in Armenia,* p. 152.

44. Sarafian, *United States Official Documents on the Armenian Genocide,* vol. 3, p. 28.

45. Atkinson, *"The German, the Turk and the Devil Made a Triple Alliance,"* p. 58.

46. Riggs, *Days of Tragedy in Armenia,* p. 152.

47. Davis report of February 9, 1918, in Sarafian, *United States Official Documents on the Armenian Genocide,* vol. 3, pp. 87–90.

48. Ibid., p. 91.

49. Ibid., p. 86.

50. Riggs, *Days of Tragedy in Armenia,* p. 139.

51. Ehmann to Metternich, January 14, 1916, PA, Botsch. K./98 (fiche 7214).

52. Dadrian, *History of the Armenian Genocide,* p. 325.

53. FO 608/247/8109.

54. "A List of Those Responsible for the Massacres and Deportations of the Armenians," *Armenian Review* 35 (1982): 442.

55. British Embassy to Curzon, July 13, 1921, FO 371/6504/E 8519.

56. Rumbold to Curzon, April 24, 1922, FO 371/7882/4425.

57. Jacobsen, *Diaries of a Danish Missionary,* p. 93.

58. Krikor M. Zahigian, *One Page of Armenia's Tragedy: A Story of the Years Wherein We Have Seen Evil,* p. 22.

59. Riggs, *Days of Tragedy in Armenia,* p. 101.

60. The orders of the minister of the interior, issued on August 3 and 15, 1915, are reprinted in Orel and Yuca, *The Talât Pasha 'Telegrams,'* p. 122.

61. Davis report of February 9, 1918 in Sarafian, *United States Official Documents on the Armenian Genocide,* vol. 3, pp. 73–74. See also Riggs, *Days of Tragedy in Armenia,* p. 105.

62. Ruth A. Parmelee, *A Pioneer in the Euphrates Valley,* p. 19.

63. Sarafian, *United States Official Documents on the Armenian Genocide,* vol. 3, pp. 31–32.

64. Riggs, *Days of Tragedy in Armenia,* p. 112.

65. Ahmad, *Kurdistan during the First World War,* p.173.

66. Parmelee, *A Pioneer in the Euphrates Valley,* p. 22.

67. Alice Muggerditchian Shipley, *We Walked, Then Ran,* p. 116. For another such account see Boghos Jafarian, *Farewell Kharpert: Autobiography of B.J.,* p. 108.

68. "Statement by Isabelle Harley," in Barton, *"Turkish Atrocities,"* p. 70.

69. Jacobsen, *Diaries of a Danish Missionary,* p. 81.

70. Riggs, *Days of Tragedy in Armenia,* p. 158.

71. Jacobsen, *Diaries of a Danish Missionary,* p. 168.

72. *Sonnen-Aufgang* 20, no. 1 (October 1917): 2.

73. Riggs, *Days of Tragedy in Armenia,* pp. 175, 185.

74. Ernst Kwiatkowski to Vienna, January 30 and March 10, 1914, in Ohandjanian, *Österreich-Armenien,* vol. 6, pp. 4300, 4338.

75. Bergfeld to Wangenheim, July 9, 1915, PA, T. 183/37/A22559 (fiche 7123).

76. Ibid.

77. Oscar S. Heizer to Morgenthau, June 28, 1915, in Sarafian, *United States Official Documents on the Armenian Genocide,* vol. 2, p. 26; Leon Z. Surmelian, *I Ask You Ladies and Gentlemen,* p. 89.

78. The complete text of this proclamation was included in Heizer's dispatch of June 28, 1915, in Sarafian, *United States Official Documents on the Armenian Genocide,* vol. 2, pp. 15–16.

79. Ibid., pp. 1–2.

80. Bergfeld to Wangenheim, June 25 and 27, 1915, PA, Botsch. K./169 (fiche 7248).

81. Ibid.

82. Heizer to Morgenthau, June 30, 1915, in Sarafian, *United States Official Documents on the Armenian Genocide,* vol. 2, pp. 7–8.

83. Ibid., p. 12.

84. Surmelian, *I Ask You Ladies and Gentlemen,* p. 97.

85. Heizer to Morgenthau, July 10, 1915, in Sarafian, *United States Official Documents on the Armenian Genocide,* vol. 2, p. 19.

86. Heizer to Morgenthau, July 28, 1915, in ibid., pp. 26–27.

87. Heizer to Secretary of State, April 11, 1919, in ibid., p. 38.

88. Bergfeld to Berlin, August 27, 1917, PA, T. 183/38/A28189 (fiche 7128).

89. Bergfeld to embassy, September 9, 1915, PA, Botsch. K./170 (fiche 7253).

90. Bergfeld to Berlin, July 25, 1915, PA, T. 183/38/A23905 (fiche 7124).

91. Bergfeld to Berlin, August 27, 1917, PA, T. 183/38/A28189 (fiche 7128).

92. Karl Ranzi to Vienna, February 15, 1916, in Ohandjanian, *Österreich-Armenien,* vol. 7, p. 5021.

93. Heizer to Morgenthau, July 28, 1915, in Sarafian, *United States Official Documents on the Armenian Genocide,* vol. 2, p. 26.

94. Heizer to Secretary of State, April 11, 1919, in ibid., p. 38.

95. Kwiatkowski to Vienna, July 31, 1915, in Ohandjanian, *Österreich-Armenien,* vol. 6, p. 4646.

96. Ibid., p. 4725.

97. Ara Sarafian, "Correspondence," *Armenian Forum* 2, no. 4 (February 2003): 144.

98. Akcam, *Armenien und der Völkermord,* pp. 176–78.

99. Heizer to Morgenthau, July 28, 1915, in Sarafian, *United States Official Documents on the Armenian Genocide,* vol. 2, p. 26.

100. Peter to Morgenthau, August 26, 1915, in ibid., pp. 52–53.

101. Pailadzo Captanian, *1915: Der Völkermord an den Armeniern: Eine Zeugin berichtet,* trans. Meliné Pehlivanian, pp. 42–43.

102. Kerr, *The Lions of Marash,* p. xxi.

103. Great Britain, Parliament, *The Treatment of Armenians in the Ottoman Empire,* p. 543.

104. Telegram of Talaat to the governor of Adana, May 23, 1915, quoted from the files of the Ministry of the Interior in Orel and Yuca, *The Talât Pasha 'Telegrams,'* p. 118.

105. Nathan to Morgenthau, August 7, 1915, in Sarafian, *United States Official Documents on the Armenian Genocide,* vol. 2, p. 84.

106. See my discussion of this topic in chapter 7.

107. Einstein, *Inside Constantinople,* p. 184.

108. Sarafian, *United States Official Documents on the Armenian Genocide,* vol. 2, p. 78.

109. Büge to Hohenlohe, August 12, 1915, PA, Botsch. K./170 (fiche 7252).

110. Sarafian, *United States Official Documents on the Armenian Genocide,* vol. 2, p. 87.

111. Büge to Hohenlohe, September 2, 1915, PA, Botsch. K./96 (fiche 7207).

112. Büge to Hohenlohe, September 10, ibid., Botsch. K./170 (fiche 7253).

113. Nathan to Morgenthau, September 11, 1915, in Sarafian, *United States Official Documents on the Armenian Genocide,* vol. 2, p. 87.

114. Great Britain, Parliament, *The Treatment of Armenians in the Ottoman Empire,* p. 503.

115. Hohenlohe to Bethmann Hollweg, September 14, 1915, PA, T. 183/38/A27578 (fiche 7127).

116. Ibid., Botsch. K./170 (fiche 7253).

117. Nathan to Morgenthau, September 22, 1915, in Sarafian, *United States Official Documents on the Armenian Genocide,* vol. 2, p. 91.

118. Sarafian, *United States Official Documents on the Armenian Genocide,* vol. 2, p. 96.

119. Ibid., p. 102.

120. Telegram of Talaat to the governor of Marash, May 23, 1915, quoted from the files of the Ministry of the Interior in Orel and Yuca, *The Talât Pasha 'Telegrams,'* p. 118.

121. Sarafian, *United States Official Documents on the Armenian Genocide,* vol. 1, p. 25.

122. PA, Botsch. K./170 (fiche 7252).

123. Paren Kazanjian, *The Cilician Armenian Ordeal,* p. 328.

124. Statement of March 1, 1916, PA, Botsch. K./100 (fiche 7219).

125. "Aufzeichnung über die armenische Frage," by embassy secretary Van Hoesch, n.d., forwarded to Berlin on September 18, 1916, PA, T. 183/44/A25749 (fiche 7153); Rössler to Berlin, April 27, 1916, PA, T. 183/42/A12911 (fiche 7145).

126. Kerr, *The Lions of Marash,* p. 25.

127. Kazanjian, *The Cilician Armenian Ordeal,* p. 128.

128. Uwe Feigel, *Das evangelische Deutschland und Armenien: Die Armenierhilfe deutscher evangelischer Christen seit dem Ende des 19. Jahrhunderts im Kontexte der deutsch-türkischen Beziehungen,* p. 194.

129. Cf. Hilmar Kaiser, "The Baghdad Railway and the Armenian Genocide, 1915–1916: A Case Study of German Resistance and Complicity," in *Remembrance and Denial,* ed. Hovannisian, p. 75.

130. William S. Dodd, "Report of Conditions Witnessed in the Armenian Deportations in Konia, Turkey," in Barton, *"Turkish Atrocities,"* pp. 146–47.

131. Report of September 3, 1915, in Great Britain, Parliament, *The Treatment of Armenians in the Ottoman Empire,* p. 428.

132. Barton, *"Turkish Atrocities,"* p. 155.

133. Sarafian, *United States Official Documents on the Armenian Genocide,* vol. 2, pp. 122–23.

134. Letter of Dr. Wilfred M. Post to William W. Peet, November 25, 1915, in Great Britain, Parliament, *The Treatment of Armenians in the Ottoman Empire,* p. 435.

135. Friedrich Freiherr Kress von Kressenstein, *Mit den Türken zum Suezkanal,* p. 132.

136. Nathan to Morgenthau, November 4, 1915, in Sarafian, *United States Official Documents on the Armenian Genocide,* vol. 2, p. 99.

137. Report of November 16, 1915, PA, AA, T 183/40 (fiches 7137–38).

138. Ibid. (fiche 7138). Copies of these reports are also included in Great Britain, Parliament, *The Treatment of Armenians in the Ottoman Empire,* pp. 455–57.

139. Rössler to Berlin, November 8, 1915, PA, T. 183/40/A35045 (fiche 7134).

140. Vahram Daderina, "Our Story," manuscript quoted in Hilmar Kaiser, *At the Crossroads of Der Zor: Death, Survival, and Humanitarian Resistance in Aleppo, 1915–1917,* p. 19.

141. Reprinted from the Ministry of the Interior files in Orel and Yuca, *The Talât Pasha 'Telegrams,'* p. 120.

142. PA, T. 183/38/A24524 (fiche 7124).

143. Becker, *Äskulap zwischen Reichsadler und Halbmond,* pp. 200–201; Kress von Kressenstein, *Mit den Türken zum Suezkanal,* p. 137; Rössler to Berlin, November 8, 1915, PA, T. 183/40/A35045 (fiche 2134).

144. Reprinted from the Ministry of the Interior files in Orel and Yuca, *The Talât Pasha 'Telegrams,'* p. 118.

145. Sarafian, *United States Official Documents on the Armenian Genocide,* vol. 1, p. 18.

146. Ibid., pp. 94–95.

147. Rössler to Berlin, September 27, 1915, PA, T. 183/39/A30049 (fiche 7130).

148. Martin Niepage, *The Horrors of Aleppo: Seen by a German Eyewitness,* pp. 4–5. The German original was published as *Ein Wort an die berufenen Vertreter des deutschen Volkes* (Potsdam, 1916).

149. PA, Botsch. K./97 (fiche 7210).

150. Niepage, *The Horrors of Aleppo,* p. 10.

151. Great Britain, Parliament, *The Treatment of Armenians in the Ottoman Empire,* pp. xxxiii–xxxiv; Rössler to Berlin, November 11, 1915, PA, T. 183/45/A3181 (fiche 7157).

152. Kerop Bedoukian, *The Urchin: An Armenian's Escape,* p. 40.

153. Rössler to Berlin, September 27, 1915, PA, T. 183/39/A30049 (fiche 7130).

154. Hoffmann to embassy, November 8, 1915, PA, T. 183/41/A2889 (fiche 7139).

155. Jackson summary report, March 4, 1918, in Sarafian, *United States Official Documents on the Armenian Genocide,* vol. 1, p. 146.

156. PA, T. 183/44/A 25739 (fiche 7153).

157. Kaiser, *At the Crossroads of Der Zor,* pp. 37–49; Jackson summary report, March 4, 1918, in Sarafian, *United States Official Documents on the Armenian*

Genocide, vol. 1, p. 152; Karl Meyer, *Armenien und die Schweiz: Geschichte der schweizerischen Armenierhilfe,* p. 108; John Minassian, *Many Hills Yet to Climb: Memoirs of an Armenian Deportee,* p. 86, 107.

158. Reprinted from the Ministry of the Interior files in Orel and Yuca, *The Talât Pasha 'Telegrams,'* p. 124.

159. See, for example, Peet to Mordtmann, January 17, 1916, PA, Botsch. K./98 (fiche 7214).

160. Morgenthau diary, January 6 and 22, 1916, LC, reel 5.

161. Rössler to Berlin, June 17, 1916, PA, T. 183/43/A17939 (fiche 7148).

162. Rössler to Berlin, September 20, 1916, PA, T. 183/45/A28162 (fiche 7156).

163. Rössler to Berlin, February 14, 1917, PA, T. 183/46/A8613 (fiche 7163).

164. Jackson letter of September 3, 1916, forwarded to the State Department by his wife, in Sarafian, *United States Official Documents on the Armenian Genocide,* vol. 1, p. 119.

165. Jackson summary report, March 4, 1918, in ibid., p. 154.

166. Kaiser, *At the Crossroads of Der Zor,* p. 55.

167. Hoffmann to embassy Constantinople, April 28, 1916, PA, Botsch. K./100 (fiche 7219); Foreign Ministry to embassy, June 30, 1916, PA, Botsch. K./101 (fiche 7221).

168. Foreign ministry to Schuchardt, November 27, 1916, PA, T. 183/45/A30662 (fiche 7157).

169. Rössler to embassy, March 16, 1917, PA, Botsch. K./101 (fiche 7223).

170. Meyer, *Armenien und die Schweiz,* p. 109.

171. Karekin [Garegin] Pasdermajian, "My Last Interview with Talaat Pasha," *Armenian Review* 35 (1982): 126 (n. 7) (reprint of a 1922 article); George Mouradian, *Armenian Infotext,* p. 94.

172. Kazarian, "A Catalogue of Those Principally Responsible for the 1915–18 Massacres," p. 255.

173. James Kay Sutherland, *The Adventures of an Armenian Boy,* p. 146.

174. Dadrian, *Key Elements in the Turkish Denial of the Armenian Genocide,* p. 54 (n. 64).

175. Djemal Pasha, *Memories of a Turkish Statesman,* p. 279. See also his article "Zur Frage der Greuel in Armenien."

176. PA, Botsch. K./169 (fiche 7249).

177. Ibid., T. 183/38/A23991 (fiche 7124).

178. Ibid., T. 183/43/A16612 (fiche 7147).

179. Kress von Kressenstein, *Mit den Türken zum Suezkanal,* p. 130.

180. Pomiankowski, *Der Zusammenbruch des Ottomanischen Reiches,* p. 199.

181. Djemal Pasha, *Memories of a Turkish Statesman,* pp. 277, 279.

182. Metternich to Berlin, December 9, 1915, PA, T. 183/40/A36483 (fiche 7136).

183. Yair Auron, *The Banality of Indifference: Zionism and the Armenian Genocide*, p. 377; Beylerian, *Les grandes puissances, l'Empire Ottoman*, p. 287.

184. Kazemzadeh, *The Struggle for Transcaucasia (1917–1921)*, pp. 28–29; Frank G. Weber, *Eagles on the Crescent: Germany, Austria, and the Diplomacy of the Turkish Alliance, 1914–1918*, p. 153; David Fromkin, *A Peace to End All Peace: Creating the Modern Middle East 1914–1920*, p. 214. A. L. Macfie in *The End of the Ottoman Empire, 1908–1923*, p. 138, doubts that Djemal Pasha would "ever have undertaken so risky an adventure, particularly as he was noted for his patriotism."

185. Künzler, *Im Lande des Blutes und der Tränen*, pp. 10–11.

186. Leslie's report of June 14 was forwarded by Consul Jackson to Morgenthau on June 28. It is reprinted in Sarafian, *United States Official Documents on the Armenian Genocide*, vol. 1, pp. 30–32 (the quotation is on p. 32).

187. Jernazian, *Judgment unto Truth*, p. 60.

188. Ibid., p. 62. The report of the governor is summarized in a dispatch from the Ministry of Interior to the governor of Diarbakir, dated July 6, and is reprinted in Orel and Yuca, *The Talât Pasha 'Telegrams,'* pp. 132–33.

189. Künzler, *Im Lande des Blutes und der Tränen*, p. 39.

190. Henry W. Glockler, *Interned in Turkey, 1914–1918* (written in 1918), pp. 25–26; Jernazian, *Judgment unto Truth*, p. 65.

191. Künzler, *Im Lande des Blutes und der Tränen*, p. 38.

192. Bruno Eckart, "Meine Erlebnisse in Urfa," *Der Orient* 3 (1921): 120–21 (several of these articles were published under the same title as a book in 1922); Künzler, *Im Lande des Blutes und der Tränen*, p. 17.

193. Glockler, *Interned in Turkey*, p. 27.

194. Edelman report of August 26, 1915, in Sarafian, *United States Official Documents on the Armenian Genocide*, vol. 1, pp. 73–75.

195. Eckart, "Meine Erlebnisse in Urfa," p. 122; Künzler, *Im Lande des Blutes und der Tränen*, pp. 22–23.

196. Jernazian, *Judgment unto Truth*, p. 75; the order of August 29 is reprinted from the Ministry of the Interior files in Orel and Yuca, *The Talât Pasha 'Telegrams,'* p. 129.

197. Jernazian, *Judgment unto Truth*, p. 75.

198. Ibid., p. 84; Künzler, *Im Lande des Blutes und der Tränen*, pp. 39–40.

199. Hilmar Kaiser, ed., *Eberhard Count Wolffskeel von Reichenberg, Zeitoun, Mousa Dagh, Ourfa: Letters on the Armenian Genocide*, p. xv.

200. Jernazian, *Judgment unto Truth*, p. 87; Lepsius, *Deutschland und Armenien*, p. lvii.

201. Künzler, *Im Lande des Blutes und der Tränen*, p. 65.

202. Glockler, *Interned in Turkey*, p. 47.

203. Archive of the chief-of-staff, reprinted in Orel and Yuca, *The Talât Pasha 'Telegrams,'* pp. 134; Rössler to Berlin, November 8, PA, T. 183/40/A35045 (fiche 7134).

204. Glockler, *Interned in Turkey,* p. 49.

205. Eckart, "Meine Erlebnisse in Urfa," p. 142.

206. Künzler report of December 5, 1915, contained in Rössler to Berlin, January 3, 1916, PA, T. 183/41/A2888 (fiche 7139).

207. Jackson summary report, March 4, 1918, in Sarafian, *United States Official Documents on the Armenian Genocide,* vol. 1, p. 148.

208. Ibid., p. 155.

209. Rössler to Berlin, February 14, 1917, PA, T. 183/46/A8613 (fiche 7163).

210. Jernazian, *Judgment unto Truth,* p. 110.

211. Jackson summary report, March 4, 1918, in Sarafian, *United States Official Documents on the Armenian Genocide,* vol. 1, p. 155; Künzler to German consulate Aleppo, April 8, 1917, forwarded by Rössler to Berlin, April 20, 1917, PA, T. 183/47/A15054 (fiche 7165).

212. Künzler, *Im Lande des Blutes und der Tränen,* pp. 64–65. See also his posthumous autobiography, *Köbi: Vater der Armenier,* p. 141; and Meyer, *Armenien und die Schweiz,* pp. 110–11.

213. Andreas Vischer, "Urfa im Sommer 1919," *Mitteilungen über Armenien* (Basel) 12 (October 1919): 598.

214. Wangenheim to Berlin, June 25, 1915, PA, T. 183/37/A20447 (fiche 7122); Dadrian, "The Secret Young-Turk Ittihadist Conference," p. 191.

215. See, for example, Richard G. Hovannisian, ed., *The Armenian Genocide in Perspective,* p. 29.

216. Johannes Lepsius, *Der Todesgang des armenischen Volkes: Bericht über das Schicksal des armenischen Volkes in der Türkei während des Weltkrieges,* p. 230.

217. Michael M. Gunter, *"Pursuing the Just Cause of Their People": A Study of Contemporary Armenian Terrorism,* p. 23.

218. Horton to Morgenthau, July 30, 1915, in Sarafian, *United States Official Documents on the Armenian Genocide,* vol. 2, p. 108.

219. Quoted from the Prime Minister's Archive by Orel and Yuca, *The Talât Pasha 'Telegrams,'* p. 133.

220. Einstein, *Inside Constantinople,* p. 286.

221. Austrian consul Vladimir Radimsky to Vienna, November 9, 1915, in Ohandjanian, *Österreich-Armenien,* vol. 6, pp. 4839–40.

222. Radimsky to Vienna, November 21, 1915, quoted in Ohandjanian, *Armenien,* p. 122.

223. PA, T. 183/45/A31505 (fiche 7157).

224. Ibid.

225. Marjorie Housepian, *Smyrna 1922: The Destruction of a City,* p. 46.

226. Dr. Weber to embassy, March 6, 1917, PA, Botsch. K./174 (fiche 7268).

227. Foreword of the editor to Agnacia Manuelian, *Unending Journey,* p. 15.

228. Quoted from the Ministry of the Interior files by Orel and Yuca, *The Talât Pasha 'Telegrams,'* p. 129.

229. Pallavicini to Vienna, November 11, 1915, in Ohandjanian, *Österreich-Armenien*, vol. 6, p. 4838.

230. Metternich to Berlin, December 7, 1915, PA, T. 183/40/A36184 (fiche 7135).

231. Metternich to Berlin, December 18, 1915, PA, T. 183/40/A37207 (fiche 7136).

232. Quoted from the Ministry of the Interior files by Orel and Yuca, *The Talât Pasha 'Telegrams,'* pp. 124–25.

233. Ibid., p. 125.

234. Metternich to Berlin, March 21, 1916, PA, T. 183/41/A8090 (fiche 7142).

235. Quoted from the Ministry of the Interior files by Orel and Yuca, *The Talât Pasha 'Telegrams,'* pp. 125–26.

236. Kühlmann to Berlin, February 16 and 24, 1917, PA, T. 183/46/A5919 and A6742 (fiche 7162).

237. Pallavicini to Vienna, March 24, 1917, in Ohandjanian, *Österreich-Armenien*, vol. 7, p. 5302.

238. Embassy minute, December 11, 1917, PA, Botsch. K./174 (fiche 7270).

239. Mary Mills Patrick, *Under Five Sultans,* p. 283.

Chapter 11. RESETTLEMENT

1. Minister of the Interior to the governors of Mosul, Urfa, and Zor, May 23, 1915, quoted from the Ministry of the Interior files in Orel and Yuca, *The Talât Pasha 'Telegrams,'* p. 117.

2. "Regulations Related to Settlement and Board and Lodging and Other Affairs…," printed in Sarafian, *United States Official Documents on the Armenian Genocide,* vol. 1, p. 170.

3. Report of the German engineer Bastendorff to Rössler, December 18, 1915, PA, T. 183/41/A2888 (fiche 7139); Rössler to Berlin, November 30, 1915, PA, T. 183/40/A36213 (fiche 7135); Jackson to Morgenthau, February 8, 1916, in Sarafian, *United States Official Documents on the Armenian Genocide,* vol. 1, p. 113.

4. Mae M. Derdarian, *Vergeen: A Survivor of the Armenian Genocide,* p. 66.

5. Bastendorff to Rössler, December 18, 1915, PA, T. 183/41/A2888 (fiche 7139).

6. Waldemar Frey, *Kut-el-Amara: Kriegsfahrten und Erinnerungsbilder aus dem Orient,* p. 305.

7. Rössler to Berlin, April 27, 1916, PA, T. 183/42/A12911 (fiche 7145).

8. *Arabian Report,* n.s. 11 (September 27, 1916), FO 371/2781/201201. This report can also be found in Beylerian, *Les grandes puissances, l'Empire Ottoman, et les Arméniens,* p. 250.

9. Eckart, "Meine Erlebnisse in Urfa," p. 23.

10. Litten to Rössler, February 6, 1916, forwarded to Berlin on February 9, 1916, PA, T. 183/41/A5498 (fiche 7141).

11. Bernau to Jackson, September 10, 1916, in Sarafian, *United States Official Documents on the Armenian Genocide*, vol. 1, pp. 129–32.

12. Ibid., p. 134.

13. Litten to Rössler, February 6, 1916, forwarded to Berlin on February 9, 1916, PA, T. 183/41/A5498 (fiche 7141).

14. "Reisebericht unseres Vertrauensmannes," June 26, 1916, forwarded by Rössler to Berlin, June 29, 1916, PA, T. 183/43/A18552 (fiche 7148). This report is reprinted in Kaiser, *At the Crossroads of Der Zor*, pp. 63–66.

15. Bernau to Jackson, September 10, 1916, in Sarafian, *United States Official Documents on the Armenian Genocide*, vol. 1, pp. 131–32.

16. Ibid.; Rössler to Berlin, July 29, 1916, PA, T. 183/44/A21969 (fiche 7151).

17. Rössler to Berlin, February 14, 1917, T. 183/46/A8613 (fiche 7163).

18. Jackson to Morgenthau, February 8, 1916, in Sarafian, *United States Official Documents on the Armenian Genocide*, vol. 1, p. 113.

19. Report of an eyewitness in the Armenian newspaper *Arew*, August 21 and 25, 1916, PA, T. 183/45/A30202 (fiche 7156).

20. Bernau to Jackson, September 10, 1916, in Sarafian, *United States Official Documents on the Armenian Genocide*, vol. 1, pp. 132–33.

21. Hratch A. Tarbassian, *Erzurum (Garin): Its Armenian History and Traditions*, p. 242.

22. Rössler to Berlin, February 14, 1917, PA, T. 183/46/A8613 (fiche 7163).

23. Künzler, *Im Lande des Blutes und der Tränen*, p. 82.

24. Rössler to Berlin, May 2, 1917, PA, T. 183/47/A16719 (fiche 7165).

25. Künzler, *Im Lande des Blutes und der Tränen*, p. 86; Künzler report of December 9, 1917, PA, Botsch. K./102 (fiche 7225).

26. Jackson to Morgenthau, February 8, 1916, September 10, 1916, and summary report of March 4, 1918, in Sarafian, *United States Official Documents on the Armenian Genocide*, vol. 1, pp. 113, 134, 148.

27. Rössler to Berlin, March 20, 1916, PA, Botsch. K./99 (fiche 7216); Kaiser, *At the Crossroads of Der Zor*, p. 59.

28. Joseph Kiera, *Ins Land des Euphrat und Tigris: Kriegserinnerungen*, p. 228.

29. Kévorkian, *L'Extermination des déportés arméniens ottomans dans les camps de concentration de Syrie-Mésopotamie*, vol. 2, p. 224.

30. Jackson summary report of March 4, 1918, in Sarafian, *United States Official Documents on the Armenian Genocide*, vol. 1, p. 148.

31. Morgenthau diary, September 26, 1915, LC, reel 5.

32. Rössler to Berlin, July 31, 1915, PA, T. 183/38/A24524 (fiche 7124).

33. Rössler to Berlin, November 11, 1915, PA, T 183/40/A35047 (fiche 7135).

34. Rössler to Andreas Vischer, Basel, April 12, 1916, PA, Botsch. K/100 (fiche 7219).

35. Rössler to Berlin, April 27, 1916, PA, T. 183/42/A12911 (fiche 7145).

36. Report of Sister Rohner, June 26, 1916, in Rössler to Berlin, June 29, 1916, PA, T. 183/43/A18552 (fiche 7148).

37. Kévorkian, *L'Extermination des déportés arméniens ottomans dans les camps de concentration de Syrie-Mésopotamie,* pp. 40, 44.

38. Quoted from the Ministry of Interior files by Gürün, *The Armenian File,* p. 212.

39. Rössler to Berlin, July 29, 1916, PA, T. 183/44/A. 21969.

40. Kévorkian, *L'Extermination des déportés arméniens ottomans dans les camps de concentration de Syrie-Mésopotamie,* pp. 176, 180, 185; Garabed Kapikian, *Yeghernabadoum,* trans. Aris Sevag, p. 61.

41. Jackson summary report of March 4, 1918, in Sarafian, *United States Official Documents on the Armenian Genocide,* vol. 1, p. 149.

42. Report of Lieutenant Bünte, May 11, 1917, in Rössler to Berlin, May 15, 1917, PA, T. 183/47/A18747 (fiche 7166).

43. Rössler to Berlin, November 5, 1916, PA, T. 183/45/A31831 (fiche 7157).

44. Ludwig Schraudenbach, *MUHAREBE {War}: Der erlebte Roman eines deutschen Führers im Osmanischen Heere, 1916/17,* p. 352; Dadrian, *German Responsibility,* p. 195 (n. 179).

45. Ranzi to Vienna, September 24, 1915, in Ohandjanian, *Österreich-Armenien,* vol. 6, pp. 4741–43.

46. Ranzi to Vienna, February 15, 1916, in ibid., vol. 7, pp. 5019–21.

47. Manouk Chakalian, *Journey for Freedom (Armenian Massacres, Deportation),* p. 37.

48. Wiegand, *Halbmond im letzten Viertel,* p. 220.

49. Hardegg to Berlin, May 30, 1916, PA, T. 183/43/A16612 (fiche 7147).

50. Ranzi to Vienna, August 4, 1916 in Ohandjanian, *Österreich-Armenien,* vol. 7, pp. 5177–79; Hardegg to embassy, June 30, 1916, PA, Botsch. K./173 (fiche 7263).

51. Hardegg to Berlin, March 23, 1917, in Gust, "Revidierte Ausgabe der von Johannes Lepsius 1919 unter dem Titel 'Deutschland und Armenien' herausgegebenen Sammlung diplomatischer Aktenstücke," pp. 305–6.

52. Maud Mandel, book review [of Kévorkian, *L'Extermination des déportés arméniens ottomans dans les camps de concentration de Syrie-Mésopotamie*], *Armenian Forum* 1, no. 3 (Autumn 1998): 81.

Chapter 12. WHO WERE THE PERPETRATORS OF THE MASSACRES?

1. Cf. Sureya Bedr Khan, *The Case of Kurdistan against Turkey,* pp. 33–34.

2. Walter Guinness Moyne, *Impressions of Armenia,* p. 7.

3. Zürcher, "Between Death and Desertion," p. 246.

4. McCarthy, *Death and Exile,* p. 195.

5. The words are those of the Kurdish historian Kamal Madhar Ahmad in his *Kurdistan during the First World War,* p. 55. See also Arshak Safrastian, *Kurds and Kurdistan,* p. 74; Robert Olson, *The Emergence of Kurdish Nationalism and the Sheikh Said Rebellion, 1880–1925,* pp. 10–11; Hamit Bozarslan, "Les relations kurdo-arméniennes 1894–1966," in *Die Armenische Frage und die Schweiz (1896–1923),* ed. Hans-Lukas Kieser, p. 334.

6. Martin van Bruinessen, *Agha, Shaikh and State: The Social and Political Structure of Kurdistan,* p. 189.

7. Ahmad, *Kurdistan during the First World War,* p. 157; Hamit Bozarslan, "Histoire des relations kurdo-arméniennes," in *Kurdistan und Europa: Einblicke in die Kurdische Geschichte des 19. und 20. Jahrhunderts,* ed. Hans-Lukas Kieser, p. 165.

8. Jacobsen, *Diaries of a Danish Missionary,* p. 136.

9. The text of this memorandum is reprinted in Mukhitarian, *An Account of the Glorious Struggle of Van-Vasbouragan,* pp. 11–16.

10. Ibid., p. 3. See also Hilmar Kaiser, "'A Scene from the Inferno': The Armenians of Erzurum and the Genocide, 1915–1916," in *Der Völkermord an den Armeniern und die Shoah,* edited by Hans-Lukas Kieser and Dominik J. Schaller, p. 164.

11. Ahmad, *Kurdistan during the First World War,* pp. 156, 166.

12. Hepworth, *Through Armenia on Horseback,* p. 226.

13. Glen W. Swanson, "The Ottoman Police," *Journal of Contemporary History* 7, nos. 1–2 (January–April 1972): 257.

14. Report of Col. Claude Hawker, November 1, 1913, FO 371/1773/50846.

15. Riggs, *Days of Tragedy in Armenia,* pp. 127–28.

16. Victor Pietschmann, *Durch kurdische Berge und armenische Städte: Tagebuch der österreichischen Armenierexpedition 1914,* p. 251.

17. Morgenthau diary, November 12, 1915, LC, reel 5.

18. Quoted in Chaliand and Ternon, *The Armenians,* p. 96.

19. J. W. Ernst Sommer, *Die Wahrheit über die Leiden des armenischen Volkes in der Türkei während des ersten Weltkrieges* (Frankfurt/Main, 1919), p. 6, quoted in Walker, "World War I and the Armenian Genocide," p. 246.

20. Morgenthau to Washington, November 18, 1915, NA, RG 59, 867.00/798 (M 353, roll 6, fr. 561).

21. Davis to Morgenthau, December 30, 1915, in Sarafian, *United States Official Documents on the Armenian Genocide,* vol. 3, p. 28.

22. Davis summary report of February 9, 1918, in ibid., p. 86.

23. Faiz el-Ghassein, *Die Türkenherrschaft und Armeniens Schmerzensschrei,* pp. 80–81.

24. Captanian, *1915: Der Völkermord an den Armeniern,* p. 86.

25. Ahmad, *Kurdistan during the First World War,* p. 155.

26. Hoffmann to embassy, November 8, 1915, PA, T. 183/41/A2889 (fiche 7139).

27. Jackson to Morgenthau, August 3, 1915, in Sarafian, *United States Official Documents on the Armenian Genocide,* vol. 1, p. 39.

28. Kemal H. Karpat, *Ottoman Population 1830–1914: Demographic and Social Characteristics,* p. 27.

29. Rössler to Berlin, July 27, 1915, PA, T. 183/38/A23991 (fiche 7124).

30. Rössler to Wangenheim, June 29, 1915, PA, Botsch. K./169 (fiche 7249).

31. Stange to the German military mission, Constantinople, August 23, 1915, PA, Botsch. K./170 (fiche 7254).

32. Scheubner-Richter to Berlin, August 5, 1915, PA, T. 83/39/A28584 (fiche 7129).

33. Davis to Morgenthau, July 24, 1915, in Sarafian, *United States Official Documents on the Armenian Genocide,* vol. 3, p. 18.

34. Ibid., p. 26.

35. Statement of Dr. Ida S. Stapleton, in Barton, *"Turkish Atrocities,"* p. 24.

36. Manuelian, *Unending Journey,* p. 36.

37. FO 371/6500/3557. See also Hans-Lukas Kieser, "Dr. Mehmed Reshid (1873–1919): A Political Doctor," in *Der Völkermord an den Armeniern und die Shoah,* ed. Kieser and Schaller, p. 264.

38. Morgenthau, *Ambassador Morgenthau's Story,* p. 315.

39. Toynbee, *The Western Question in Greece and Turkey,* pp. 278–79.

40. James L. Gelvin, *Divided Loyalties: Nationalism and Mass Politics in Syria at the Close of the Empire,* p. 82.

41. J. H. Monahan to ambassador, Constantinople, October 14, 1914, FO 371/21461/70602.

42. Order no. 8682, quoted in Gürün, *The Armenian File,* p. 205. Zürcher ("Ottoman Labour Battalions in World War I," in *Der Völkermord an den Armeniern und die Shoah,* ed. Kieser and Schaller, p. 192) considers February 25 the date of the original order, but this ignores the phrase "announce again."

43. This order was discovered by British troops. It can be found in FO 371/9158/E5523.

44. Shiroyan, *Smiling through the Tears,* p. 176.

45. Quoted from the Central Zionist Archives by Auron, *The Banality of Indifference,* p. 339.

46. Germany, Reichskriegsministerium, *Sanitätsbericht über das deutsche Heer (Deutsches Feld- und Besatzungsheer) im Weltkriege 1914/18,* p.802.

47. Nogales, *Four Years beneath the Crescent,* p. 177.

48. Rössler to Berlin, April 27, 1916, PA, T. 183/42/A12911 (fiche 7145).

49. Eckart, "Meine Erlebnisse in Urfa," pp. 122–26; Künzler, *Im Lande des Blutes und der Tränen,* pp. 17–21; Glockler, *Interned in Turkey,* p. 33.

50. Rössler to embassy, September 3, 1915, PA, Botsch. K./170 (fiche 7253).

51. Davis summary report of February 9, 1918, in Sarafian, *United States Official Documents on the Armenian Genocide,* vol. 3, p. 98.

52. Heizer to Morgenthau, July 28, 1915, in ibid., vol. 2, p. 28.

53. Ernst von Kwiatkowski to Vienna, September 4, 1915, in Ohandjanian, *Österreich-Armenien,* vol. 6, p. 4724.

54. The recollections of survivors, collected by Aram Andonian, are printed in Raymond H. Kévorkian, "Recueil de témoignages sur l'extermination des *amele tabouri* ou bataillons de soldats-ouvriers arméniens de l'armée ottomane pendant la première guerre mondiale," *Revue d'Histoire Arménienne Contemporaine* 1 (1995).

55. Christoffel, *Zwischen Saat und Ernte,* p. 112.

56. Erickson, *Ordered to Die,* p. 104.

57. Künzler, *Köbi: Vater der Armenier,* p. 151.

58. Atamian, *The Armenian Community,* p. 263.

59. Becker, *Äskulap zwischen Reichsadler und Halbmond,* p. 190.

60. The text of this order can be found in FO 371/9158/E5523.

61. Kaiser, "The Baghdad Railway and the Armenian Genocide, 1915–1916," p. 94.

62. Rössler to embassy, July 10, 1916, PA, Botsch. K. 170/101 (fiche 7221).

63. Künzler, *Im Lande des Blutes und der Tränen,* pp. 76–77.

64. Erickson, "The Turkish Official Military Histories of the First World War," p. 198 (n. 7).

65. Ökte, *Ottoman Archives,* p. 74.

66. Bergfeld to embassy, February 25, 1914, PA, Botsch. K./167 (fiche 7242).

67. Hohenlohe to Berlin, September 25, 1915, PA, T. 183/39/A28578 (fiche 7129).

68. H. Philip to Washington, September 1, 1916, NA, RG 59, 867.4016/296 (M 353, roll 45, fr. 254-59).

69. Liman von Sanders, *Five Years in Turkey,* p. 157.

Chapter 13. THE NUMBER OF VICTIMS

1. Meir Zamir, "Population Statistics of the Ottoman Empire in 1914 and 1919," *Middle Eastern Studies* 17 (1981): 86.

2. Karpat, *Ottoman Population 1830–1914,* p. 10.

3. Marashlian, *Politics and Demography,* p. 48.

4. Zamir, "Population Statistics of the Ottoman Empire," p. 87.

5. McCarthy, *Muslims and Minorities,* p. 51.

6. Dennis R. Papazian, *What Every Armenian Should Know...,* p. 29.

7. See, for example, Gürün, *The Armenian File,* p. 96; Shaw and Shaw, *History of the Ottoman Empire and Modern Turkey,* p. 337.

8. As given in Shaw and Shaw, *History of the Ottoman Empire and Modern Turkey,* p. 337.

9. The figure for Anatolia in McCarthy, *Muslims and Minorities,* p. 110, is 1,493,276. The figure used here is the one adjusted for the empire by Marashlian, *Politics and Demography,* p. 58.

10. The patriarchate figures are 1,847,900 for 1910 and 2,100,000 for 1912. I have used the average of these two statistics.

11. Marashlian, *Politics and Demography,* p. 36.

12. Sarkis Karajian, "An Inquiry into the Statistics of the Turkish Genocide of the Armenians, 1915–1918," *Armenian Review* 25 (Winter 1972): 17.

13. Great Britain, Parliament, *The Treatment of Armenians in the Ottoman Empire,* p. 664.

14. Charles J. F. Dowsett, "Armenia," in *Encyclopaedia Britannica* (1967 ed.), vol. 2, p. 421.

15. Hovannisian, *Armenia on the Road to Independence,* p. 37.

16. Yapp, *The Making of the Modern Near East,* p. 197;. Zürcher, *Turkey: A Modern History,* p. 119.

17. U.S. Congress, Senate, *Conditions in the Near East: Report of the American Military Mission to Armenia,* appendix, p. 7.

18. "Memorandum on Relief Work That May Arise Out of an Armistice with Turkey," October 30, 1918, FO 371/4363/PID 490.

19. Sonyel, "Turco-Armenian Relations and British Propaganda during the First World War," p. 429.

20. Kévorkian, *L'Extermination des déportés arméniens ottomans dans les camps de concentration de Syrie-Mésopotamie,* p. 14.

21. Nubar to Foreign Minister Gout, December 11, 1918, reprinted from the archive of the French Foreign Ministry in Simsir, *The Deportees of Malta,* p. 55.

22. Yusuf Halacoglu, *Facts on the Relocation of Armenians (1914–1918),* p. 104.

23. Khoren K. Davidson, *Odyssey of an Armenian of Zeitoun,* p. 127.

24. Boghos Nubar, "The Armenian Question and the Peace Congress," May 24, 1917, forwarded to the U.S. secretary of state on October 25, 1917, NA, RG 59, 867.4016/364 (M 353, roll 46, fr. 312).

25. Boghos Nubar to the French foreign minister, M. Gout, of December 11, 1918, reprinted in Simsir, *The Deportees of Malta,* p. 55.

26. Albert Howe Lybyer, "Turkey under the Armistice," *Journal of International Relations* 12 (1922): 458.

27. James Barton, *Story of Near East Relief (1915–1930): An Interpretation,* p. 82.

28. William Linn Westermann, "The Armenian Problem and the Disruption of Turkey," in *What Really Happened at Paris: The Story of the Peace Conference, 1918–1919, by American Delegates,* ed. Edward Mandell House and Charles Seymour, p. 202.

29. Barton to Col. House, April 9, 1919, NA, RG 59, 867.00/153 (M 820, roll 537, fr. 204).

30. Kerr, *The Lions of Marash*, p. 36.

31. George R. Montgomery, "The Non-Arab Portion of the Ottoman Empire," NA, RG 59, 867.00/31 (M 820, roll 536, fr. 109).

32. Georg Mesrop, *L'Arménie du point de vue géographique, historique, éthnographique, statistique et culturel*, p. 81.

33. Johannes Lepsius, "Die Überlebenden," *Der Orient* 3, nos. 10–11 (1921): 131.

34. Azarya, *The Armenian Quarter of Jerusalem*, p. 74.

35. Richard G. Hovannisian, "The Ebb and Flow of the Armenian Minority in the Arab Middle East," *Middle East Journal* 28 (1974): 20.

36. Karajian, "An Inquiry into the Statistics of the Turkish Genocide," pp. 22–23.

37. Halacoglu, *Facts on the Relocation*, p. 104.

38. Gürün, *The Armenian File*, p. 219.

39. Sonyel, *The Ottoman Armenians*, p. 301.

40. Ökte, *Ottoman Archives*, p. 74.

41. Great Britain, Parliament, *The Treatment of Armenians in the Ottoman Empire*, p. 651.

42. McCarthy and McCarthy, *Turks and Armenians*, p. 65.

43. Kévorkian, *L'Extermination des déportés arméniens ottomans dans les camps de concentration de Syrie-Mésopotamie*, p. 61.

44. Youssef Courbage and Philippe Fargues, *Christians and Jews under Islam*, trans. Judy Mabro, p. 111.

45. Udo Steinbach, *Die Türkei im 20. Jahrhundert: Schwieriger Partner Europas*, p. 50.

46. Zürcher, *Turkey: A Modern History*, p. 120.

47. Morgenthau, *Ambassador Morgenthau's Story*, p. 322.

48. Suny, "Empire and Nation," p. 50.

49. Declaration of Ministry of the Interior, May 15, 1919, in Akcam, *Armenien und der Völkermord*, p. 76. The well-known Turkish historian Hikmet Bayur is said to have accepted this figure as correct (ibid.).

50. Lepsius, *Deutschland und Armenien*, p. lxiii.

51. Ternon, *The Armenians*, p. 291, n. 32.

52. Dadrian, *Key Elements in the Turkish Denial of the Armenian Genocide*, p. 20.

53. Haigazn K. Kazarian, "The Turkish Genocide of the Armenians: A Premeditated and Official Assault," *Armenian Review* 30 (1977): 14.

54. Karajian, "An Inquiry into the Statistics of the Turkish Genocide," p. 6.

55. Ara Sarafian, "The Absorption of Armenian Women and Children into Muslim Households as a Structural Component of the Armenian Genocide," in *In God's Name: Genocide and Religion in the Twentieth Century*, ed. Omer Bartov and Phyllis Mack, p. 211.

56. McCarthy, *Death and Exile*, p. 230.

Chapter 14. CONCLUSION: THE QUESTION OF PREMEDITATION

1. Dadrian, "The Documentation of the World War I Armenian Massacres in the Proceedings of the Turkish Military Tribunal," p. 564.

2. Dadrian, "The Armenian Genocide and the Pitfalls of a 'Balanced' Analysis," p. 129.

3. Sarafian, "The Archival Trail," p. 51.

4. Hacobian, *Armenian and the War,* pp. 39, 44–45.

5. Toynbee, *Armenian Atrocities,* p. 69.

6. Chaliand and Ternon, *The Armenians,* p. 18.

7. Leo Kuper, "The Concept of Genocide and Its Applicability to the Turkish Massacres of Armenians in 1915–16," in *A Crime of Silence,* ed. Permanent People's Tribunal, p. 188.

8. Christopher J. Walker, "British Sources on the Armenian Massacres, 1915–1916," in *A Crime of Silence,* ed. Permanent People's Tribunal, pp. 54–55, and "World War I and the Armenian Genocide," in *The Armenian People from Ancient to Modern Times,* ed. Hovannisian, p. 272.

9. Efraim Karsh and Inari Karsh, *Empires of the Sand: The Struggle for Mastery in the Middle East, 1798–1923,* pp. 153–54.

10. Jackson to Morgenthau, June 5, 1915, in Sarafian, *United States Official Documents on the Armenian Genocide,* vol. 1, pp. 19–20.

11. Morgenthau to Washington, August 11, 1915, in U.S. Department of State, *Papers Relating to the Foreign Relations of the United States, 1915: Supplement,* p. 986.

12. Wangenheim to Berlin, July 7, 1915, PA, T. 183/37/A21257 (fiche 7122).

13. Sonyel, *The Ottoman Armenians,* p. 300.

14. Simsir, *The Deportees of Malta,* p. 40.

15. Shaw and Shaw, "The Authors Respond," p. 399.

16. Ökte, *Ottoman Archives,* p. 357.

17. Christian Gerlach, "Nationsbildung im Krieg: Wirtschaftliche Faktoren bei der Vernichtung der Armenier und beim Mord an den ungarischen Juden," in *Der Völkermord an den Armeniern und die Shoah,* ed. Kieser and Schaller, pp. 358–59.

18. Suny, "Empire and Nation," pp. 46, 51, and "Reply to My Critics," p. 134. See also his *Armenia in the Twentieth Century,* pp. 16–18.

19. Kaiser, "'A Scene from the Inferno,'" p. 172; Donald Bloxham, "The Armenian Genocide of 1915–1916: Cumulative Radicalization and the Development of a Destruction Policy," *Past and Present* 181 (2003): 143.

20. Yalman, *Turkey in My Time,* p. 219.

21. Andrew Mango, "Remembering the Minorities," *Middle Eastern Studies* 21, no. 4 (October 1985): 129.

22. Toynbee letter of March 16, 1966, quoted in Lillian Etmekjian, "The Evidence for the Armenian Genocide in the Writings of Two Prominent Turks," *Armenian Review* 35 (1982): 184.

23. Willis, *Prologue to Nuremberg,* p. 24.

24. McCarthy and McCarthy, *Turks and Armenians,* p. 53.

25. Nathan to Morgenthau, September 27, 1915, in Sarafian, *United States Official Documents on the Armenian Genocide,* vol. 2, pp. 93–94.

26. Rössler to Berlin, June 25, 1914, PA, T. 134/33/A13394 (R13194).

27. Rössler to Constantinople, September 14, 1915, PA, Botsch. K./170/A53a (fiche 7253), and Rössler to Berlin, December 20, 1915, PA, T. 183/40/A468 (fiche 7137).

28. Kate E. Ainslee to James Barton, July 6, 1915, in Great Britain, Parliament, *The Treatment of Armenians in the Ottoman Empire,* p. 477.

29. George Abel Schreiner, *The Craft Sinister: A Diplomatic-Political History of the Great War and Its Causes,* pp. 124–25.

30. The memoir was published in Istanbul in 1992. It is discussed by Ronald Grigor Suny, "Religion, Ethnicity, and Nationalism: Armenians, Turks, and the End of the Ottoman Empire," in *In God's Name,* ed. Bartov and Mack, p. 54.

31. Von Hoesch, "Aufzeichnung über die armenische Frage," n.d. [1916], PA, T.183/44/A25749 (fiches 7153–54).

32. Erickson, *Ordered to Die,* p. 103.

33. Rössler to Berlin, July 27, 1915, PA, T. 183/38/A23991 (fiche 7124).

34. Morgenthau to Washington, November 18, 1915, NA, RG 59, 867.00/798 (M 353, roll 6, fr. 561).

35. Dyer, "Letter to the Editor," *Middle Eastern Studies* 9 (1973): 130, and "Turkish 'Falsifiers' and Armenian 'Deceivers,'" p. 107.

Epilogue: THE POLITICIZATION OF HISTORY

1. For further details, see Francis P. Hyland, *Armenian Terrorism,* pp. 21–22.

2. Chaliand and Ternon, *The Armenians,* pp. 6–7; Gunter, *"Pursuing the Just Cause of Their People."*

3. Suny, *Looking toward Ararat,* p. 228.

4. Simon Payaslian, "After Recognition," *Armenian Forum* 2, no. 3 (Autumn 1999): 36–41.

5. Andrew Corsun, "Armenian Terrorism: A Profile," *Department of State Bulletin* 82 (August 1982): 35, cited by Vigen Guroian, "The Politics and Morality of Genocide," in *The Armenian Genocide,* ed. Hovannisian, p. 316.

6. Cf. Guroian, "The Politics and Morality of Genocide," pp. 316–17.

7. Ibid., p. 325. See also Vryonis, *The Turkish State and History,* pp. 100–102.

8. "Attention Members of the U.S. House of Representatives," *New York Times,* May 19, 1985.

9. Richard Falk, "Foreword" to "The Armenian Genocide in Official Turkish Records: Collected Essays by Vahakn N. Dadrian," *Journal of Political and Military Sociology* 22, no. 1 (Summer 1994): i.

10. Akcam, *Armenien und der Völkermord,* p. 12.

11. This is the suggestion of Guroian, "The Politics and Morality of Genocide," p. 335.

12. Philip Kennikot in the *Washington Post,* November 24, 2002.

13. Roger R. Trask, *The United States Response to Turkish Nationalism and Reform, 1914–1939,* p. 91.

14. Edward T. Linenthal, *Preserving Memory: The Struggle to Create America's Holocaust Museum,* pp. 230–34.

15. Israel W. Charny, "The Turks, Armenians and the Jews," in *Book of the International Conference on the Holocaust and Genocide,* Book 1: *The Conference Program and Crisis,* pp. 269–315; Gunter, *"Pursuing the Just Cause of Their People,"* p. 140.

16. "Riss im türkisch-israelitischen Verhältnis," *Neue Zürcher Zeitung,* May 17, 2000. For a detailed discussion of this episode, see Yair Auron, *The Banality of Denial: Israel and the Armenian Genocide,* ch. 7.

17. *New York Times,* January 24, 2001.

18. "European Parliament Accuses Turkey of Genocide," *Washington Post,* November 16, 2000; "Turkey: New Genocide Charges," *New York Times,* November 16, 2000.

19. Salahi R. Sonyel, "Turco-Armenian Relations in the Context of the Jewish Holocaust," *Belleten* 54 (1990): 769–70.

20. Joachim Hoffmann, *Die Ostlegionen 1941–1943: Turkotartaren, Kaukasier und Wolgafinnen im deutschen Heer,* pp. 39, 76; Hans Werner Neulen, *An deutscher Seite: Internationale Freiwillige von Wehrmacht und Waffen-SS,* pp. 324–32.

21. Dadrian, "The Complicity of the Party, the Government, and the Military," p. 31.

22. In a 1931 interview with the newspaper editor Richard Breiting, Hitler similarly linked the Armenian deportations to his plan to colonize the East. See Edouard Calic, *Unmasked: Two Confidential Interviews with Hitler in 1931,* trans. Richard Barry, p. 81.

23. Heath W. Lowry, "The United States Congress and Adolf Hitler on the Armenians," *Political Communication and Persuasion* 3 (1985): 123.

24. Winfried Baumgart, "Zur Ansprache Hitlers vor den Führern der Wehrmacht am 22. August 1939: Eine quellenkritische Untersuchung," *Vierteljahrshefte für Zeitgeschichte* 16 (1968): 139.

25. For the argument that the quotation is authentic and should have been accepted at Nuremberg, see Kevork B. Bardakjian, *Hitler and the Armenian Genocide,* p. 24.

26. Bernard Lewis, *The Emergence of Modern Turkey,* p. 350.

27. The third edition was published in New York by Oxford University Press in 2002.

28. Quoted in Yves Ternon, "Freedom and Responsibility of the Historian: The 'Lewis Affair,'" in *Remembrance and Denial,* ed. Hovannisian, pp. 243–44.

29. The court's verdict is summarized in Marc Nichanian, "The Truth of the Facts: About the New Revisionism," in *Remembrance and Denial,* ed. Hovannisian, p. 253.

30. Ternon, "Freedom and Responsibility of the Historian," p. 245.

31. *Washington Post,* September 9, 1995, quoted in Rouben Paul Adalian, "The Ramifications in the United States of the 1995 French Court Decision on the Denial of the Armenian Genocide and Princeton University," *Revue du Monde Arménien Moderne et Contemporaine* 3 (1997): 105.

32. Ternon, "Freedom and Responsibility of the Historian," pp. 240, 242.

33. Henry C. Theriault, "Denial and Free Speech: The Case of the Armenian Genocide," in *Looking Backward, Moving Forward: Confronting the Armenian Genocide,* edited by Richard G. Hovannisian, pp. 231–61.

34. See the lengthy discussion on the pro-Turkish French website www.tetede-turc.com.

35. *Chronicle of Higher Education,* February 2, 1996.

36. James H. Tashjian, "On a 'Statement' Condemning the Armenian Genocide of 1915–18 Attributed in Error to Mustafa Kemal, Later 'The Atatürk,'" *Armenian Review* 35 (1982): 237.

37. Gunter, "Why Do the Turks Deny They Committed Genocide against the Armenians?" p. 491.

38. News release. See also Gerard J. Libaridian, *Modern Armenia: People, Nation, State,* pp. 278–79.

39. Cf. Göcek, "Reconstructing the Turkish Historiography," pp. 223–30.

40. Bruno Blaser, "Von der schweren Last der Geschichte: Versuch eines Armenisch-Türkischen Dialog," *Hilfsbundbote* (Bad Homburg) 103, no. 2 (2001): 10.

41. Bill Broadway, "Armenians' Bittersweet Pilgrimage," *Washington Post,* June 23, 2001.

42. Mehmet Necef, "The Turkish Media Debate on the Armenian Massacres," in *Genocide: Cases, Comparisons, and Contemporary Debates,* edited by Steven L. B. Jensen, pp. 232–40.

43. Douglas Frantz, "Unofficial Commission Acts to Ease Turkish-Armenian Enmity," *New York Times,* July 10, 2001.

44. Paul Glastris, "Armenia's History, Turkey's Dilemma," *Washington Post,* March 11, 2001.

45. Sebouh Aslanian, "'The Treason of the Intellectuals': Reflections on the Uses of Revisionism and Nationalism in Armenian Historiography," *Armenian Forum* 2, no. 4 (February 2003): 37.

46. A somewhat optimistic appraisal of the work of the commission is given by David L. Phillips in *Unsilencing the Past: Track Two Diplomacy and Turkish-Armenian Reconciliation.*

47. *Hürriyet,* October 18, 2000, cited by Necef, "The Turkish Media Debate," p. 236. Other such views are quoted on p. 249.

48. Sina Aksin, "A General Appraisal of the Armenian Issue," *Turkish Review Quarterly Digest* 1, no. 4 (Summer 1986): 53. (This digest is published by the Directorate General of Press and Information, Ankara.)

49. Deringil, "In Search of a Way Forward," pp. 70–71. See also Fikret Adanir, "Die armenische Frage und der Völkermord an den Armeniern im Osmanischen Reich: Betroffenheit im Reflex nationalistischer Geschichtsschreibung," in *Erlebnis—Gedächtnis—Sinn: Authentische und konstruierte Erinnerung,* ed. Hanno Loewy and Bernhard Moltmann, p. 256; and Taner Akcam, *Dialogue across an International Divide: Essays towards a Turkish-Armenian Dialogue.*

50. Suny, "Reply to My Critics," p. 136.

Works Cited

Unpublished Sources

Library of Congress, Manuscript Collection

National Archives, College Park, MD

Politisches Archiv des Auswärtigen Amtes, Berlin

Public Record Office, London

Published Sources

COLLECTIONS OF DOCUMENTS

Adalian, Rouben Paul, ed. *The Armenian Genocide in the United States Archives,*
1915–1918 (microfiche). Alexandria, VA: Chadwyck-Healey, 1994.

Beylerian, Arthur, comp. *Les grandes puissances, l'Empire Ottoman, et les Arméniens*
dans les archives françaises (1914–1918). Paris: Université de Paris I, 1983.

Ghazarian, Vatche, ed. and trans. *Boghos Nubar's Papers and the Armenian Question*
1915–1918: Documents. Waltham, MA: Mayreni, 1996.

Great Britain. Foreign Office. *British Documents on the Origin of the War 1898–1914.*
Vol. 9, part 1. London: HMSO, 1933.

———. *Documents on British Foreign Policy 1919–1939.* First series, vol. 4. London:
HMSO, 1952. Vol. 13. London: HMSO, 1963.

Great Britain. House of Commons. *Sessional Papers (Commons).* Vol. 95 (1896).
Turkey nos. 1, 3, 6, 8.

Great Britain. Parliament. *The Treatment of Armenians in the Ottoman Empire:*
Documents Presented to Viscount Grey of Fallodon, Secretary of State for Foreign
Affairs (1916). Reprinted Astoria, NY: J. C. and A. L. Fawcett, 1990.

Great Britain. Parliamentary Papers. *Key to Names of Persons and Places Withheld*
from Publication in "The Treatment of Armenians in the Ottoman Empire, 1915–16."
Miscellaneous, No. 31 (1916).

Gust, Wolfgang, ed. "Revidierte Ausgabe der von Johannes Lepsius 1919 unter
dem Titel 'Deutschland und Armenien' herausgegebenen Sammlung diplomatischer Aktenstücke." At http://home.t-online.de/home/wolfgang.gust/ehome.
htm, 1998.

Lepsius, Johannes, ed. *Deutschland und Armenien, 1914–1918: Sammlung diplomati-*
scher Aktenstücke. Potsdam: Tempelverlag, 1919.

Lepsius, Johannes, et al., eds. *Die grosse Politik der Europäischen Kabinette 1871–1914: Sammlung der diplomatischen Akten des Auswärtigen Amtes.* Vols. 9, 10, 12. Berlin: Deutsche Verlagsgesellschaft für Politik und Geschichte, 1927.

Ohandjanian, Artem, comp. *Österreich-Armenien, 1872–1936: Faksimilesammlung diplomatischer Aktenstücke.* 2nd rev. ed. 12 vols. Vienna: Ohandjanian Selbstverlag, 1995.

Ökte, Ertugrul Zekai, ed. *Ottoman Archives, Yildiz Collection: The Armenian Question, Talori Incidents.* Istanbul: Historical Research Foundation, 1989.

Pokrowski, M. N., ed. *Die internationalen Beziehungen im Zeitalter des Imperialismus: Dokumente aus den Archiven der Zarischen und der Provisorischen Regierung.* Translated by Erich Boehme. 2nd series. Vol. 7. Berlin: Reimar Hobbing, 1935.

Sarafian, Ara, comp. *United States Official Documents on the Armenian Genocide.* 3 vols. Watertown, MA: Armenian Review, 1993–95.

Simsir, Bilal N., ed. *British Documents on Ottoman Armenians.* 4 vols. Ankara: Türk Tarih Kurumu Basivemi, 1989–90.

———, ed. *Documents diplomatiques Ottomans: Affaires arméniens.* Vol. 1: 1886–93. Ankara: Société d'Histoire, 1985.

Turkey, Prime Ministry. *Documents on Ottoman Armenians.* 2 vols. Ankara: Directorate General of Press and Information, 1982–83.

U.S. Department of State. *Papers Relating to the Foreign Relations of the United States, 1895, Part 2.* Washington, DC: GPO, 1896.

———. *Papers Relating to the Foreign Relations of the United States, 1914: Supplement, The World War.* Washington, DC: GPO, 1928.

———. *Papers Relating to the Foreign Relations of the United States, 1915: Supplement.* Washington, DC: GPO, 1928.

Other Sources

Adalian, Rouben Paul. "The Ramifications in the United States of the 1995 French Court Decision on the Denial of the Armenian Genocide and Princeton University." *Revue du Monde Arménien Moderne et Contemporaine* 3 (1997): 99–122.

Adanir, Fikret. "Die armenische Frage und der Völkermord an den Armeniern im Osmanischen Reich: Betroffenheit im Reflex nationalistischer Geschichtsschreibung." In *Erlebnis—Gedächtnis—Sinn: Authentische und konstruierte Erinnerung,* edited by Hanno Loewy and Bernhard Moltmann, pp. 237–63. Frankfurt/M.: Campus, 1996.

Ahmad, Feroz. "Unionist Relations with the Greek, Armenian, and Jewish Communities of the Ottoman Empire, 1908–1914." In *Christians and Jews in the Ottoman Empire: The Functioning of a Plural Society,* edited by Benjamin Braude and Bernard Lewis, pp. 401–34. New York: Holmes and Meier, 1982.

———. *The Young Turks: The Committee of Union and Progress in Turkish Politics 1908–1914.* Oxford: Clarendon Press, 1969.

Ahmad, Kamal Madhar. *Kurdistan during the First World War.* Trans. Ali Maher Ibrahim. London: Saqui Books, 1994.

Ajay, Nicholas Z. "Political Intrigue and Suppression in Lebanon during World War I." *International Journal of Middle East Studies* 5 (1974): 140–60.

Akarli, Engin Deniz. "Particularities of History: A Response to Ronald Grigor Suny." *Armenian Forum* 1, no. 2 (Summer 1998): 53–64.

Akcam, Taner. *Armenien und der Völkermord: Die Istanbuler Prozesse und die türkische Nationalbewegung.* Hamburg: Hamburger Edition, 1996.

———. *Dialogue across an International Divide: Essays towards a Turkish-Armenian Dialogue.* Toronto: Zoryan Institute, 2001.

———. *From Empire to Republic: Turkish Nationalism and the Armenian Genocide.* London: Zed Books, 2004.

———, ed. "The Proceedings of the Turkish Military Tribunal as Published in *Takvim-i Vekayi, 1919–1920.*" Dearborn, MI: Armenian Research Center, 2001.

Aksin, Sina. "A General Appraisal of the Armenian Issue." *Turkish Review Quarterly Digest* 1, no. 4 (Summer 1986): 49–67.

Alexander, Edward. *A Crime of Vengeance: An Armenian Struggle for Justice.* New York: Free Press, 1991.

Allen, William Edmond D., and Paul Muratoff. *Caucasian Battlefields: A History of the Wars on the Turco-Caucasian Border, 1828–1921.* Cambridge: At the University Press, 1953.

Altug, Yilmaz, trans. *The Turkish Code of Criminal Procedure.* London: Sweet and Maxwell, 1962.

Andonian, Aram, comp. *The Memoirs of Naim Bey: Turkish Official Documents Relating to the Deportations and Massacres of Armenians.* Newton Square, PA: Armenian Historical Research Association, 1965.

Aprahamian, Souren. *From Van to Detroit: Surviving the Armenian Genocide.* Ann Arbor, MI: Gomidas Institute, 1993.

Argyll, George Douglas Campbell, Duke of. *Our Responsibilities for Turkey: Facts and Memories of Forty Years.* London: John Murray, 1896.

Armenian Revolutionary Federation. "A List of Those Responsible for the Massacres and Deportations of the Armenians." *Armenian Review* 35 (1982): 290–312, 438–49.

Armstrong, Harold. *Turkey in Travail: The Birth of a New Nation.* London: John Lane/Bodley Head, 1925.

Ash, Timothy Garton. "On the Frontier." *New York Review of Books,* November 7, 2002, p. 60.

Aslanian, Sebouh. "'The Treason of the Intellectuals': Reflections on the Uses of Revisionism and Nationalism in Armenian Historiography." *Armenian Forum* 2, no. 4 (February 2003): 1–38.

Aspirations et agissements révolutionnaires des comités arméniens avant et après la procla-mation de la Constitution Ottomane. Constantinople: n.p., 1917.

Assembly of Turkish American Associations. *Armenian Allegations: Myth and Reality, a Handbook of Facts and Documents*. Washington, DC: Assembly of Turkish American Associations, 1987.

―――. *Armenian Atrocities and Terrorism: Testimonies of Witnesses*. Washington, DC: Assembly of Turkish American Associations, 1997.

―――. *Setting the Record Straight on Armenian Propaganda against Turkey*. Washington, DC: Assembly of Turkish American Associations, 1982.

Astourian, Stephan H. "The Armenian Genocide: An Interpretation." *History Teacher* 23 (1990): 111–60.

―――. "Genocidal Process: Reflections on the Armeno-Turkish Polarization." In *The Armenian Genocide: History, Politics, Ethics*, edited by Richard G. Hovannisian, pp. 53–79. New York: St. Martin's Press, 1992.

Atamian, Sarkis. *The Armenian Community: The Historical Development of a Social and Ideological Conflict*. New York: Philosophical Library, 1955.

Ataöv, Türkkaya. *Death Caused by Disease in Relation to the Armenian Question*. Ankara: Sevinc Matbaasi, 1985.

Atkinson, Tacy. *"The German, the Turk and the Devil Made a Triple Alliance": Harpoot Diaries, 1908–1917*. Princeton, NJ: Gomidas Institute, 2000.

Auron, Yair. *The Banality of Denial: Israel and the Armenian Genocide*. New Brunswick, NJ: Transaction, 2003.

―――. *The Banality of Indifference: Zionism and the Armenian Genocide*. New Brunswick, NJ: Transaction, 2000.

Avakian, Lindy V. *The Cross and the Crescent*. 3rd ed. Fresno, CA: Golden West, 1998.

Azarya, Victor. *The Armenian Quarter of Jerusalem: Urban Life behind Monastery Walls*. Berkeley: University of California Press, 1984.

Balakian, Peter. *The Burning Tigris: The Armenian Genocide and America's Response*. New York: HarperCollins, 2003.

Barby, Henry. *Au pays de l'épouvante: L'Arménie martyre*. Paris: n.p., n.d.

Bardakjian, Kevork B. *Hitler and the Armenian Genocide*. Cambridge, MA: Zoryan Institute, 1985.

Barker, A. J. *The Neglected War: Mesopotamia 1914–1918*. London: Faber and Faber, 1967.

Barrows, John Otis. *In the Land of Ararat: A Sketch of the Life of Mrs. Elizabeth Freeman Barrows Ussher*. New York: Fleming H. Revelle, 1916.

Barton, James L., comp. *Story of Near East Relief (1915–1930): An Interpretation*. New York: Macmillan, 1930.

―――. *"Turkish Atrocities": Statements of American Missionaries on the Destruction of Christian Communities in Ottoman Turkey, 1915–1917*. Edited by Ara Sarafian. Ann Arbor, MI: Gomidas Institute, 1998.

Bartov, Omer, and Phyllis Mack, eds. *In God's Name: Genocide and Religion in the Twentieth Century*. New York: Berghahn Books, 2001.

Bass, Gary Jonathan. *Stay the Hand of Vengeance: The Politics of War Crimes Tribunals.* Princeton, NJ: Princeton University Press, 2000.

Baumgart, Winfried. "Zur Ansprache Hitlers vor den Führern der Wehrmacht am 22. August 1939: Eine quellenkritische Untersuchung." *Vierteljahrshefte für Zeitgeschichte* 16 (1968): 120–49. Also "Erwiderung." *Vierteljahrshefte für Zeitgeschichte* 19 (1971): 301–4.

Bayur, Yusuf Hikmet. *Türk Inkilabi Tarihi.* Vol. 3. Ankara: Tarih Kurumu, 1983.

Becker, Helmut. *Äskulap zwischen Reichsadler und Halbmond: Sanitätswesen und Seuchenbekämpfung im türkischen Reich während des ersten Weltkriegs.* Herzogenrath: Murken-Altrogge, 1990.

Bedoukian, Kerop. *The Urchin: An Armenian's Escape.* London: John Murray, 1978.

Bedr Khan, Sureya. *The Case of Kurdistan against Turkey.* Stockholm: Sara Publishing, 1995 (originally published in 1928).

Berkes, Niyazi. *The Development of Secularism in Turkey.* Montreal: McGill University Press, 1964.

Bernstorff, Count Johann von. *Memoirs of Count Bernstorff.* Translated by Eric Sutton. New York: Random House, 1936.

Bihl, Wolfdieter. *Die Kaukasus-Politik der Mittelmächte.* Part l. Vienna: Hermann Böhlaus, 1975.

Binark, Ismet. "Letter to the Editor." *Zeitschrift für Türkeistudien* 7 (1994): 287–89; 8 (1995): 265–67.

Blaser, Bruno. "Von der schweren Last der Geschichte: Versuch eines Armenisch-Türkischen Dialog." *Hilfsbundbote* (Bad Homburg) 103, no. 2 (2001): 10.

Bliss, Edwin Munsell. *Turkish Cruelties upon the Armenian Christians.* Philadelphia, PA: Imperial, 1896.

Bloxham, Donald. "The Armenian Genocide of 1915–1916: Cumulative Radicalization and the Development of a Destruction Policy." *Past and Present* 181 (2003): 141–91.

———. "Power Politics, Prejudice, Protest and Propaganda: A Reassessment of the German Role in the Armenian Genocide of World War I." In *Der Völkermord an den Armeniern,* edited by Hans-Lukas Kieser and Dominik J. Schaller, pp. 213–44. Zurich: Chronos, 2002.

Bogazici University, ed. *Armenians in the Ottoman Empire and Modern Turkey (1912–1926).* Istanbul: Tasvir Press, 1984.

Bonsal, Stephen. *Suitors and Suppliants: The Little Nations at Versailles.* New York: Prentice-Hall, 1946.

Bozarslan, Hamit. "Histoire des relations kurdo-arméniennes." In *Kurdistan und Europa: Einblicke in die kurdische Geschichte des 19. und 20. Jahrhunderts,* edited by Hans-Lukas Kieser, pp. 151–86. Zurich: Chronos, 1997.

———. "Les relations kurdo-arméniennes 1894–1966." In *Die Armenische Frage und die Schweiz (1896–1923),* edited by Hans-Lukas Kieser, pp. 329–40. Zurich: Chronos, 1999.

Broadway, Bill. "Armenians' Bittersweet Pilgrimage." *Washington Post,* June 23, 2001.

Browning, Christopher R. *Nazi Policy, Jewish Workers, and German Killers.* Cambridge: Cambridge University Press, 2000.

Bruinessen, Martin van. *Agha, Shaikh and State: The Social and Political Structure of Kurdistan.* London: Zed Books, 1992.

Bryce, James. *Transcaucasia and Ararat: Being Notes of a Vacation Tour in the Autumn of 1876.* London: Macmillan, 1896.

Calic, Edouard. *Unmasked: Two Confidential Interviews with Hitler in 1931.* Translated by Richard Barry. London: Chatto and Windus, 1971.

Captanian, Pailadzo. *1915: Der Völkermord and den Armeniern: Eine Zeugin berichtet.* Translated by Meliné Pehlivanian. Leipzig: Gustav Kiepenheuer, 1993 (first published in French in 1919).

Carzou, Jean-Marie. *Un génocide exemplaire: Arménie 1915.* Paris: Flammanion, 1975.

Center for Strategic Research. *Armenian Claims and Historical Facts.* Ankara: Center for Strategic Research, 1998.

Chakalian, Manouk. *Journey for Freedom (Armenian Massacres, Deportation).* New York: Carlton Press, 1976.

Chalabian, Antranig. *General Andranik and the Armenian Revolutionary Movement.* N.p., 1988.

——. *Revolutionary Figures.* Translated by Arra S. Avakian. N.p.: A. Chalabian, 1994.

Chaliand, Gerard, and Yves Ternon. *The Armenians: From Genocide to Resistance.* Translated by Tony Berrett. London: Zed Press, 1983.

Charny, Israel W. "The Turks, Armenians and the Jews." In *Book of the International Conference on the Holocaust and Genocide,* Book 1, *The Conference Program and Crisis,* pp. 269–315. Tel Aviv: Institute of the International Conference on the Holocaust and Genocide, 1983.

Chorbajian, Levon, and George Shirinian, eds. *Studies in Comparative Genocide.* New York: St. Martin's Press, 1999.

Christoffel, Ernst J. *Zwischen Saat und Ernte: Aus der Arbeit der christlichen Blindenmission im Orient.* Berlin: Christliche Blindenmission im Orient, n.d.

Comité de Défense de la Cause Arménienne. *Justicier du génocide arménien: Le procès de Tehlirian.* Paris: Editions Diasporas, 1981.

Cook, Ralph Elliot. "The United States and the Armenian Question, 1894–1924." Ph.D. dissertation, Fletcher School of Law and Diplomacy, 1957.

Copeland, Libby. "Survivor." *Washington Post,* September 24, 2000.

Courbage, Youssef, and Philippe Fargues. *Christians and Jews under Islam.* Translated by Judy Mabro. London: I. B. Tauris, 1997.

Criss, Nur Bilge. *Istanbul under Allied Occupation, 1918–1923.* Leiden: Brill, 1999.

Cruikshank, A. A. "The Young Turk Challenge in Postwar Turkey." *Middle East Journal* 22 (1968): 17–28.

Dabag, Mihran. "Jungtürkische Visionen und der Völkermord an den Armeniern." In *Genozid und Moderne,* edited by Mihran Dabag and Kristin Platt, vol. 1, pp. 152–205. Opladen: Leske and Budrich, 1998.

Dadrian, Vahakn N. "The Armenian Genocide and the Pitfalls of a 'Balanced' Analysis: A Response to Ronald Grigor Suny." *Armenian Forum* 1, no. 2 (Summer 1998): 73–130.

————. "The Armenian Question and the Wartime Fate of the Armenians as Documented by the Officials of the Ottoman Empire's World War I Allies: Germany and Austria-Hungary." *International Journal of Middle East Studies* 34 (2002): 59–85.

————. "The Complicity of the Party, the Government, and the Military: Select Parliamentary and Judicial Documents (Recently Uncovered and Obtained)." *Journal of Political and Military Sociology* 22 (1994): 29–96.

————. "The Convergent Roles of the State and Governmental Party in the Armenian Genocide." In *Studies in Comparative Genocide,* edited by Levon Chorbajian and George Shirinian, pp. 92–124. New York: St. Martin's Press, 1999.

————. "Documentation of the Armenian Genocide in German and Austrian Sources." In *The Widening Circle of Genocide: A Critical Bibliographical Review,* edited by Israel W. Charny, vol. 3, pp. 77–125. New Brunswick, NJ: Transaction Books, 1994.

————. "The Documentation of the World War I Armenian Massacres in the Proceedings of the Turkish Military Tribunal." *International Journal of Middle East Studies* 23 (1991): 549–76.

————. "Genocide as a Problem of National and International Law: The World War I Armenian Case and Its Contemporary Legal Ramifications." *Yale Journal of International Law* 14 (1989): 221–334.

————. *German Responsibility in the Armenian Genocide: A Review of the Historical Evidence of German Complicity.* Cambridge, MA: Blue Crane Books, 1996.

————. *The History of the Armenian Genocide: Ethnic Conflict from the Balkans to Anatolia to the Caucasus.* 2nd rev. ed. Providence, RI: Berghahn, 1997.

————. *The Key Elements in the Turkish Denial of the Armenian Genocide: A Case Study of Distortion and Falsification.* Toronto: Zoryan Institute, 1999.

————. "The Naim-Andonian Documents on the World War I Destruction of Ottoman Armenians: The Anatomy of a Genocide." *International Journal of Middle East Studies* 18 (1986): 311–60.

————. "Ottoman Archives and Denial of the Armenian Genocide." In *The Armenian Genocide: History, Politics, Ethics,* edited by Richard G. Hovannisian, pp. 280–310. New York: St. Martin's Press, 1992.

————. "The Role of the Special Organization in the Armenian Genocide during the First World War." In *Minorities in Wartime: National and Racial Groupings in Europe, North America and Australia during the Two World Wars,* edited by Panikos Panayi, pp. 50–82. Oxford: Berg, 1993.

————. "The Role of Turkish Physicians in the World War I Genocide of Ottoman Armenians." *Holocaust and Genocide Studies* 1 (1986): 169–92.

————. "The Secret Young-Turk Ittihadist Conference and the Decision for the World War I Genocide of the Armenians." *Holocaust and Genocide Studies* 7 (1993): 173–201.

————. "The Secret Young-Turk Ittihadist Conference and the Decision for the World War I Genocide of the Armenians." *Journal of Political and Military Sociology* 22 (1994): 173–98.

————. "A Textual Analysis of the Key Indictment of the Turkish Military Tribunal Investigating the Armenian Genocide." *Journal of Political and Military Sociology* 22 (1994): 133–72.

————. "The Turkish Military Tribunal's Prosecution of the Authors of the Armenian Genocide: Four Major Court-Martial Series." *Holocaust and Genocide Studies* 11 (1997): 28–59.

————. *Warrant for Genocide: Key Elements of Turko-Armenian Conflict.* New Brunswick, NJ: Transaction Books, 1999.

Dasnabedian, Hratch. *History of the Armenian Revolutionary Federation Dashnaktsutiun 1890–1924.* Translated by Bryan Fleming and Vahe Habeshian. Milan: Oemme Edizioni, 1990.

Davidson, Khoren K. *Odyssey of an Armenian of Zeitoun.* New York: Vantage Press, 1985.

Davis, Leslie A. *The Slaughterhouse Province: An American Diplomat's Report on the Armenian Genocide, 1915–1917.* Edited by Susan K. Blair. New Rochelle, NY: Aristide D. Caratzas, 1989.

Davison, Roderic H. "The Armenian Crisis, 1912–1914." *American Historical Review* 53 (1948): 481–505.

————. *Turkey.* Englewood Cliffs, NJ: Prentice-Hall, 1968.

————. "Turkish Attitudes concerning Christian-Muslim Equality in the Nineteenth Century." *American Historical Review* 59 (1954): 844–64.

Derdarian, Mae M. *Vergeen: A Survivor of the Armenian Genocide.* Los Angeles, CA: Atmus, 1997.

Deringil, Selim. "In Search of a Way Forward: A Response to Ronald Grigor Suny." *Armenian Forum* 1, no. 2 (Summer 1998): 65–71.

————. *The Well-Protected Domains: Ideology and Legitimation of Power in the Ottoman Empire, 1876–1909.* London: I. B. Tauris, 1998.

Deutscher Hilfsbund für christliches Liebeswerk. *1896–1921, 25 Jahre im Orient: Ein Gang durch die Arbeit des Deutschen Hilfsbundes für christliches Liebeswerk im Orient.* Frankfurt/M: Orient, 1921.

Devereux, Robert. Preface to Ziya Gökalp, *The Principles of Turkism.* Trans. Robert Devereux. Leiden: Brill, 1968 (originally published in Turkish in 1923).

Dinkel, Christoph. "German Officers and the Armenian Genocide." *Armenian Review* 44, no. 1 (Spring 1991): 77–133.

Dixon-Johnson, C. F. *The Armenians.* Northgate: Toulmin and Sons, 1916.

Djemal Pasha, Ahmed. *Memories of a Turkish Statesman, 1913–1919.* New York: George H. Doran, 1922.

———. "Zur Frage der Greuel in Armenien: Eine Rechtfertigungsschrift." *Frankfurter Zeitung,* September 3, 1919.

Dowsett, Charles J. F. "Armenia." *Encyclopedia Britannica* (1967 ed.), vol. 2, pp. 418–21.

Duguid, Stephen. "The Politics of Unity: Hamidian Policy in Eastern Anatolia." *Middle Eastern Studies* 9 (1973): 139–55.

Dunn, Robert. *World Alive: A Personal Story.* New York: Crown, 1956.

Dyer, Gwynne. "Letter to the Editor." *Middle Eastern Studies* 9 (1973): 129–30, 377–85.

———. "Turkish 'Falsifiers' and Armenian 'Deceivers': Historiography and the Armenian Massacres." *Middle Eastern Studies* 12 (1976): 99–107.

Earle, Edward Mead. "American Missions in the Near East." *Foreign Affairs* 7 (1929): 398–417.

Eckart, Bruno. "Meine Erlebnisse in Urfa." *Der Orient* 3 (1921): 54–58, 119–26, 133–46, 154–60; 4 (1922): 20–24.

Ehmann, Johannes. "Letter." *Sonnen-Aufgang* 20, no. 1 (October 1917): 2.

Ehrhold, Käthe. *Flucht in die Heimat: Aus dem Kriegserlebnis deutscher Missionsschwestern in der asiatischen Türkei.* Dresden: C. Ludwig Ungelenk, 1937.

Einstein, Lewis. *Inside Constantinople: A Diplomatist's Diary during the Dardanelles Expedition, April–September, 1915.* London: John Murray, 1917.

Eliot, Charles. *Turkey in Europe.* New York: Barnes and Noble, 1965 (reprint of 2nd edition, 1907).

Ergil, Dogu. "A Reassessment: The Young Turks, Their Politics and Anti-Colonial Struggle." *Balkan Studies* 16, no. 2 (1975): 26–72.

Erickson, Edward J. *Ordered to Die: A History of the Ottoman Army in the First World War.* Westport, CT: Greenwood Press, 2001.

———. "The Turkish Official Military Histories of the First World War: A Bibliographical Essay." *Middle Eastern Studies* 39 (2003): 190–98.

Ertürk, Hüsameddin. *Iki Devrin Perde Arkasi.* Istanbul: Dinar Yayincilik, 1957.

Erzberger, Mathias. *Erlebnisse im Weltkrieg.* Stuttgart: Deutsche Verlagsanstalt, 1920.

Etmekjian, Lillian. "The Evidence for the Armenian Genocide in the Writings of Two Prominent Turks." *Armenian Review* 35 (1982): 183–91.

———. "Toynbee, Turks, and Armenians." *Armenian Review* 37, no. 3 (Autumn 1984): 61–65.

Evans, Laurence. *United States Policy and the Partition of Turkey, 1914–1924.* Baltimore, MD: Johns Hopkins University Press, 1965.

Falk, Richard. Foreword to "The Armenian Genocide in Official Turkish Records: Collected Essays by Vahakn N. Dadrian." *Journal of Political and Military Sociology.* 22, no. 1 (Summer 1994): i–ii.

Feigel, Uwe. *Das evangelische Deutschland und Armenien: Die Armenierhilfe deutscher evangelischer Christen seit dem Ende des 19. Jahrhunderts im Kontexte der deutsch-türkischen Beziehungen.* Göttingen: Vandenhoeck und Ruprecht, 1989.

Feigl, Erich. *A Myth of Terror: Armenian Extremism, Its Causes and Its Historical Context.* Freilassing: Edition Zeitgeschichte, 1987.

Foreign Policy Institute. "The Turkish Argument: The Armenian Issue in Nine Questions and Answers." In *A Crime of Silence: The Armenian Genocide,* edited by Permanent People's Tribunal, pp. 132–67. London: Zed Books, 1985.

Foss, Clive. Book review of Vahakn Dadrian, *German Responsibility in the Armenian Genocide. Institute for the Study of Genocide Newsletter* 19 (Fall 1997): 12–16.

Frantz, Douglas. "Unofficial Commission Acts to Ease Turkish-Armenian Enmity." *New York Times,* July 10, 2001.

Frey, Waldemar. *Kut-el-Amara: Kriegsfahrten und Erinnerungsbilder aus dem Orient.* Berlin: Brunnen, 1932.

Friedman, Isaiah. *Germany, Turkey, and Zionism, 1897–1918.* Oxford: At the Clarendon Press, 1977.

Fromkin, David. *A Peace to End All Peace: Creating the Modern Middle East, 1914–1920.* New York: Henry Holt, 1989.

FRUSA (Papers Relating to the Foreign Relations of the United States of America). "FRUSA's Documentation of the Appearance of the Ottoman Turkish Delegation before the Council of Four, Paris June 17, 1919." *Armenian Review* 35 (1982): 67–80.

Gawrych, George W. "The Culture and Politics of Violence in Turkish Society, 1903–14." *Middle Eastern Studies* 22 (1986): 307–30.

Gelvin, James L. *Divided Loyalties: Nationalism and Mass Politics in Syria at the Close of the Empire.* Berkeley, CA: California University Press, 1998.

Gerlach, Christian. "Nationsbildung im Krieg: Wirtschaftliche Faktoren bei der Vernichtung der Armenier und beim Mord an den ungarischen Juden." In *Der Völkermord an den Armeniern und die Shoah,* edited by Hans-Lukas Kieser and Dominik J. Schaller, pp. 347–422. Zurich: Chronos, 2002.

Germany, Reichskriegsministerium. *Sanitätsbericht über das deutsche Heer (Deutsches Feld- und Besatzungsheer) im Weltkriege 1914/18.* Vol. 2. Berlin: E. S. Mittler, 1938.

Germany, Turkey and Armenia: A Selection of Documentary Evidence Relating to the Armenian Atrocities from German and Other Sources. London: J. J. Keliher, 1917.

Ghassein, Faiz el-. *Die Türkenherrschaft und Armeniens Schmerzensschrei.* 2nd ed. Zurich: Institut Orell, Füssli, 1918.

Ghazarian, Vatche, ed. *Village Remembered: The Armenians of Habousi.* Waltham, MA: Mayreni, 1997.

Gidney, James B. *A Mandate for Armenia.* Kent, OH: Kent State University Press, 1967.

Glastris, Paul. "Armenia's History, Turkey's Dilemma." *Washington Post,* March 11, 2001.

Glockler, Henry W. *Interned in Turkey, 1914–1918.* Beirut: Sevan Press, 1969.

Göcek, Fatma Müge. "Reconstructing the Turkish Historiography on the Armenian Massacres and Deaths of 1915." In *Looking Backward, Moving Forward: Confronting the Armenian Genocide,* edited by Richard G. Hovannisian, pp. 209–30. New Brunswick, NJ: Transaction Books, 2003.

Gökalp, Ziya. *The Principles of Turkism.* Translated by Robert Devereux. Leiden: Brill, 1968.

———. *Turkish Nationalism and Western Civilization: Selected Essays.* Translated by Niyazi Berkes. Westport, CT: Greenwood Press, 1959.

Gossoian, Haig. *The Epic Story of the Self-Defense of Armenians in the Historic City of Van.* Translated by Samuels S. Tarpinian. N.p.: Raven Publishers, 1980.

Graves, Robert. *Storm Centres of the Near East: Personal Memories 1879–1929.* London: Hutchinson, 1933.

Gunter, Michael M. *The Kurds in Turkey: A Political Dilemma.* Boulder, CO: Westview, 1990.

———. *"Pursuing the Just Cause of Their People": A Study of Contemporary Armenian Terrorism.* New York: Greenwood Press, 1986.

———. "Why Do the Turks Deny They Committed Genocide against the Armenians?" *Orient* (Leverkusen, Germany) 30 (1989): 490–93.

Guroian, Vigen. "Collective Responsibility and Official Excuse Making: The Case of the Turkish Genocide of the Armenians." In *The Armenian Genocide: A Perspective,* edited by Richard G. Hovannisian, pp. 135–52. New Brunswick, NJ: Transaction Books, 1986.

———. "The Politics and Morality of Genocide." In *The Armenian Genocide: History, Politics, Ethics,* edited by Richard G. Hovannisian, pp. 311–39. New York: St. Martin's Press, 1992.

Gürün, Kamuran. *The Armenian File: The Myth of Innocence Exposed.* London: Weidenfeld and Nicolson, 1985.

Guse, Felix. "Der Armenieraufstand 1915 und seine Folgen." *Wissen und Wehr* 6 (1925): 609–21.

———. *Die Kaukasusfront im Weltkrieg: Bis zum Frieden von Brest.* Leipzig: Koehler und Amelang, 1940.

Gust, Wolfgang. *Der Völkermord an den Armeniern: Die Tragödie des ältesten Christenvolkes der Welt.* Munich: Carl Hauser, 1993.

Hacobian, A. P. *Armenia and the War: An Armenian's Point of View with an Appeal to Britain and the Coming Peace Conference.* New York: George H. Doran, n.d.

Halacoglu, Yusuf. *Facts on the Relocation of Armenians (1914–1918).* Ankara: Turkish Historical Society, 2002.

Hanioglu, Sükrü M. *The Young Turks in Opposition.* New York: Oxford University Press, 1995.

Hartunian, Abraham H. *Neither to Laugh Nor to Weep: A Memoir of the Armenian Genocide.* Translated by Vartan Hartunian. Boston: Beacon Press, 1968.

Hepworth, George H. *Through Armenia on Horseback.* London: Isbister, 1898.

Heyd, Uriel. *Foundations of Turkish Nationalism: The Life and Teachings of Ziya Gökalp.* London: Luzac, 1950.

Hoffmann, Joachim. *Die Ostlegionen 1941–1943: Turkotartaren, Kaukasier und Wolgafinnen im deutschen Heer.* Freiburg/Br.: Rombach, 1976.

Hofmann, Tessa. *Annäherung an Armenien: Geschichte und Gegenwart.* Munich: Beck, 1997.

———. *Armin T. Wegner: Writer, Eyewitness and Photographer of the Armenian Genocide.* Yerevan: Apaga, 1996.

———. "German Eyewitness Reports on the Genocide of the Armenians, 1915–16." In *A Crime of Silence: The Armenian Genocide,* edited by Permanent People's Tribunal, pp. 61–92. London: Zed Books, 1985.

———. "New Aspects of the Talat Pasha Court Case: Unknown Archival Documents on the Background and Procedure of an Unintended Political Trial." *Armenian Review* 42, no. 4 (Winter 1989): 41–53.

———, ed. *Der Völkermord an den Armeniern vor Gericht: Der Prozess Talaat Pasha.* Göttingen: Gesellschaft für bedrohte Völker, 1985 (reprint of 1921 Berlin edition).

Hofmann, Tessa, and Méline Péhlivanian, "Malatia 1915: Carrefour des convois de déportés d'après le journal du missionnaire allemand Hans Bauernfeind." In *L'Extermination des déportés arméniens ottomans dans les camps de concentration de Syrie-Mésopotamie (1915–1916): La deuxième phase du génocide,* edited by Raymond H. Kévorkian, pp. 247–314. Paris, 1998 (special issue of *Revue d'Histoire Arménienne Contemporaine* 2).

Horton, George. *The Blight of Asia.* Indianapolis: Bobbs-Merrill, 1926.

Höss, Annette. "The Trial of Perpetrators by the Turkish Military Tribunals: The Case of Yozgat." In *The Armenian Genocide: History, Politics, Ethics,* edited by Richard G. Hovannisian, pp. 208–21. New York: St. Martin's Press, 1992.

Housepian, Marjorie. *Smyrna 1922: The Destruction of a City.* London: Faber and Faber, 1972.

Hovannisian, Richard G, ed. *The Armenian Genocide: History, Politics, Ethics.* New York: St. Martin's Press, 1972.

———, ed. *The Armenian Genocide in Perspective.* New Brunswick, NJ: Transaction Books, 1986.

———, comp. *The Armenian Holocaust: A Bibliography Relating to the Deportations, Massacres and Dispersion of the Armenian People, 1915–1923.* 2nd ed. Cambridge, MA: Armenian Heritage Press, 1980.

———, ed. *The Armenian People from Ancient to Modern Times,* vol. 2: *Foreign Domination to Statehood: The Fifteenth Century to the Twentieth Century.* New York: St. Martin's Press, 1997.

———. "The Armenian Question in the Ottoman Empire." *East European Quarterly* 6 (1972): 1–26.

———. "The Armenian Question in the Ottoman Empire, 1876–1914." In *The Armenian People from Ancient to Modern Times,* vol. 2: *Foreign Domination to*

Statehood: The Fifteenth Century to the Twentieth Century, edited by Richard G. Hovannisian, pp. 203–38. New York: St. Martin's Press, 1997.

————. *Armenian Van/Vaspurakan.* Costa Mesa, CA: Mazda, 2000.

————. *Armenia on the Road to Independence, 1918.* Berkeley: University of California Press, 1969.

————. "The Critic's View: Beyond Revisionism." *International Journal of Middle East Studies* 9 (1978): 379–88.

————. "The Ebb and Flow of the Armenian Minority in the Arab Middle East." *Middle East Journal* 28 (1974): 19–32.

————. *Looking Backward, Moving Forward: Confronting the Armenian Genocide.* New Brunswick, NJ: Transaction, 2003.

————. "The Question of Altruism during the Armenian Genocide of 1915." In *Embracing the Other: Philosophical, Psychological, and Historical Perspectives on Altruism,* edited by Pearl M. Oliner et al., pp. 282–305. New York: New York University Press, 1992.

————, ed. *Remembrance and Denial: The Case of the Armenian Genocide.* Detroit: Wayne State University Press, 1999.

Hulme-Beaman, Ardern. *Twenty Years in the Near East.* London: Methuen, 1898.

Hyland, Francis P. *Armenian Terrorism.* Boulder, CO: Westview Press, 1991.

Institut für armenische Fragen. *The Armenian Genocide: Documentation.* Vols. 1, 2, 8. Munich: IfAF, 1987–91.

Jackh, Ernest. *The Rising Crescent: Turkey Yesterday, Today, and Tomorrow.* New York: Farrar and Rinehart, 1944.

Jacobsen, Maria. *Diaries of a Danish Missionary: Harpoot, 1907–1919.* Translated by Kristen Vind. Princeton, NJ: Gomidas Institute, 2001.

Jafarian, Boghos. *Farewell Kharpert: Autobiography of B.J.* N.p., 1989.

Jäschke, Gotthard. *Der Turanismus der Jungtürken: Zur Osmanischen Aussenpolitik im Weltkriege.* Leipzig: Otto Harrassowitz, 1941.

Jernazian, Ephraim K. *Judgment unto Truth: Witnessing the Armenian Genocide.* Translated by Alice Haig. New Brunswick, NJ: Transaction Books, 1990.

Johnson, Clarence R., ed. *Constantinople Today, or the Pathfinder Survey of Constantinople: A Study in Oriental Social Life.* New York: Macmillan, 1922.

Kaiser, Hilmar. *At the Crossroads of Der Zor: Death, Survival, and Humanitarian Resistance in Aleppo, 1915–1917.* Princeton, NJ: Gomidas Institute, 2002.

————. "The Baghdad Railway and the Armenian Genocide, 1915–1916: A Case Study of German Resistance and Complicity." In *Remembrance and Denial: The Case of the Armenian Genocide,* edited by Richard G. Hovannisian, pp. 67–112. Detroit, MI: Wayne State University Press, 1999.

————, ed. *Eberhard Count Wolffskeel von Reichenberg, Zeitoun, Mousa Dagh, Ourfa: Letters on the Armenian Genocide.* Princeton, NJ: Gomidas Institute, 2001.

————. "Germany and the Armenian Genocide: Reply to Vahakn N. Dadrian's Response." *Journal of the Society for Armenian Studies* 9 (1996–99): 135–40.

————. "Germany and the Armenian Genocide: A Review Essay." *Journal of the Society for Armenian Studies* 8 (1995–97): 127–42; 9 (1996–99): 135–40.

————. "'A Scene from the Inferno': The Armenians of Erzurum and the Genocide, 1915–1916." In *Der Völkermord und den Armeniern und die Shoah,* edited by Hans-Lukas Kieser and Dominik J. Schaller, pp. 129–86. Zurich: Chronos, 2002.

Kansu, Aykut. *Politics in Post-Revolutionary Turkey, 1908–1913.* Leiden: Brill, 2000.

Kapikian, Garabed. *Yeghernabadoum.* Translated by Aris Sevag. New York: Rehabilitation Union, 1978.

Karajian, Sarkis. "An Inquiry into the Statistics of the Turkish Genocide of the Armenians, 1915–1918." *Armenian Review* 25 (Winter 1972): 3–44.

Karal, Enver Ziya. *Armenian Question (1878–1923).* Translated by Sekip Engineri. Ankara: Gündüz, 1975.

Karayan, Sarkis. "An Inquiry into the Number and Causes of Turkish Human Losses during the First World War." *Armenian Review* 35 (1982): 284–89.

Karpat, Kemal H. *Ottoman Population 1830–1914: Demographic and Social Characteristics.* Madison: University of Wisconsin Press, 1985.

Karsh, Efraim, and Inari Karsh, *Empires of the Sand: The Struggle for Mastery in the Middle East, 1798–1923.* Cambridge, MA: Harvard University Press, 1999.

Kash, Sarkis H. *Crime Unlimited.* Milwaukee, WI: Journal Printing Co., 1965.

Kazanjian, Paren, ed. *The Cilician Armenian Ordeal.* Boston: Hye Intentions, 1989.

Kazarian, Haigazn K. "A Catalogue of Those Principally Responsible for the 1915–1918 Massacres." *Armenian Review* 29 (1976): 253–72.

————. "The Genocide of Kharpert's Armenians: A Turkish Judicial Document and Cipher Telegrams Pertaining to Kharpert." *Armenian Review* 19 (Spring 1966): 16–23.

————. "Minutes of Secret Meetings Organizing the Turkish Genocide of Armenians." *Armenian Review* 18, no. 3 (Autumn 1965): 18–40.

————. "Turkey Tries Its Chief Criminals: Indictment and Sentence Passed Down by Military Court of 1919." *Armenian Review* 24 (Winter 1971): 3–26.

————. "The Turkish Genocide of the Armenians: A Premeditated and Official Assault." *Armenian Review* 30 (1977): 3–25.

————. "Unpublished Turkish Document No. 289 on the Deportations." *Armenian Review* 34 (1981): 195–98.

Kazemzadeh, Firuz. *The Struggle for Transcaucasia (1917–1921).* New York: Philosophical Library, 1951.

Keeling, Edward Herbert. *Adventures in Turkey and Russia.* London: John Murray, 1924.

Kemal Bey, Ismail. *The Memoirs of Ismail Kemal Bey.* London: Constable, 1920.

Kerr, Stanley E. *The Lions of Marash: Personal Experiences with American Near East Relief, 1919–1922.* Albany: State University of New York Press, 1973.

Kévorkian, Raymond H. *L'Extermination des déportés arméniens ottomans dans les camps de concentration de Syrie-Mésopotamie (1915–1916): La deuxième phase du* génocide. (Special issue of *Revue d'Histoire Arménienne Contemporaine* 2 [1996–98].)

————. "Recueil de témoignages sur l'extermination des *amele tabouri* ou bataillons de soldats-ouvriers arméniens de l'armée ottomane pendant la première guerre mondiale." *Revue d'Histoire Arménienne Contemporaine* 1 (1995): 289–303.

————. "R. P. Yervant P'Erdahdjian: Evénements et faits observés à Constantinople par le vicariat [patriarcal] (1914–16)." *Revue d'Histoire Arménienne Contemporaine* 1 (1995): 247–87.

Kiera, Joseph. *Ins Land des Euphrat und Tigris: Kriegserinnerungen.* Breslau: Frankes, 1935.

Kieser, Hans-Lukas. "Dr. Mehmed Reshid (1873–1919): A Political Doctor." In *Der Völkermord an den Armeniern und die Shoah,* edited by Hans-Lukas Kieser and Dominik J. Schaller, pp. 245–80. Zurich: Chronos, 2002.

————. *Kurdistan und Europa: Einblicke in die Kurdische Geschichte des 19. und 20. Jahrhunderts.* Zurich: Chronos, 1997.

————. *Der verpasste Friede: Mission, Ethnie und Staat in den Ostprovinzen der Türkei, 1839–1938.* Zurich: Chronos, 2000.

Kieser, Hans-Lukas, and Dominik J. Schaller, eds. *Der Völkermord an den Armeniern.* Zurich: Chronos, 2002.

Kirakossian, John S. *The Armenian Genocide: The Young Turks before the Judgment of History.* Translated by Shoshan Altunian. Madison, WI: Sphinx Press, 1992.

Knapp, Grace Higley. *The Mission at Van: In Turkey in War Time.* Privately printed, 1915.

————. *The Tragedy of Bitlis.* New York: Fleming H. Revell, 1919.

Korganoff, Gabriel. *La participation des Arméniens à la guerre mondiale sur la front du Caucasus (1914–1918).* Paris: Massis, 1927.

Kress von Kressenstein, Friedrich Freiherr. *Mit den Türken zum Suezkanal.* Berlin: Vorhut, 1938.

Künzler, Jakob. *Im Lande des Blutes und der Tränen: Erlebnisse in Mesopotamien während des Weltkrieges.* Potsdam: Tempel, 1921.

————. *Köbi: Vater der Armenier.* Kassel: Johannes Stauda, 1967.

Kuper, Leo. "The Concept of Genocide and Its Applicability to the Turkish Massacres of Armenians in 1915–16." In *A Crime of Silence: The Armenian Genocide,* edited by Permanent People's Tribunal, pp. 186–92. London: Zed Books, 1985.

Kuru, Baki. "Law of Procedure." In *Introduction to Turkish Law,* edited by T. Ugrul Ansay and Don Wallace, pp. 175–208. The Hague: Kluwer Law International, 1996.

Kuscubasi, Esref. *The Turkish Battle at Khaybar.* Translated and edited by Philip H. Stoddard and H. Basri Danisman. Istanbul: Arba Yayinlari, 1999.

Kushner, David. *The Rise of Turkish Nationalism: 1876–1908.* London: Frank Cass, 1977.

Kutay, Cemal. *Birinci Dünya Harbinde Teskilat-I Mahsusa ve Hayber'de Türk Cengi.* Istanbul: Tarih Yayinlari, 1962.

Landau, Jacob M. *Pan-Turkism in Turkey: From Irredentism to Cooperation.* 2nd ed. Bloomington: Indiana University Press, 1995.

Lang, David Marshall. *The Armenians: A People in Exile.* London: George Allen and Unwin, 1981.

Langer, William L. *The Diplomacy of Imperialism: 1890–1902.* 2 vols. New York: Alfred A. Knopf, 1935.

Larcher, Maurice. *La guerre turque dans la guerre mondiale.* Paris: E. Chiron, 1926.

Lepsius, Johannes. *Armenien und Europa: Eine Anklageschrift wider die christlichen Grossmächte und ein Aufruf an das christliche Deutschland.* Berlin: Akademische Buchhandlung, 1897.

———. "Der Prozess Teilirian-Talaat." *Der Orient* 3, no. 6 (1921): 65–80, 88–95.

———. *Der Todesgang des armenischen Volkes: Bericht über das Schicksal des armenischen Volkes in der Türkei während des Weltkrieges.* 4th ed. Potsdam: Missionshandlung und Verlag, 1930.

———. "Die Überlebenden." *Der Orient* 3, nos. 10/11 (1921): 130–33.

Leverkuehn, Paul. *Posten auf ewiger Wache: Aus dem abenteuerlichen Leben des Max von Scheubner-Richter.* Essen: Essener Verlagsanstalt, 1938.

Lewis, Bernard. *The Emergence of Modern Turkey.* New York: Oxford University Press, 1966.

Libaridian, Gerard J. *Modern Armenia: People, Nation, State.* New Brunswick, NJ: Transaction, 2004.

Liman von Sanders, Otto. *Five Years in Turkey.* Translated by Carl Reichmann. Annapolis, MD: U.S. Naval Institute, 1927.

Lindley, John M. *"A Soldier Is Also a Citizen": The Controversy over Military Justice, 1917–1920.* New York: Garland, 1990.

Linenthal, Edward T. *Preserving Memory: The Struggle to Create America's Holocaust Museum.* New York: Viking, 1995.

Loftus, Elizabeth F., and James M. Doyle. *Eyewitness Testimony: Civil and Criminal.* 3rd ed. Charlottesville, VA: Lexis Publishing, 1997.

Longrigg, Stephen H. *Syria and Lebanon under French Mandate.* New York: Octagon Books, 1972.

Lowry, Heath W. *The Story behind Ambassador Morgenthau's Story.* Istanbul: Isis Press, 1990.

———. "The United States Congress and Adolf Hitler on the Armenians." *Political Communication and Persuasion* 3 (1985): 111–40.

Lust-Okar, Ellen Marie. "Failure of Collaboration: Armenian Refugees in Syria." *Middle Eastern Studies* 32, no. 1 (January 1996): 53–68.

Lybyer, Albert Howe. "Turkey under the Armistice." *Journal of International Relations* 12 (1922): 447–73.

McCarthy, Justin. *Death and Exile: The Ethnic Cleansing of Ottoman Muslims, 1821–1922.* Princeton, NJ: Darwin Press, 1995.

————. *Muslims and Minorities: The Population of Ottoman Anatolia and the End of the Empire.* New York: New York University Press, 1983.

————. *The Ottoman Peoples and the End of Empire.* New York: Oxford University Press, 2001.

————. *The Ottoman Turks: An Introductory History to 1923.* London: Longman, 1997.

————. "The Report of Niles and Sutherland: An American Investigation of Eastern Anatolia after World War I." *XI. Türk Tarih Kongresi,* pp. 1809–52. Ankara: n.p., 1994.

McCarthy, Justin, and Carolyn McCarthy. *Turks and Armenians: A Manual on the Armenian Question.* Washington, D.C.: Assembly of Turkish American Associations, 1989.

Macfie, A. L. *The End of the Ottoman Empire, 1908–1923.* London: Longman, 1998.

McKale, Donald M. *War by Revolution: Germany and Great Britain in the Middle East in the Era of World War I.* Kent, OH: Kent State University Press, 1998.

Maechler, Stefan. *The Wilkomirski Affair: A Study in Biographical Truth.* Translated by John E. Woods. New York: Schocken, 2001.

Mandalian, James G., ed. and translator. *Armenian Freedom Fighters: The Memoirs of Rouben der Minasian.* Boston: Hairenik Association, 1963.

Mandel, Maud. "Book Review." *Armenian Forum* 1, no. 3 (Autumn 1998): 79–82.

Mandelstam, André N. *Das armenische Problem im Lichte des Völker- und Menschenrechts.* Berlin: Georg Stilke, 1931.

————. *Le sort de l'Empire Ottoman.* Lausanne: Librairie Payot, 1917.

Mango, Andrew. "Remembering the Minorities." *Middle Eastern Studies* 21, no. 4 (October 1985): 118–40.

————. "Turks and Kurds." *Middle Eastern Studies* 30 (1994): 975–97.

————. "Understanding Turkey." *Middle Eastern Studies* 18 (1982): 194–213.

Manuelian, Agnacia. *Unending Journey.* London: Thornton Butterworth, 1939.

Marashlian, Levon. "Finishing the Genocide: Cleansing Turkey of Armenian Survivors, 1920–1923." In *Remembrance and Denial: The Case of the Armenian Genocide,* edited by Richard G. Hovannisian, pp. 113–45. Detroit, MI: Wayne State University Press, 1999.

————. *Politics and Demography: Armenians, Turks, and Kurds in the Ottoman Empire.* Cambridge, MA: Zoryan Institute, 1991.

Mazian, Florence. *Why Genocide?: The Armenian and Jewish Experiences in Perspective.* Ames: Iowa State University Press, 1990.

Melson, Robert F. "Provocation or Nationalism: A Critical Inquiry into the Armenian Genocide of 1915." In *The Armenian Genocide: A Perspective,* edited by Richard G. Hovannisian, pp. 61–84. New Brunswick, NJ: Transaction Books, 1986.

————. *Revolution and Genocide: On the Origins of the Armenian Genocide and the Holocaust.* Chicago: University of Chicago Press, 1992.

————. "A Theoretical Inquiry into the Armenian Massacres of 1894–1896." *Comparative Studies in Society and History* 25 (1982): 481–509.

Mesrop, Georg. *L'Arménie du point de vue géographique, historique, éthnographique, statistique, et culturel.* Constantinople: Conseil Consultatif National Arménien, 1919.

Messerlian, Zaven M. *The Premeditated Nature of the Genocide Perpetrated on the Armenians.* Antelias: Armeni Catholicosate of Cilicia, 2001.

Messinger, Gary S. *British Propaganda and the State in the First World War.* Manchester: Manchester University Press, 1992.

Meyer, Karl. *Armenien und die Schweiz: Geschichte der schweizerischen Armenierhilfe.* Berlin: Blaukreuz, 1974.

Miller, Donald E., and Lorna Touryan Miller. *Survivors: An Oral History of the Armenian Genocide.* Berkeley: University of California Press, 1993.

Minassian, Gaidz F. "Les relations entre le Comité Union et Progrès et la Fédération Révolutionnaire Arménienne à la veille de la Première Guerre Mondiale après les sources arméniennes." *Revue d'Histoire Arménienne Contemporaine* 1 (1995): 45–99.

Minassian, John. *Many Hills Yet to Climb: Memoirs of an Armenian Deportee.* Santa Barbara, CA: Jim Cook, 1986.

Mohl, Hedwig von. "Erinnerungen an ein türkisches Lazarett im Weltkrieg." *Der Neue Orient* 8 (1920): 43–47.

Moravian, Suzanne Elizabeth. "Bearing Witness: The Missing Archives as Evidence of the Armenian Genocide." In *The Armenian Genocide: History, Politics, Ethics,* edited by Richard G. Hovannisian, pp. 103–28. New York: St. Martin's Press, 1992.

Morgenthau, Henry. *Ambassador Morgenthau's Story.* Garden City, NY: Doubleday, 1918; Ann Arbor, MI: Gomidas Institute, 2000.

Mouradian, George. *Armenian Infotext.* Southgate, MI: Bookshelf Publishers, 1995.

Moyne, Walter Guinness. *Impressions of Armenia.* London: Spottiswoode, Ballantyne, 1918.

Mugerditchian, Esther. *From Turkish Toils: The Narrative of an Armenian Family's Escape.* New York: George H. Doran, n.d.

Mühlmann, Carl. *Das Deutsch-Türkische Waffenbündnis im Weltkriege.* Leipzig: Koehler und Amelang, 1940.

Mukhitarian, Onnig. *An Account of the Glorious Struggle of Van-Vasbouragan.* Translated by Samuels S. Tarpinian. N.p.: Raven Publishers, 1980.

Nalbandian, Louise. *The Armenian Revolutionary Movement: The Development of Armenian Political Parties through the Nineteenth Century.* Los Angeles: University of California Press, 1963.

Naslian, Jean. *Les Mémoires de Mgr. Jean Naslian, évêque de Trébizonde, sur les événements politico-religieux en Proche Orient de 1914 à 1928.* Vol. 1. Vienna: Imprimerie Mechitariste, 1955.

Nassibian, Akaby. *Britain and the Armenian Question: 1915–1923.* London: Croom Helm, 1984.

National Congress of Turkey. *Documents relatifs aux atrocités commises par les Arméniens sur la population musulmane.* Constantinople: n.p., 1919.

———. *The Turco-Armenian Question: The Turkish Point of View.* Constantinople: n.p., 1919.

Necef, Mehmet. "The Turkish Media Debate on the Armenian Massacre." In *Genocide: Cases, Comparisons, and Contemporary Debates,* edited by Steven L. B. Jensen, pp. 225–62. Copenhagen: Danish Center for Holocaust and Genocide Studies, 2003.

Neulen, Hans Werner. *Adler und Halbmond: Das deutsch-türkische Bündnis 1914–1918.* Frankfurt/M: Ullstein, 1994.

———. *An deutscher Seite: Internationale Freiwillige von Wehrmacht und Waffen-SS.* Munich: Universitas, 1985.

Nichanian, Marc. "The Truth of the Facts: About the New Revisionism." In *Remembrance and Denial: The Case of the Armenian Genocide,* edited by Richard G. Hovannisian, pp. 249–70. Detroit, MI: Wayne State University Press, 1999.

Nicolai, Walter. *The German Secret Service.* Translated by George Renwick. London: Stanley Paul, 1924.

Niepage, Martin. *The Horrors of Aleppo: Seen by a German Eyewitness.* London: T. Fisher Unwin, n.d.

Nogales, Rafael de. *Four Years beneath the Crescent.* Translated by Muna Lee. New York: Charles Scribner's 1926.

Ohandjanian, Artem. *Armenien: Der verschwiegene Völkermord.* Vienna: Böhlau, 1989.

Öke, Mim Kemal. *The Armenian Question 1914–1923.* Nicosia: K. Rustem and Brother, 1988.

———. "The Response of the Turkish Armenians to the 'Armenian Question,' 1919–1926." In *Armenians in the Ottoman Empire and Modern Turkey (1912–1926),* edited by Bogazici University, pp. 71–88. Istanbul: Tasvir Press, 1984.

Olson, Robert. *The Emergence of Kurdish Nationalism and the Sheikh Said Rebellion, 1880–1925.* Austin: University of Texas Press, 1989.

Orel, Sinasi, and Süreyya Yuca. *The Talât Pasha 'Telegrams': Historical Fact or Armenian Fiction?* Nicosia: K. Rustem and Brother, 1986.

Papazian, Dennis R. *What Every Armenian Should Know....* Dearborn, MI: Armenian Research Center, n.d. [1991].

Papazian, Kapriel Serope. *Patriotism Perverted: A Discussion of the Deeds and Misdeeds of the Armenian Revolutionary Federation, the So-Called Dashnagtzoutune.* Boston: Baikar Press, 1934.

Parla, Taha. *The Social and Political Thought of Ziya Gökalp, 1876–1924.* Leiden: E. J. Brill, 1985.

Parmelee, Ruth A. *A Pioneer in the Euphrates Valley.* N.p., 1967.

Pasdermadjian, Garegin (aka Armen Garo). *Armenia: A Leading Factor in the Winning of the War.* Translated by A. Torossian. New York: Council for Armenia, 1919.

———. *Bank Ottoman: Memoirs of Armen Garo.* Translated by Haig T. Partizian. Detroit, MI: Armen Topouzian, 1990.

———. "My Last Interview with Talaat Pasha." *Armenian Review* 35 (1982): 115–27 (reprint of a 1922 article).

———. *Why Armenia Should Be Free: Armenia's Role in the Present War.* Translated by A. Torossian. Boston: Hairenik, 1918.

Patrick, Mary Mills. *Under Five Sultans.* New York: Century, 1929.

Payaslian, Simon. "After Recognition." *Armenian Forum* 2, no. 3 (Autumn 1999): 33–56.

Pears, Edwin. *Forty Years in Constantinople: The Recollections of Sir Edwin Pears, 1873–1915.* London: Herbert Jenkins, 1916.

Peet, Louise Jenison. *No Less Honor: The Biography of William Wheelock Peet.* Chattanooga, TN: E. A. Andrews, 1939.

Permanent People's Tribunal, ed. *A Crime of Silence: The Armenian Genocide.* London: Zed Books, 1985.

Peters, Jensine Oerts. *Tests and Triumphs of Armenians in Turkey and Macedonia.* Grand Rapids, MI: Zondervan, 1940.

Peterson, Horace. *Propaganda for War: The Campaign against American Neutrality, 1914–1917.* Norman: University of Oklahoma Press, 1939.

Phillips, David L. *Unsilencing the Past: Track Two Diplomacy and Turkish Armenian Reconciliation.* New York: Berghahn, 2005.

Pickthall, Marmaduke. "Massacres and the Turks: The Other Side." *Foreign Affairs* (London) (July 1920, special supplement): xiv–xvi.

Pietschmann, Victor. *Durch kurdische Berge und armenische Städte: Tagebuch der österreichischen Armenienexpedition 1914.* Vienna: Adolf Luser, 1940.

Pomiankowski, Joseph. *Der Zusammenbruch des Ottomanischen Reiches: Erinnerungen an die Türkei aus der Zeit des Weltkrieges.* Vienna: Amalthea, 1928.

Price, M. Philips. *War and Revolution in Asiatic Russia.* New York: Macmillan, 1918.

Ramsaur, Ernest E., Jr. *The Young Turks: Prelude to the Revolution of 1908.* Princeton, NJ: Princeton University Press, 1957.

Ramsay, William M. *The Revolution in Constantinople and Turkey: A Diary.* London: Hodder and Stoughton, 1909.

Read, James Morgan. *Atrocity Propaganda: 1914–1919.* New York: Arno Press, 1972 (originally published by Yale University Press in 1941).

Reid, James. "The Armenian Massacres in Ottoman and Turkish Historiography." *Armenian Review* 37, no. 1 (Spring 1984): 22–40.

Riggs, Henry H. *Days of Tragedy in Armenia: Personal Experiences in Harpoot, 1915–1917.* Ann Arbor, MI: Gomidas Institute, 1997.

Safrastian, Arshak. *Kurds and Kurdistan.* London: Harvill Press, 1948.

Salt, Jeremy. "Britain, the Armenian Question and the Cause of Ottoman Reform: 1894–96." *Middle Eastern Studies* 26 (1990): 308–28.

———. *Imperialism, Evangelism and the Ottoman Armenians, 1878–1896.* London: Frank Cass, 1993.

Sanders, Michael L., and Philip M. Taylor. *British Propaganda during the First World War, 1914–18.* London: Macmillan, 1982.

Sandes, E. W. C. *In Kut and Captivity with the 6th Indian Division.* London: John Murray, 1919.

Sanjian, Avedis K. *The Armenian Communities in Syria under Ottoman Dominion.* Cambridge, MA: Harvard University Press, 1965.

Sarafian, Ara. "The Archival Trail: Authentication of *The Treatment of Armenians in the Ottoman Empire, 1915–16.*" In *Remembrance and Denial: The Case of the Armenian Genocide,* edited by Richard G. Hovannisian, pp. 51–65. Detroit, MI: Wayne State University Press, 1999.

———. "Correspondence." *Armenian Forum* 2, no. 4 (February 2003): 143–45.

———. "The Issue of Access to Ottoman Archives." *Zeitschrift für Türkeistudien* 6 (1993): 93–99.

———. "Letter to the Editor." *Zeitschrift für Türkeistudien* 7 (1994): 287–89; and "Comment," 8 (1995): 267.

———. "The Ottoman Archives Debate and the Armenian Genocide." *Armenian Forum* 2, no. 1 (Spring 1999): 35–44.

———. "The Paper Trail: The American State Department and the *Report of Committee on Armenian Atrocities.*" *Revue du Monde Arménien Moderne et Contemporaine* 1 (1994): 127–32.

———. "Research Note: The Issue of Access to Ottoman Archives Revisited." *Zeitschrift für Türkeistudien* 7 (1994): 290–93.

Sarian, Nerses S. *I Shall Not Die: A Tribute to the Faithfulness of God.* London: Marshall, Morgan and Scott, 1967.

Sarkisian, E. K., and R. G. Sahakian. *Vital Issues in Modern Armenian History: A Documented Exposé of Misrepresentation in Turkish Historiography.* Translated by Elisha B. Chrakian. Watertown, MA: Armenian Studies, 1965.

Sazonov, Serge D. *Fateful Years, 1909–1916: The Reminiscences of Serge Sazonov.* New York: Frederick A. Stokes, 1928.

Schatkowski Schilcher, L. "The Famine of 1915–1918 in Greater Syria." In *Problems of the Modern Middle East in Historical Perspective,* edited by John p. Spagnolo, pp. 229–58. Reading: Ithaca Press, 1992.

Schemsi, Kara [pseudonym for Rechid Safet Bey]. *Turcs et arméniens devant l'histoire: Nouveaux témoignages russes et turcs sur les atrocités arméniens de 1914 à 1918.* Geneva: Imprimerie Nationale, 1919.

Schilling, Victor. "Kriegshygienische Erfahrungen in der Türkei." In *Zwischen Kaukasus und Sinai: Jahrbuch des Bundes der Asienkämpfer,* vol. 2, pp. 71–89. Berlin: Deutsche Orientbuchhandlung, 1922.

Schraudenbach, Ludwig. *MUHAREBE: Der erlebte Roman eines deutschen Führers im Osmanischen Heere 1916/17.* Berlin: Drei Masken, 1925.

Schreiner, George Abel. *The Craft Sinister: A Diplomatic-Political History of the Great War and Its Causes.* New York: G. Albert, Geyer, 1920.

———. *From Berlin to Bagdad: Behind the Scenes in the Near East.* New York: Harper and Brothers, 1918.

Sener, Hikmet. "A Comparison of the Turkish and American Military Systems of Nonjudicial Punishment." *Military Law Review* 27 (1965): 111–52.

Serman, E. *Mit den Türken an der Front.* Berlin: August Scherl, 1915.

Seton-Watson, R. W. *Disraeli, Gladstone and the Eastern Question: A Study in Diplomacy and Party Politics.* London: Frank Cass, 1971.

Shaw, Stanford J., and Ezel Kural Shaw. "The Authors Respond." *International Journal of Middle East Studies* 9 (1978): 388–400.

———. *History of the Ottoman Empire and Modern Turkey.* Vol. 2. Cambridge: Cambridge University Press, 1977.

Sheffey, Yigal. *British Military Intelligence in the Palestine Campaign 1914–1918.* London: Frank Cass, 1998.

Shipley, Alice Muggerditchian. *We Walked, Then Ran.* Phoenix, AZ: Alice M. Shipley, 1983.

Shiroyan, Haig. *Smiling through the Tears.* Flushing, NY: n.p., 1954.

Simsir, Bilal N. *The Deportees of Malta and the Armenian Question.* Ankara: Foreign Policy Institute, 1984.

———. "The Deportees of Malta and the Armenian Question." In *Armenians in the Ottoman Empire and Modern Turkey (1912–1926),* edited by Bogazici University, pp. 26–41. Istanbul: Tasvir Press, 1984.

Sonyel, Salahi R., ed. *Displacement of the Armenians: Documents.* Ankara: n.p., 1978.

———. *The Great War and the Tragedy of Anatolia: Turks and Armenians in the Maelstrom of Major Powers.* Ankara: Turkish Historical Society, 2001.

———. *Greco-Armenian Conspiracy against Turkey Revived.* London: Cyprus Turkish Association, 1975.

———. *The Ottoman Armenians: Victims of Great Power Diplomacy.* London: K. Rüstem and Brothers, 1987.

———. "Turco-Armenian Relations and British Propaganda during the First World War." *Belleten* 58 (1994–95): 381–449.

———. "Turco-Armenian Relations in the Context of the Jewish Holocaust." *Belleten* 54 (1990): 757–72.

Steinbach, Udo. *Die Türkei im 20. Jahrhundert: Schwieriger Partner Europas.* Bergisch Gladbach: Gustav Lübbe, 1996.

Steuber, Werner. *Arzt und Soldat in drei Erdteilen.* Berlin: Vorhut, 1940.

Stoddard, Philip H. "The Ottoman Government and the Arabs, 1911 to 1918: A Preliminary Study of the Teskilat-i Mahsusa." Ph.D. dissertation, Princeton University, 1963.

Suny, Ronald Grigor. *Armenia in the Twentieth Century*. Chico, CA: Scholars Press, 1983.

———. "Empire and Nation: Armenians, Turks and the End of the Ottoman Empire." *Armenian Forum* 1, no. 2 (Summer 1998): 17–51.

———. *Looking toward Ararat: Armenia in Modern History*. Bloomington: Indiana University Press, 1993.

———. "Religion, Ethnicity, and Nationalism: Armenians, Turks, and the End of the Ottoman Empire." In *In God's Name: Genocide and Religion in the Twentieth Century*, edited by Omar Bartov and Phyllis Mack, pp. 23–61. New York: Berghahn Books, 2001.

———. "Reply to My Critics." *Armenian Forum* 1, no. 2 (Summer 1998): 131–36.

Surmelian, Leon Z. *I Ask You Ladies and Gentlemen*. New York: E. P. Dutton, 1945.

Süslü, Azmi, ed. *Russian View on the Atrocities Committed by the Armenians against the Turks*. Ankara: Köksav-Kök, 1991.

Sutherland, James Kay. *The Adventures of an Armenian Boy*. Ann Arbor, MI: Ann Arbor Press, 1964.

Svajian, Stephen G. *A Trip through Historic Armenia*. New York: Greenhill, 1977.

Swanson, Glen W. "The Ottoman Police." *Journal of Contemporary History* 7, nos. 1–2 (January–April 1972): 243–60.

Talaat Pasha, Mehmet. "Posthumous Memoirs of Talaat Pasha." *Current History* 15 (1921): 287–95.

Tamcke, Martin. *Armin T. Wegner und die Armenier: Anspruch und Wirklichkeit eines Augenzeugen*. Göttingen: Cuvillier, 1993.

Tarbassian, Hratch. A. *Erzurum (Garin): Its Armenian Heritage and Traditions*. Translated by Nigol Schahgaldian. N.p.: Garin Compatriotic Union of the United States, 1975.

Tarzian, Mary Mangigian. *The Armenian Minority Problem 1914–1934: A Nation's Struggle for Security*. Atlanta, GA: Scholars Press, 1992.

Tashjian, James H. "The Armenian 'Dashnag' Party: A Brief Statement." *Armenian Review* 21, no. 4 (Winter 1968): 49–57.

———. "On a 'Statement' Condemning the Armenian Genocide of 1915–18 Attributed in Error to Mustafa Kemal, Later 'The Ataturk.'" *Armenian Review* 35 (1982): 227–44.

Ter Minassian, Anahide. *Nationalism and Socialism in the Armenian Revolutionary Movement (1887–1912)*. Translated by A. M. Berrett. Cambridge, MA: Zoryan Institute, 1984.

———. "Van 1915." *Guerres Mondiales et Conflits Contemporains* 39, no. 153 (January 1989): 35–59.

Ternon, Yves. *The Armenian Cause*. Translated by Anahid Apelian Mangouni. Delmar, NY: Caravan Books, 1985.

———. *The Armenians: History of a Genocide*. Translated by Rouben C. Cholakian. Delmar, NY: Caravan Press, 1981.

———. *Enquête sur la négation d'un génocide*. Marseille: Parenthèses, 1989.

————. "Freedom and Responsibility of the Historian: The 'Lewis Affair.'" In *Remembrance and Denial: The Case of the Armenian Genocide,* edited by Richard G. Hovannisian, pp. 237–48. Detroit, MI: Wayne State University Press, 1999.

————. "La qualité de la preuve: A propos des documents Andonian et de la petite phrase de Hitler." In *L'actualité du génocide des Arméniens,* edited by Comité de Défense de la Cause Arménienne, pp. 135–41. Paris: Edipol, 1999.

Theriault, Hank. "Universal Social Theory and the Denial of Genocide: Norman Itzkowitz Revisited." *Journal of Genocide Research* 3 (2001): 241–56.

Toynbee, Arnold J. *Acquaintances.* London: Oxford University Press, 1967.

————. *Armenian Atrocities: The Murder of a Nation.* London: Hodder and Stoughton, 1915.

————. *The Western Question in Greece and Turkey: A Study in the Contact of Civilizations.* 2nd edition. New York: Howard Fertig, 1970 (originally published in 1922).

Trask, Roger R. *The United States Response to Turkish Nationalism and Reform, 1914–1939.* Minneapolis: University of Minnesota Press, 1971.

Trumpener, Ulrich. *Germany and the Ottoman Empire: 1914–1918.* Princeton, NJ: Princeton University Press, 1968.

————. "Suez, Baku, Gallipoli: The Military Dimensions of the German-Ottoman Coalition, 1914–18." In *Coalition Warfare: An Uneasy Accord,* edited by Keith Neilson and Roy A. Prete. Waterloo, Ontario: Wilfrid Laurier University Press, 1983.

Tverdokhlebov. *Notes of Superior Russian Officer on the Atrocities at Erzeroum: Drawn from the Memoirs of Lt.-Col. Tverdokhlebov.* N.p., 1919.

U.S. Air Force Reserve Officer Training Corps. *Military Law.* Montgomery, AL: Maxwell Air Force Base, 1978.

U.S. Congress. Senate. *Conditions in the Near East: Report of the American Military Mission to Armenia.* 66th Cong., 2nd sess., Senate Doc. 266, appendix, 1920.

U.S. Provost Marshal General. *Second Report of the Provost Marshal General to the Secretary of War on the Operations of the Selective Service System to December 20, 1918.* Washington, DC: GPO, 1919.

Uras, Esat. *The Armenians in History and the Armenian Question.* Translated from 2nd ed. by Süheyla Artemel. Ankara: Documentary Publications, 1988.

Ussher, Clarence D., and Grace H. Knapp. *An American Physician in Turkey: A Narrative of Adventures in Peace and War.* Boston: Houghton Mifflin, 1917.

Valyi, Felix. *Spiritual and Political Revolutions in Islam.* London: Kegan Paul, 1925.

Vambéry, Arminius. "Personal Recollections of Abdul Hamid II and His Court." *Nineteenth Century and After* 65 (June 1909): 980–93; 66 (July 1909): 69–88.

Van der Dussen, W. J. "The Question of Armenian Reform in 1913–1914." *Armenian Review* 39, no. 1 (Spring 1986): 11–28.

Vérité sur le Mouvement Révolutionnaire Arménien et les mesures gouvernementales. Constantinople: n.p., 1916.

Vischer, Andreas. "Urfa im Sommer 1919." *Mitteilungen über Armenien* (Basel) 12 (October 1919): 598.

Vratzian, Simon. "The Armenian Revolution and the Armenian Revolutionary Federation." *Armenian Review* 3, no. 3 (Autumn 1950): 3–31.

Vryonis, Speros, Jr. "Stanford J. Shaw, History of the Ottoman Empire and Modern Turkey, vol. 1 (1976): A Critical Analysis." *Balkan Studies* 24 (1983): 163–286.

———. *The Turkish State and History: Clio Meets the Grey Wolf.* 2nd ed. New Rochelle, NY: Aristide D. Caratzas, 1993.

Walker, Christopher J. *Armenia: The Survival of a Nation.* Rev. 2nd ed. New York: St. Martin's Press, 1990.

———. "British Sources on the Armenian Massacres, 1915–1916." In *A Crime of Silence: The Armenian Genocide,* edited by Permanent People's Tribunal, pp. 53–58. London: Zed Books, 1985.

———. "Letter to the Editor." *Middle Eastern Studies* 9 (1973): 376.

———. "World War I and the Armenian Genocide." In *The Armenian People from Ancient to Modern Times,* edited by Richard G. Hovannisian, pp. 239–73. New York: St. Martin's Press, 1997.

Washburn, George. *Fifty Years in Constantinople and Recollections of Robert College.* Boston: Houghton Mifflin, 1909.

Weber, Frank G. *Eagles on the Crescent: Germany, Austria, and the Diplomacy of the Turkish Alliance, 1914–1918.* Ithaca, NY: Cornell University Press, 1970.

Wegner, Armin T. *Der Weg ohne Heimkehr: Ein Martyrium in Briefen.* 2nd ed. Dresden: Sibyllen, 1920.

Weldon, Lewen. *"Hard Lying": Eastern Mediterranean 1914–1919.* London: Herbert Jenkins, 1926.

Westermann, William Linn. "The Armenian Problem and the Disruption of Turkey." In *What Really Happened at Paris: The Story of the Peace Conference, 1918–1919, by American Delegates,* edited by Edward Mandell House and Charles Seymour, pp. 176–203. New York: Charles Scribner's Sons, 1921.

Whitman, Sidney. *Turkish Memories.* New York: Charles Scribner's Sons, 1914.

Wiegand, Theodor. *Halbmond im letzten Viertel: Briefe und Reiseberichte aus der alten Türkei von Theodor und Marie Wiegand 1895 bis 1918.* Munich: Bruckmann, 1970.

Wigram, W. A., and E. T. A. Wigram. *The Cradle of Mankind: Life in Eastern Kurdistan.* London: Adam and Charles Black, 1914.

Willis, James F. *Prologue to Nuremberg: The Politics and Diplomacy of Punishing War Criminals of the First World War.* Westport, CT: Greenwood Press, 1982.

Willmore, J. Selden. *The Great Crime and Its Moral.* New York: George H. Doran, n.d.

Wilson, Arnold T. *Loyalties Mesopotamia, 1914–1917: A Personal and Historical Record.* New York: Greenwood Press, 1969 (originally published in London by Oxford University Press in 1931).

Woods, H. Charles. *The Danger Zone of Europe: Changes and Problems in the Near East*. London: T. Fisher Unwin, 1911.

Yalman, Ahmed Emin. *Turkey in My Time*. Norman: University of Oklahoma Press, 1956.

———. *Turkey in the World War*. New Haven, CT: Yale University Press, 1930.

Yapp, Malcolm E. *The Making of the Modern Near East, 1792–1923*. London: Longman, 1987.

———. Review of *The History of the Armenian Genocide* by V. N. Dadrian. *Middle Eastern Studies* 32 (1996): 395–97.

Yeghiayan, Vartkes. *The Armenian Genocide and the Trials of the Young Turks*. La Verne, CA: American Armenian International College Press, 1990.

Yilmaz, Suhnaz. "An Ottoman Warrior Abroad: Enver Pasha as an Expatriate." *Middle Eastern Studies* 35, no. 4 (October 1999): 40–69.

Young, George. *Corps de droit ottoman*. Vol. 7. Oxford: Clarendon Press, 1906.

Zahigian, Krikor M. *One Page of Armenia's Tragedy: A Story of the Years Wherein We Have Seen Evil*. Cleveland: n.p., 1923.

Zamir, Meir. "Population Statistics of the Ottoman Empire in 1914 and 1919." *Middle Eastern Studies* 17 (1981): 85–106.

Zetterberg, Seppo. *Die Liga der Fremdvölker Russlands 1916–1918: Ein Beitrag zu Deutschlands antirussischem Propagandakrieg unter den Fremdvölkern Russlands im ersten Weltkrieg*. Helsinki: Akateeminen Kirjakauppa, 1978.

Ziemke, Kurt. *Die Neue Türkei: Politische Entwicklung 1914–1929*. Stuttgart: Deutsche Verlags-Anstalt, 1930.

Zürcher, Erik Jan. "Between Death and Desertion: The Experience of the Ottoman Soldier in World War I." *Turcica* 28 (1996): 235–58.

———. "Ottoman Labour Battalions in World War I." In *Der Völkermord und den Armeniern und die Shoah,* edited by Hans-Lukas Kieser and Dominik J. Schaller, pp. 187–95. Zurich: Chronos, 2002.

———. *Turkey: A Modern History*. Rev. ed. London: I. B. Tauris, 1997.

———. *The Unionist Factor: The Role of the Committee of Union and Progress in the Turkish National Movement 1905–1926*. Leiden: E. J. Brill, 1984.

Index

Abdul Hamid II (sultan), 9, 11, 23, 30, 38; and Adana massacre of 1809, 33; attempted assassination of, 32; blamed for 1894–95 massacres, 27; suspends 1876 constitution, 6

Abdul Mejid I (sultan), 4

Abdulahad Nuri Bey, 67, 76, 81

Abdülhalik Bey, Mustafa, 68

Abou Herrera, 56

Acar, 8

Adana: deportations from, 184–86; massacre of 1909, 33–34; role of CUP branch, 184–86, 232

Afghanistan, 83

Ahmad, Feroz, 39

Ahmad, Kamal Madhar, 52, 176, 223, 226

Ahmed Bey, Cerkez, 112, 200

Ainslee, Kate, 254

Akcam, Taner, 74–75, 88, 112, 262

Akif Pasha, Resit, 89

Aksin, Sina, 271

Aleppo: deportation committee of, 64–65; exemption from deportation for, 191, 251; factories employing Armenians in, 195; hiding of deportees in, 194; orphanages in, 194–96; relief program run from, 194–97; size of Armenian population of, 191; typhus epidemic, 60, 191

Alevi Kurds, 224. See also Dersim Kurds

Alexandretta (Iskenderun), 104, 157, 183–84

Allemby, Edmund, 108

Amassia, 182

Ambassador Morgenthau's Story, 140–42, 305n48

Amele Tabouri. See Labor battalions

American Baptist Missionary Union, 143

American Board of Commissioners for Foreign Missions (ABCFM), 137, 139, 142–43

American relief program, 57, 65, 178, 194–95

American Research Institute (Ankara), 261

Andonian, Aram: collects testimonies of survivors, 63, 146; on courts-martial, 77; on Naim Bey's character, 68–69; transmits Memoirs of Naim Bey, 69

Andranik, 31, 36, 101, 147

Angora (Ankara), 28

Aprahamian, Souren, 102

Ararat (film), 262

Ardahan, 8

Argyll, George Douglas Campbell, Duke of, 8

Armenakan party, 11, 14

Armenia, historic, 3, 11

Armenian Assembly of America, 267

Armenian Atrocities: The Murder of a Nation (Toynbee), 137

Armenian Bureau of London, 70

Armenian Church. See Gregorian Church

Armenian General Benevolent Union, 67

Armenian-Greek section of British high commissioner, 123–25

Armenian interpreters, 146

Armenian Legion, 107, 120

Armenian National Council (Constantinople), 239

Armenian National Defense Committee (Cairo), 105–106

Armenian National Defense Committee of America, 105

Armenian National Delegation, 104, 237

Armenian nationalism, 6

Armenian National Union, 69

Armenian patriarchate (Constantinople), 67, 75, 101, 123–25, 128, 158, 207, 234–35

Armenian patriarchate (Jerusalem), 114

Armenian Review, 124

Armenian Revolutionary Federation. See Dashnaks

Armenian Secret Army for the Liberation of Armenia (ASALA), 259

Armenians, Ottoman: attitude toward revolutionaries, 13–14; adopted by Muslim families, 168, 236; conscription of, 90, 228; economic status of, 3; genocide recognition demand by descendants of, 259–60; Kurds, relations with, 4; military role in World War I, 100–109; number of deported, 236; number of killed, 240–42; number of survivors, 236–39; population statistics for, 5, 234–35 sympathy for Entente, 91; as volunteers for Russian army, 101–103, 106, 118, 157

Armenian volunteers in Hitler's armies, 264

Armistice of Mudros (1918), 73, 107

Askeri Bey, Sulayman, 83

Aspirations et agissements révolutionnaires des comités arméniens (1916), 97, 168

Asquith, Herbert Henry, 109

Assembly of Turkish American Associations, 143, 260

Assyrian Christians, 161

Astourian, Stephen, 45, 66

Atamian, Sarkis, 230

Atkinson, Herbert, 168, 173

Atkinson, Tacy, 167, 173

atrocities, Armenian, 97–98, 115–21

atrocities, Turkish, 14, 118–19, 137, 147

"Attention Members of the U.S. House of Representatives" (open letter of 1985), 260–61

Auschwitz lie, 262

Austria-Hungary, 35, 37

Azerbaijan, 157

Azmi Bey, Djemal, 182

Baghdad railway, 135, 154–55, 184, 197, 251; camps alongside of, 187–90; exemption from deportation for workers of, 230; tunnels, unfinished, 56, 187; use of British prisoners of war at, 62; vulnerability of, 104

Bahri Pasha, 22

Balakian, Peter, 45, 282n3

Balkans, Muslim refugees from, 3, 29, 35–36, 231, 253

Balkan wars (1912–13), impact of, 35–36

Barton, James L., 139, 143, 237, 304n31

Basra, 157

Batum, 8

Bauernfeind, Hans, 145

Bauer, Yehuda, 268

Baumgart, Winfried, 265

Bayazid, 8

Bayur, Yusuf Hikmet, 92

Bedel (military service exemption tax), 228

Beersheba Desert, 229

Behic Bey (colonel), 86

Bergfeld, Heinrich, 145–46, 178–82, 231

Bericht über die Lage des armenischen Volkes in der Türkei (Report on the Situation of the Armenian People in Turkey) (Lepsius), 134

Berkes, Niyazi, 45

Berliner Tageblatt, 111

Bernau, Auguste, 212–13

Bernstorff, Count Johann von, 56, 65

Bezjian, Zenop, 216

Bibliothèque Nubar (Paris), 67, 146

Bihl, Wolfdieter, 72

Bilezkian, Levon G., 187

Binark, Ismet, 132

Bitlis (city), 22–23, 116, 119

Bitlis (*vilayet*), 3, 144

Blair, Susan, 173

Bliss, Edwin Munsell, 15, 27, 29

Bloxham, Donald, 88, 161, 249

Bookbinder, Hyman, 263

Bosnia-Herzegovina, 8, 35

Böttrich (German officer), 160

Bozanti transit camp, 188–89

brigands, 164, 166, 222, 225, 227

Bristol, Mark, 146

British prisoners of war. *See* prisoners of war, treatment of British

Browning, Christopher R., 148–49

Bryce, James, 8, 137–39

Buchanan, G., 137

Büge, Eugen, 184–85

Bulgaria, 35; revolt of 1876, 7, 18, 21

Bureau d'information arménienne (Constantinople), 124

Butz, Arthur, 262

Calthorpe, Arthur G., 73, 81
Carter, Jimmy, 263
Catholic Armenians, 27, 165, 180, 184,
  205–206, 252
Caucasus: Armenian population in, 11,
  36; Armenian survivors in, 237–39;
  Armenian volunteers in, 101, 122,
  168; as base for Armenian revolu-
  tionaries, 13, 19; Special Organiza-
  tion operations in, 82; Turkish
  winter offensive in, 91, 102, 157
Cemal (Turkish official), 81
Central Turkey College (Aintab), 186
Cevdet Pasha, Tahir, 99
Chaliand, Gerard, 246
Chambers, William, 185
Chavous, Kevork, 31
Chechens, 217
*chette*s, 84, 89, 227–28
Christoffel, Ernst, 121
Chronicles of Higher Education, 267
Chulussi Bey, 164
Cilicia, 3, 33, 37, 103, 105, 107, 147, 221
Circassians, 3, 7, 210, 217, 226–27, 229,
  253–54
"Civil war within a global war" thesis,
  115, 122, 252, 261
Cölasan, Emin, 271
Commission of Responsibilities and
  Sanctions, 123, 175
Committee for the Defense of the
  Armenian Cause, 267
Committee of Union and Progress (CUP):
  and Adana massacre, 34; alleged role
  in extermination of Armenians, 88;
  alleged secret meeting of February
  1915, 51–53; establishes dictatorship
  in 1913, 36; hostility toward Chris-
  tian states, 35; ideology of, 34–35;
  inner workings of, 150; last congress
  of, 112; nationalist wing of, 32; at
  Paris Congress (1902), 32; role of
  local branches of, 223, 230–32,252;
  Saloniki Congress (1910), 44; seizure
  of power (1908) by, 33
Compatriotic studies, 147
Concerned Scholars and Writers, 267
Congress of Berlin (1878), 9
Constantinople agreement (1915), 74

Constantinople (Istanbul): Armenian
  community of, 3, 203, 251; arrests of
  April 24, 1915 in, 150, 203; demonstrations against Allies, 77; exemption from deportation for Armenians
  of, 251; Massacre of 1895 in, 22;
  occupation by Allies, 77–78, 122;
  Ottoman Bank seizure, 24–26; starvation in, 208
Constitution of 1876, 6, 32–33
conversions, 177, 208, 219, 241, 252
convicts, release of, 83–84, 95, 223–24,
  227–28, 291n98
Cook, Ralph Elliot, 141
Courbage, Youssef, 240
courts-martial of 1915–22: and Armenian
  atrocities, 117; lack of due process of,
  78–79; loss of documentation for, 80;
  reasons for establishment of, 74–75;
  reliability of findings of, 72, 78, 82;
  role of judge in, 79
CUP. *See* Committee of Union and
  Progress
Cyprus, 107
Cyprus Convention (1878), 8

Dadrian, Vahakn N., 14, 44, 91, 218,
  264, 268; on Andana massacre, 33;
  on Armenian defenselessness,
  121–22; on Armenians killed, 240;
  on Armenian volunteers in Russian
  army, 102; on 1894–95 massacres,
  33; on content verification method,
  71–72; on courts-martial of 1915–
  22, 71, 73–74, 76, 78, 81–82, 86; on
  covert nature of Armenian genocide,
  88–89; on Djemal Pasha, 113; on
  Esref Kuscubasi, 85; on genocidal
  consequences, 53, 250; on German
  foreign ministry archive, 135; on
  German role in deportations,
  160–61; on Gökalp, 46, 280n28;
  on Guse, 94; on Malta prisoners,
  127–28; on *Memoirs of Naim Bey*, 67,
  71–73; on military crisis of 1915,
  157; on Morgenthau memoirs, 140,
  142; on premeditation, 43, 245; on
  punishment of excesses, 114; on
  Resad Bay, 117; on Resit Akif Pasha,

89; on Special Organization, 76, 82–83, 86, 88 ; on Stange, 85; on "Ten Commandments," 47, 49–50; on Turkish archives, 132; on Van uprising, 98

Damad Ferid (grand vizier), 75

Damascus, 191, 218–20

Dardanelles, British attack on, 92, 104, 157, 256

Dashnaks, 90, 147, 151; assassinations, resort to, 13, 32

attitude of Armenian community toward, 13–14; Congress of Erzurum (1914), 100; Fifth Congress (1909), 34; Fourth General Convention (1907), 13; Khanasor raid (1897), 30; plans for a general uprising by, 93; and revolutionary justice, 12–15, 31; and socialism, 12; suspend armed struggle, 33

Davis, Leslie A., 59–60, 139, 165–71, 174, 176, 226–27, 229

Davison, Roderic H., 156, 260

Defenders of the Fatherland (Erzurum), 11

Deirmendere River, 145, 181

Denmark, 75

Department of Public Security, 155

Department for the Settlement of Tribes and Immigrants, 155

Deportation program: antecedents for, 150–51; differences in implementation of, 162, 251; dispersal of deportees, 153–54, 307n4; end of, 205–208; exemptions from, 165, 175–76, 180, 191, 203–205, 231, 236, 251–52; German role in, 159–61; lack of guards for, 163, 225; Muslims help Armenians in, 175–176; reasons for, 39, 155–59, 256, 307n7; scope of program, 307n4; transportation problem for, 253, 255. See also names of cities

Der Boghosian, Bedros, 259,

Der-el-Zor, 158, 209, 215–18, 227

Deringil, Selim, 272

Dersim Kurds, 176–224

deserters from Ottoman army, 58, 91, 95, 103, 118, 198, 222, 228

Deutsche Orient-Mission (German Mission for the Orient), 143

Deutscher Hilfsbund für Christliches Liebeswerk im Orient (German League of Assistance for Works of Christian Charity in the Orient), 143, 194–95

Deutschland und Armenien 1914–1918: Sammlung diplomatischer Aktenstücke (Gemany and Armenia 1914–1918: Collection of Diplomatic Documents) (Lepsius), 133–34

Diarbekir (city), 118, 223

Diarbekir (vilayet), 3, 110, 112

Diaspora, Armenian, 265, 271

Dinkel, Christoph, 160

Dixon-Johnson, C.F., 99

Djavid Bey, 207

Djemal Pasha, Ahmed, 33, 104, 190, 193; and Armenian relief program, 194–95; assassination of, 259; forbids photographing deportees, 192; helps Armenian deportees, 76, 218–19, 254; offers separate peace, 198, 317n184; orders artisans to Urfa, 203, 215; orders deportation from Marash, 186–87; punishes killers of Armenians, 112–13; role in deportations, 196–98, 206; tried in absentia, 76; on Turkish deaths, 115

Documents officiels concernant les massacres arméniens (Naim Bey–Andonian), 64

Dodd, William S., 187–88

Dorbeller, Anna von, 145

Dört Yöl, 105

Dowsett, Charles J. F., 235

Drasdamat Kanayan, Igdir (Dro), 101

Dro. See Drasdamat Kanayan, Igdir

Droshag (Standard), 14

Durkheim, Emile, 45

Dyer, Gwynne, 50, 52, 87, 95, 99, 116, 133, 256

Eckart, Bruno, 198, 200–202

Edelman, Samuel, 200

Edmonds, W. S., 127

Egypt, 55, 82–83, 157

Ehmann, Johannes, 169–70, 175, 177

Eighth Infantry Regiment (Turkish), 84–85

Einstein, Lewis, 157, 184

Elashkird-Bayizid Plain, 117
Elections of 1912, Ottoman, 36
Eliot, Charles, 6, 14, 26–27
Emergence of Modern Turkey, The (Lewis),
    265
Enver Pasha, Ismail, 33, 141, 150, 256;
    and deportations, 152, 156, 206;
    directs Special Organization, 82–83;
    and food shortages, 55; killing of,
    259; meets Murad of Sebastia, 157;
    tried in absentia, 73, 76; and two-
    track system of orders, 89; warns
    Armenian patriarch in 1915, 101;
    and winter offensive in Caucasus, 255
Ergil, Dogu, 83
Erickson, Edward J., 60, 94, 133, 157,
    230, 254
Erzinjan, 119, 145, 163, 166, 181
Erzurum, 11; CUP radicals, role of,
    164–65; Dashnak congress of 1914
    in, 100; deportation from, 163–67;
    killing of Muslims in, 119; number
    of Armenians in, 162
Eskijian, Hovhannes, 194–95
Essad Bey, 47, 49–50
ethnic cleansing, 46
Euphrates College (Harput), 58, 165, 169
Euphrates River, 56, 164, 176
European intervention in Turkish affairs,
    8–9, 17, 36, 38
European Parliament, 259, 264, 267
Evangelical Academy (Mühlheim), 270

Faik Pasha, Suleiman, 126
Fargues, Philippe, 240
Faurisson, Robert, 262
*fedayee*s, 13, 31, 147
Fein, Helen, 268,
Feldmann, Otto von, 160
Fenerdjian, A., 125
Fifth Army (Turkish), 204
Fifth column role of Armenian revolu-
    tionaries, 249, 257, 269
Final Solution of the Jewish Question,
    250–51, 265
Ford, Gerald, 259
Forty Days of Musa Dagh, The (Werfel), 262
Forum of the Armenian Associations of
    France, 266

Fourteenth Infantry Division (Turkish), 56
Fourth Army (Turkish), 157
Fragments: Memories of a Wartime Childhood
    (Wilkomirski), 148
France: and Armenian Legion, 107; de-
    signs on Middle East, 106; presses for
    reforms in Ottoman Empire, 21, 37
Francis Ferdinand, archduke, assassina-
    tion of, 38
Frearson, Ms. (resident of Aintab), 172,
    183
French Civil Code, article 1382 of, 266
French Foreign Legion, 108
French Parliament, 259, 264

Galib Bey, 44
Gallipoli landing, 157
Garmudj (Germüs), 199, 202
Garo. *See* Pasdermadjian, Garegin
Gayssot Act, 267
Geary, Arthur B., 44
Geddes, A., 126
Geddes, Walter M., 188–89
gendarmes, 86, 224–26, 229, 252
genocidal consequences, 53–54, 250
genocide concept, 262, 265, 268
Gerlach, Christian, 248
German Foreign Ministry archive, 133–35
German military mission, 135, 204
Germany; assistance to deportees by, 160,
    195; censorship of massacre reports
    by, 134; and deportation order,
    159–61; presses for reforms in
    Ottoman Empire, 37; refuses extra-
    dition of CUP leaders, 258
Gevorg V (*catholicos*), 101, 104
Gevorgian, Ardavesh, 259
Ghazarian, Vatche, 118
Gladstone, William Ewart, 15, 27
Glockler, Henry, 198, 200, 202
Gökalp, Ziya, 35; alleged role in extermi-
    nation plans, 45; arrested and tried
    in 1919, 46, 125; espouses Turanism,
    44–45; *Principles of Turkism, The*, 45;
    role in CUP, 45; taken to Malta,
    125; and Turkish nationalism, 45
Göljük, Lake (Lake Hazar), 172, 174
Gordon, Adolf von, 66
Goulkévich, M., 38

Graffam, Mary L., 144
Gräter, E., 192
Graves, Robert, 18–19, 23, 26
Great Britain, 21, 37
Greece, 35
Gregorian church, 3–4
guerillas, Armenian, 13, 31, 92, 103–04, 156, 233
Gunter, Michael M., 53, 73
Gürün, Kamuran, 113, 137, 240
Guse, Felix, 93–94, 99, 117, 120
Gust, Wolfgang, 134

Hagopian, Hagop S., 141
Halacoglu, Yusuf, 236, 240
Halil Bey, Galatali, 112, 200, 206, 225
Halim Pasha, Said, 85, 98, 159, 258
Hama, 191, 218–19
Hamidiye regiments, 9, 20–21, 37, 223
Hamlin, Cyrus, 17
Harbord, James G., 119, 236
Hardegg, Julius Loytved, 197, 219–20
Harley, Isabelle, 177
Harput (Elazig): arrests of revolutionaries in, 168–69, 171; deportations from, 170–72; killing of prisoners in, 169; searches for arms in, 168. See also Mamouret-ul-Aziz
Harput trial, 81
Hartunian, Abraham, 116
hate-speech, 267
Heck, Lewis, 49, 77, 80
Heizer, Oscar, 163, 178–80, 182, 229
Hendrick, Burton J., 141
Hepworth, George H., 19, 22–23, 26–28, 224
Heyd, Uriel, 46
Hilberg, Raul, 268
Hilfsbund. See Deutscher Hilfsbund…
Hilmi Bey, 164–65
historians, responsibility of, 261, 266, 272
History of the Ottoman Empire and Modern Turkey (Shaw), 259
Hitler, Adolf, 204, 251, 264–65
Hoesch, Alexendar von 254
Hoff, Nicholas, 38
Hoffmann, Hermann, 192, 194–95, 226
Hoffman, Philip, 142

Hofmann, Tessa, 136
Hohenlohe-Waldenburg, Ernst Wilhelm, 111–12, 185, 231
Hollis (American consul), 146
Holocaust, Jewish, 262, 264–65, 268
Holocaust Memorial Council, 263
Homs, 191, 218
Horton, George, 54, 204
hospitals, conditions in Turkish, 59
House, Edward M., 143
House Joint Resolution 192, 261
Hovannisian, Richard G., 17, 90, 101, 268; on Armenian genocide, 43; on courts-martial of 1919–22, 78; on Dashnaks, 100; on Mevzanlade Rifat, 52; on population statistics, 235; on reform agreement of 1914, 38; on religious conversions, 168; on Special Organization, 88; on rebellion of Van, 96
Huber (Aleppo school official), 192
Hulme-Beaman, Ardern, 28
Humann, Hans, 156
Hunchak (Bell), 11
Hunchaks: Congress of Constanza (1913), 36; founding of, 11; intent to provoke reprisals, 16; organize Constantinople demonstration, 22; plans for uprising in 1915, 93; plot assassination of Talaat, 36, 203; program of 1880s, 92; role in Sassun uprising, 20–21; role in Zeitun uprising, 24; use of terror by, 12
Hurewitz, J. C., 260
Hürriyet (Istanbul), 271

Ihsan Bey, 81
"Increased Security Precautions" (Turkish army directive), 92
India, 83
Inquiry, The (research group), 143, 174
Institute of Turkish Studies, 261
interpreters, Armenian, 146
irregulars, 223, 228
Islahia transit camp, 113, 190
Italy, 37
Ittihad ve Terraki. See Committee of Union and Progress

Jackson, Jesse, 142, 191–93, 195, 202–203, 215, 247
Jacobson, Maria, 58–59, 168, 175, 177, 223
Janikian, Aram, 186
Jäschke, Gotthard, 45
Jernazian, Ephraim, 198, 201
Johannsen, Alma, 225
Justice Commandos for the Armenian Genocide (JCAG), 259

Kafir, 4
Kaiser, Hilmar, 72, 133, 161, 249, 282n3
Kaloustian, Krikor, 187
Kamakh Gorge, 164
Kamar-Katiba (poet), 11
Kamil Pasha, Mahmud, 163, 165
Kamphövener Pasha, 25
Karagöz (Constantinople), 91
Karajian, Sarkis, 235, 240
Karal, Enver Ziya, 137
Karlukh transit camp, 193
Karpat, Kemal H., 132, 234–35
Kars, 8
Kasim Bey, Hussein, 219
Katma transit camp, 190
Kazanjian, Paren, 147
Kazarian, Haigazn K., 45, 87, 124, 126, 196, 240
Kazin, Alfred, 268
Kemal, Mustafa (Atatürk), 127, 175, 263
Kemal Bey, Yusuf, 86
Kemal, Mehmet, 77
Kerr, Stanley, 116, 239
Kévorkian, Raymond H., 146, 236, 240
Khabar River, 217
Khanasor raid (1897), 30
Khirimian (archbishop), 9–10
Knapp, Grace Higley, 99, 118, 121, 144, 159
Konia transit camp, 187–88
Kress von Kressenstein, Friedrich Freiherr, 135, 189–90, 195, 197
Kuckhoff (German vice consul), 93
Kühlmann, Richard von, 207
Künzler, Jakob, 60, 198, 200, 202–203, 215, 230–31
Kuper, Leo, 17, 246
Kurdemlik, 173

Kurdistan, demand for, 52
Kurds: alliance with Armenians against Kemalist regime, 52–53; and Andana massacre of 1809, 34; attacks on Armenian villages, 4, 23, 96; as brigands, 164, 222 enrolled in militias, 95, 223; relations with Armenians, 4, 9; role in Constantinople massacre of 1895, 25; role in World War I Armenian massacres, 167, 173–74, 182, 222–24, 253; and Sassun rebellion of 1894, 16; in war of 1877–78, 7
Kuscubasi Bey, Esref, 85
Kut-al-Amara, 61
Kutay, Cemal, 85
Kwiatkowski, Ernst von, 181

Labor battalions, 164, 228–31
Lamb, Harry, 124
Landau, Jacob Lang, 83
Lang, David, 66
Langer, William L., 16, 30
Laz, 3, 23, 25, 85
Lebanon, 55
Légion d'Orient, 107–108
legislatures pressured to recognize Armenian genocide, 259
Lepsius, Johannes, 66, 133–34, 136, 239–40
Leslie, F. H., 198
Levantine exaggerations, 144–45
Lewis, Bernard, 260, 265–67
Liberal Union party, 75
Libya, 83
Liman von Sanders, Otto, 56, 135, 204–205, 225, 231
Liparit (German missionary), 65
Litten, Wilhelm, 212–13
Lloyd George, David, 109
locust plague of 1915, 54–55
Loris-Melikov, Mikayel, 7
Lowry, Heath W., 140–42, 265
Lulejian (Euphrates College professor), 169
Lybber, Albert, 237

McCarthy, Carolyn, 16, 121, 143, 240
McCarthy, Justin, 16, 92, 121–22, 132, 143, 155, 234–35, 240–241, 250

McFie, A. L., 317n184
McKale, Donald, 83
Mallet, Louis, 65
Malta prisoners: appeal for release of, 81,
    126; dossiers of, 69, 124–25; escape
    of, 127; number of, 123;
    significance of release of, 122–23,
    127–28; traded for British hostages,
    127; trials abandoned, 127; transfer
    from Constantinople of, 77, 122
Mamouret-ul-Aziz (*vilayet*), 3, 176–77.
    See also Harput
Mandelstam, André N., 37, 93
Mango, Andrew, 44, 73, 249
Manoukian, Aram, 96
Marash (district), 186–87
Marsovan, 14
Marashlian, Levon, 128, 235
massacres of 1894–1896, 7, 19; casualties
    of, 26; causes of, 29; role of Abdul
    Hamid in, 26–28
Maxwell, Sir John, 104–106
Mazian, Florence, 52
Medz Vodjiru (The Great Crime) (Naim
    Bey–Andonian), 63
Melson, Robert F., 17, 46, 66, 78
Memoirs of Naim Bey, The (Andonian),
    250; authenticity of, 72–73; differ-
    ences between editions of, 64, 71;
    used as propaganda, 70; British
    attitude towards, 123–25
Merrill, John E., 186
Mersina, 183–84
Meskene transit camp, 213–14
Mesopotamia, 82–83
Methodist Episcopal Church, 143
Metro-Goldwyn-Mayer, 263
Mezreh, 168, 173
military tribunals, U.S., 79
militia, 165, 223, 227
Miller, Arthur, 268
Miller, Donald, 147–48
Miller, Lorna Touryan, 147–48
millet system, 3–4
Mishlayevsky (Russian general), 101
mohadjirs (refugees), 159
Mohammed II (sultan), 3
Mohammed V (sultan), 34
Mohahan, J. H., 165

Monde, Le (Paris), 266
Montenegro, 8
Montgomery, George, 239
Mordtmann (German embassy official),
    158
Morgenthau, Henry, 240; *Ambassador
    Morgenthau's Story*, 140; on Armenian
    guerillas, 92, 103; attitude towards
    Germany of, 140–41; on Der-el-Zor,
    216; diary of, 140; on 1894–1896
    massacres, 27; entertains Talaat, 141,
    150; intervenes on behalf of Smyrna
    Armenians, 204; on punishment of
    excesses, 110; on purpose of deporta-
    tions, 247, 255
Mosul, 209, 216–17, 237
Muammer Bey, Ahmed, 125
Mukhitarian, Onnig, 97
Munif bey, Ali, 184
Murad of Sebastia, 31, 93, 157
Musa Dagh, 106
Muslim refugees during World War I,
    120–21, 159, 241, 257
Mush (district), 31
Musheg (archbishop), 33–34

Nail Bey, Yenibahceli, 180–82
Naim Bey, 63, 68–69
Nalbandian, Louise, 12, 14, 18
Narodnaya Volya, 12
Naslian, Jean (bishop), 44
Nassibian, Akaby, 138
Nathan, Edward, 114, 183–85, 189, 253
National Congress of Turkey, 75, 93
National Day of Remembrance of Man's
    Inhumanity to Man, 259–60
Nazim (Dr.), 47, 51
Necati (CUP delegate), 81
Nemesis (Dashnak organization), 258
Netherlands, 75
Neukirch (Red Cross physician), 163
New York Times, 260, 267
Nicholas II (tsar), 101
Nicolson, Sir Harold, 106
Niepage, Martin, 192–93
Niles, Emory N., 119
Noel, E. W. C., 118
Nogales, Rafael de, 96, 117, 229
North Atlantic Treaty Organization
    (NATO), 259

Nubar Pasha, Boghos, 69, 104, 106–109,
    183, 236–37
Nuremberg trials, 72, 80

Oates, Joyce Carol, 268
Ohandjanian, Artem, 72, 160
Öke, Mim Kemal, 115, 154–55
Ökte, Ertugrul Zekai, 240
open letter of 1985. *See* "Attention
    Members of the U.S. House of
    Representatives"
oral history, 147–48
Orel, Sinasi, 67–71, 73, 123, 127
Orly airport attack (1983), 259
orphanages for Armenian children,
    194–96
Osmania transit camp, 189, 253
Ostlegionen (eastern legions), 264
Ottoman Bank, seizure of (1896), 24–25
Ottoman Empire, 3–4, 28, 35; bureau-
    cratic ineptitude of, 253; civilian
    war deaths, 115; corruption in, 55;
    declares holy war, 221; enters World
    War I, 90; famines during World
    War I in, 54–57; military alliance
    with Germany, 39; orders general
    mobilization in 1914, 38; population
    statistics of, 115; reform proposals
    for, 23, 37–38, 221; transportation
    problems of, 55–56, 301n179
Ottomanism, 35

Palestine, 55, 107, 191, 237, 252
Pallavicini, Johann Merkgraf von, 206
Pan-Islamism, 35
Papazian, Mrs. (Erzurum), 227
Paris Peace Conference (1919), 108,
    236–37
Parmelee, Ruth, 176
Pasdermadjian, Garegin (Garo), 101–103,
    117
Patriotic Society of Van, 11
Pears, Edwin, 19, 33
Peet, William Wheelock, 65, 194
Persia, 30, 237
Peter, W., 182
Petra, 219
Pichon, Stephen, 108
Pickthall, Marmaduke, 146

Picot, Georges, 74
pilgrimage to Anatolia (2001), 270
political correctness, 269
Pomiankowski, Joseph, 135, 157, 197
population statistics, 3, 234–35
Post, Wilfred M., 188–89
premeditation, 245–47, 252, 256
Presbyterian Church, 143
Price, M. Philips, 118
Principles of Turkism, The (Gökalp), 45
prisoners of war, treatment of British,
    61–62
property of Armenian deportees, 153–54
Protestant Armenians, 165, 176, 184,
    186, 205–206, 216, 252
Protestant missionaries, 6, 142–44
Provisional Law Concerning the Measures
    to be Taken...(1915), 153
"provocation" thesis, 16–17

Rakka, 57, 214–15
Rakka transit camp, 214
Rahmi Bey, 204–205
Ranzi, Karl, 113, 218–19
Ras-ul-Ain transit camp, 191, 209–210,
    227
Rathenau, Walter, 136
Rawlinson, Alfred, 127
Rawlinson, Henry, 127
Reconciliation Commission.
    See Turkish-Armenian Reconciliation
    Commission
reform proposals for Ottoman Empire,
    23, 37–38, 221
Reid, James, 45
Renaissance (Constantinople), 50
*Report of the Committee on Alleged German
    Outrages* (Bryce), 137
Resad Bey, 117
resettlement: in Del-el-Zor, 212, 215–18;
    official orders for, 209; in Ras-ul-
    Ain, 209–10; in *vilayet* of Damascus,
    218–20
Resid Bey, 254
restitution, Armenian demand for, 269
Revue d'Histoire Arménienne Contemporaine,
    146
Rifat, Mevlanzade, 51–53
Riggs, Henry, 58, 120, 143, 165–66,
    169–71, 174–76, 224–25

Riggs, Mary W., 172
Riza, Ahmed, 32
Riza Bey, Yusuf, 86
Robeck, John de, 81
Robert College (Constantinople), 17
Robin Hood, legend of, 13
Rohner, Beatrice, 194–96, 213, 217
Rössler, Walter, 112, 193, 195–97, 210;
    on Armenian deportees, 57, 172;
    on Armenians in Der-el-Zor, 215–
    17; on Baghdad railway workers,
    230; on Circassians, 227, 229; on
    exemption for Protestant Armenians,
    186; on Katma transit camp, 190;
    on Memoirs of Naim Bey, 66–67, 70;
    on Meskene transit camp, 214; on
    Ottoman ineptitude, 253, 255;
    on released convicts, 84
Rumania, 8
Rumbold, Horace, 125,175
Russia: designs on Turkish Armenia of, 7;
    presses for reforms in Ottoman
    Empire, 21; proposes reform agree-
    ment in 1913, 37; supports
    Armenian revolutionaries, 31, 95,
    102, 156, 178; and Sykes-Picot
    agreement, 74
Russian Marxism, 11
Russian Revolution of 1917, 118
Russo-Turkish war of 1828–29, 7
Russo-Turkish war of 1877–78, 7, 29, 36
Ryan, Andrew, 123

Sabaheddin, Mehmed, 32
Sabit Bey, 126, 174–75
Saint James Church (Jerusalem), 263
Sakir, Behaeddin, 47, 51–52, 80–81, 88,
    164–65, 258–59
Salt, Jeremy, 21
Samsun, 182
Sarafian, Ara, 132–33, 137–39, 143, 182,
    270
Sarid, Yossi, 263
Sarikamis, battle of, 102, 157, 296n82
Sassun, 16, 20–21, 31
Sazonov, Serge D., 37, 99
Schäfer, Paula, 186, 189–90
Scheubner-Richter, Max Erwin von, 93,
    99, 159, 163–65, 227

Schmavonian, Arshag K., 141–42, 146
Schraudenbach, Ludwig, 135, 218
Schreiner, George Abel, 104, 254
Schuchardt, Friedrich, 196
Sefi (colonel), 47
Serbia, 8
Shaw, Ezel Kural, 154, 248, 259
Shaw, Stanford J., 132, 154, 248, 259
Shevki Bey, 227
Shipley, Alice, 176
Shiradjian, Aaron, 194
Shirakian, Arshavir, 258
Shiroyan, Haig, 116
Shoukrie (minister of education), 51
Simsir, Bilal, 124
Sivas (vilayet), 3
Sixth Army (Turkish), 56
"Slaughterhouse Province," 168, 173, 178
Smyrna (Izmir), 77, 204–205, 251,
    289n62
socialism, role in Armenian revolutionary
    ideology of, 11–12
Sofia, 105
Sonyel, Salaki R., 117, 154, 236, 240,
    248, 264
Soviet Armenia, 258
Spain, 75
Special Organization (SO): accused of
    massacres, 76, 221; alleged link to
    CUP, 87; origins of, 82–83; and war
    ministry, 83, 87
speculators, 55
Spiecker, Marie, 192
Stange (colonel), 84–85, 227
Stange Detachment, 85
Steinbach, Udo, 240
Stoddard, Philip H., 82
Strummer, Deli, 148
Suat Bey, Ali, 216–17
Suez Canal, 83, 157
Suny, Ronald Grigor, 4, 53, 159, 240,
    248, 259, 269–70, 272
Surabian, Dikran, 44
survivor testimony, Armenian, 147–49
Sutherland, Arthur E., 119
Sweden, 75
Sykes, Mark, 74
Sykes-Picot agreement (1915), 74

Tahsin Bey, Hasan, 163
"Taking a Stand against the Turkish
    Government's Denial of the
    Armenian Genocide..." (1996),
    267–68
Takvim-i Vekayi, 80
Talat Pasha, Mehmet, 33, 92, 141, 148,
    256; aborted assassination of, 36;
    assassination of, 66, 258; and depor-
    tation program, 152, 156, 158, 184,
    230; disputed telegrams of, 64,
    66–67; disputed character of, 65;
    and end of deportations, 205–207;
    escapes from Constantinople, 73;
    orders arrest of revolutionary leaders,
    150–51; and punishment of excesses,
    110–11, 114; role in "Ten Command-
    ments," 47; secret speech at Saloniki
    congress, 44; and two-track system
    of orders, 89, 112
Tamcke, Martin, 136
Tanzimat, 4
Tashjian, James H., 44
Taurus Mountains, 188, 254
Tehlirian, Soghomon, 66, 258
Tel Aviv Holocaust and Genocide Confer-
    ence (1982), 263
"Ten Commandments," 47–49
Ter Minassian, Anahide, 12
Ternon, Yves, 44, 66, 119, 240, 246
"Terrible Turk," concept of, 7, 144, 262
Teskilat-i Mahsusa. See Special Organiza-
    tion
Third Army (Turkish), 76, 80, 157, 163,
    222
Thrace, 74
Tiflis convention (1892), 12
torture in Ottoman prisons, 14, 16, 20,
    169, 198–99
Toynbee, Arnold J., 116, 137–38, 145,
    162, 235, 240, 246, 249
*Treatment of Armenians in the Ottoman
    Empire (1915–16), The* (British Blue
    Book), 137–39, 304n28
Treaty of Berlin (1878), 8–9, 11, 37
Treaty of Lausanne (1923), 258
Treaty of San Stefano (1878), 7–8
Treaty of Sèvres (1920), 78, 123, 125

Trebizond (Trabzon), 22, 229; deportation
    from, 178–82; drownings, 181–82;
    exemptions from deportation, 180;
    killing of Muslims, 119; revolution-
    ary organization in, 178; role of
    CUP committee of, 179–81; rumors
    about killings, 145; searches for
    weapons, 178; size of Armenian
    population in, 178
Trebizond trial, 81
Tripoli, 35, 159, 253
Triumvirate, rule of, 150, 196
Trumpener, Ulrich, 159–60
Tseghasban Turkeh (The Genocidal Turk)
    (Kazarian), 124
Tur Abdin Mountains, 161
Turanism, 35, 44–45, 159, 249
Turkey, Republic of: strategic relationship
    with the United States, 259–60;
    threats against proponents of geno-
    cide charge, 262–64
Turkish archives, 124, 131–33, 261
Turkish-American Workshop (Chicago,
    2000), 269
Turkish-Armenian Reconciliation Com-
    mission, 270–71
Turkish army, World War I casualties of,
    60–61
Turkish Foreign Policy Institute, 155
Turkish General Staff archive, 88, 133
Turkish historiography, 90, 270
Turkish Military Criminal Code and
    Military Criminal Procedure, 80
Turkish nationalism, 45
Turkish officials, assassination of, 259
Turkish soldiers, treatment of, 57–60
Türkiye Inkilabinin ic Yübü (The Inner
    Aspects of the Turkish Revolution)
    (Rifat), 51
Tverdokhlebov (Russian officer), 300n172
typhus epidemics, 55–56, 60, 189–91,
    214, 219, 229

Uniform Code of Military Justice (U.S.),
    79
U.S. Congress, 264
U.S. Department of State, 126, 137, 139,
    175, 260, 263

U.S. House of Representatives, 259
U.S. Holocaust Memorial Museum, 263
Updike, John, 268
Urfa, 227,229; artisans sent to, 203; deportations from, 202–203; famine in, 55; role of CUP radicals, 200; searches for weapons in, 198, 200; size of Armenian population in, 198; uprising in, 201
Ussher, Clarence D., 97, 99, 159
Ussher, Elizabeth, 97, 99

Van (city): atrocities during 1915 rebellion, 97; attempted assassination of governor of, 13; Russian occupation of, 96, 157, 256; strength of Dashnaks in, 95; uprising in 1895, 24; uprising in 1915, 92, 95–99, 156
Van, Lake, 31, 118, 152
Van (vilayet), 3
Vehib Pasha, Mehmet, 76, 80, 113
Verchinlour (Constantinople), 49
Vérité sur le mouvement révolutionnaire Arménien et les mesures gouvernementales (1916), 111, 113
Von der Goltz, Colmar, 135, 160–61

Waffen-SS, 264
Walker, Christopher J., 19, 47, 52, 72, 87, 247
Wangenheim, Hans Freiherr von, 158, 247
Washington Post, 260, 267
"We Commemorate the Armenian Genocide of 1915 ...," 5–36
Werfel, Franz, 262
Werth, Carl, 121
Westenenk, L. C., 38
Westermann, William L., 237

Whitman, Sidney, 28
Wiegand, Theodor, 135
Wilkomirski, Benjamin, 148
Willis, James, 249
Wilson, Woodrow, 136, 140, 143
Wolff-Metternich, Paul von, 78, 111, 195, 197–98, 206
Wolffkeel von Reichenberg, Eberhard, 200–201
Women and Children of the Armenian Genocide (oral history project), 147
Woods, H. Charles, 34
wounded soldiers, treatment of Turkish, 57–60

Yalman, Ahmed Emin, 87, 101, 113, 117, 249
Yapp, Malcolm, E., 235, 282n3
Yeghiayan, Vartkes, 73
Yerevan State University, 271
Yotneghparian, Mugerditch, 199, 201–202
Young, Greg, 145
Young Turks. See Committee of Union and Progress
Yozgat trial, 50, 75–76, 80–81
Yuca, Süreyya, 67–71, 73, 123, 127

Zahigian, Krikor, 175
Zavan (archbishop), 36
Zeitun, 24, 103–104
Zeki Bey, 216
Zeve, 98
Zimmermann, Arthur, 141
Zohrab, Krikor, 112, 200
Zollinger, Emil, 195
Zürcher, Erik, 73, 83, 88, 133, 235, 240